# THE SANCTUARY CITY

# THE SANCTUARY CITY

IMMIGRANT, REFUGEE, AND
RECEIVING COMMUNITIES IN
POSTINDUSTRIAL PHILADELPHIA

## DOMENIC VITIELLO

CORNELL UNIVERSITY PRESS
*Ithaca and London*

Thanks to generous funding from the University of Pennsylvania Stuart Weitzman School of Design and the Andrew Mellon Foundation, the ebook editions of this book are available as open access volumes through the Cornell Open initiative.

First published 2022 by Cornell University Press

Library of Congress Cataloging-in-Publication Data

Names: Vitiello, Domenic, author.
Title: The sanctuary city: immigrant, refugee, and receiving communities in postindustrial Philadelphia / Domenic Vitiello.
Description: Ithaca [New York]: Cornell University Press, 2022. | Includes bibliographical references and index. |
Identifiers: LCCN 2021051816 (print) | LCCN 2021051817 (ebook) | ISBN 9781501764691 (hardcover) | ISBN 9781501764806 (paperback) | ISBN 9781501764707 (pdf) | ISBN 9781501764714 (epub)
Subjects: LCSH: Refuge (Humanitarian assistance)—Pennsylvania—Philadelphia. | Sanctuary movement—Pennsylvania—Philadelphia. | Refugees—Pennsylvania—Philadelphia—Social conditions. | Immigrants—Pennsylvania—Philadelphia—Social conditions. | Political refugees—Pennsylvania—Philadelphia—Social conditions. | Noncitizens—Government policy—United States. | Philadelphia (Pa.)—Emigration and immigration—Government policy.
Classification: LCC JV7078 .V58 2022 (print) | LCC JV7078 (ebook) | DDC 362.8709748/11—dc23/ eng/20220308
LC record available at https://lccn.loc.gov/2021051816
LC ebook record available at https://lccn.loc.gov /2021051817

# CONTENTS

# PREFACE

My relationships with the subjects of this book—immigrant, refugee, and receiving communities in Philadelphia since the 1970s—bear some explaining, since they are more intimate than research often entails. To some extent I grew up around them, and I have spent most of my career working with them.

I like to joke that my parents were the only people crazy enough to move to Philadelphia in 1974, when I was one year old. The city lost over a quarter of a million residents in the 1970s due to deindustrialization and white flight. But my father's job at Temple University drew us there, and my mother would soon work for a large hospital. "Meds and eds" were among the only parts of the city's economy that were growing. Generally, though, people with choices did not choose Philadelphia in those years.

When my parents split up a few years later, my mother began to rent out the third floor of our house in the Mt. Airy neighborhood of Northwest Philadelphia. Our first tenant was a man named Hap, who had recently arrived from Vietnam. I was four years old and did not know what that meant. But I knew he was an electrical engineer who took English classes at night, and he seemed to have no family. The next tenant I remember was in the 1980s, an American man named Robert who was very involved in St. Vincent de Paul Catholic church in nearby Germantown. Every weekend he cooked a big pot of soup or beans, packed them in glass jars, loaded them into a milk crate on the back of his bicycle, and delivered them to the First United Methodist Church of Germantown (FUMCOG), which was hosting a family from Guatemala. Our next tenant was a man named Onesmo, from Nigeria, where he was apparently a prince. This made me wonder why he worked as a low-paid security guard on the night shift.

My father lived mostly in South Philadelphia in the 1980s, where for several years he organized a festival that brought together Italian, African American, and Southeast Asian performing artists and neighbors. I only later came to understand which streets in the neighborhood were the color lines dividing these groups. For a few years he lived in West Philadelphia, a block off Baltimore

Avenue, where Southeast Asian and African merchants were reopening old storefronts. My most regular interaction with people from these communities was playing pickup basketball and soccer at neighborhood recreation centers, where I witnessed a mix of intergroup tension and peace.

The summer after my first year in college, in 1992, my mother got me a job with a landscaper whose crew mostly came from Guatemala. Some people had come in the 1980s, smuggled and hosted by nearby congregations, including FUMCOG, and by the 1990s had been granted asylum. But others, including some of their cousins, had come more recently and lacked those protections. I spent some years thereafter visiting lawyers' offices with my friend Omar, interpreting and inquiring if there were ways to legalize his status, as he had fled the military in Guatemala at age fifteen. They all told us he had come just a year too late to qualify for asylum.

I worked several summers on the same crew and played for the Guatemalan team in the Hispanic Soccer League of Philadelphia. We wore jerseys embroidered with the national symbol of the Quetzal bird, as if we represented the nation itself. At the time, the guys on the team did not know enough Guatemalans in the city to field a good squad, so they invited me, and I recruited two men from West Africa and the Caribbean whom I met playing pickup in West Philadelphia.

After graduate school, in 2005, immigrant communities in Philadelphia became the center of my research and practice. At the same time, my colleagues and mentors at the University of Pennsylvania (Penn for short), historians Michael Katz, Wendell Pritchett, and Mark Stern and anthropologist Kathleen Hall, started the Philadelphia Migration Project. Mathew Creighton did most of the number crunching and mapping through which we compared different groups' experiences. We collaborated with Audrey Singer and David Park from the Brookings Institution on a report that helped reintroduce many Philadelphians to our region as an immigrant destination. Mark and his partner, Susan Seifert, also involved me in their Social Impact of the Arts Project, studying African, Asian, and Latin American community organizations. I am forever indebted to these colleagues for supporting what was the start of my research for this book.

The other key vehicle at Penn through which I have engaged with immigrant communities is teaching in our Urban Studies and City Planning programs. Since 2005, thanks to Elaine Simon, I have taught a course called "The Immigrant City." It was the experience of sitting with my students that first term at the Al-Aqsa mosque, listening to our host, Marwan Kreidie, discuss the city's Palestinian community, that first gave me the idea that I could write a book comparing the experiences of different immigrant communities. This seemed like a good way to make sense of how urban America was changing and how my own city was recovering from a half-century of decline. Most of my research assistants for the book came from this class over the years. My colleague Eugénie Birch's Penn Institute for Urban Research and her urban humanities initiative supported by the Andrew Mellon Foundation funded much of my research assistants' work.

The more direct ways I have been involved in newcomer communities range from board service to collaboration on projects and research. In 2006 I joined the board of Juntos, an organization started by my former student Peter Bloom, working with the Mexican community in South Philadelphia. My students and I became involved in various parts of Juntos's work. Among other projects, we worked with Ruben Chico, Maximino "Charro" Sandoval, Jaime Ventura, and other colleagues to develop an agricultural cooperative in their hometown in Mexico. I am deeply thankful to these colleagues for engaging me in all this, and to our other colleagues on Juntos's board and staff, including Rita Banegas, Rosemary Barbera, Gabriel Berrios, Gloria and Guadalupe Canchola, Leticia Cortes, Isabel Garcia, Mark Lyons, Leticia Roa Nixon, Carlos Pascual Sanchez, Carlos Perez Vega, Christina Phillips-Ramos, Mario Ramirez, Estela Reyes-Bugg, Alfonso Rocha, Eugenio Saenz, Zac Steele, and Irma Zamora.

Other communities have been exceptionally welcoming to me, too. In 2007 I became a member of AFRICOM, the Coalition of African and Caribbean Communities in Philadelphia. When Lansana Koroma, from Sierra Leone, proposed that I join, I responded, perplexed, "Ok, my mother lives in Morocco," where she had recently moved for work, "but I'm not of African descent." My father's family came from Italy and Germany and my mother's people were Eastern European Jews, all of whom came to the United States around the turn of the twentieth century. Lansana smiled and replied, "But we all come from Africa," referring to the migration of early humans from the African continent many thousands of years ago. Lansana and other colleagues in AFRICOM, including Dr. Bernadine Ahonkhai, Megan Doherty, Eric Edi, Siddiq Hadi, Rev. John Jallah, Giordani Jean-Baptiste, Tiguida Kaba, Elhadji Ndiaye, Vincent N'gadi, Raphia Noumbissi, Alisa Orduña-Sneed, Sam Osirim, Samuel Quartey, Stanley Straughter, Vera Tolbert, Alou Traoré, Philip Udo-Inyang, Lanfia Waritay, and many others, were invaluable in helping me understand the diversity and complexity of Black Philadelphia. I consider their invitations to help referee their annual soccer tournament and to chair AFRICOM's bylaws revision committee, along with my service on the board of the African Cultural Alliance of North America (ACANA) in the late 2000s, among the greatest honors in my career.

My position as a professor of urban studies and community development has afforded me many opportunities to work on research, program development, and advocacy with colleagues at immigrant-led organizations and other institutions that serve newcomers. They include Josephine Blow, Rev. John Gblah, Voffee Jabateh, and Musa Trawally at ACANA; Agatha Johnson of the AfriCaribe Micro-Enterprise Network; Zeina Halabi and Marwan Kreidie at the Arab American Development Corporation; Jenny Chen, Helen Gym, Ed Nakawatase, and Ellen Somekawa at Asian Americans United; Lan Dinh and Nancy Nguyen at Boat People SOS and VietLead; Manuel Portillo at Guate en Philly; Judi Bernstein-Baker, Jessi Koch, and Sarah Peterson at HIAS-PA; Israel Colon and Jennifer Rodriguez at the Mayor's Office of Immigrant Affairs; Mike Dunn and Juliane Ramic at Nationalities Service Center; Blanca Pacheco, Peter Pedemonti, Jen Rock, Margaret Sawyer, and others at the New Sanctuary Movement of Philadelphia; Javier Garcia Hernandez and Barbara Rahke at PhilaPOSH; Matthew O'Brien at Puentes de Salud; and Amanda Bergson-Shilcock, Peter Gonzalez, Fatima Muhammad, and Anne O'Callaghan at the Welcoming Center for New Pennsylvanians. These collaborations all enabled and enriched the research for this book.

Many of the people mentioned here generously assisted me in vetting and editing the various chapters. So did Amnah Ahmad; Hajer Al-Faham; Luis Argueta; Chioma Azi; Jacob Bender; Angela and Phil Berryman; Michael Blum; Marion Brown; Terry Clattenburg; Nelson Diaz; Ricardo Diaz Soto; Nora El-marzouky; Bill Ewing; David Funkhouser; Elinor Hewitt; Aziz Jalil; Nelly Jimenez-Arévalo; Portia Kamara; Mary Day Kent; Mia-lia Boua Kiernan; Elizabeth Killough; Jean Marie Kouassi; Steve Larson; Sr. Margaret McKenna; Sr. Dana Mohamed; Betsy and Ron Morgan; Dalia O'Gorman; Cristina Perez; David Piña; Edgar Ramirez; Oni Richards-Waritay; Carlos Rojas; Rosalva Ruth-Bull; Marlena Santoyo; Nasr Saradar; Hazami Sayed; Sam Togba Slewion; Ludy Soderman; Marcos and Alma Romero Tlacopilco; Cristobal Valencia; Ted Walkenhorst; Debbie Wei; and Alexandra Wolkoff. René Luís Alvarez and Clara Irazábal gave helpful and inspiring comments on early versions of the introduction and chapter 1 at conferences of the Urban History Association and the Association of Collegiate Schools of Planning. Michael Jones-Correa and the readers for the press gave invaluable feedback on the entire manuscript. So did Andrew Sandoval-Strausz, who has been my closest and most supportive reader, on multiple drafts.

I owe my deepest thanks to the people who shared the personal stories that introduce the five main chapters of this book: Joel Morales, Thoai Nguyen, Sarorng "Rorng" Sorn, Rev. John Jallah, Mohammed (now Ethan) Al Juboori, and Carmen Guerrero. I cannot thank them enough.

The other people who deserve a great share of the credit for producing this book, though of course none of the blame for its shortcomings, are my research assistants. Arthur Acolin, Daniel Schwartz, Mena Shanab, and Rachel Van Tosh played outsized roles in this research. Others who made large contributions include Mengyuan Bai, Oscar Benitez, Benjamin Dubow, Natasha Menon, Yareqzy Muñoz, Juliana Pineda, Leah Whiteside, and Hannah Wizman-Cartier. Tyler Bradford, Alia Burton, Paola Abril Campos, Yuri Castaño, Javier Garcia Hernandez, Haein Jung, Lea Makhloufi, Anjuli Maniam, Sheila Quintana, Amanda Wagner, Laura Wasserson, and Ariana Zeno worked on smaller parts of this project and adjacent research that informed it. Danielle Dong designed and produced the maps in each chapter, and Danielle and Arthur Acolin made the tables in the introduction.

Most of the research for this book consisted of over 150 interviews that my research assistants and I conducted with staff and leaders of community and civic organizations, including many of the people mentioned here. We asked people to relate the histories of their communities and organizations, including experiences of migration, settlement, work, housing, relations with neighbors, and transnational activities. Early chapters also draw on my own archival research in Swarthmore College's Peace Collection, Philadelphia City Council, and Temple University's Urban Archives, whose staff I thank for their assistance and excellent curation of these records.

The academic communities I inhabit have supported me in this project in many ways beyond those already noted. I thank the many colleagues at Penn in our Mellon-supported urban humanities initiative, the Department of City and Regional Planning, Urban Studies Program, and Weitzman School of Design, particularly Nadine Beauharnois, Tiara Campbell, Roslynne Carter, Chris Cataldo, Alisa Chiles, Kate Daniel, Caroline Golab, Vicky Karkov, Brianna Reed, Mary Rocco, Stephanie Whaley, and Christine Williams; in Penn's Center for the Study of Ethnicity, Race, and Immigration, including Amada Armenta, Fernando Chang-Muy, Chenoa Flippen, Michael Jones-Correa, Anne Kalbach, Sarah Paoletti, and Emilio Parrado; and at the *Encyclopedia of Greater Philadelphia*, especially Howard Gillette and Charlene Mires. I am particularly grateful to Fritz Steiner, dean of the Weitzman School, for providing the funds that, along with funding from our Mellon initiative, make this book open access.

At Cornell University Press, I thank my editor Michael McGandy and his colleagues Martyn Beeny, Adriana Ferreira Barboza, Jonathan Hall, Clare Jones, David Mitchell, Sarah Noell, Ange Romeo-Hall, and Brock Schnoke; and also Nicole Balant and Kristen Bettcher for their gracious assistance with the many steps in the process of publication. I am grateful to Terry Clattenburg and Sabrina Vourvoulias for providing photographs for chapters 1 and 5; and to the artists Pose II, Juice, Hera, Base, Prisco, Nom/Oliver, Zenith, Cern, Aware, and Yours, who together painted the mural *Liberty Forsaken*, a portion of which adorns the book's cover.

Finally, I thank my family for their love and patience over the many years I have worked on this book. My wife, Soumya, has supported me in every way possible, not least indulging my years of serving on boards and other "after five-o'clock jobs" with immigrant communities.

My greatest hope is that this book informs, and complicates, my own and other people's students' understandings of American history, cities, and communities. As I often tell my students, it is not only acceptable, but in many ways it is entirely appropriate, to be confused and frustrated by immigration, particularly the ways in which our governments and communities respond to newcomers. I hope that people who read this book are alternately horrified and heartened, enraged and inspired, by the things people do to and for one another. For immigration and immigrant, refugee, and receiving communities are among the richest, most complex subjects through which to consider the best and worst parts of our humanity and history.

# ABBREVIATIONS

| | |
|---|---|
| AADC | Arab American Development Corporation |
| ACANA | African Cultural Alliance of North America |
| ACLAMO | Latin American Community Action of Montgomery County |
| AFAHO | African Family and Health Organization |
| AFRICOM | Coalition of African and Caribbean Communities in Philadelphia |
| AFSC | American Friends Service Committee |
| AMEN | Afri-Caribe Micro-Enterprise Network |
| BPSOS | Boat People SOS |
| CASA | Central American Sanctuary Alliance of Delaware County |
| CCATE | Centro de Cultura, Arte, Trabajo y Educación |
| CDC | Community development corporation |
| CIA | Central Intelligence Agency |
| CISPES | Committee in Solidarity with the People of El Salvador |
| DACA | Deferred Action for Childhood Arrivals |
| DED | Deferred Enforced Departure |
| DHS | Philadelphia Department of Human Services |
| ECOWAS | Economic Community of West African States |
| ESL | English as a Second Language |
| FB | Foreign-born |
| FBI | Federal Bureau of Investigation |
| FUMCOG | First United Methodist Church of Germantown |
| HIAS-PA | Hebrew Immigrant Aid Society—Pennsylvania |
| ICE | Immigration and Customs Enforcement |
| ICNA | Islamic Circle of North America |
| INS | Immigration and Naturalization Service |
| JEVS | Jewish Employment and Vocational Service |
| LCFS | Lutheran Children and Family Services |
| LGBTQ | Lesbian, Gay, Bisexual, and Transgender |
| MAA | Mutual Assistance Association |
| MYCP | Muslim Youth Center of Philadelphia |

| | |
|---|---|
| NAFTA | North American Free Trade Agreement |
| NISGUA | Network in Solidarity with the People of Guatemala |
| NPFL | National Patriotic Front of Liberia |
| NSC | Nationalities Service Center |
| NSM | New Sanctuary Movement |
| PEACE | Program for Emergency Assistance, Cooperation and Education |
| PhilaPOSH | Philadelphia Area Project on Occupational Safety and Health |
| SEAFN | Southeast Asian Freedom Network |
| SEAMAAC | Southeast Asian Mutual Assistance Associations Coalition |
| SHAMS | Social Health and Medical Services Clinic |
| SHARE | Salvadoran Humanitarian Aid, Research and Education |
| SIV | Special Immigrant Visa |
| TPS | Temporary Protected Status |
| ULAA | Union of Liberian Associations in the Americas |
| UN | United Nations |
| UNICCO | United Nimba Citizens' Council |
| USAID | United States Agency for International Development |
| Volag | Voluntary agency |
| WOAR | Women Organized Against Rape |

# THE SANCTUARY CITY

# Introduction

## Sanctuary and the Immigrant City

> At different times and places, under varied circum-
> stances, the significance of sanctuary has been
> recovered and taken on new meanings.
>
> Chicago Religious Task Force on Central America and
> Tucson Ecumenical Council Central America Task
> Force (1982)

"We do not need a policy that draws lines in our
community and still subjects part of our community to deportation," testified Cristobal Valencia, who came to the United States from Puebla, Mexico.
Representing the organization Juntos, he outlined advocates' demand that Philadelphia police and prisons stop holding people for detention by federal Immigration and Customs Enforcement (ICE).[1] This hearing in the gilded
chambers of city council, on a rainy Wednesday in March 2014 before the
council's Committee on Public Safety, would help yield one of the strongest
sanctuary city policies in the nation. But it remained disputed. In his ensuing
executive order, Mayor Michael Nutter made an exception for people being
released from prison after serving time for a violent first- or second-degree felony. To organizers in the Cambodian American 1Love Movement and other
advocates in the Philadelphia Family Unity Network, this continued "to draw
lines of who is deserving and who is not."[2]

Americans' fights over sanctuary and sanctuary cities are, at their heart,
about which newcomers deserve protection and support and of what kinds.
Despite activists' appeals for universal protections, the immigrants and refugees at the hearing were already distinguished and divided in so many ways.
They had different relationships to the United States and its national government, with different rights and limits in their different statuses. They had different experiences of migration, settlement, and relations with receiving

communities in the city. Their distinct histories made sanctuary matter for diverse reasons.

People fleeing violence and poverty in Central America were among the fastest-growing communities in the city at the time, and most lacked legal status. "I live in constant fear that my mother who is undocumented could be at the wrong place in the wrong time at any moment," testified Tamara Jimenez, from Honduras, a board member of the New Sanctuary Movement of Philadelphia. They did not report robberies at the store her mother owned, she explained, to avoid the risk of losing the business and being deported back to one of the most violent places in the Americas. "Immigrant communities don't feel safe and protected."[3]

Philadelphia was a major center of African and Caribbean settlement and had the second largest Muslim population in the nation. "Deportation is a big part of our work" with African and Caribbean immigrants, declared Nigerian American Chioma Azi, staff attorney from the African Cultural Alliance of North America, an organization led by Liberians. One of several people at the hearing who stressed how these issues mattered to Black immigrants, she cited "legal and human rights abuses that I have been made aware of and . . . [been] witnessing."[4] The Jewish director of the local chapter of the Council on American-Islamic Relations, Jacob Bender, added that police collaboration with ICE "breeds resentment and distrust, especially among Muslim immigrants who have been the principal targets of improper immigration practices in recent years."[5]

Some people testified to the ways their community's vulnerability to deportation derived from its historical relationships with the United States and with the city. Naroen Chhin, a community organizer with 1Love Movement, explained why many Cambodian refugees like himself were convicted of felonies, which later allowed those who had not acquired US citizenship to be deported. "When my community was resettled here . . . we were living in extremely poor neighborhoods where day to day the only thing we saw was drugs, gangs and racial conflict. Our parents were still . . . facing their own trauma of having survived a genocide" unleashed after the United States pulled out of Southeast Asia at the end of the Vietnam War. "'Gangs' started because kids wanted to protect themselves" in the absence of protection in schools and on the streets. "This city," he concluded, "was not prepared for refugee resettlement."[6]

Each community of immigrants and refugees represented at the hearing could have told a parallel story of the ways in which US involvement in their country and their history of migration and settlement in the city made sanctuary relevant for them. Whether from Central America, Southeast Asia, West Africa, the Middle East, or Mexico, the United States played a significant role in their people's displacement. They had different statuses and experiences of the city, its neighborhoods and receiving communities. But for all these groups, debates over what protections and assistance they deserved at both the federal and local levels remained contested and in many ways unresolved, making sanctuary important to so many communities.

This book tells five stories about these different groups' experiences of migration and settlement in Philadelphia and how they and their allies in receiving communities organized to address the problems they faced, to seek their own forms of sanctuary. This is but a small part of the history of sanctuary and sanctuary cities. Yet it reflects much of the experiences of immigrant communities and sanctuary in US cities at large in the late twentieth and early twenty-first centuries. The diversity of those experiences illuminates the consequences, ironies, and injustices of how and why US governments and communities treat different newcomers so differently from one another. It helps us appreciate why our immigration debates and immigration system are such a mess and what is at stake for different communities in that mess.

## What Is a Sanctuary City?

To most Americans, a sanctuary city means a local government that refuses to collaborate with federal authorities in detaining or deporting people who are in the country illegally.[7] Sanctuary city declarations typically instruct, for example, that "no agent or agency, including the Philadelphia Police Department and its members, shall request information about or otherwise investigate or assist in the investigation of the citizenship or residency status of any person unless such inquiry or investigation is required by statute, ordinance, federal regulation or court decision."[8] Sanctuary policies in US cities also usually affirm something to the effect that "no agent or agency shall condition the provision of City . . . benefits, opportunities or services on matters related to citizenship or residency status."[9] These clauses aim to guarantee people's access to public schools, libraries, health clinics, business licensing, and other city services.

But sanctuary—providing refuge for vulnerable foreigners—entails much more than government policies and services. It means both a contested set of protections and various forms of support for newcomers, often provided by newcomers themselves. Other lines in the same declaration explained this second aspect of sanctuary:

> RESOLVED: That the City Council supports and commends the citizens of Philadelphia who are providing humanitarian assistance to those seeking refuge in our City; and be it further
> RESOLVED: That the people of Philadelphia be encouraged to work with the existing sanctuaries to provide the necessary housing, transportation, food, medical aid, legal assistance and friendship that will be needed.[10]

These acts of sanctuary as help with critical human needs typically come from family, friends, and neighbors, and from civil society—community and civic organizations and social movements. Institutions ranging from congregations to social service agencies, ethnic associations, and human rights groups mobilize to address newcomers' shelter, work, health, legal, and other necessities. In this broader perspective, sanctuary cities are the places, the safe spaces, where immigrants, refugees, and their allies help one another rebuild their lives and communities.

The clauses excerpted here come not from Philadelphia's twenty-first-century sanctuary declarations but rather from an earlier era of sanctuary activism. Largely copied from San Francisco's "City of Refuge" resolution, this draft resolution for city council was prepared by people involved with the Philadelphia-based Central America Organizing Project in the winter of 1986. Their sanctuary city campaign was one of dozens of similar efforts launched across the country at the time, as media publicized the Sanctuary Movement during a federal trial of some of its leaders in Tucson, Arizona.

In the trial, the government accused the defendants of human smuggling, reflecting the state's view of sanctuary. In fact, the defendants, mostly religious leaders, did operate a sort of underground railroad for people from El Salvador and Guatemala who were fleeing torture, murder, and genocide carried out by US-backed regimes. They helped people travel across Mexico and the US border, to cities in the Southwest and to congregations hosting people in sanctuary around the country, including in Philadelphia and surrounding suburbs. People involved in the movement offered protection and support as long as the administration of President Ronald Reagan refused to grant Central Americans political asylum and persisted in labeling them "illegal economic immigrants." Sanctuary city campaigns were one of several lines of political advocacy that people in the movement pursued, most of which targeted US foreign and asylum policy.[11]

"In response to our national government's policy of deporting Central American refugees and harassing their supporters," proclaimed one of the Philadelphia campaign's appeals for support, "a number of cities, including San Francisco, Berkeley, Cambridge, Mass., Chicago, Seattle, and Ithaca have declared themselves to be Cities of Refuge or Sanctuary Cities."[12] So had other liberal cities and suburbs, including New York City; Burlington, Vermont; Ann Arbor, Michigan; and Takoma Park, Maryland—none of which were home to large numbers of Central Americans. Los Angeles, with some 300,000 Central American residents, passed the first sanctuary policy in the country in 1979, even before the Sanctuary Movement arose, and reaffirmed its status as a sanctuary city in 1985. New Mexico and Wisconsin became sanctuary states the next year.[13] These were leading centers of leftist activism, as was Philadelphia, which was a major center of civil rights, interfaith, peace, and other movements.

In rejecting the national government's assessment of which newcomers deserved protection, sanctuary cities articulated their responsibilities toward immigrants and refugees as a matter of larger geopolitics. Sympathetic politicians and advocates labeled the Central America crisis "another Vietnam" and cast Guatemalans, Salvadorans, and sometimes other immigrants as equally deserving of refugee status as the Southeast Asians being resettled in American cities at the same time.[14] In another outreach letter, the campaign's leaders wrote, "We also need to think about what it means that this country is so attractive: that we are an island of plenty in an impoverished world, and that our government is supporting oppressive governments . . . in many countries (Chile, the Philippines, South Africa, and many more). In the long run," they concluded, "we need to think about changing that situation rather than guarding our borders against the influx which might result from it."[15]

By 1987, some twenty-four cities in the United States had declared themselves sanctuaries—or "declared sanctuary," as activists often put it.[16] However, Philadelphia would not have a sanctuary city policy until the twenty-first century. The organizers of the sanctuary city campaign in 1986 dissolved the effort after a few meetings. City council members, who were already sympathetic to the movement and almost certain to pass the resolution, never saw their draft.[17]

These activists' decision to abandon the campaign underscores the fact that sanctuary city policies are often not the most important parts of the broader practices of sanctuary. Even at the campaign's outset in January 1986, the leaders of the Central America Organizing Project acknowledged the limited need for a sanctuary city policy. "There is a belief" among some activists, wrote the group's founder, Rev. David Funkhouser, that "city government could approve the sanctuary proposal within a few months. But, since Philadelphia has very few refugees" from Central America, "there is no need to rush the proposal through." The group saw this effort more "as an educational tool" to increase support for the movement.[18]

By the spring, the campaign's organizers decided that they and their fellow activists were busy with more critical work. Their ongoing community outreach and education about Central America through congregations and other institutions made the educational function of the campaign redundant.[19] Moreover, as sanctuary activist Anne Ewing noted, "We're facing mayoral and council elections this year, and we felt such a complex issue would get lost in the shuffle."[20] Most significantly, however, as she explained, "We've decided to spend our energies on direct work with refugees" from El Salvador and Guatemala.[21]

Their decision to abandon the sanctuary city campaign signaled a larger ambivalence about sanctuary city policies among activists, including refugees involved in the movement. Direct action—humanitarian assistance, protection of refugees, and advocacy for peace in Central America—took priority among most activists. Moreover, sanctuary city declarations had limited utility even in places where many Central Americans lived. Sanctuary Movement cofounder Jim Corbett, one of the defendants in Tucson, complained, "Even where the local government declares sanctuary," Salvadorans and Guatemalans "live in constant fear that someone will report them directly to the INS [Immigration and Naturalization Service]. Anyone can exploit this fear." This vulnerability only increased with passage of the Immigration Reform and Control Act of 1986, which further criminalized illegal immigration and the employment of people who were in the country illegally.[22] Sanctuary city governments could do nothing—at least nothing legal—to stop the federal officers operating inside their cities. The most they could do was withhold information and decline to participate in the work of federal agencies.

Only asylum, or temporary legal protection as long as the civil wars and threats of violence lasted, could change the vulnerable status of Central American refugees in the United States. Moreover, only the federal government could grant those protections. And only the federal governments and militaries of the United States, El Salvador, and Guatemala could end the wars and the disappearances—the state-sponsored abduction and murder of innocent people. Cities could do none of these things. As a result, sanctuary city declarations and policies in most places had limited value beyond publicity for the movement and its causes; though they held greater practical significance in Los Angeles and other parts of the West, where more Central Americans lived.[23]

But sanctuary cities in the other sense, as places where people and institutions mobilized to offer help, were necessary, most immediately for the safety and well-being of refugees. Tucson was a sanctuary city, in the functional sense, largely as a result of Corbett and his colleagues' network of churches and goat herders who helped people move from Mexico into the United States.[24] Philadelphia was a sanctuary city of a different, more common, sort, much like the San Francisco Bay area, Seattle, Chicago, Boston, and New York: a major center of sanctuary congregations, organizations, and activists, including Central Americans, who were engaged in national and transnational work for peace and justice. These places were not, however, major centers of Central American population until the twenty-first century.

In their work between these cities and Central America, refugees and their allies gave further meanings to sanctuary and the sanctuary city. Sanctuary congregations, cities, and the movement at large represented spaces in which not only to find protection and restore people's lives, but also from which to work to end the wars and rebuild communities in Central America.[25] Some sanctuary cities established sister city relationships, like Burlington, Vermont, whose Mayor Bernard Sanders traveled to Puerto Cabezas, Nicaragua, in the late 1980s to deliver medical and other supplies.[26] Sanctuary activists sent aid to displaced people in Mexico and Guatemala during the wars and accompanied refugees home after the conflicts ended. Some founded institutions that continued to fight for human rights and fund grassroots community health, education, and other work in Central America.

The geography of sanctuary thus transcended the confines of sanctuary congregations and sanctuary cities. The Sanctuary Movement encompassed national and transnational networks of people, institutions, and cities working for peace and community development. The places where they "built sanctuary"—meaning spaces, practices, and communities of protection and support—extended from their churches and safe houses to workplaces, schools and universities, cities and towns with sanctuary policies, temporary encampments in the Guatemalan jungle where displaced people took refuge, and Central American villages, towns, and cities that people resettled and rebuilt after the civil wars.

These diverse meanings, critiques, and practices of sanctuary are not particular to the Central American crisis and the Sanctuary Movement of the 1980s. Rather, they expose larger patterns in the relationships between migration and cities. Disputes about who deserves a place in the nation and its cities and what sorts of support, if any, should be offered to newcomers have enflamed many episodes of American history, from colonial times to the twenty-first century.[27] Migrant and receiving communities have mobilized to confront the social, economic, and legal challenges faced by different newcomer groups. Their varied definitions, practices, and critiques of refuge, sanctuary, and sanctuary cities expose the great diversity and central tensions of America's immigrant and receiving communities. Their civil society organizations manifest what protection and assistance have meant for different individuals and communities. Their migration and their transnational work and lives reveal the ways in which US cities are linked to other parts of the world, especially places where our government has fueled violence and displacement.

This book examines the history of sanctuary, defined broadly as protection and assistance for vulnerable groups, in Philadelphia and the United States since the 1970s. The five chapters that follow this introduction explore the histories of Central American; Southeast Asian; Liberian; Iraqi, Syrian, and Palestinian; and Mexican migration, community building, and civil society. These groups have had different places in debates about immigration and US society and about newcomers in the city. They have each been prominent and controversial in some way. Together they illuminate most of the central lines of America's debates over immigration and many of the most important issues facing cities in the late twentieth and early twenty-first centuries.

## Migration, Sanctuary, and Cities

The multifaceted notion of sanctuary, this book contends, offers an important way to understand the relationships between migration, migrants, and cities. It affords a broad perspective across the arc of people's migration, settlement, and continued relationships with their homelands as well as receiving communities' relationships with newcomers over time. Considering sanctuary helps us relate the politics and geopolitics of immigration to people's everyday experiences. It offers a lens through which to trace the disputed, evolving positions of different newcomer groups in US society and in the city, its neighborhoods and communities.

The concept of sanctuary demands that we consider not only municipal policies and politics but also the relationships between the local, national, and transnational contexts of different migrations. Why are particular groups here? What sorts of protection do our governments and communities afford them, and why? Protection from what? Answering these questions can help us make sense of the United States' and its cities' relationships with different nations and peoples of the world.

Attention to the contested nature of sanctuary, including refugees' and immigrants' critiques of the limits and ironies of their protection, underscores global and local struggles over power and human rights. Scholars of critical refugee studies have advocated a departure from predominant views of refugees as helpless victims, objects of rescue, and crises or problems in themselves. Rather, refugees' experiences make visible the ongoing processes of imperialism, conflict, state violence, displacement, and the racialized and gendered ways in which people are made subjects of the nations and cities that receive them.[28] In a broader sense, this applies to immigrants at large.

Parsing the variety of humanitarian assistance entailed in sanctuary illuminates the everyday experiences of immigrant, refugee, and receiving communities in housing, work, legal aid, safety, friendship, and other key dimensions of communities' well-being. What sorts of problems do different groups face? What help are they offered and by whom? How do the answers to these questions shape people's experiences of settlement, relations between newcomer and receiving communities, and people's ability to transcend social, economic, and other challenges over time? More simply, in the words of urban planner Leonie Sandercock, "How can we . . . strangers live together without doing each other too much violence?"[29] Exploring these questions forces us to reflect on what we owe one another as human beings, as neighbors and inhabitants of a deeply interconnected world.

As an analytical framework, sanctuary elevates the interests and agency of both newcomers and old-timers more explicitly than inquiries that mainly ask, "What have immigrants done for cities?" This latter line of questioning commonly refers to economic outcomes, population growth, and other statistics that matter but that fail to capture the most immediate, intense, and meaningful impacts of immigrant and refugee settlement for most city residents, new and old. Exploring sanctuary illuminates much about urban revitalization and the economic costs and benefits of immigration for the United States, for cities, and for migrant and receiving communities. But it also reveals something more human and more complex. Examining people's everyday experiences, their problems and how they address them, removes immigration and its impacts from the realm of the abstract. *Sanctuary* as a set of practices, a term activists use as both a noun and a verb, invites us to understand people, especially newcomers, as the central actors in shaping the relationships between migration and cities, partly through the civil society institutions they form and run.

Sanctuary has existed in tension with other ways in which Americans understand the relationships between immigration (or immigrants) and cities, whether popular concerns about the "invasion" of "aliens," costs and benefits, or more affirmative ideas about revitalization.[30] The Philadelphia sanctuary city campaign in 1986 addressed people who feared sanctuary cities would "open up our country to hundreds of millions of refugees if we set this precedent," asserting in response that "it's not clear that we would be harmed" by the arrival of "more illegal immigrants." They cited "economic studies in California" showing that "these people pay considerably more into the government in taxes than they receive in social services, government benefits, public school expenditures. . . . In other words, they subsidize our governments," and as low-wage workers, they "are benefitting the private sector as well."[31] More recently, sanctuary activists have celebrated immigrants' contributions to urban revitalization while citing similar studies that demonstrate the positive impacts of immigration on America's economy and public safety.[32]

However, such arguments have made many sanctuary activists uncomfortable given their reduction of immigrants and their merits to economic units and their apparent celebration of inequality and low-wage, precarious work. Still, this narrative of economic contributions as a justification for immigrants' right to stay played well with politicians and other allies in the 1980s. It was even more powerful in the 2000s and 2010s, when people witnessed immigrant-led revitalization across the country. The commitment of some local politicians to sanctuary city policies stemmed narrowly from a desire to perpetuate that growth. Therefore, while they continued to employ the narratives of revitalization and benefits (more than costs), activists in the late twentieth and early twenty-first centuries also articulated more humanistic and more sacred justifications for sanctuary and sanctuary cities. They stressed religious traditions, moral imperatives, and cities' historical commitments to offering protection and assistance to vulnerable people.

Scholars have less often conceived of cities as sanctuaries and have commonly viewed sanctuary policies and movements with skepticism. Some argue that the relationships between hosts and guests always limit the possibility for people to accept one another unconditionally. The host country's laws of immigration, asylum, and refugee protection are only the most obvious limits on the rights and acceptance of guests. They produce an ever-present imbalance of power among people that neither city governments nor civil society can overcome.[33]

Social scientists have cast sanctuary city policies as a form of urban citizenship and governance that allows cities to delimit the rights of migrants. Their guarantee of access to services enables cities to manage undocumented populations and their impacts on the city, including its health and safety and its budget, in part by limiting who gets specific protections and support—once again distinguishing between deserving and undeserving immigrants.[34] Some critics charge that sanctuary policies do little more than sustain an unjust status quo in which migrants who lack legal status continue to do precarious work that enriches the city and its more privileged classes.[35]

Activists and scholars have also lamented the limits of social movements and civil society to offer migrants fuller protections, which might enable people to transcend their social, economic, and legal insecurity. Congregations offering sanctuary help shield a small number of immigrants from detention but do little to alter communities' fundamental vulnerabilities.[36] Charity and community support, according to some critics, should never be expected to provide an enduring system to welcome and protect vulnerable newcomers.[37] Yet to varying degrees in different places and communities, such systems do exist in US cities: witness the long-term work and larger impacts of sanctuary movements and a broader set of civil society institutions.

Historically, sanctuary city protections have been episodic, but civil society has a long record of assistance to migrants in the United States, with substantial continuities. In the nineteenth century, middle-class reformers established missions, settlement houses, and other organizations to aid newcomers in cities across the nation. Immigrants themselves started mutual aid associations and other organizations. Some of these institutions survive today as social service providers, community centers, and refugee resettlement agencies.

Civil society gives the humanitarian assistance aspects of sanctuary a bigger history than just sanctuary city protections or even sanctuary movements. The story of the Sanctuary Movement and some of the institutions it produced, as recounted in this chapter and the next one, indicates this. Civil society also exposes and helps to make up for the limits of protections and assistance from the state, including the resettlement system, which is the most concerted support the United States offers to vulnerable people from abroad. To be sure, some parts of civil society, such as white supremacist movements and militias, promote violence and oppression. Moreover, civil society has never had the resources to fully compensate for the failures of the state. Its powers and success are limited, and tensions between different parts of civil society persist. Nonetheless, from human rights organizations and health clinics to employment and legal services and from soccer leagues to transnational hometown associations, the spaces and supports that civil society offers people matter deeply to most immigrant and receiving communities. In the words of political scientist Els de Graauw, civil society is key to "making immigrant rights real" by helping people seek, claim, and exercise rights, needs, and privileges.[38]

This book explores sanctuary in large part through the work of civil society, tracing the ways in which different communities have organized and addressed the challenges they faced. Injustice and violence fill many pages—both physical violence and structural violence, meaning political and economic structures or systems that produce oppression. Yet it presents a more optimistic view of civil society, and of sanctuary, than some of the criticism noted previously, even if it shares many of the same critiques of sanctuary city politics and policies. Local and transnational community revitalization are important parts of this story. As suggested in this chapter, however, revitalization does not fully describe the deeper, more challenging problems and processes of building and repairing communities in US cities and the regions around the world to which migration has increasingly tied us.

As indicated by the people who testified at the Philadelphia City Council hearing in 2014, sanctuary has often meant different things for different immigrant, refugee, and receiving communities. The city is a sanctuary *from* something different for each community—sometimes for each individual or family—and communities' and individuals' experiences of sanctuary in the city vary widely. The United States' relationships with nations and peoples around the world condition the position of all immigrants in the country. The state divides newcomers into categories that grant distinct rights and privileges to different people.

The further protections and support that newcomer and receiving communities seek and build illuminate their diverse processes of community formation and development over time. Their civil society organizations have evolved in ways that are sometimes similar but often different, befitting communities' specific legal, work, and housing problems; religious institutions; cultural practices; and transnational ties. They have also experienced diverse trajectories of wealth and mobility, community relations, and places in local, national, and international debates about migration. Their experiences, geographies, visions, and critiques of sanctuary (and its closest synonym, refuge) thus help us grasp some of the tremendous diversity of America's immigrants and refugees and of our cities and receiving communities.

Ultimately, all, or almost all, the groups featured in this book have become part of the fabric of the city and region. They have all built protections and support systems, with varying levels of help, resistance, and collaboration with receiving communities. Their experiences in the late twentieth and early twenty-first centuries are particular to their time, though they echo broader patterns in the history of migration, cities, and sanctuary.

## Sanctuary and Cities in History

The protections and assistance that migrants find in sanctuary cities have varied over time, as have the reasons why cities and communities offer sanctuary. Another clause in the draft resolution of the 1986 Philadelphia campaign underscored that sanctuary was a core function of the city and the nation since their founding:

WHEREAS: Both the United States and the City of Philadelphia have for centuries served as a haven for refugees of religious and political persecution from all parts of the world, and much of the historical and moral tradition of our nation is rooted in the provision of sanctuary to persecuted peoples.[39]

Philadelphia was "the city to which religious dissidents of all kinds could come during the colonial era," and later "a major link in the Underground Railroad," the campaign's organizers emphasized in another outreach letter. They likened declaring sanctuary city status to the refusal of certain cities and states to cooperate with the Fugitive Slave Act, which required the return of escaped slaves to their owners in the South before the Civil War.[40] People at the 2014 city council hearing cited each of these historical reference points, among others.

Cities have functioned as places of sanctuary for millennia, while empires and nations have fluctuated in their willingness to offer legal and physical protections. Religious and state authorities selected certain cities and towns as sanctuaries in ancient Hebrew, Indian, Hawaiian, later-medieval European, and colonial-era Native American societies. "Tell the Israelites to designate the cities of refuge," states the Bible (Josh. 20:2), while Moses proclaimed that areas in the Promised Land "shall be a refuge, for the children of Israel, and for the stranger" (Num. 35:15). As the Bible also explains (Exod. 21:12–14), ancient sanctuary cities commonly shielded people from retribution for involuntary manslaughter, to prevent blood feuds, or after defeat in battle. Local authorities typically vetted people seeking refuge to confirm they deserved protection and assistance. The Greeks, Romans, and early Christians shared this tradition, though their sanctuaries were usually temples and churches, not entire cities.[41]

In Judeo-Christian tradition, the term *sanctuary* came to mean both the sacred space where a community of faith worshipped and a place of refuge. People supporting and offering sanctuary have commonly seen these two meanings, and by extension the love of God and love of one's neighbor, as inseparable.[42] Advocates emphasize the biblical values of compassion, forgiveness, and mercy—of "welcoming the stranger" and "loving him as thyself"—which are also found in Muslim, Buddhist, Hindu, Native American, and other traditions.[43]

In modern history, African American towns from Texas to New Jersey, as well as some white towns and congregations, protected Blacks who were fleeing slavery and later racial violence. They provided shelter, food, and employment. People who stayed often gained broader rights of membership, including property. In France, Italy, and other European countries, sanctuary villages and towns, which were usually organized by Catholic congregations, harbored Jewish refugees during the Spanish Civil War and World War II.[44]

Sanctuary cities in the late twentieth and early twenty-first centuries evoked these histories but were centrally focused on immigrants and refugees. The sanctuary policies of US cities in the 2000s used much the same language as those of the 1980s and the sanctuary movements of these decades shared many similarities. But the immigrants and refugees for whom they mattered, as well as the ways in which they mattered, were different. While the 1980s movement focused on Central America, the newest wave of American sanctuary cities grew out of a more general opposition to federal immigration and deportation policies and a growing anti-immigrant movement. Some cities' policies predated the eruption of immigration debates in late 2001, 2005, and 2016. The events of these years, however, helped give sanctuary and sanctuary cities their specific meanings in this period, just as debates over what the nation owed—and what it did—to Central American and Southeast Asian refugees helped give sanctuary and refuge their meanings in the 1980s.

Philadelphia's twenty-first-century sanctuary policy was prompted by federal efforts to involve local police in enforcing immigration. The Illegal Immigration Reform and Immigrant Responsibility Act of 1996 allowed the INS to partner with local jurisdictions and deputize officers as immigration agents. Shortly after Nelson Diaz became city solicitor in early 2001, INS agents approached the city's police department about entering into a 287g agreement (named for a clause in that act). A former judge and general counsel at the US Department of Housing and Urban Development, Diaz had experience in quietly heading off attempts to exclude Latinos and undocumented immigrants from public housing. "Generally, Puerto Ricans," like himself, "have always been very pro-immigration," he explained.[45]

With a formal opinion issued in May 2001, "I instructed all officials in the entire city that they had no obligation with regard to enforcing any immigration issues, and that if anyone had any issues of health care or police issues, they were to get services, irrespective of their status."[46] Under the US Constitution, state and local governments are not required to do the work of the federal government, and regulating immigration is a federal matter. Diaz and his boss, Mayor John Street, an African American, asked Police Commissioner John Timoney, an immigrant from Ireland, to issue a separate memo establishing a formal policy for the police department. It read:

A. While the City has various services available to immigrants, few take advantage of these services because they fear that any contact with these agencies may bring their immigration status to the attention of the federal authorities.

B. All immigrants should be encouraged to utilize these City services without fear of any reprisals because the city has no obligation to report any illegal immigrants to the federal government as long as they are law abiding. The Police Department will preserve the confidentiality of all information regarding law abiding immigrants to the maximum extent permitted by law.[47]

However, this police policy stipulated that when immigrants were "suspected of engaging in criminal activity," the department would "continue to cooperate with federal authorities in investigating and apprehending" them.[48]

"I very quietly didn't say anything to anybody" in the media or outside of city agencies, Diaz stressed. "Then I got a call" from Allegheny County several months later. In response, he helped Pittsburgh and neighboring local governments in the county to replicate the policy.[49] In Philadelphia, though, authorities were so quiet about the policy that people in immigrant communities and later administrations in city hall rarely knew about it, including most of the activists who launched sanctuary city campaigns in the next decade.

That September, sanctuary almost became a far less important issue, if not entirely irrelevant. On Tuesday evening, September 4, 2001, President Vicente Fox of Mexico arrived in Washington, DC. Over the next three days, he would address a joint session of Congress and help President George W. Bush initiate immigration reform that would offer most of the roughly thirteen million people who were in the United States illegally a path to citizenship. However, the following Tuesday morning, Al-Qaeda terrorists hijacked commercial airplanes and slammed them into the World Trade Center towers in New York and the Pentagon outside the capitol. National security concerns immediately took over immigration debates. The Patriot Act increased government surveillance powers and restricted civil liberties. The Department of Justice expanded collaboration with local law enforcement in detaining and deporting people who were in the country illegally.[50] A new era in America's immigration history began, one in which sanctuary became increasingly relevant.

The act that intensified America's fight over immigration and its relationship to cities, even more than the terrorist attacks of September 11, 2001, came in December 2005. The US House of Representatives passed a bill that month making it a felony, no longer just a civil offense, to be in the country illegally or to provide any type of assistance to people who were in the country illegally.[51]

Starting in Philadelphia on Valentine's Day 2006, a series of "Day Without an Immigrant" marches ensued in cities across the country. After the US Senate rejected the House bill later that spring, local and state governments attempted to take immigration control into their own hands. In July, the small city of Hazleton, Pennsylvania, passed the nation's first Illegal Immigration Relief Act, claiming local action was necessary if politicians in Washington would not pass immigration reform. This was the opposite of a sanctuary city policy. It threatened to fine and revoke licenses of landlords and employers of people who were in the country illegally, and also declared that Hazleton's official language was English, opposing federal directives to translate public documents for speakers of other languages.[52]

A polarized landscape of sanctuary and anti-immigrant cities and states took form across the United States.[53] Other local governments immediately copied Hazleton's act, especially old mining and manufacturing centers in eastern Pennsylvania. By mid-October, the state was home to twenty-seven of the forty-nine such bills that had been introduced across the country. In the Philadelphia suburbs, the old factory towns of Riverside, New Jersey, and Bridgeport, Pennsylvania, passed acts that were copied word-for-word from Hazleton. Riverside later repealed its act as residents and local politicians regretted that it had sparked an exodus of Brazilian immigrants who had buoyed the town's housing market and economy. They were also embarrassed by national media attention. This reversal made Riverside what urban planner Teresa Vazquez-Castillo called a "repentant city."[54]

Other cities affirmed or reaffirmed their commitments to sanctuary. By April 2008, more than seventy municipalities and four states had established sanctuary policies.[55] Between 2009 and 2014, in response to pressure from advocates and following cities such as New Haven, Connecticut, and Chicago, Philadelphia incrementally phased out most of its collaboration in federal immigration enforcement.[56] In December 2015, however, outgoing Mayor Michael Nutter rescinded most of the sanctuary policy, only promising that the police would withhold the identities of victims and witnesses of crime. He apparently sought to curry favor with the administration of President Barack Obama, which had been pressuring the city to abandon its sanctuary policy. But new Mayor Jim Kenney signed the fuller protections back into effect on his first day in office in January 2016.[57]

The election of Donald Trump to the presidency later that year threatened immigrants and sanctuary cities. Straight away, Philadelphia and other cities began preparing to defend their sanctuary policies in court and mobilizing to support immigrant communities. In California, legislators passed a sanctuary state law. In his first week in office, President Trump signed executive orders to strip federal funding from sanctuary cities, build a wall on the border with Mexico, suspend the United States' refugee resettlement program, temporarily ban migration and travel from majority-Muslim nations, and permanently end the resettlement of Syrian refugees.[58] In summer 2018, Philadelphia, Chicago, and the state of California all defeated federal legal challenges to their sanctuary policies, while the Supreme Court upheld the third version of Trump's "Muslim ban."

With Trump's election, hundreds of congregations and thousands of people joined the New Sanctuary Movement, which had been established in Washington, DC; Chicago; New York; Philadelphia; and other cities starting in 2006. Under the Trump administration, member congregations in Philadelphia and other cities began to host more people in sanctuary who were claiming asylum but threatened with deportation. The city was again a major hub of sanctuary activism, partly since it had become something it was not in the 1980s, an important center of immigration.

The sanctuary movements of the late twentieth and early twenty-first centuries took place in distinct yet similar eras of US political history but very different periods of American urban and immigration history. The United States remained a global power throughout these decades, though the end of the Cold War shifted the nation's priorities concerning whom should be offered refuge.[59] Refugees in the 1970s and 1980s experienced a resettlement system that was just beginning to formalize. People arriving in Philadelphia and most of the country in these decades settled in cities and towns whose histories of immigration lay generations in the past and whose neighborhoods and public services were suffering from disinvestment. In contrast, people arriving in the twenty-first century largely experienced places that were growing again, thanks mainly to increased immigration.

## Migration to Philadelphia

The immigrant and refugee groups featured in this book represent much but not all of the recent history of immigration in Philadelphia and other urban regions of the United States. The Philadelphia region is a particular sort of immigrant destination, what sociologist Audrey Singer has termed a "re-emerging gateway."[60] It does not share the continuous history of large-scale immigration that New York, Chicago, and the Southwest experienced across the twentieth century. But Philadelphia does manifest the predominant patterns and trends in late twentieth- and early twenty-first-century immigration and cities that are shared by most of the rest of the country.

Internal migrations influenced the city and region's population and neighborhoods most profoundly from the 1940s to the end of the twentieth century. The arrival of African Americans and Puerto Ricans and the departure of whites and many manufacturers that employed them to the suburbs and the Sun Belt transformed the racial and economic geography of the city and region. Even after the 1965 immigration act reopened US borders following an era of immigration restriction that began in the 1920s, in the Philadelphia region, applications for citizenship declined. "The reason," reported the Philadelphia *Evening Bulletin,* "seems to be a drop in the number of older immigrants coming to the United States, and an increase in the number of younger arrivals." This mattered for the region, since "older immigrants tended to remain here, while the younger ones are moving to other parts of the country to seek jobs," following "big companies and corporations . . . moving southward."[61] Philadelphia's deindustrialization in this era made it a less attractive destination for immigrants of working age, even as internal migrants were recruited to fill some of the factory jobs that remained.[62] Big and small cities across the Rust Belt had much the same experience.

The population of the city and region remained predominantly native-born whites, Blacks, and Puerto Ricans, but at the end of the twentieth century the foreign-born population grew and diversified. The city became a major site of refugee resettlement in the late 1970s and 1980s, before it revived as a significant destination for other immigrants in the 1990s. Most of the European immigrants who made up the great majority of the region's foreign-born population in 1970 and 1980 were older people who had come during the first half of the century. Italians and Germans were the largest foreign-born groups in the region as late as 1990. But that year, people from Korea, India, Vietnam, and the Philippines were also among the region's top ten immigrant groups. Tables I.1 and I.2 document the ten largest foreign-born groups, as well as native-born groups, in the city of Philadelphia and the metropolitan area in 1970, 1990, and 2010.

By 2010, Indians and Mexicans were the largest immigrant groups in the region, followed by people from China, Vietnam, Korea, Germany, and the Dominican Republic. Inside the city, Haitians, Jamaicans, Cambodians, and Liberians were also in the top ten. Smaller communities hailed from around the world: refugees from East and West Africa, the Middle East, and South and Southeast Asia and immigrants from everywhere arriving on family, work, and diversity visas or crossing the border illegally, especially from Mexico and Central America. Philadelphia was still not as diverse as global cities such as Los Angeles, Miami, or New York, which all had much higher proportions of immigrants. But foreign-born Philadelphians generally embodied the diversity

Table I.1  Population of the City of Philadelphia (1970, 1990, and 2010)

| 1970 | | 1990 | | 2010 | |
|---|---|---|---|---|---|
| Total Population | 1,949,100 | Total Population | 1,577,804 | Total Population | 1,504,736 |
| Foreign-born Population | 131,900 | Foreign-Born Population | 111,385 | Foreign-Born Population | 182,449 |
| Italy | 28,300 | USSR/Russia | 11,597 | Vietnam | 14,114 |
| USSR/Russia | 25,800 | Italy | 9,372 | China | 13,719 |
| Germany | 15,300 | Korea | 5,695 | India | 12,256 |
| Poland | 9,100 | Vietnam | 5,598 | Dominican Republic | 10,654 |
| United Kingdom | 8,500 | Poland | 5,400 | Mexico | 7,201 |
| Ireland | 4,500 | Germany | 5,031 | Ukraine | 6,426 |
| Ukraine | 4,400 | India | 4,454 | Haiti | 6,346 |
| Austria | 3,700 | China | 4,031 | Jamaica | 6,274 |
| Canada | 2,400 | Jamaica | 3,402 | Cambodia | 4,988 |
| Yugoslavia | 2,400 | Cambodia | 3,384 | Liberia | 4,272 |
| Native-Born (NB) Population | 1,817,200 | Native-Born (NB) Population | 1,466,419 | Native-Born (NB) Population | 1,322,287 |
| NB White | 1,136,300 | NB White | 769,624 | NB White | 509,671 |
| NB Black | 645,400 | NB Black | 611,103 | NB Black | 615,622 |
| NB Asian and Pacific Islander | 2,800 | NB Asian and Pacific Islander | 9,028 | NB Asian and Pacific Islander | 29,344 |
| NB Native American | 1,300 | NB Native American | 1,908 | NB Native American | 1,917 |
| NB Hispanic (any race) | 30,600 | NB Hispanic (any race) | 73,549 | NB Hispanic (any race) | 144,371 |
| NB Other | 800 | NB Other | 26,711 | NB Other | 21,262 |

Source: US Census Bureau: 1970 and 1990 Decennial Census, 2006–2010 American Community Survey from IPUMS USA (Steven Ruggles, Sarah Flood, Sophia Foster, Ronald Goeken, Jose Pacas, Megan Schouweiler and Matthew Sobek. IPUMS USA: Version 11.0 [dataset]. Minneapolis, MN: IPUMS, 2021). Table by Danielle Dong and Arthur Acolin.

The table lists the ten largest foreign-born groups in each year, along with native-born groups.

Table I.2   Population of the Philadelphia Primary Metropolitan Statistical Area (1970, 1990, and 2010)

| 1970 | | 1990 | | 2010 | |
| --- | --- | --- | --- | --- | --- |
| Total Population | 4,796,100 | Total Population | 4,834,728 | Total Population | 5,278,069 |
| Foreign-Born Population | 262,500 | Foreign-Born Population | 276,476 | Foreign-Born Population | 520,593 |
| Italy | 50,300 | Italy | 23,485 | India | 51,916 |
| Germany | 34,800 | Germany | 18,356 | Mexico | 42,179 |
| USSR/Russia | 32,900 | United Kingdom | 18,285 | China | 28,203 |
| United Kingdom | 27,700 | Korea | 16,842 | Vietnam | 25,877 |
| Poland | 16,000 | USSR/Russia | 16,504 | Korea | 24,733 |
| Canada | 11,000 | India | 14,141 | Germany | 18,219 |
| Ireland | 9,800 | Vietnam | 9,255 | Dominican Republic | 16,795 |
| Austria | 6,400 | Poland | 9,200 | Philippines | 15,703 |
| Hungary | 5,900 | Philippines | 9,158 | Italy | 14,879 |
| Greece | 5,400 | Canada | 8,217 | Ukraine | 14,494 |
| Native-Born (NB) Population | 4,533,600 | Native-Born (NB) Population | 4,558,252 | Native-Born (NB) Population | 4,757,476 |
| NB White | 3,645,100 | NB White | 3,497,898 | NB White | 3,308,286 |
| NB Black | 829,200 | NB Black | 887,705 | NB Black | 1,003,274 |
| NB Asian and Pacific Islander | 5,700 | NB Asian and Pacific Islander | 24,851 | NB Asian and Pacific Islander | 77,770 |
| NB Native American | 2,500 | NB Native American | 6,738 | NB Native American | 5,271 |
| NB Hispanic (any race) | 49,500 | NB Hispanic (any race) | 138,018 | NB Hispanic (any race) | 286,885 |
| NB Other | 1,600 | NB Other | 3,042 | NB Other | 75,990 |

Source: US Census Bureau: 1970 and 1990 Decennial Census, 2006–2010 American Community Survey from IPUMS USA (Steven Ruggles, Sarah Flood, Sophia Foster, Ronald Goeken, Jose Pacas, Megan Schouweiler and Matthew Sobek. IPUMS USA: Version 11.0 [dataset]. Minneapolis, MN: IPUMS, 2021). Table by Danielle Dong and Arthur Acolin.

The table lists the ten largest foreign-born groups in the city and eight surrounding suburban counties in Pennsylvania and New Jersey in each year, along with native-born groups.

of immigrants in the twenty-first-century United States at large, in terms of ethnic and national origins as well as educational backgrounds, wealth, occupations, and legal status.

The city and suburbs shared with most of the rest of the nation the take-off in immigration in the 1990s and the spread of immigrant settlement to new and re-emerging gateways in the Rust Belt, the South, and the Mountain West. In 2008, the US Census Bureau announced that after losing close to one-third of its population since 1952 (from 2.2 million to less than 1.5), the city was growing again, thanks to immigration.[63] This was another trend that it shared with most cities, as immigrants played a central role in reversing decades-long declines. Indeed, without immigration every metropolitan area in the US would have lost population in the early twenty-first century.[64] Since more than one-quarter of all immigrants in the country lacked legal status in this era, even without illegal immigration alone, many cities and suburbs would have shrunk.[65]

Philadelphia also became a prominent center of activism for both sanctuary and immigration restriction in the early twenty-first century, in part because it became home to many people who were in the country illegally. They ranged from Mexicans who came after the agricultural economies of small towns crashed in the 1990s to their neighbors in South Philadelphia from Indonesia, who were Christians whose asylum claims were often denied. They included people from China, Haiti, Ireland, and all over the globe who had stayed past the expiration date of their tourist, work, or student visas. They also included some people who came as refugees, particularly from Southeast Asia, who were eligible for citizenship but then targeted for deportation following changes in federal law and international agreements. In the 2010s, many people arrived from Central America, fleeing violence and often claiming asylum, yet again federal authorities were reluctant to grant it.

As the following map shows, new immigrants settled across the city and region. In the city, they concentrated especially in row house neighborhoods and sometimes in apartments in Northeast, South, West, and Southwest Philadelphia. Many also settled in working-class suburbs such as Upper Darby, Bensalem, and Norristown and across the river in the city of Camden and adjacent towns in New Jersey. Wealthier immigrants tended to settle in more dispersed patterns around the region, from condominiums downtown to large single homes in the far suburbs.

The groups profiled in this book are predominantly refugees and working-class immigrants with tenuous legal status, whether illegal, temporary, or otherwise contested. The chapters focus mostly on first-generation migrants and relate the experiences of later generations more concisely. Many of the

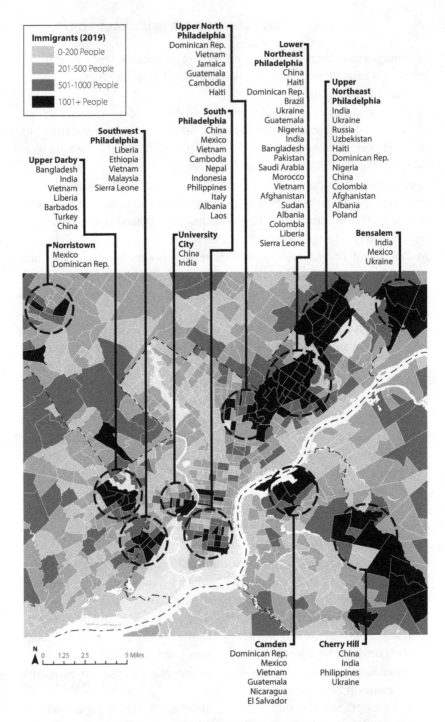

**Immigrants (2019)**
- 0–200 People
- 201–500 People
- 501–1000 People
- 1001+ People

**Upper North Philadelphia**
Dominican Rep.
Vietnam
Jamaica
Guatemala
Cambodia
Haiti

**Lower Northeast Philadelphia**
China
Haiti
Dominican Rep.
Brazil
Ukraine
Guatemala
Nigeria
India
Bangladesh
Pakistan
Saudi Arabia
Morocco
Vietnam
Afghanistan
Sudan
Albania
Colombia
Liberia
Sierra Leone

**Upper Northeast Philadelphia**
India
Ukraine
Russia
Uzbekistan
Haiti
Dominican Rep.
Nigeria
China
Colombia
Afghanistan
Albania
Poland

**South Philadelphia**
China
Mexico
Vietnam
Cambodia
Nepal
Indonesia
Philippines
Italy
Albania
Laos

**Southwest Philadelphia**
Liberia
Ethiopia
Vietnam
Malaysia
Sierra Leone

**Upper Darby**
Bangladesh
India
Vietnam
Liberia
Barbados
Turkey
China

**Norristown**
Mexico
Dominican Rep.

**University City**
China
India

**Bensalem**
India
Mexico
Ukraine

**Camden**
Dominican Rep.
Mexico
Vietnam
Guatemala
Nicaragua
El Salvador

**Cherry Hill**
China
India
Philippines
Ukraine

N
0   1.25   2.5        5 Miles

**FIGURE I.1.**   Map of the largest concentrations of immigrant settlement in Philadelphia and adjacent suburbs in 2019, listing predominant foreign-born groups in different neighborhoods and towns in order of their prevalence in those areas. (Source: American Community Survey; map by Danielle Dong.)

refugees in this book came from middle-class backgrounds. But middle-class immigrant groups, especially those working in the region's robust medical, pharmaceutical, and higher education industries and living in more affluent suburbs, are under-represented in this study. They are arguably the people for whom sanctuary matters least, though this varies and can change quickly.

Central Americans, Southeast Asians, Liberians, Arabs, and Mexicans present a set of communities that are especially well suited to excavating the various meanings and manifestations of sanctuary in recent US history. Chapter 1 explores the Sanctuary Movement of the 1980s and the solidarity movements that gave sanctuary in that era much of its meanings. It also traces Guatemalans' and Salvadorans' later experiences of settlement and sanctuary in the twenty-first-century city. The next chapter relates the experiences of refugees from Vietnam, Cambodia, and Laos and the evolution of the resettlement system that grew up in response to their displacement. This and the following two chapters reflect on changes and continuities in resettlement and on different refugees' experiences of the city in the period between the depths of its decline in the 1970s and 1980s and its revitalization since the 1990s.

On the surface, sanctuary may not seem like the right term to describe the experiences of people with formal refugee status. Refuge is the more obvious word. But Southeast Asians, Liberians, Arabs, and other refugees have been contested, politically and popularly, their acceptance into American society and our cities and neighborhoods disputed in ways that made protections and support beyond their refugee status and resettlement services necessary. Structural and physical violence shaped not just their displacement but also their lives in America. Thus, they still faced challenges of safety and survival as individuals, families, and communities. Moreover, their legal status in the United States has been neither monolithic nor static and has sometimes changed in traumatic ways.

The Temporary Protected Status and Deferred Enforced Departure status of many Liberians offers one illustration of this, which is detailed in chapter 3. Since the 1990s, when Liberians migrated and were resettled during and after their country's civil war, the United States increasingly granted certain groups more limited protections than permanent refuge or asylum. The transatlantic and local history of Liberian Philadelphia also illuminates multiple diasporas of people of African descent. Like other chapters but to an even greater degree, this chapter explores the complex relationships among immigrants and the city's largely African American receiving communities.

The next two chapters discuss what many Americans consider to be the focal points of twenty-first-century immigration debates. Chapter 4 examines refugee and immigrant groups from the Middle East, mainly Palestinians, Iraqis, and Syrians, in the years before and after 2001 and the subsequent US invasion of Iraq. It grapples with some of the myths and realities of Arabs' position in American society and in the city, including the ways in which Muslims and their allies confront the words and actions of people who believe they do not belong in the United States at all.[66] Chapter 5 explores recent Mexican migration and the pro- and anti-immigrant movements of the twenty-first century, including the New Sanctuary Movement, parsing the new and old meanings it gave to sanctuary and the sanctuary city.

Each chapter begins with the story of one individual or family's reasons for and experience of migration to Philadelphia and introduces their homeland's historical relationship with the United States. The second section of each chapter reflects on what protections and support the United States owed people from their country. The subsequent sections then detail each group's experiences of settlement in the city, including employment, housing, neighborhoods, and relationships with neighbors, and then examine how civil society evolved to address these and other challenges, both locally and transnationally. Each chapter concludes by carrying forward the story to the start of the 2020s, considering how sanctuary remained or became newly relevant.

While it charts several decades of recent history, this is also a book that engages ongoing realities: what we still owe one another and what we do to and for and with one another in the present. It is about receiving communities as well as immigrants. It is not just a history we can leave in the past, nor one we can see as simply other people's problem.

# CHAPTER 1

# Sanctuary in Solidarity

## Central Americans and the Sanctuary Movement

"Being forced to leave your country causes a pain that stays with you for the rest of your life. It is not the same as choosing to come here," observed Joel Morelos (a pseudonym).[1] "I was born and raised in a very bad situation," in the small city of Escuintla in southern Guatemala, on one of the country's largest plantations, a few years before civil war broke out in 1960. The war would last for thirty-six years, as the US-backed military abducted and murdered activists, bombed indigenous communities, and battled leftist rebels.[2] "When you are born in that kind of situation, you start saying 'what's going on?' I mean, you see all kinds of things and you start asking questions."[3]

His father was a union organizer, and from an early age Joel had a well-developed sense of the injustices of their government and military. At eight or nine years old he broke their curfew to get medicine for his sick mother, but soldiers cornered him on his way back, threatening to beat and kill him. A couple of years after primary school, he went to work as a carpenter in the maintenance shop of a sugar cane plantation and also picked coffee to help feed the family. He joined a group of youth who petitioned the government for high school classes at night, as young people were doing in other parts of the country, so those who worked could continue their education. This movement angered authorities with its demonstrations in Guatemala City and the countryside, though after two years of advocacy, Escuintla did start a night school.[4]

As a teen, Joel joined a group of peasants demanding greater rights and representation in local government. As a mestizo of mixed European and indigenous descent, he was treated better than most of the peasants, who were Maya and lacked access to schooling or political power and experienced greater poverty. "I had good luck because I had food," Joel explained. "A lot of people didn't have that. Seeing that situation pushed me to be active, to tell my opinions."[5] But this along with his involvement in student organizing and the sugar industry workers' union all put him in bad standing with government leaders.[6]

In 1977, following a student march, armed men in plain clothes whom Joel, then age twenty, did not recognize grabbed him, pushed him into a car, blindfolded him, and drove to an empty cinderblock house. They spent two hours torturing him, kicking him in the head, stabbing him in the shoulder, extinguishing cigarettes on his skin, and interrogating him about student groups in which he had been active. They accused him of teaching revolutionary Communist theories, though he had barely heard of Communism and did not know any Communists.[7]

Unlike most of the roughly 45,000 Guatemalans who were "disappeared" by military death squads between the mid-1970s and mid-1980s, Joel survived.[8] This was unintentional, as his captors left him in a garbage heap by the road, assuming he would die. Instead, he was able to crawl home and get treatment for his wounds, though he would forever be deaf in one ear and bear scars on his hands and arms. The only reason the squads did not come after him again, he believed, was that he had come upon the son of the local police chief after a motorcycle accident and took him to the hospital.[9]

But in May 1980, three days after Joel married his girlfriend, Gabriela, his name appeared on a "death list" circulated at the plantation where he worked by a group that called itself Squadron of Death. For the next two years the couple hid with friends, taking different routes to work each day. A gunman shot at Joel in the marketplace one day but missed, and Gabriela narrowly avoided abduction. Her brother, also a union member, was disappeared, and most of Joel's colleagues in the leadership of the union and student groups were killed or fled the country. In 1983, the couple decided to leave too, after Joel's name appeared on another death list put out by a squad calling itself the Secret Anticommunist Army.[10]

Joel and Gabriela joined the over 400,000 Guatemalans, including many activists, who fled their country's repressive military dictatorships during the civil war, especially at the height of violence in the 1980s.[11] This was on top of more than one million people who were displaced internally within the country by 1982.[12] Carrying their infant daughter, Lucy, Joel and Gabriela walked through the mountains and took back-road buses two hundred miles to the Mexican border, where they met friends who had left before them. After crossing into Mexico, they avoided the camps where Mexican authorities were herding people to deport them back to Guatemala. Instead, they tried to pass for Mexicans. Joel found a job selling photo albums door to door and they rented a small room. He went to talk with a lawyer at the local United Nations office but the lawyer told him that Mexico was not granting asylum.[13]

Getting asylum in the United States was virtually impossible thanks to its long-standing allegiances in Central America. As far back as 1954 the US Central Intelligence Agency (CIA) had helped overthrow a civilian government in Guatemala and install a military government. It did this after the democratically elected president, Colonel Jacobo Arbenz, began taking land from some of the 2 percent of landowners in the country who owned 70 percent of its arable land and redistributing it among landless peasants. The administration of President Dwight Eisenhower intervened covertly at the urging of the New Orleans–based United Fruit Company, the largest landowner in Guatemala since the 1930s. CIA director Allen Dulles had served on the company's board and had done legal work for it with his brother, Eisenhower's secretary of state, John Foster Dulles. In addition to more than 40 percent of the nation's land, which was acquired largely in a deal negotiated by John Foster Dulles, United Fruit owned Guatemala's telephone and telegraph systems and almost all its railroad infrastructure. This mix of corporate, political, and military influence made Central American countries what Americans since the start of the twentieth century called "banana republics." And even though less than 0.1 percent of Guatemalans were Communists, Arbenz's decision to allow them to participate in politics amidst the Cold War alarmed US officials.[14]

By the 1980s, military dictatorships and death squads that were armed and trained by the United States made Guatemala and El Salvador the most violent and oppressive places in the Americas. These regimes abducted, tortured, and murdered indigenous people and union and student organizers at least as much as they did leftist guerrillas, leaving people's bodies in the streets, often decapitated or with their ears, nose, or genitals cut off. They bombed indigenous villages to deter support for the rebels. Still, the Reagan administration argued that the people fleeing this violence, which human rights advocates and the United Nations considered genocide, were economic migrants rather than political refugees. It granted asylum to less than 1 percent of Guatemalan asylum claimants and not many more Salvadorans, since they were fleeing anti-Communist regimes supported by the US government.[15] This inspired the Sanctuary Movement.

After the Morelos family had lived in southern Mexico for a year and a half, a man from a local church knocked on their door. He said he had heard they were seeking help and that congregations in the United States would pay for their journey and their legal and medical expenses when they arrived if they would speak in public along with their hosts about the reasons why they had fled.[16] Joel was looking, as he put it, to tell his story and that of Guatemala.[17] According to Anne Ewing, cochair of the Sanctuary Committee at First United Methodist Church of Germantown (FUMCOG) in Philadelphia, the move-ment was "looking for articulate people" with a personal story that illuminated the larger political dimensions of the struggle. "So, after the decision-making process," sanctuary workers "decided to take care of them if they could get across the border."[18] The Morelos family would be among the small minority, less than 1 percent, of Central Americans formally sponsored by sanctuary con-gregations in the United States. FUMCOG would be their host.

Notwithstanding the exceptional nature of Joel, Gabriela, and Lucy's for-mal sanctuary, in their voyage to Philadelphia they were fairly typical of the thousands of people whose migration sanctuary workers assisted in the 1980s. Mexicans and Central Americans in the movement helped them travel to Mex-ico City, then by airplane to Hermosillo, and on to Nogales, Mexico, where they arrived in late June 1984. There they stayed at the home of Catholic lay worker Maria Aguilar, where they met Quaker goat rancher Jim Corbett from across the border in Tucson. Aguilar and Corbett's colleague Father Dagoberto Quiñones showed them a hole in the border fence and the steeples of Sacred Heart Church just beyond it in Nogales, Arizona. This crossing in the Sonora Desert was the Sanctuary Movement's main gateway into the United States at the time. Traveling separately from Joel on the night of June 26, Gabriela and Lucy were immediately caught and returned to Mexico. The US Border Patrol arrested Joel, who feigned a Mexican accent to avoid being sent back to Guatemala. They bussed him across the border six days later.[19]

The family made it across on their next attempts, reuniting at Sacred Heart on July 6. From there, Jesus Cruz drove them to Rev. John Fife's Southside Pres-byterian Church in Tucson, where a big sign reading "This Is The Sanctuary For The Oppressed of Central America" hung outside on the light blue stucco walls. This was the first congregation in the country to declare sanctuary. Cruz then drove them to Sister Darlene Nicgorski's apartment in Phoenix. She ar-ranged with colleagues in Chicago to send them east to Philadelphia.[20] Later that month they embarked on a string of car rides across the country.[21]

"We never knew where we were going" along the way, Joel recalled, even as they knew very well the personal and political reasons for their journey. "This is a very secret way to travel—house by house, city by city, church by church," and "synagogues, meetings."[22] This secrecy was a necessary irony of what may people in the 1980s called the Public Sanctuary Movement, which was highly protective of migrants yet very public in its diverse lines of activism and direct action.

## Saving Our Lives

"Some of us think the Sanctuary Movement saved our lives," said Manuel Portillo, who helped fellow Central Americans travel from the Guatemalan border to Mexico City and later organized Guatemalans in sanctuary around the United States. Not just the lives of people in sanctuary, he stressed. Sanctuary served as a therapeutic space for refugees to cope with their trauma and from which to work for peace in Central America, "saving our lives" in a larger sense.[23]

These were the core meanings of sanctuary from the perspective of Central American refugees, especially those who accepted the burdens of living in isolation in host congregations. Their commitment to public speaking and advocacy grew out of their struggles in labor, student, church, and human rights activism in their own countries. This work had made them targets for disappearances, torture, and murder by armies and death squads, which in turn caused their flight. It also made the Sanctuary Movement very much their own movement, especially once they dismantled the initial paternalism of many of their hosts, which was sometimes tinged with racism and classism, even if North Americans often continued to present it as *their* movement.[24]

For receiving communities in the United States, sanctuary meant something similar but with different emphasis. "Sanctuary is in essence a public welcoming of undocumented Central American refugees into the protection and care of the church," explained the main instructional manual of the Sanctuary Movement, first issued in 1982. More than this, it entailed a broad commitment to "supporting and assisting the refugees in their struggle . . . assuming their burdens as our own," and "communicat[ing] visibly and dramatically to the North American people a call to national responsibility." To congregations considering sanctuary, the manual declared, "The bottom line of sponsorship *is not money*. The real bottom line is the opportunity for expressing love/justice; of helping; of caring; the offering of time, talent, patience, and eventual ending of violence and terror in Central America so that the refugees may return to their homelands."[25] Sanctuary congregations approached these commitments in different ways, but most practiced sanctuary as "an act of hospitality" in a most expansive sense.[26] It involved material support and protection for individuals

and families, legal petition for their asylum, spiritual fellowship, political advocacy, community organizing, public speaking with the refugees, and help rebuilding people's lives and communities.

The vetting process the Morelos family underwent weighed serious practical
and personal as well as political questions. Angela Berryman of the Philadelphia-
based American Friends Service Committee (AFSC), another key coordinator of
the movement, emphasized that sanctuary in a congregation demanded people
who could handle the stress of putting themselves "out there publicly," deal with
the media, and "take a little bit of isolation, too." They also needed to be willing
to take the risk of putting their family in Central America in danger if the wrong
people discovered their involvement in the movement.[27]

This vetting process also revealed one of the movement's core tensions, concerning which Central Americans should be assisted, with what sorts of help,
and what in turn should be asked of them. In other words, what should be
the Sanctuary Movement's relationship with migrants? Some activists, especially in Chicago, argued for supporting just the few refugees who would speak
out publicly with their hosts. Many Central Americans in sanctuary also argued against hosting just anyone in congregations. Rather, only people who
were already politically engaged should receive this level of support, since sanctuary was an outgrowth of their own movements. They also warned against
aiding those who had served in the army or government of Guatemala or El
Salvador.[28] Past experience gave good reason to doubt claims of desertion and
to fear espionage, which endangered their families back home.

However, for people along the US-Mexico border who were helping Central
Americans get to safety, discriminating between people who were all in need,
all fleeing violence and injustice, was unfair and impossible. This was the view
of the movement's cofounders in the Southwest, Jim Corbett and Reverend
Fife in Tucson and Father Quiñones across the border in Nogales, Mexico. For
them and their colleagues, it mattered little whether people were headed for a
sanctuary congregation, a neighborhood in Los Angeles, or a better shot at asylum in Canada. As Corbett wrote in 1988, "everywhere along the border sanctuary services are provided by religious rather than political groups, and the
religious groups respond according to refugees' needs rather than their political alignments or usefulness."[29] Sanctuary workers, especially in the Southwest,
still helped people who did not "pass" the vetting process. They transported
and connected them to decent places to settle and to landlords, employers, legal
aid, and community organizations, especially the Catholic Church in Los Angeles, Santa Fe, and other cities.[30] Many Central Americans who were not hosted
by a sanctuary congregation, including a small number already settled in Phila-

delphia, also participated in the movement's public education and advocacy campaigns.

Unlike other immigrant rights movements in US history, the Sanctuary Movement of the 1980s and early 1990s was fundamentally an antiwar movement. People held protest vigils, marches, and letter-writing and phone campaigns pressing Congress and the White House to change foreign policy and stop US aid to repressive governments, militaries, and death squads in Central America. They urged authorities in Guatemala and El Salvador to end the disappearances, torture, and bombing of indigenous communities.

Sanctuary activists also demanded changes in US asylum policy. They argued that by not granting asylum to people fleeing death and persecution in these countries, the United States was violating its own Refugee Act of 1980 as well as the United Nations agreements on refugees that the US had signed. These included the 1949 Geneva Conventions on War and War Victims and the 1967 UN Protocol Relating to the Status of Refugees. The Reagan administration's policies therefore lacked legitimacy, activists in the movement claimed, and sanctuary constituted an effort to comply with these just laws.[31]

Activists from Central and North America also often cited a "higher law." As Marlena Santoyo, a member of Germantown Friends (Quaker) Meeting in Philadelphia, explained her congregation's declaration of sanctuary, "the meeting decided to follow God's law above the government's."[32] Or as Sister Margaret McKenna, another Philadelphia activist, said, "We all believed that our faith was calling us to do this, to help the Salvadorans, more than we believed it was illegal and therefore wrong."[33]

Far from the border and without a large Central American population, Philadelphia in some ways stood on the sidelines of the debate over which refugees to help. Its history of congregations mobilizing to host refugees resembled that of other centers of the movement around the country, which coordinated with, but took the lead from, Chicago and Tucson. Yet its activists and the organizations they built played a particularly large role in certain forms of national organizing and in transnational solidarity work.

Similar to the refugees, for some of the leading sanctuary activists from the United States, the movement grew out of their work in solidarity movements in Latin America before the height of the Central American civil wars and refugee crisis in the 1980s.[34] This was particularly important for establishing Philadelphia as a center of the Sanctuary Movement, as it was in San Francisco, Los Angeles, New York, and Washington, DC.[35] In partnership with their Central American colleagues, these activists continued to operate transnationally during the wars. They organized delegations for US politicians and journalists to witness conditions in Central America, sent emergency aid to displaced people, and supported refugees' organizing and planning to return after the wars.

The Sanctuary and solidarity movements and Central American human rights movements were inextricably linked, led and supported by many of the same people. In a broad sense, they may be understood as different parts of the same work, operating at different scales. The Sanctuary Movement was a movement and not an organization. But it produced new institutions and shaped the work of others in ways that generated formal political action and community development. These institutions enabled not just the temporary protection of asylum seekers and other displaced people. They also supported the formation of immigrant communities in the United States and reconstruction of communities in Central America.

Sanctuary activists called themselves "workers" and developed a well-organized system for supporting the people they called "refugees," a political statement that highlighted the injustice of the US government's refusal to grant them that status. The authors of the sanctuary manual, the Chicago Religious Task Force on Central America and the Tucson Ecumenical Council Central America Task Force, coordinated the movement's "underground railroad" network in the United States. The Tucson group's members helped mostly Salvadorans and Guatemalans, as well as some Nicaraguans, get into the country. They worked with the Chicago group to match Central Americans with churches, synagogues, and Quaker meetings around the country and arrange their transit to these destinations. Once people were in the protection of a sanctuary congregation, their manual instructed, "offering sanctuary must usually include . . . the commitment to provide for their basic human needs and to assist them in becoming independent and self sufficient."[36]

Congregants formed networks of hosts, cooks, drivers, employers, attorneys, and other allies who made their churches, homes, cars, and workplaces safe spaces. Sanctuary workers mobilized "supporting congregations" to assist in this. Together they helped Central Americans find decent employment and gain levels of economic security not enjoyed by most refugees who were recognized by the government and resettled in US cities in the same era. Indeed, sanctuary and supporting congregations' mostly middle-class social networks and neighborhoods explain much of Central American refugees' comparatively good experiences of housing and work.

To the question of "how long must we be responsible" for the people they hosted, the Chicago and Tucson groups' manual told congregations that refugees become self-sufficient at varying paces, but underscored, "WE HOPE THAT THERE WOULD BE A FRIENDSHIP DEVELOPED BETWEEN THE SPONSOR AND THE REFUGEE(S) THAT WOULD CONTINUE

FOREVER."[37] After the civil wars in El Salvador and Guatemala ended in the 1990s, sanctuary and solidarity activists helped rebuild people's hometowns and livelihoods, and sometimes accompanied them on their journeys home. Some solidarity groups invested in small enterprises, training, schools, and other community projects. Others supported democratic elections, human rights activism, and reconciliation after the wars. Some of this work continues today.

Looking beyond the Sanctuary Movement's "underground railroad" and political advocacy in Washington, DC, is crucial for grasping its impacts and meanings for cities, towns, and communities in the United States and in Central America. Sanctuary and solidarity work ultimately took the form of community organizing and development, direct actions through which people from Philadelphia and other US cities supported the rights and well-being of their relatives and neighbors both locally and transnationally. This yields a portrait of sanctuary as something that transcends the confines of an individual sanctuary congregation or sanctuary city, occupying a longer chronology and more diverse set of spaces. Again, for Central Americans this grew out of their own longer struggles at home.

This chapter relates the origins and evolution of the Sanctuary Movement in Philadelphia. But it also carries forward the story beyond the 1980s and early 1990s, revealing a more complicated history of Central American migration to Philadelphia and the United States, at the end of the chapter. Just as the Sanctuary Movement did not abruptly cease with the formal end of the Central American civil wars, migration did not stop but rather grew and diversified thereafter, thanks to continued violence and US complicity in displacement. Yet the experiences of Central Americans differed greatly between those who came to Philadelphia in the 1980s and later, as did the meanings they helped give to sanctuary and the sanctuary city.

## Sanctuary in Philadelphia

When the Morelos family arrived in 1984, Philadelphia was an increasingly important center of the Sanctuary Movement, and a logical one. It had a long history as a destination for persecuted peoples and a home to active congregations, social movements, and international institutions on the left. Some of the relationships that had been fostered in interfaith movements since World War II helped grow the Sanctuary Movement in the 1980s, as liberal Methodists, Baptists, Quakers, Jews, Catholics, Presbyterians, and other sects influenced one another. Moreover, the presence of peace and justice institutions that were already engaged in Latin America, especially AFSC, played a key role in making Philadelphia a major node in national and transnational sanctuary work.

As in other regions, for many of the leading sanctuary activists from Philadelphia, the work of sanctuary grew out of involvement in earlier Latin American solidarity movements.[38] Mary Day Kent, a Quaker, spent most of the 1970s first working for AFSC's program on Latin America and the Caribbean and then staffing the US Committee for Panamanian Sovereignty. In the 1980s, she worked for the Philadelphia Yearly Meeting's Peace Committee, supporting the Sanctuary Movement. She and a colleague broadcast a weekly Central America Report for fifteen minutes of the *Third World News Hour* on WXPN, the University of Pennsylvania's student radio station, in the early 1980s.[39]

David Funkhouser volunteered in the Peace Corps in Colombia after college and was later ordained as an Episcopal priest. In 1979, he became the first national coordinator of the Nicaraguan Solidarity Network, which was modeled after a solidarity group that was involved in Chile. Around the same time, he began volunteering in AFSC's Latin America and Caribbean division. In the early 1980s he started the Central America Organizing Project to do "political education work" and build relations between communities in Philadelphia and Central America.[40]

Angela Berryman's career likewise reflects the longer arc of the history of the solidarity and Sanctuary Movements in Central America, Philadelphia, and the United States. In 1976, she and her husband, Phil, moved to Guatemala to serve as AFSC's Central America representatives. Both had previously worked with the Catholic Church in Latin America. They arrived in Guatemala a few months after a devastating earthquake, so they became involved in rural reconstruction projects. They also monitored conditions in Guatemala and nearby countries, supporting social movements and reporting to AFSC, Amnesty International, and other groups on the growing violence in Central America. As Angela related, in 1980 they left "under duress . . . even followed at the airport."[41]

Settling in Philadelphia, the Berrymans worked for AFSC and with others "trying to build a movement here" to counter the violence in Central America and the US government's involvement in it.[42] Angela spent years at AFSC, supporting the sanctuary work of Quaker meetings nationwide. After leaving AFSC, Phil taught at Philadelphia-area universities and wrote multiple books about Central America, including a seminal volume on liberation theology, a tradition that originated in Latin America in the 1960s and prioritized solidarity with oppressed and impoverished people above all other spiritual goals.[43]

The Berrymans and fellow Philadelphia-area activists launched a variety of national and local solidarity organizations. They helped establish the Committee in Solidarity with the People of El Salvador (CISPES) in 1980 and the Network in Solidarity with the People of Guatemala (NISGUA) in 1981. These groups became the main coordinators of public outreach, education, and advocacy at the national and transnational levels. The Berrymans were also involved with the Pledge of Resistance and Witness for Peace, two groups that did similar work focused on Nicaragua.[44]

Beyond these larger groups, as Mary Day Kent described it, a core of activists would regularly meet "in Angie and Phil's living room" to start and do the business of other independent projects. These groups could operate more nimbly than bigger ones, especially Quaker institutions, which made decisions via consensus. The process of consensus was too slow for some of the more time-sensitive needs of refugees and people who had been abducted.[45]

Personal encounters with Central Americans who had experienced torture, bombings, threats, and assassination were another crucial factor in birthing the Sanctuary Movement in Philadelphia and other places far from the border. In July 1980, the US National Council of Churches sponsored a tour of four Salvadoran academics who had served as ministers for the Frente Democratico Revolucionario, the opposition party that was critical of the current regime, who visited Quakers and other activists in the city. On their return to El Salvador a few months later, three of the four men were killed.[46] Around the same time, FUMCOG hosted a group of Guatemalan refugees who were on the run with several Catholic priests, who likewise spoke about the situation in Central America and the need for help. Then, in 1982, a former nun and a Salvadoran refugee gave a presentation at a church potluck. As FUMCOG Sanctuary Committee cochair Dick Cox observed, this all "pricked our consciences and emotions." Echoing many colleagues, Anne Ewing stated, "There's nothing as powerful as the incarnation of the oppressed in front of your face."[47]

After the Philadelphia Yearly Meeting hosted Jim Corbett for a conference with activists from various faiths in 1983, six congregations declared sanctuary within the next several years. Tabernacle United Presbyterian Church in West Philadelphia was the first, hosting Linda and Ernesto (pseudonyms), a young couple from El Salvador whose names ended up on death lists due to their respective occupations as a trade unionist and relief worker helping peasants from villages destroyed by the government. They soon moved to New York to study at Union Theological Seminary, which was a sanctuary campus. Tabernacle also became home to the local chapters of CISPES and NISGUA, as well as other sanctuary and solidarity groups.[48]

By the end of the 1980s, ten sanctuary congregations and an eleventh organization in the region hosted Central American refugees: Tabernacle and Beth

David synagogue in West Philadelphia; FUMCOG, Chestnut Hill Friends, Germantown Friends, and Mishkan Shalom synagogue in Northwest Philadelphia; Central Baptist Church, Media Friends, Southampton Friends, and Concord Friends in the near and far suburbs; and the Catholic Coalition for Sanctuary. Another thirty-seven congregations and organizations in the region made formal declarations of support for sanctuary, coordinating with these host congregations. Their members provided refugees with meals, rides, legal aid, friendship, links to employment, and more.[49]

This work in Philadelphia reflected national patterns. Sanctuary workers estimated that some 42,000 people nationwide were involved in this work in the mid-1980s. They represented almost 350 sanctuary congregations, 15 universities, and 4 other groups that declared sanctuary by 1987, and roughly two thousand supporting congregations by the early 1990s.[50]

In Philadelphia and around the country, these congregations and their members generally resided in white middle-class neighborhoods and had been influenced by liberation theology. As FUMCOG Sanctuary Committee member Marion Brown explained, "Liberation theology gave the Sanctuary Movement a standard text." Opposition to the United States' war in Vietnam had given her, like many other Americans, reasons to question the government she had grown up trusting. "Once you tune into one particular global aggression situation, it makes you more aware and tuned into others. You have a framework" in which "the aggression of our government becomes real and believable, even if you don't want to believe it."[51]

FUMCOG was part of a long tradition of radical religious activism in Germantown. Just down the road, Quakers had launched the first public petition against slavery 300 years earlier. Anne Ewing and others in the FUMCOG Sanctuary Committee had backgrounds in community organizing for racial integration. They reached out to the Chicago Religious Task Force for guidance in organizing the congregation for sanctuary.[52] Their committee worked for over a year educating fellow members about the Central American refugee crisis and the historical and spiritual roots of the Sanctuary Movement, through meetings and the church's newsletter.[53]

FUMCOG's members voted to declare "public sanctuary" a few months before the Morelos family reached Philadelphia. Immediately after the vote, congregants quickly set up committees to support their housing and health care—funding and lining up rides to doctor, dentist, and emergency room visits—and a jail bond committee. "The choir begrudgingly agreed to let us have" the room they used for putting on their robes, remembered Dick Cox. With few bilingual members, the church initially hired translators from two nearby congregations, St. Vincent de Paul and Germantown Friends. When they felt ready, the committee contacted people at the Tucson Ecumenical Council who would arrange for refugees to travel to Philadelphia.[54]

When Joel, Gabriela, and Lucy arrived, along with another Guatemalan couple and their infant son who were on their way to sanctuary at Riverside Church in Manhattan, a member of the Sanctuary Committee hosted a welcome picnic. Colored lanterns hung around the backyard to light the late summer evening. Pastor Ted Loder and committee members prepared a welcoming service for church on Sunday to formally introduce the Morelos family to the congregation. Some eight hundred people attended. Joel and Gabriela danced an indigenous Maya dance to a cassette tape of Guatemalan music provided by a FUMCOG member. Local Congressman Bill Gray, a Black Baptist minister, gave one of the sermons. As Loder recounted, Gray "stressed the racism implicit in the policies of the Justice Department and the Immigration and Naturalization Service which keep the Statue of Liberty pointed toward Western Europe, but not toward Central America, or Haiti, or South Africa."[55]

The Morelos family initially stayed at the church, where members of FUMCOG, St. Vincent's, Germantown Friends, and other congregations visited them, bringing their kids and sleeping bags to spend the night together.[56] The Chicago and Tucson groups' manual recommended that refugees "stay in the church building for one to two weeks," with "24-hour monitors . . . maintained on the church premises," to enable "an assessment of how INS will react and [give] refugees an opportunity to feel secure."[57] The family soon moved to an apartment above a child care center owned and operated by Marion Brown in the adjacent neighborhood of Mt. Airy. Brown characterized "this particular living situation" as another "protected environment . . . on a diverse block in an intentionally integrated neighborhood, on my property, set back from the road." Plus, a different member of the congregation still came to stay with them every night.[58]

In addition to shelter, food, and other material support, congregation members connected Joel and Gabriela with safe, decent employment. Joel worked with construction contractors, mainly doing carpentry and home repair. As at other sanctuary congregations, FUMCOG members made sure that employers paid him fair wages and posed no threat of deportation.[59] In this way, the church also helped ensure a "protected work environment," as Marion Brown put it.[60]

Joel, Gabriela, and Lucy appeared publicly and spoke to the press even before they reached Philadelphia. When they reached Phoenix, Sister Nicgorski arranged an interview with local newspaper and TV reporters. In Philadelphia, like others in sanctuary, they regularly visited churches and colleges around the region to share their story and educate Americans about human rights abuses in Guatemala.[61] On the wall of their apartment, they hung a poster with the Central American refugee slogan, "If you knew the truth, then surely you would help us."[62] They also testified at a briefing in Congress and traveled to meetings of Guatemalans in sanctuary at Riverside Church in New York and elsewhere.[63]

When speaking in public, the Morelos family wore bandanas covering their faces and hats pulled down over their foreheads (see figure 1.1). They knew the US government was spying on church audiences. They especially sought to avoid detection by the Guatemalan authorities, who would kill their relatives in retribution for their continued activism.[64] Sanctuary workers found it comical that the Federal Bureau of Intelligence (FBI) sent agents to their meetings disguised in loose shirts and pants, colorful bandanas, and Birkenstock sandals because they mistook activists, especially the Quakers, for hippies. But threats to Central Americans' safety were a real and delicate matter.[65] As one Guatemalan refugee remembered, "It was terrifying when we heard someone speaking Spanish . . . because we thought that somebody was a spy."[66] Echoing others, Linda at Tabernacle United Church told a journalist in 1985, "We come from terror" in El Salvador, "and we are not free from terror here."[67]

FIGURE 1.1.    Photo of the "Morelos" family at the First United Methodist Church of Germantown in 1984. (Photo courtesy of Joel Morales.)

The experiences of the Morelos family and their hosts at FUMCOG were fairly typical of Central Americans in sanctuary congregations in Philadelphia and other US cities. The welcoming ceremonies; the assistance with housing, employment, legal and other aid that congregations offered; and refugees' involvement in the movement were all pretty standard. Still, each congregation took its own approach to organizing and practicing sanctuary, as did individual refugees and sanctuary committee members.

Chestnut Hill Friends Meeting, where Mary Day Kent was a member and other congregants had assisted refugees in Germany after World War II, readily endorsed sanctuary. Their dozen-member Sanctuary Committee held fundraisers with Latin American food, music, and decorations, raising money and supplies as well as interest among neighbors in the city's most affluent neighborhood.[68] In declaring sanctuary on February 10, 1985, they noted, "We make this declaration with the hope of support from the wider community."[69]

The meeting expressed a geography of sanctuary focused on congregants' homes, the main space most refugees inhabited in sanctuary congregations. "Just as Friends [Quakers] believe that 'there is that of God in everyone,' so do we believe that God is everywhere—no more in our meeting House than in our homes," they explained in their declaration of sanctuary. "We offer, then, a Community of Refuge rather than a sacred building. We offer our Meeting House and our Family Houses as asylum."[70]

At a Meeting for Worship and Celebration attended by over two hundred people, including the Morelos family and Ernesto and Linda from Tabernacle, in September 1985, Chestnut Hill Friends welcomed eighteen-year-old Paz (a pseudonym meaning "peace") from El Salvador "into Public Sanctuary." Her brother had disappeared a year earlier, she told them through an interpreter. Bombings and napalm spraying had "caused hundreds of thousands of Salvadorans to leave our country. People have this question on their minds: are we going to be alive this afternoon?" Sanctuary, she said, "provides us with both a means of satisfying our needs and to educate the people here on what is happening in El Salvador. Sanctuary is a commitment to our struggle."[71]

In Paz's first ten weeks in Chestnut Hill, the meeting mobilized a characteristically intense web of support, the details of which its Sanctuary Committee recorded in a report. Fifty volunteers provided "round-the-clock companionship . . . 26 of them members/attenders of the Chestnut Hill Mtg., 6 from other Friends Meetings, 18 from 8 different religious denominations and no religious denomination." Twenty-seven people offered to translate, including Mary Day Kent, though "not all have been called upon. Paz now does her public speaking in English." Two doctors, three dentists, and multiple lawyers, including attorneys from other sanctuary congregations, were working with Paz or available on-call. "Friends and friends have provided clothing (Paz prefers books to clothing but has discovered new needs such as mittens and thermal underwear), food (Russian tea, fruit and peanut butter are favorites)"; and "Showers, laundry facilities, sewing machine use are being provided in various households."[72]

"Friends and friends" worked to connect Paz to her host community and to a growing network of people in sanctuary locally and across the Northeast. Many offered orientation to Philadelphia through "dinner invitations, concerts, . . . political events, shopping trips, English lessons, newspapers, books, museum visits." The father of one meeting member "provided material and instruction for an evening of silk-screening in the Meeting House—5 Central American refugees produced 66 posters (graphics by Paz) now being sold for donations to Sanctuary." Congregants drove Paz to Ithaca, New York, to spend Thanksgiving "with Esperanza who is in Sanctuary with Ithaca Friends Mtg.," and two weeks later, the report noted, "she will attend the N.E. Regional Sanctuary Mtg. at Riverside Church in NYC."[73] When Paz's mother, "Libertad"; sister, "Victoria"; and brother-in-law, "Luis," reached the United States, they took sanctuary at Germantown Friends Meeting, three miles down Germantown Avenue from Chestnut Hill Friends and less than a mile from FUMCOG.[74]

Central Baptist Church, in the wealthy suburb of Wayne, played a somewhat different role in the movement, after declaring sanctuary in 1984. Congregant Betsy Morgan stressed it "wasn't always a political sanctuary space." Beginning in 1985, the two-hundred-member church hosted a Salvadoran businessman named Mauricio (another pseudonym), who fled because death squads mistook him for his politically active cousin.[75] "Mauricio's life in El Salvador was very much like ours here" in the region's affluent suburbs, said another congregant, "and the fact that this kind of abuse can be exercised against somebody like him shows how bad the situation in El Salvador really is." Soldiers stopped a bus he was riding and detained him, hung him by his thumbs from a tree all night, then imprisoned him for a week and told him to leave the country upon his release. When he did not depart, men with machine guns came to his house three times, beating his mother on the last occasion and forcing him to flee out the back door; he escaped with only a single change of clothes and without his wife and children.[76]

Though in need of protection, Mauricio was not politically engaged. But then Central Baptist began hosting refugees traveling to other destinations, in collaboration with CISPES and the Salvadoran Humanitarian Aid, Research and Education (SHARE) Foundation, another nonprofit supporting displaced Salvadorans in Central America and the United States. "So, when these people were passing through, that gave Mauricio a connection to the movement. We had him go to a variety of places and . . . civic organizations and other churches," Morgan explained. In the process, he became radicalized in the United States instead of in El Salvador. Central Baptist "had people coming through the early '90s," including the orphan son of a Baptist woman killed in El Salvador, who also did not quite fit the typical profile of "political refugees" in sanctuary who spoke for the movement.[77]

Some sanctuary activists formed new institutions in response to opposition from within their religious organizations. Mishkan Shalom ("sanctuary of peace"), which hosted a family from Guatemala, was founded in 1988 by a rabbi who had been voted out of his suburban synagogue over his criticism of Israel and his insistence on offering sanctuary for Central Americans.[78] The Catholic Church in Mexico and much of the United States played a central role in the Sanctuary Movement, but Cardinal John Krol and his successor, Anthony Bevilaqua, forbade congregations in the Archdiocese of Philadelphia from sponsoring Central Americans. Sister Margaret McKenna, a member of the Medical Mission Sisters, helped found American Christians Against Torture after visiting El Salvador in the early 1980s, and tried unsuccessfully to convince her sisters to declare public sanctuary. Though progressive in their politics, they were "prudent people" and "feared meeting the service requirements and pulling it off," she recalled.[79] So, in 1987, she organized some twenty-five Catholics to form the Catholic Coalition for Sanctuary, a group not affiliated with any congregation. She had also started an organization called Peacemakers Reflection Center, which had space on the grounds of the Medical Mission where its members sold Latin American art and promoted sanctuary and solidarity with Latin Americans. They hosted a Salvadoran man there.[80]

The Medical Mission's property in Northeast Philadelphia, named Peace Hermitage, was another sort of sanctuary space, an old estate secluded in wooded grounds. Religious campuses like this have long sheltered refugees and asylum seekers, and the stresses of sanctuary made such spaces of quiet retreat and therapeutic reflection all the more valuable.[81] Peace Hermitage also gave over a large expanse of lawn for a community garden planted by Hmong refugees from Laos, who had fought alongside the United States in the Vietnam War.[82]

For all the protections that sanctuary congregations offered, they were not impenetrable to federal authorities. In October 1984, someone broke into the Morelos family's apartment, apparently as part of the INS undercover investigation targeting sanctuary workers and the people they hosted. The intruder stole Joel's wallet, which contained names and addresses of the people who had helped the family get from Arizona to Philadelphia, along with books, tapes, and envelopes with the address of Gabriela's family in Guatemala.[83]

Three months later, on the morning of Monday, January 14, 1985, Marion Brown looked out of her window around 7:30, just after the church member who stayed with the family that night had left and as the staff and families at the childcare center were arriving. "About two inches of light snow covered the parking lot of the childcare center," she remembered, "so I could see from the footprints in the snow that someone had gone upstairs to the apartment." She found Gabriela and Lucy, who had just turned four, there with three INS agents. They "were eating pieces of Lucy's leftover birthday cake that Gabriela had served them, thinking that they were old friends and now guests in their home." The agents had knocked on the door, presenting themselves as sanctuary workers from Tucson and claiming to carry birthday presents for Lucy and messages from people the family had met in Arizona. "Between mouthfuls of birthday cake, they announced to Gabriela that they were arresting her and demand[ed] to know where Joel was. It was a panicky moment!"[84]

Brown contacted FUMCOG member and attorney Ted Walkenhorst and Pastor Loder, on a phone line they presumed was not secure, but rather was likely tapped by the FBI. Joel was out working with a carpenter, but they soon located him and he turned himself in, accompanied by Walkenhorst, who got him and Gabriela, with Lucy in tow, released on bail that afternoon. They were arrested to serve as government witnesses against the people who had helped them along the border. The agents had obtained their address from Jesus Cruz, who had driven the family from Nogales to Tucson and then to Phoenix. He later contacted them through the Sanctuary network, saying he had gifts to send for Lucy. In fact, Cruz was an undercover informant, a key witness in the ensuing trial of Aguilar, Corbett, Fife, Nicgorski, Quiñones, and seven other sanctuary workers in the Southwest. People at FUMCOG heard of similar arrests of Central Americans in sanctuary in several other cities, as federal agents detained sixty Guatemalans and Salvadorans that same day.[85]

About three weeks later, in Guatemala, Joel's younger brother was abducted while waiting for a bus, by men in a white Toyota pickup with tinted glass. The same thing happened to his cousin two days later. As Pastor Loder explained, these abductions, which were reported in the newspaper in Guatemala, would help validate Joel's petition for asylum. "But our deeper reaction was grief and the sobering realization that Joel's participation in Public Sanctuary (and of course, ours) may well have precipitated the kidnapping of these two young men." They had been involved in union and human rights activism, and the "method of abduction is chillingly familiar to thousands of families of disappeared persons in Guatemala," Loder observed. FUMCOG held a memorial service for the two men. This compounded Joel's emotional fatigue from public speaking about his own torture and flight, and he withdrew from this activity for a time.[86]

Happier events punctuated the winters of 1985 and 1986 for the Morelos family. At the same time that they held the memorial service for his brother, FUMCOG members were organizing a religious wedding for Joel and Gabriela. They had been previously married in a civil service, but now Gabriela was pregnant with their second child and Joel was on notice to testify in the upcoming trial of sanctuary workers in Tucson, which started in October 1985. Moreover, as Pastor Loder noted, "our church family slowly had become theirs."[87]

In winter 1986, several of the people who were presently on trial in Tucson (the same ones who had assisted Joel's family), helped his other brother, Julio (also a pseudonym), to cross the border and get to sanctuary at FUMCOG. Julio stayed with Joel, Gabriela, and Lucy in the apartment above the childcare center behind Marion Brown's home. After a few months, they relocated to an apartment over the garage at the home of Anne Ewing and her family.[88]

Another FUMCOG member connected Julio to a landscaper who would employ him for the next six years. Going to work, he recalled, was "something that helped us . . . it's like psychology . . . instead of being home wondering if immigration was going to come, or worry all the time." As soon as he arrived, he went to speak at congregations, schools, and universities, and "wherever we were to go," sanctuary workers "would accompany us." But he, too, tired of public speaking, "especially when you talk about my brother" who was disappeared.[89]

Sanctuary was challenging for both hosts and hosted, and Central American refugees varied in their levels of engagement in the movement. In congregations and households hosting refugees, most relationships were warm, even loving. "Sanctuary has given us the opportunity of feeling like human beings," Joel told one journalist.[90] Still, in addition to the isolation, risks, and other stresses of sanctuary, in some congregations and households religious, cultural, and other personal differences led to some conflicts. "You can be very idealistic and say, 'of course I will take in another human being,'" reflected Angela Berryman, "but there's a lot more entailed in taking someone into your house, or into your church."[91] Sometimes refugees and their hosts formed "wonderful bonds," recalled Mary Day Kent, but as in any group, some Central American refugees and North American hosts were "feisty, demanding, difficult people." Some refugees made romantic advances toward members of their host congregations, and vice versa. Sometimes this was welcome, but other times it was not.[92]

Like the Sanctuary Movement more broadly, the relationships between refugees and their hosts evolved in Philadelphia and nationally. "Initially there was a lot of paternalism, treating us like kids" in some congregations around the country, remembered Manuel Portillo, who lived in sanctuary in Connecticut and later moved to Boston and then Philadelphia. "So, we began to take matters into our hands as well." Refugees organized themselves, and "it became more of a partnership" in which refugees were involved in planning meetings and decisions in the movement.[93]

Mary Day Kent described sanctuary congregations as "very hands-on," with a "sincere attitude," "but . . . also kind of tone deaf," as the movement was tied to "deeply rooted US cultural" views about "adopting refugees" into "wholesome host communities." It took some hosts time to adjust their idealistic assumptions, to see refugees as more than objects of their charity, and to grasp cultural differences and the political activism and perspectives of Central Americans. In her view, the intimate relationships between Central Americans in sanctuary and their hosts, like the movement at large, benefited from "shifting the framework from charity to solidarity."[94]

In the mid-1980s, the movement also became a well-known cause, thanks largely to national media coverage of the Tucson trial. This occasioned the wave of sanctuary city and state resolutions across the country, including two successful campaigns outside Philadelphia. In February 1986, activists in the Delaware County Pledge of Resistance, a chapter of the national organization, convinced the overwhelmingly Republican town council of the suburb of Swarthmore to adopt a sanctuary city resolution. The council president, who voted against the bill, declared it "has no teeth." The borough solicitor, who coauthored the bill, agreed that "there is no such thing as sanctuary." The INS took issue, however, calling it "tantamount to 'lawlessness or anarchy,'" and sent a representative to speak against it, unsuccessfully, before the largest crowd ever to witness a council meeting in the borough. Later that year, a similar scene played out in Allentown, a small city north of Philadelphia, where the Central America Organizing Project had helped form the Lehigh Valley Sanctuary Support Group. The Democratic-majority city council passed a resolution similar to Swarthmore's, which drew sharp rebukes from the mayor, the police chief, and an INS spokesman who labeled sanctuary "un-American."[95]

When Joel took the stand in Tucson in spring 1986, the judge forbade any mention of his political persecution in Guatemala, as part of a larger farce in which the government sought to make the case purely about human smuggling. As one of the FUMCOG members who traveled with him to Tucson for the trial remembered it, "The prosecutor asked Joel something about slipping across the border, and Joel put his hand to his ear and said, 'I'm sorry, I couldn't hear you because soldiers in Guatemala beat me so hard I've gone deaf in this ear.'"[96]

At the beginning of May, eight of the eleven defendants who finished the trial were found guilty. But none went to prison and none of the refugees who had been rounded up to testify were deported. In this and other trials, neither the government nor sanctuary workers won what they hoped for—in the government's case a clear indictment of the movement, and for the movement a recognition of refugees' right to asylum.[97] Instead, advocacy to change federal asylum and foreign policy gained more traction for the movement.

## Asylum and Peace

Joel, Gabriela, and Lucy won asylum in November 1986, several years before most Guatemalans or Salvadorans. After their arrest the prior year, Ted Walkenhorst filed their application, consisting of a dossier six inches thick and over 1,000 pages long, which he prepared with a team of volunteers and other lawyers. "The facts in Joel's case were so compelling," he recalled, including the marks of his persecution that were literally visible on his body, that US authorities "concluded he did meet the definition of political refugee."[98] Pastor Loder added, "When the refugees explain their deeply religious motivation for opposing the repression and injustice in their countries, it is not stretching the truth to suggest that they are, in fact, *religious* refugees, as well as political ones."[99]

Asylum allowed Joel, Gabriela, and five-year-old Lucy to become permanent residents. Nine-month-old Joelito was already a citizen, having been born in Philadelphia.[100] The United States granted Joel's brother Julio asylum in 1989, an effort likewise aided by Walkenhorst.[101]

One of the most important results of Sanctuary Movement lobbying was a change in US policy toward asylum for Central Americans. But this larger shift only began in 1989, when the federal government settled a lawsuit granting Temporary Protected Status (TPS) to Guatemalans and Salvadorans and ordered the review of asylum denials dating back to 1980. Another settlement allowed Central Americans to reapply for asylum. Finally, in 1997, Congress passed the Nicaraguan Adjustment and Central American Relief Act, which allowed people who arrived during key parts of the civil wars to apply for permanent residence.[102]

But asylum solved only some problems, mainly the threat of deportation. Until the wars and violence ended, Central Americans in the United States still lived in fear for the safety of their families and themselves. From the mid-1980s into the 1990s, sanctuary activists, spurred mainly by the refugees and experienced solidarity workers among them, intensified their transnational efforts to promote peace and safety for Central Americans who had been displaced and remained under threat.[103]

Between 1985 and 1989, David Funkhouser of the Central America Organizing Project led eleven delegations to Central America for politicians and community leaders. The aim was "mostly . . . trying to awaken people" to the links between US foreign policy and the suffering of everyday Central Americans.[104] Philadelphia congressman Tom Foglietta and councilman Angel Ortiz joined the delegation in 1987, along with journalists from the *Philadelphia Inquirer*. Foglietta became an enthusiastic supporter of the movement. A Republican congressman from Virginia on a separate delegation that year observed that the situation was "somewhat parallel to the early days of the Nazis in Germany" in the late 1930s. Still, this did not deter his continued support for US aid to the Contra rebels in Nicaragua and the regimes of Guatemala and El Salvador.[105]

Notwithstanding responses like this one, such trips led by Funkhouser and others helped inspire political and congregation action. Sanctuary and solidarity activists in Philadelphia succeeded in swaying some key figures in Congress, including Republican senator Arlen Specter, to oppose continued aid to El Salvador and the Contras. A resident of Northwest Philadelphia, Specter's support was one of their greatest political wins.[106]

Central Baptist in Wayne embodied as well as any congregation the movement's shift toward direct action in Central America, what its pastor, Rev. Stephen Jones, termed the "core of the problem." By the late 1980s, "the real thrust of the ministry," he explained, was "not focusing on housing Central Americans as much as it is being advocates for them."[107] Congregation members organized delegations to El Salvador and neighboring countries, visiting church and union leaders, educators, community organizations, government officials and US embassies, refugee camps in Honduras, and on their return, legislators in the United States.[108] Part of the solution to Central America's problems, Reverend Jones averred, is to get "more North Americans to go down to El Salvador . . . [to] get a picture of what our government is doing down there," and then lobby Congress. "There aren't too many ambiguities in El Salvador," he declared, adding, "It's not very difficult to understand."[109]

While El Salvador's civil war ended in 1991, Guatemala's civil war continued until 1996. In the early 1990s, the Guatemala Focus Group of the Central America Organizing Project, including the Morelos brothers, Anne Ewing, Sister McKenna, and others, developed the Philadelphia Rapid Response Network for Guatemala. They coordinated with other activists in the NISGUA network, monitoring news from Central America, and rallying fellow activists to immediately phone and write to US and Guatemalan officials in an attempt to save people who had recently been disappeared. They also pressured Guatemalan authorities to stop targeting social movements, civil society, and communities; and they held events publicizing continued violence and human rights abuses.[110]

Asylum and the end of the civil wars meant more than legal protections and diminished fears for Central American refugees. For the Morelos family and others who had lived in hiding, whether formally in sanctuary or not, it meant they could now reclaim their true names and identities. They gave up the pseudonym Morelos and used their real name, Morales. Julio became Jorge again. Joel kept his adopted first name and later also used his original name, Manuel. When asked why they had chosen pseudonyms so close to their real names, Jorge replied that they had wanted to never "get too far from our names, our identity." He took some comfort in the fact that he could sign his initials, "JM," which still "felt like me."[111]

## Solidarity and Development

In September 1993, a reporter from the *Philadelphia Inquirer* visited Joel's family at the home they had bought in Mt. Airy to cover a reunion that FUMCOG members, especially Ted Walkenhorst, had worked for two years to help arrange: "'This is my Grandma,' Joelito announced proudly. She spoke to him in Spanish. In reply, Joelito, 7, could manage only a few words. But his Spanish has been getting better ever since the two met for the first time, three weeks ago."[112]

The reporter penned an article titled, "A New Meaning for Sanctuary." Guatemala's civil war was not quite over, but due to changes in Central America and in US policy, the number of people fleeing had declined. As a result, sanctuary activists "redirected their energies to helping refugees find a more peaceful, prosperous and just place to live—either here or back home," Rev. John Fife in Tucson explained. "We really shifted from a public resistance movement to the delivery of social services and ministry to Central Americans and Central American communities in the United States."[113]

Helping families reunite across borders was a big part of this work. After the signing of Guatemala's peace accords in 1996, Dick Cox accompanied Joel, Gabriela, and their children on their first trip back to Guatemala, and Walkenhorst joined Joel on a subsequent visit.[114] The Morales brothers continued to live in Philadelphia, visiting their parents in Guatemala periodically. Jorge later married a woman from Escuintla whom he met on these trips.

One often-repeated interpretation of the Sanctuary Movement is that in the 1990s its workers helped "refugees return home or establish new lives in the

US," and then they "moved on to other progressive social causes like the anti-apartheid movement or LGBTQ equality," the civil war in Bosnia, or the continuing crises in Haiti.[115] The evolution of activist committees at FUMCOG and many other sanctuary congregations surely followed this path.[116] Joel, Jorge, and many other refugees also became less involved in local and transnational activism over time.

But other people and congregations involved in the Sanctuary Movement, both Central and North Americans, carried on its work in solidarity initiatives. They supported refugees' planning for postwar reconstruction, and then peace and reconciliation processes, including lawsuits against former military and political leaders. As refugees returned home, solidarity work focused on helping people rebuild their lives, livelihoods, and communities, at least as much in Guatemala and El Salvador as in Philadelphia and other US cities. This took various forms: accompanying returning refugees; partnerships and sister relationships between congregations and towns; educational exchanges; monitoring of elections; and nonprofits funding transnational community organizing and development. Nearly all the core leaders of sanctuary work in Philadelphia as well as people from all the sanctuary congregations in the region remained deeply involved in this work through the mid-1990s, and some are still active today.[117]

Following earlier patterns of bearing witness, visiting Central America and seeing how people lived forced Americans to think about poverty relief and development there. On a trip in 1990, Peter Kostmayer, a Democratic Congressman from the Philadelphia suburbs, penned one of many missives distributed to activists and politicians to lay out the case. "I visited the lush Guatemalan countryside (where the Tarzan movies were made) and the urban slums of Guatemala City," he wrote, "where in one place . . . eighty thousand squatters have been camped," most of them displaced by the war, "some for nearly a decade, living in houses made of plastic and cardboard, without electricity or water." In the cities "and the wretchedly poor countryside," he reported, "there are children everywhere, many suffering from malnutrition and denied at the very onset of their tender lives any real chance to succeed." Kostmayer lamented the abuse of US economic aid, which the rich used to purchase US imports instead of assisting the poor.[118]

Philadelphia area groups engaged in diverse solidarity campaigns during and after the civil wars. Members of the Delaware County Pledge of Resistance organized people to attend antiwar rallies in Washington, DC, and advocate for peace and human rights in Central America as well as Haiti, South Africa, and elsewhere. Their Guatemala Program hosted speakers, promoted labor rights at US-owned factories in Guatemala, and circulated petitions and letters to Congress urging support for the peace process, a ban on commercial weapons sales to Guatemala, and land and civil rights for returning refugees. They also advocated and raised funds for the Permanent Commissions of Guatemalan Refugees in Mexico. These were made up of some eighty commissioners, "themselves refugees, who share the responsibilities of travel, negotiations" with governments, "and most importantly, planning for the 'collective and organized return' of the 46,000 refugees in the camps."[119]

People in Philadelphia sent material aid to displaced people during and after the war through PEACE (Program for Emergency Assistance, Cooperation and Education) for Guatemala, which was founded in 1983 and based at Tabernacle United in West Philadelphia. Angela Berryman, Reverend Funkhouser, and Joel Morales served on its board, as did others with connections to Guatemala.[120] Its members raised funds in the United States and distributed grants for small farm businesses, training, and leadership development for women in the regions of Guatemala from which most of the refugees had come.

PEACE for Guatemala also funded "integrated support for the displaced," sending emergency supplies for people who had fled to different parts of the country. In 1990, for example, it furnished two communities that had resettled in the Peten jungle with "mosquito netting, rubber boots, lanterns and batteries . . . seeds and tools for vegetable production . . . simple medicines and medical instruments," as well as training for "members of the community in nutrition and basic health care." This all aimed "to stabilize a community and build skills for the long term." For other groups of internally displaced people in Guatemala, PEACE rented land and purchased "cloth and buttons, thread, needles and basic cooking implements and agricultural tools and seeds" and fertilizer.[121]

Most of its grants helped Guatemalan peasants rebuild lives and livelihoods. In spring and summer 1991, PEACE for Guatemala spent $13,610 on its Program for Support of the Campesino Population of the Guatemalan Altiplano, mainly to boost animal husbandry among small farmers. "We're providing one hamlet with 20 pairs of piglets, to raise and breed for local use," its newsletter announced. "Medicines, vaccines and feed are also being provided, along with instruction on how to care for the animals." Another village got poultry: "100 hens, 20 roosters, 40 turkey hens and 20 tom turkeys, to create a self-sustaining flock that would provide both eggs and occasional meat. Widows and orphans will be the first to receive poultry." Another part of this project involved agricultural training, consisting of five courses in "organic farming, vegetable production, latrine construction, energy-efficient stoves, and non-chemical insect control." It also included a weaving initiative with both young and older women as well as literacy and leadership training. In the same grant period, PEACE gave $6,000 to "Widows helping widows: An agricultural project for survival." For refugees who had left Guatemala, PEACE donated $720 for "a self-survey" by the Permanent Commissions in Mexico, "to determine who owned land inside Guatemala, in whose hands that land now lies, and whether it would be available if a return home became possible."[122]

In the early 1990s, as conditions in Guatemala improved, the Morales brothers and other members of the Central America Organizing Project's Guatemala Focus Group partnered with the Philadelphia chapter of the Pledge of Resistance to keep in touch with people in the camps in Mexico. Members made their own plans for accompaniment and material aid to returning refugees. They raised funds and supplies for community health, education, and rebuilding in Central America and supported the salaries of sanctuary workers at the US-Mexico border.[123]

Some congregations mobilized to support community development in Central America well beyond the end of the wars and return of refugees. Central Baptist formed a sister city relationship with the Salvadoran town of Las Anonas and partnered with churches in three other towns. "The first place we met [the people of Anonas] was on top of a rock mountain. They had wandered around for 10 years," remembered Ron Morgan, Betsy's husband. "When these people came back, they planted first and lived in tents and houses that they made out of sticks and plastic and cardboard." The Morgans and fellow congregants raised funds and sent supplies to help rebuild homes and a school for Las Anonas.[124] Over the years, they participated in emergency relief and rebuilding in Salvadoran towns after hurricanes, earthquakes, and floods.[125] Three other sanctuary and supporting congregations, Tabernacle United, Mishkan Shalom, and St. Vincent's, formed the Romero Interfaith Center in 1990 to assist this work in Las Anonas, "improving the everyday lives of rural Salvadorans to ensure the values of dignity, justice and peace." They affiliated with the larger grassroots US-El Salvador Sister Cities network.[126]

Activists from Swarthmore Friends and eight neighboring congregations in the Philadelphia suburbs followed a path much like that of Central Baptist. They formed the Central American Sanctuary Alliance of Delaware County (CASA) in 1987 and later renamed it the Central American Solidarity Association. After providing sanctuary for a Salvadoran family at Media Friends, CASA formed a partnership with the Nuevo Gualcho community, which was established by returning refugees in El Salvador. CASA helped fund its school and the development of its water supply until the organization ceased operating in 2007, as members aged and died.[127] Other transnational partnerships helped rebuild different institutions. Several professors at Swarthmore College created a faculty exchange program with the University of Central America in El Salvador. In addition to teaching classes and translating colleagues' writing, the Swarthmore professors served as election monitors for the nation's first free elections in 1994.[128]

While some of the transnational solidarity and development activities of Philadelphia-area organizations faded away in the later 1990s and 2000s, others continued, like the partnerships of Central Baptist and the Romero Center in El Salvador. At the end of Guatemala's civil war, the Episcopal Dioceses of Guatemala and Pennsylvania formed a Companion Diocese relationship. Under these auspices, St. Martin in the Fields Episcopal Church in Chestnut Hill partnered with three congregations in Guatemala's Northwest highlands, one of the main regions from which people fled in the 1980s. Members of St. Martin's Companion Parish Committee continued to visit Guatemala, and several parishioners participated in two medical missions organized by the Pennsylvania diocese (see figure 1.2). The committee collected donations of clothing and household goods and regularly sent funds to support scholarships and social programs. This helped one of their companion parishes, San Marcos in Quetzaltenango, sustain its work with people living with HIV, women in prison, and the LGBTQ

FIGURE 1.2.   Visitors from St. Martin's behind members of a women's chocolate-making cooperative composed mainly of people with HIV in Quetzaltenango, Guatemala, in 2018. St. Martin's companion parish San Marcos helped them organize and some of St. Martin's funding supported continued work with the co-op. (Photo courtesy of Terry Clattenburg.)

community, along with the training of volunteer health workers. Leaders and members of the Guatemalan parishes occasionally visited Philadelphia.[129]

For St. Martin's, these postwar partnerships grew out of earlier solidarity activism. Back in 1985, a group of parishioners traveled with Reverend Funkhouser on his first delegation to Central America. At his urging, in 1987 St. Martin's formed a Central America Cluster Group, a vehicle for solidarity work that the Central America Organizing Project convinced other congregations and organizations to establish, too. The St. Martin's group helped sponsor a women's health clinic in Nicaragua, collecting and delivering medicine and supplies, and other types of aid.[130]

Rev. Funkhouser's trips in the 1980s helped inspire community development work outside of congregations as well. Participants included people who were interested in what became known as *fair trade*, such as Philadelphia's local food pioneer Judy Wicks. Others went on to work in Mexico and Central America, helping to organize worker-owned cooperatives, nutrition programs, and aid to squatter settlements. Funkhouser became involved in fair trade in 2004 and worked in this area for almost a decade. In 2013, he began regular visits to Honduras, the most violent country in the Americas in the twenty-first century, to work with human rights groups providing restorative therapy for people who were impacted by violence.[131]

The three national Central American solidarity networks, the Nicaraguan Network (now based in Arizona) and NISGUA and CISPES in Washington, DC, all continued to operate as well.[132] NISGUA supported community organizing, legal work, and delegations promoting human rights, land rights, and the Guatemalan peace and reconciliation process. Similarly, CISPES organized delegations and assisted social movements and elections monitoring in El Salvador, where the SHARE Foundation also continued to invest in community development and in "building a new system of democracy."[133] AFSC ran programs for preventing youth violence in schools and neighborhoods of Guatemala City and conducted advocacy related to peace and displacement in El Salvador. PEACE for Guatemala merged with the Guatemala Health Rights Support Project in 1994 to form Guatemala Partners, which became Rights Action four years later. Based in Washington, DC, Toronto, and Guatemala, it continued to fund community groups "carrying out their own development, environmental defense, human rights, and emergency relief projects" in Guatemala, El Salvador, Honduras, and southern Mexico.[134]

This transnational human rights and development work has become permanent, it seems, sustained by decades-old organizations and relationships. "The sanctuary movement's real victory" by the early 1990s, Jim Corbett argued, "had been the development of sanctuary as an enduring institution," particularly among congregations and communities for which "providing sanctuary has become integral to being faithful."[135] As Ted Walkenhorst put it, "Those of us in the church have learned a lot about our faith and how it's supposed to be practiced."[136] Peace and community development were an integral part of that practice.

Unfortunately, this work remained relevant, as poverty and violence in Central America persisted and escalated in the twenty-first century. "Literally people did give their lives" in Central America in the 1980s and 1990s, Angela Berryman reflected, to build "a better society, which really never came to fruition."[137] As Betsy Morgan said, "The way the global economy was playing out, people were having to come here and make enough money."[138] Gangs in El Salvador, Guatemala, and Honduras increasingly extorted, raped, and forced people, especially youth, to join, marry, and live in servitude to them. The United States continued to support Central American governments and their militaries, which allowed organized crime to rule much of these countries. In 2004 they ratified the Central American Free Trade Agreement, which drove prices for small farmers' harvests down to unlivable levels. These conditions continued to inspire the migration of people illegally crossing borders into Mexico and the United States seeking safety, asylum, and economic survival. As one American journalist who covered the civil war in El Salvador wrote in 2019, "The effects of that war are still sending migrants north."[139]

## Guate en Philly

The Morales brothers and other refugees in sanctuary in Philadelphia went on to enjoy successful careers, especially compared to later Central American immigrants. Jorge quickly became the foreman of his landscaping crew, which also hired other Guatemalans who were in sanctuary and their brothers, cousins, and friends who arrived in the 1990s. In 1992 he started his own landscaping business with a pickup truck, two lawnmowers, a chainsaw, and some other equipment. It would remain a successful small business for over twenty years, owning two trucks and employing other Guatemalans of the sanctuary and later generations. Joel worked for over a decade, ultimately becoming foreman, for one of the area's high-end carpentry and home remodeling companies, which also hired other Guatemalans. He later became head of maintenance at one of the region's elite Quaker colleges.[140]

Central Americans who came to Philadelphia in sanctuary in the 1980s and early 1990s helped shape some of the subsequent migration and settlement. Some, including Jorge, used family reunification visas to bring over spouses, children, and other family members. Through sanctuary and supporting congregations, they were connected with networks of decent landlords, employers, and customers in relatively comfortable, well-off neighborhoods in leafy areas such as Germantown, Mt. Airy, and Chestnut Hill and suburbs like Media and Swarthmore. This aided their family members and friends who came later too.

But most Central Americans in twenty-first century Philadelphia were not related to the people who came during the civil wars. In the 1980s, a good portion of the few dozen Guatemalans and Salvadorans in the city and suburbs had settled there with the help of the Sanctuary Movement. This changed in the 1990s, however, as over 500 Guatemalans and 300 Salvadorans lived in the city by 2000 according to the US Census (which almost surely undercounted them), with more in the suburbs. Migration grew in the 2000s, as people fled violence and poverty. Close to 7,000 Guatemalans, 4,000 Hondurans, and 3,000 Salvadorans lived in the region by the early 2010s, according to the census.[141]

Recent Central American immigrants came from different backgrounds from refugees like the Morales brothers and their experiences in the United States diverged sharply. In Guatemalan Philadelphia, "there is this divide" between the different generations of migrants, acknowledged Manuel Portillo. Most Guatemalans who arrived between the late 1990s and 2020s came from the rural east of the country, while the refugees of the 1980s came largely from the south and west. They therefore "had a different understanding of the conflict." The east was the military's stronghold during the civil war, where less fighting occurred, though some families had lost relatives in the war. In recent years Guatemalans across the country suffered the extortion of their land and businesses, murders, beatings, rapes, and coercion, especially of young family members. But those from the west and south were more often targets of the army and state-sponsored death squads during the preceding decades of the war. Moreover, new Guatemalan immigrants were more often Evangelical and often hostile to the political left, while the earlier generation was more Catholic, connected to liberation theology, and generally more educated.[142]

People who came before and after 1991, the cutoff year for asylum in most cases, also experienced distinct contexts of settlement in the city. The Sanctuary Movement's intensely personal and supportive practices helped a small number of people settle in peaceful, middle-class neighborhoods, work in good jobs, and travel and support community development in Central America. Most Guatemalans and Salvadorans, and also Hondurans, who came later experienced instead the housing, labor markets, and neighborhoods of the city and region's poor and working classes, much like other immigrants from Latin America who were in the country illegally. They settled in row house neighborhoods among Puerto Ricans, Dominicans, Mexicans, Haitians, African Americans, and other working-class groups. Dispersed around the region, larger concentrations formed in the Upper North and Lower Northeast Philadelphia neighborhoods of Logan, Olney, Feltonville, Juniata, and Oxford Circle; in Bensalem, just outside Northeast Philadelphia; in Upper Darby and other suburbs near West Philadelphia; and across the river in Camden, New Jersey, and the adjacent suburb of Pennsauken.

Both generations held similar occupations in construction, landscaping, and housekeeping. But generally, those who came in the 1980s enjoyed better wages, benefits, workplace conditions, and career trajectories than later immigrants. This sort of bifurcation of social, economic, and neighborhood experiences became a defining feature of immigration at the end of the twentieth century.[143]

These divergent pathways resulted in part from dramatically different contexts of reception for different generations of Central Americans. Later migrants enjoyed nothing like the assistance of the Sanctuary Movement, its acts of hospitality and its transnational community building. Americans who had been involved in the movement generally paid little attention to, and were often unaware of, these new immigrants.

Even as their numbers grew, the region's Central American communities remained small and fragmented. Community organizations included a handful of Evangelical churches with Central American pastors and a couple of teams in the city's Hispanic Soccer League. Beyond this, they lacked institutions of civil society to assist people's settlement, housing, employment, and cultural preservation.

The spike in unaccompanied children arriving in the United States from Central America beginning in 2014, however, inspired greater support. Refugee resettlement agencies in Philadelphia found new legal avenues to work with this group of asylum seekers. These included the Obama administration's Central American Minors programs, which granted refugee status to over 1,600 children and TPS to another 1,400 (mostly Salvadorans).[144] La Puerta Abierta ("the open door"), an organization based in the suburbs that worked for years in Ecuador with families experiencing trauma and violence resulting from displacement, began therapeutic and mentoring programs for Latin American immigrant youth locally.[145] As in the 1980s, some of Philadelphia's twenty-first-century sanctuary work thus grew out of earlier solidarity work.

In 2015, a group of Guatemalan pastors and community leaders including Manuel Portillo established Guate en Philly (meaning Guatemala or Guatemalan in Philadelphia), aiming to organize people in local and transnational projects. They started by hosting construction worker safety trainings and visits

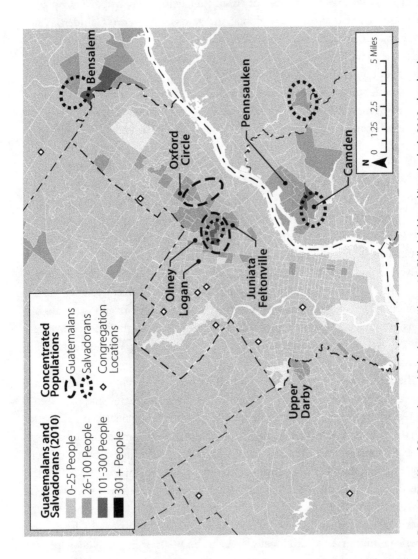

**Figure 1.3.** Map of Guatemalan and Salvadoran settlement in Philadelphia and its suburbs in 2010, also showing locations of 1980s sanctuary congregations. (Source: US Census; map by Danielle Dong.)

from the consulate in New York, which offered passport and other document services, to address some of people's immediate needs.[146] This work stalled with the election of Donald Trump as president, though, as fear of deportation limited public gatherings in this and other communities in which many people were in the United States illegally. But it soon picked up again as Guatemalans and other Central Americans continued to migrate. Guate en Philly helped convince the Guatemalan consular service to establish an office in the city in 2019.

Some Central Americans gained asylum and many received TPS in the 2010s, but in 2018 the Trump administration announced that for most it would not renew TPS, which was set to expire in early January 2021. The administration also began separating families, detaining people who had crossed the border indefinitely, and then forcing asylum seekers at the border to wait in dangerous conditions in Mexico. It cut off aid to El Salvador, Guatemala, and Honduras and pressured their governments to accept and resettle asylum seekers themselves. Still, conditions in Central America led to another spike in migrants seeking to enter the United States in the late 2010s and early 2020s.[147]

For immigrants from Central America in the twenty-first century, sanctuary meant different things than it did in the 1980s. While Central Americans again experienced acute crises of violence and migration, the US government's culpability was less obvious. The strong association with the Sanctuary Movement was gone, though a small number of Central Americans became active in the New Sanctuary Movement of Philadelphia and some of its member congregations would again harbor people from Central America (detailed further in chapter 5). Most of the thousands of Guatemalans and Salvadorans in the region in this century enjoyed nothing like the solidarity and support, either local or transnational, that sanctuary workers and congregations offered. They largely fended for themselves, working low-paid, often precarious jobs in service of wealthier Philadelphians, yet interacting relatively little with them. Some, however, found other forms of sanctuary in the emotional, spiritual, legal, and sometimes material support of their churches, legal aid organizations, and small nonprofits such as La Puerta Abierta and Guate en Philly.

Sanctuary for most Central Americans who arrived since the early 1990s mainly meant the limited municipal protections forbidding city police, prisons, and other city agencies from participating in their detention and deportation. This policy had greater practical value for the bigger number of people from Central America in twenty-first-century Philadelphia than such a policy could have in the 1980s. For the large proportion who lacked legal status, at worst sanctuary represented the tenuous hope that police officers inside the city would comply with local policy instead of deciding to turn them over to federal authorities for detention, as some did. Still, outside city boundaries, where the majority of Central Americans in the region lived, even that protection was usually absent.

Though relatively small populations, the Guatemalan and Salvadoran communities in Philadelphia illuminate the broader diversity of immigrant and receiving communities and of the opportunities and challenges they faced over time. The asylum claims of different generations of Central Americans reveal the frequently ambiguous, contested, and sometimes contradictory nature of people's status as immigrants or refugees. Their migration points up how closely related the causes and effects of immigration are to the United States' actions abroad and how inadequate and unjust our immigration system has often been. The Sanctuary Movement and more recent mobilization to assist people who were fleeing violence, persecution, and deprivation illustrate the generosity and humanity of some North and Central Americans, but also the challenges and limits of civil society's responses to immigration.

These arguments apply just as well to another group of refugees who came to Philadelphia in much larger numbers from 1975 to the 1990s. But these people, who were from Vietnam, Cambodia, and Laos, were granted refugee status from the start. They were resettled by government-sponsored nonprofit agencies that were responsible for arranging housing, health care, school, work, and putting refugees on a path to self-sufficiency. Still, in this era when the US refugee resettlement system grew up, specifically what refugees deserved and what place they might hold in the nation and its cities were open and contested questions. Ironically, despite their legal status and formal supports, not to mention their anti-Communism and the fact many had fought on the American side in the Vietnam War, in many ways Southeast Asians enjoyed less sanctuary in Philadelphia and other parts of urban America. Once resettled, they faced greater violence, less support, and other injustices in their neighborhoods.

## CHAPTER 2

# Refugee Resettlement
## Southeast Asians and the Resettlement System

"What I remember most about that period was seeing dead bodies strewn through the rice fields," recalled Thoai Nguyen. "When my father was prioritized for evacuation, we moved to a southern city called Can Tho." It was March 1975, "about a month-and-a-half prior to" what some people call the "fall of Saigon" and others see as the "liberation of Vietnam" from its colonial oppressors.[1] This was the end of what Americans call the Vietnam War, which began in 1955, after the French, with US support, had fought the North Vietnamese for the prior decade in a failed attempt to retake their former colony.[2] This would be the United States' biggest and longest direct military conflict of the twentieth century.

Thoai was nine years old in spring 1975. But up to that point, he acknowledged, "I was largely protected from everything." His father "came from . . . old money," with "large tracts of land," and had served first in the South Vietnamese army, then as an attaché for the French, and then with the US State Department. Yet as the war reached its final stage, two years after the North and the United States signed a treaty to end it, North Vietnamese, South Vietnamese, and US forces continued to fight each other. "So you had battles and dead bodies basically everywhere."[3]

"We lived a very fragile existence in those month-and-a-half that led to the final evacuation," Thoai remembered. Pulled out of school and staying in a hotel, he and his two brothers and five sisters each had a backpack, with a "change of clothing, dry food, pictures and family information." Their parents "adorned us with gold because that was a mode of exchange if we were to get lost. So each of us got a golden bracelet, gold chains, extra money stitched into the bag. Everywhere we went, we all had these backpacks, so we looked really nerdy, probably just like the Swiss Family Robinson in Vietnam."[4]

On the evening of April 28, "a huge pitch battle" broke out around Can Tho. Thoai's father took his three sons to the roof of the hotel. He "very calmly" explained "strategy and what was going on. . . . Gun ships, tanks on the bridge, and explosions" five or six miles away, "just explaining as if we were watching a movie." Around eleven that night, he was called back to the office.[5] At three a.m., Thoai was awoken by two explosions near the hotel.[6] His father "drove up with a Jeep and he said, 'We have 45 minutes to pack everything up and we're leaving.'" At the last moment, Thoai's "grandmom decided she didn't want to go, the reason being that she wanted to live the rest of her life in Vietnam." She kept Thoai's niece with her. "It wasn't an easy thing to leave them behind, but we had to make a quick decision, so we left them."[7]

The rest of the family drove back to his father's office, "air-conditioned and . . . very sterile." They waited with two other families of Vietnamese US government personnel and were told, "A couple of black cars will pull up. Just get in the cars, don't ask any questions." In the car, the driver "told us that when the car stopped, the door opens, run into the rice field. Okay, so don't ask any questions."[8]

As the three families ran toward the middle of the rice field, with Thoai holding the hand of his eleven-year-old brother, three "helicopters swooped down. We didn't see anything . . . but when the helicopters touched down, the force of the wind [was such] that we couldn't run. My brother and I were running against the wind and we couldn't go anywhere." Then "the helicopter door slides open and, then, these two GIs, huge, big GIs jumped out of the helicopter and ran towards us. So the natural reaction was, for me and my brother, we started running the other way." The GIs moved faster, scooped up the children, and pulled the families onto the helicopters.[9]

But then "they started throwing stuff out" since "there was too much weight." Thoai and his family "didn't get to choose what was thrown out. So lots of photos and things like that were thrown out, thrown overboard." As they took off, soldiers from the South Vietnamese army shot at the helicopters, since "the South did not want people to leave."[10]

The three families made it safely to a US Navy carrier, with about 300 other Vietnamese people and a smaller number of Americans from Can Tho. Other ships that were lined up nearby took on thousands of passengers, as US helicopters evacuated over 5,000 at-risk Vietnamese people on April 29 and 30, mainly airlifted from Saigon. They were mostly employees of the US, South Vietnamese military officers, and their families.[11] "It was like we were standing atop this floating city," Thoai remembered. "They had to push helicopters overboard because it was so crowded."[12]

The Vietnamese people who were evacuated at the end of the war were the allies whom US military and political leaders felt compelled to rescue. Their status as refugees was effectively guaranteed by the very fact of their evacuation, even if the details of their resettlement had yet to be worked out. Their relationships to the US government put them near the top of an emerging hierarchy of more and less privileged groups of refugees, even as their resettlement put the great majority at the bottom rung of American society.[13]

Along with other "priority evacuees," Thoai's family was among the first to be "processed" and resettled. The carrier ship transported the Nguyens to the US territory of Guam, a thirty-mile-long island strip of resorts and military bases in the Pacific where the government set up camps for processing Vietnamese evacuees. They were ordered to leave more of their things there, including Thoai and his brother's comic book collection. They buried the comics under dirt, wrapped in plastic bags, at the edge of the camp. They gathered bullet shells from the ground "which were found everywhere in Guam, to make wayfinding symbols so that we could find it again. My brother and I vowed that we would come back one day to recover our treasure."[14]

In the grander scheme of things, as Thoai put it, his was among "the few lucky families to have been evacuated by helicopter."[15] The earliest arrivals on Guam, including Thoai's family, were those airlifted by the United States, but many more people "self-evacuated" on boats, and were then picked up by US and other ships.[16] The United States admitted almost 140,000 Vietnamese refugees directly after the war. Congress supported their resettlement with $305 million from the Indochina Migration and Refugee Assistance Act of May 1975.[17]

Over the next decade, more than one million more people from Vietnam and neighboring Laos and Cambodia were resettled in the United States as people continued to flee these countries. The war took place across all three nations, making Laos and Cambodia the most heavily bombed countries on Earth, as the United States dropped more ordinance than the Allies did in all of World War II. Unexploded munitions (some with napalm), landmines, and the herbicide Agent Orange from US chemical bombing rendered rural communities perilous and agriculture impossible in the three countries.[18] In Cambodia, after the United States pulled out in early April 1975, the Khmer Rouge initiated a genocide that killed between one and two million people and displaced even more.

Compared to the family of Thoai Nguyen, the story of Sarorng "Rorng" Sorn reflected the very different experiences of Southeast Asians from less privileged backgrounds, including most Cambodians. "Born into the war," as she said, in 1968 in rural Kampong Speu Province, "just so many parts of my journey were so traumatic, and still impact me to this day." When she was one year old, the United States began a four-year campaign of carpet bombing in Cambodia, so her family lived in an underground bomb shelter. After the Khmer Rouge gained control of the country, authorities took Rorng, then age seven, to live and work in a children's labor camp, with "no freedom, no school, starving." Like most families, "my family lost family members and we were all separated, and when the war started again when Vietnamese troops invaded Cambodia" in 1978, "that's when we escaped . . . to the Thai border . . . and we . . . survived the jungle." By 1979, when they were taken into a camp in Thailand, half the people living along the border had died, Rorng remembered, their bodies dumped in holes, "and very ill people were left" by the side of the road. "Life in the camp gave me the chance to go to school, become a certified nurse, and help other Cambodian refugees."[19]

Like Rorng, most refugees from Cambodia, Laos, and Vietnam endured long journeys across land, through jungles, and in crowded and dangerous boats whose occupants were labeled "boat people." Most people were poorer than the early evacuees and people who were able to escape before Communist regimes took control; they were more often from rural areas and less connected to the US military. With greater knowledge and ability to live off the land as they fled, people from rural areas survived these journeys more often than people from the cities, though many died at sea. People who fled after spring 1975 often lived for years in refugee camps in Thailand, Indonesia, Malaysia, the Philippines, or other nearby countries.

Those nations' refusal to take in more "boat people" forced wealthy countries to create a global resettlement program through the United Nations in the late 1970s.[20] This also compelled the United States to formalize its own resettlement system. By the end of the twentieth century, more than 1.6 million Vietnamese, 580,000 Cambodian, and 320,000 Laotian refugees were resettled, a little over half of them in the United States and others in China, Canada, Australia, and Europe.[21]

Thoai's family was among the first to be cleared for resettlement from Guam. The government initially planned to resettle them in Hawaii. "However, the resettlement people basically said that Hawaii's economy is not doing so great, now, Pennsylvania, that's a land of opportunity." After a week at the Fort Indiantown Gap reception camp near the state capital Harrisburg, where

23,000 Vietnamese refugees would undergo health inspection and processing, the Nguyens were resettled in South Philadelphia in June 1975.[22]

"Privilege is a very strange thing," Thoai reflected, "because a lot of people think privilege is material things." His family was forced to abandon loved ones and possessions, and South Philadelphia was "not the best of places." Yet "even though we lost all of our wealth and privilege," Thoai's father "never felt that we—even though we lacked in material things, it was all within us to, basically, achieve all that back again."[23]

## Special Humanitarian Concern

Privilege can also be ironic, as evidenced in the history of refugee admission and resettlement. Even people who had close ties to the US government and military and were prioritized for evacuation, like the Nguyens, were resettled in a system, and in receiving communities, that imposed new forms of violence upon them. The resettlement system that grew up after the Vietnam War is the most comprehensive approach to assistance and integration of newcomers in the United States. Its history reflects both the immense generosity and resourcefulness of many people in newcomer and receiving communities and the basic inadequacy and injustices of the resettlement system for those communities. Asian American scholars have argued that the war and subsequent resettlement redefined Southeast Asians as subjects of American empire, a status that was largely codified in their visas, the resettlement system, and the welfare system to which it attached them.[24]

Southeast Asians' status as refugees should have made sanctuary in its narrower sense, as protection from deportation, irrelevant for them. But following the history of Cambodian, Laotian, and Vietnamese communities into the twenty-first century places them at the center of movements and debates about sanctuary. Some became targets for deportation due to new federal laws and international agreements. Sanctuary in all its meanings, locally and transnationally, suddenly mattered.

While the American public was ambivalent about Southeast Asian refugees from the start, they did fit the logic of refugee admission in the Cold War. These were our allies, people who had fought on the American side. Even people who had not fought were fleeing the Communist regimes that won the war. However, Americans had become deeply disenchanted with the long war, enraged by the lies presidents Lyndon Johnson and Richard Nixon told about the conflict and embarrassed by the brutal atrocities committed by the US military and by lost battles ending in a lost war.

Defeat in the Vietnam War forced the United States to reckon with what we owed a group of people who were unlike any other refugees who came to America before them. The US military played a central role in displacing people from Vietnam, Cambodia, and Laos. Unlike Jews fleeing pogroms at the turn of the twentieth century and later the Nazis, the Soviet Union, and the Eastern Bloc, Southeast Asians had no coethnics already established in America and ready to assist newcomers. The "objectives" of the US Refugee Act of 1980, therefore, were "to provide a permanent and systematic procedure for the admission to this country of refugees of special humanitarian concern" to the United States "and to provide comprehensive and uniform provisions for the effective resettlement and absorption of those refugees who are admitted."[25] In the years before and just after the passage of this landmark act, that system had to be invented and was forced to grow up quickly.[26]

The United States' answer to what refugees were owed was codified in the resettlement system, whose central aim was to make them "self-sufficient" as quickly as possible. As in most countries that resettle refugees, this was a public-private partnership. The federal Departments of State and of Health and Human Services worked with a set of mostly faith-based national networks of nonprofit organizations.[27] These voluntary agencies, "Volags" for short, were responsible for picking refugees up from processing centers, and later the airport, and then establishing them in new homes, jobs, schools, and neighborhoods.

In many ways, the resettlement and support of Southeast Asian and other refugees in the United States has been a story of profound generosity and exhausting mobilization to help people. The Volags' staff "thought we were saving lives."[28] They helped with seemingly everything, spending nights and weekends assisting refugee families with problems far beyond the scope of their programs. Surely the Volags struggled to help people achieve self-sufficiency and most of the refugees they assisted experienced the same hardships that other poor and working-class residents of US cities did. Nonetheless, they managed to resettle over a million Southeast Asians in the United States in the 1970s and 1980s and many thousands of people from the Soviet Union, Cuba, Ethiopia, Afghanistan, and other countries at the same time. They arranged housing, health care, school registration, and helped people gain employment. Put another way, they did put people on a path toward self-sufficiency.

However, that path was full of structural and interpersonal violence that reveals the core contradictions and injustices of the resettlement system. Constrained by meager funding, they placed people in deteriorating housing in declining cities and neighborhoods experiencing racial violence. These were among the places of least opportunity and most violence in the nation. The resettlement system's core strategy, since resettlement dollars themselves were insufficient, was to tie refugees to a welfare system whose limits, rules and funding cuts further destabilized their lives and limited their mobility and freedoms.[29] Arguably, the shifting requirements and repeated cuts to federal programs responsible for the social safety net have played a larger role in either bolstering or, more often, undermining the economic security of refugees since the Vietnam War than have the dollars devoted to refugee resettlement and programs. In these and other ways, self-sufficiency was an illusion, particularly for first-generation refugees—a myth repeated by people working for the government and the Volags that obscured the realities of resettlement.

For most refugees, the experience of resettlement was not only disorienting and violent; it was also degrading, oppressive, and unfair. Though Thoai's father had attained a high post in the US State Department in Asia, "when we got here, they wash[ed] their hands of him. He was completely deflated in terms of his status." Among Vietnamese refugees, Thoai noted, "I hear a lot of the same story. My dad's politics, or at least outlook, he was vehemently supportive of US involvement in the war. Then he went into, 'No, it was basically wrong they intervened,' or he went into, 'They betrayed us because they promised us this and then all they did was got us over here.'"[30] Southeast Asian refugees, especially those from families that fought and worked for the US during the war, widely shared this sense of betrayal and abandonment.[31]

The notion that resettlement was saving Southeast Asians' lives was ironic and, to some people, insulting, even if refugees were at the same time truly grateful toward the United States government and the Volags and their staff. Most Southeast Asians had escaped on their own, like Rorng Sorn. Most had saved their own lives, and one another's lives, multiple times before even being classified as refugees and assisted by the United Nations, the United States, and resettlement agencies. Hundreds of thousands had survived the isolation and privation of refugee camps. And then they survived resettlement, a system that, like other parts of what critics deride as the "poverty-industrial complex," sometimes rewarded Volag leaders and consultants far more than their clients.

It is also ironic that refugees from Southeast Asia endured such traumatic experiences of resettlement compared to Central Americans, who were denied the government's protection and support during the same period. Of course, the number of Guatemalans and Salvadorans in sanctuary in Philadelphia in the 1980s was miniscule compared to the roughly 24,000 Vietnamese, 16,000 Cambodians, and 5,000 Laotians who were resettled in the region between 1975 and 2000.[32] Over time, though, as migration in the 1990s and 2000s formed a predominantly working-class community of Central Americans in the region,

Southeast Asians became more diverse in their economic status, moving to a variety of working- and middle-class city and suburban neighborhoods.

Southeast Asian refugees broadly shared the challenges of resettlement, but they experienced divergent socioeconomic, housing, and neighborhood trajectories across generations. Generally, Vietnamese families from urban and elite or middle-class backgrounds attained more upward mobility, while rural-origin Vietnamese, Cambodian, and Hmong and other Laotian families more often lived in persistent poverty in working-class neighborhoods. These distinct outcomes appear in even sharper relief when compared to those of other groups resettled in the same era, especially Soviet Jews in Northeast Philadelphia, who enjoyed greater support than other refugees in the 1980s thanks to American Jewish community institutions.

Southeast Asian civil society in Philadelphia has evolved since the 1980s to address the alternately shifting and persistent issues of the ethnically diverse Vietnamese, Cambodian, and Laotian communities. Collaboration among those communities and with other Asian Americans has borne various work for refugee rights and protection at different times, even as organizations led by refugees have had to struggle to attain resources that enabled them to be the ones serving their own communities. The resettlement system, meanwhile, arguably exhibited greater continuity in the ways it operated and the challenges it posed for refugee and receiving communities.

Resettlement typically occurs in urban settings, yet only sometimes is it conceived in urban terms, with a focus on refugees' relationships to the city. The government and Volags have at times expressed concerns about the impacts of placing hundreds of refugees in a particular neighborhood in a short time, especially in regard to the reactions of incumbent residents and the availability of jobs. They have also alternately encouraged and discouraged the *secondary migration* of refugees leaving the place where they were resettled for another state. These moves, along with refugees' moves between parts of the same city, highlight some of the successes and failures of particular places as communities of resettlement, with different experiences of protection and assistance. Like other declining industrial centers of the American Rust Belt, Philadelphia in the 1970s and 1980s proved an especially challenging place in which to be resettled.

## Resettlement in Philadelphia

The Volags' efforts to put people on a path to self-sufficiency and to build a resettlement system that addressed the breadth and depth of their needs were thwarted by much more than a lack of funding. The labor and housing markets of the deindustrializing region, racial violence, a national recession, cuts in government funding for the resettlement and welfare systems, and the limits of the Volags' own capacity presented systemic barriers. This all compounded challenges posed by increased resettlement of Southeast Asians from rural backgrounds. In this context, refugees in Philadelphia and other cities experienced numerous economic, housing, neighborhood, and social problems.

At the start, before the 1980 act, resettlement was not much of an actual system, stressed Michael Blum, director of Nationalities Service Center (NSC), the region's largest resettlement agency. "At the present time we spend up to $200 per individual for each refugee family that we sponsor," he wrote in November 1978. "This money must pay for rent, initial food and the minimum furnishings. . . . Each individual receives a bed, including mattress and spring, sheets, and kitchen utensils."[33] By the end of the decade, the Volags developed a set of services that included English as a Second Language (ESL) classes, counseling, referrals for family planning and employment, legal services, translation, nutrition and health lessons, budgeting and consumer education, and "training in cultural values and awareness."[34]

Six resettlement programs operated in Philadelphia in the late 1970s and 1980s: NSC, Jewish Family Services along with its partner the Hebrew Immigrant Aid Society—Pennsylvania (HIAS-PA), Catholic Social Services, Lutheran Children and Family Services (LCFS), the Episcopal diocese, and Prime Ecumenical Service to Refugees. All had histories of aiding immigrants and refugees, mostly dating from the late nineteenth and early twentieth centuries, though much of their staff had no experience in such work. The state's welfare department, which disbursed federal refugee dollars, funded most of their post-1975 resettlement programs. They resettled Southeast Asians mainly in the working-class neighborhoods of West and South Philadelphia and the Logan and Olney sections of Upper North Philadelphia.

Resettlement depended on much more than the modest public resources allocated to the agencies. The Volags, city authorities, and other local institutions worked to form new webs of support from early on in 1975. They organized a refugee task force with representatives from the city's health department, school district, and human relations commission, as well as various nonprofits, to coordinate and connect refugees to services.[35] Medical care for refugees in Philadelphia was particularly strong, as city health clinics and university hospitals mobilized to offer free care.[36] Working with the family therapy division of Children's Hospital of Philadelphia, the Volags developed mental health programs for youth and families. LCFS established a Khmer

Studies Institute with a Cambodian professor of music at the University of Pennsylvania. It also ran educational programs and summer camps for Cambodian unaccompanied minors who had been brainwashed by the Khmer Rouge to teach them about Cambodian history, religion, and culture.[37]

Some of this work yielded new spaces for refugees or access to existing spaces in their neighborhoods. After widespread allegations of corruption against leaders of the Refugee Service Center in West Philadelphia, who mismanaged the state contract for post-resettlement social services in the city, in 1980 LCFS took over the center and hired Southeast Asian staff.[38] The Volags connected refugees to city libraries whose staff helped newcomers with everything from language learning and homework to seeking jobs. With support from the Penn State Agricultural Extension Urban Gardens program, Southeast Asians created or participated in some two dozen community gardens.[39] These were especially important for elders' mental health and for cultural preservation. A group of Hmong residents in Logan kept water crop cultivation alive by adapting a part of the Wingohocking Creek in nearby Belfield Park.[40] As one Catholic service agency noted, gardening "enhanced self-sufficiency by providing additional food in summer months for families on subsistence incomes." Moreover, gardens tended together by people from different backgrounds were "excellent practice ground for development of language skills and cultural interaction through daily contact with other neighborhood gardeners."[41]

Churches in West and South Philadelphia and Logan aided refugees with welfare claims, applications for green cards, and problems with landlords, schools, and neighbors.[42] Calvary United Methodist in West Philadelphia, home to the Central America Organizing Project, and nearby St. Francis de Sales church organized committees on housing, language, socialization, crime and safety, and clothing and furniture distribution.[43] A church in Logan sent twenty-six Southeast Asian children to summer camp, showed outdoor movies in the parking lot of an apartment house, ran an ESL class for mothers with small children, held clothing and furniture drives, and organized a weekly youth night with volleyball and ping-pong.[44]

Many individuals and families in Philadelphia and other communities of resettlement participated in these acts of welcoming people from Southeast Asia. They collected funds and kitchen and school supplies; volunteered with the agencies or privately accompanied and oriented newcomers to neighborhoods, schools, and health systems; invited refugees to dinner; and tutored people in English.[45] Working-class Black women in West Philadelphia and Logan gave out hundreds of breakfasts and lunches to Southeast Asian children through the state's Summer Feeding Program, including to those who were left behind when their parents went to work picking blueberries in New Jersey.[46]

These acts of kindness and personal connection, which were repeated by neighbors and congregations around the region and the country, remain among the most compassionate and humane aspects of people's experiences of resettlement. But these actions never could overcome the fundamental, structural limits and violence of the resettlement system and the welfare system nor the deeper economic and social problems of American cities. This became even more evident between the late 1970s and early 1980s, as resettlement expanded, formalized, and then suffered major funding cuts.

Southeast Asian refugee resettlement changed dramatically after 1978, in both scale and character. In the little more than three years between June 1975 and October 1978, Volags in Pennsylvania resettled 6,231 Southeast Asians and 1,479 other refugees, mainly Soviet Jews. Over the next three years, they resettled 16,846 Southeast Asians, 4,251 Soviet Jews, and 826 other refugees, including 239 Ethiopians and 110 Afghans, mostly in Philadelphia.[47] By 1982, an estimated 12,000 to 17,000 Southeast Asians lived in the city.[48]

People from Southeast Asia who arrived after 1978 mostly came from rural backgrounds and had little formal schooling or experience living in industrialized society, let alone a big city. They included many "boat people," who continued to flee Vietnam, as well as families of the Hmong ethnic group, a farming people from the highlands of Laos who fought for the United States along the Ho Chi Minh Trail during the war and were resettled after years living in refugee camps in Thailand. Cambodian refugees were overwhelmingly from rural origins since the Khmer Rouge had exterminated most of the country's urban middle class.[49]

"New wave persons have greater needs in all areas than persons arriving earlier," Blum wrote to state authorities in February 1980.[50] People from rural backgrounds had a harder time adjusting to life in the city than refugees from urban areas. Virtually all had experienced trauma, and many, especially elders, lived isolated lives as some were scared to leave their apartments or row homes.

Compounding these challenges, in the early 1980s the Reagan administration slashed resources for refugee resettlement and welfare. Reagan had been elected on a promise to dismantle government social programs, and the United States suffered recessions in 1980 and 1981–1982. At a meeting of Philadelphia's refugee service providers in August 1981, the director of the state refugee program, Gloria Guard, outlined some "proposed ideas of how to cut back by 56% (at the least) for the next" year. These included eliminating services like day care, training, legal assistance, outreach, support for the refugee service center, and more, along with "drastic reductions" in support for transportation and service referrals.[51]

This would cut refugee services to "three 'core' services," case management, job referrals, and ESL.[52] One program to be cut was Socialization and Recreation, which oriented people to schools and community institutions such as the post office, police and fire stations, banking, and public transit.[53] These tasks increasingly fell to volunteers, including a growing number of Southeast Asian community leaders and nascent mutual aid associations. But they would never make up for the limits of public investment. "Dear Gloria," wrote Blum, "The state's proposed approach appears to . . . ignore the moral and contractual leverages that influence responsible resettlement." Without these supports, the stripped-down system of resettlement "may really be more costly in the long run," for refugees and government.[54]

The state budget cut funds for ESL programs from $5.7 to $2.0 million in 1982, reducing funds for English classes so they were available to just 1,850 refugees. More than 10,000 Southeast Asian refugees in the state were on welfare that year, including almost 7,000 in Philadelphia. "The reason why they are on welfare," observed Vuong Thuy, a Vietnamese board member of the Asian American Council of Greater Philadelphia, "is that they do not know enough English to get a job."[55]

Further cuts to welfare and resettlement funding in 1983 sharply reduced the money and opportunities given to refugees. Before these cuts, all refugees received eighteen months of federal resettlement assistance and refugees in Pennsylvania could receive welfare payments as long as they were in school. After the cuts, resettlement dollars ended after three months, which would remain the standard in subsequent decades, and welfare payments ceased for able-bodied people over eighteen. This diminished refugees' ability to support family members who were still in Asia as well as the United States, as despite their own privation, some sent part of their welfare checks overseas as remittances, a practice that upset some Americans.[56]

These policy changes pushed many refugees out of school. A *Philadelphia Inquirer* reporter told the story of Tuan Le, son of a South Vietnamese police lieutenant who had served with the CIA during the war. Tuan fled in 1979 with his brother and two sisters, "largely because he wanted to get an education" and "knew that in the new Vietnam the children of former officials do not get educations and frequently do not get jobs." Like many young people, they left without their parents and were resettled in Philadelphia two years later. The three youngest siblings, ages eighteen, nineteen, and twenty, had to abandon their senior year at University City High School, where over 100 Southeast Asian students dropped out in fall 1983.[57]

"I want to go to college, you know, to study," Tuan said, "but now I cannot . . . Maybe I work in restaurant, a store." His oldest sister earned one hundred dollars a week as a seamstress, which was not enough to sustain them. Other Southeast Asian youth worked in neighborhood sandwich and pizza shops, in hotels, and bussed tables and washed dishes at restaurants. Attendance at the Volags' evening English classes consequently declined as well. A teacher at University City High told the reporter, "These kids don't fully understand what life will be like here without an education. . . . Already, they live in some of the toughest parts of town. . . . They still can't really speak the language, and it's hard to get even a bad job."[58]

Rather than promoting self-sufficiency, the rules and cuts that lawmakers made to resettlement and welfare systematically stalled Southeast Asians' integration and upward mobility. "These people came here highly motivated to get ahead," said the director of the US Office of Refugee Resettlement, Phillip Hawkes, in 1985, "but we created a welfare system in this country that inadvertently sidetracked this motivation."[59] The welfare system surely had different effects for refugees than it had for African American and Puerto Rican communities that were experiencing generational poverty and discrimination. But the limits and cuts made to welfare stalled the progress of many Southeast Asians toward better employment, language acquisition and educational attainment, thus contributing to their persistence as the group with the highest percentage of people on welfare in the United States. In 1985, nationally more than half of Southeast Asians lived in poverty and received welfare, while in Philadelphia the proportions were even higher.[60]

## Employment

Contrary to the description of Pennsylvania as a land of opportunity that Thoai Nguyen heard from resettlement functionaries in the Pacific, in 1975 it was a state where opportunities were fast disappearing. The Philadelphia region lost 100,000 factory jobs in the 1970s and tens of thousands more in the 1980s.[61] Most cities in the nation declined in these decades, especially in the Northeast and the Midwest. Jobs were hard to come by even for Southeast Asians' working-class American neighbors.

Resettlement workers and refugee community leaders in Philadelphia agreed that only about 10 percent of Southeast Asian refugees over age eighteen found steady jobs in the early 1980s.[62] At city Refugee Task Force meetings, Volag staff repeatedly "expressed concern about . . . the number of placements." They attributed this partly to the location of jobs in the suburbs, challenges of transporting refugees to those jobs, and high unemployment, which heightened competition for entry-level positions that barely paid enough to cover the costs of going to work. At the March 1982 meeting, an employee of LCFS pointed out that over 100,000 people in the Philadelphia region were seeking work.[63] The limits of English literacy and fluency among refugees, depression and posttraumatic stress, and tension in refugee families over traditional gender roles all made finding good jobs more difficult.[64]

Nonetheless, resettlement agencies actively sought out job openings and encouraged their clients to apply. Ironically, they focused on factory jobs, which were quickly disappearing. Still, many manufacturing jobs remained in the region and some refugees attained them, although they were often laid off as companies closed or moved away. The Volags formed relationships with various employers in the factory, warehouse, and service sectors.[65] The region's largest Korean social service agency partnered with the Korean Business, Dry-Cleaners, and Retail Grocery Associations to offer on-the-job training for refugees in stores; handbag, shoe, and garment factories; TV repair; and gas stations.[66] Yet the Volags struggled to fill many positions they found or were unable to even identify people to refer, usually since refugees did not speak enough English.[67]

Thoai's parents experienced some of the common employment pathways among early Vietnamese refugees, who often had more education and success in the labor market. His father, Thoai recalled, first worked as a security guard at a downtown department store, a decline in status "that really hurt him. Then he left there" in protest and "boycotted working because of systemic racism that precluded him from work that utilized his skills and professional experience." He went "back to school because none of his degrees were being recognized" and "earned his degree so he could teach while he fought the US government to regain his GS [General Schedule] level" in the federal employment hierarchy. Like other refugees who were fluent in English, he worked for HIAS-PA's resettlement program. But more exceptionally, after many years of advocacy he got his "GS level to where he left off" at the end of the war. With that status restored, "he worked for INS for a number of years as an investigator of Southeast Asian refugees who were petitioning for US citizenship. His specialty was to investigate Communist ties."[68]

Thoai's mother "couldn't participate in employment outside the home as effectively because of her lack of English. She started making . . . Vietnamese dessert food . . . in the home and, then, packaged and then brought to these Vietnamese stores." Thoai and some of his siblings—those who did not have their own jobs—got "up at six o'clock with her and we all had our sort of assembly line up. This is what we'd do for about an hour before eating breakfast and going to school."[69] Southeast Asian families often pursued such strategies,

whether preparing food or sewing at home or irregular work outside, to supplement their meager wages and insufficient support from welfare, food
stamps, and Medicaid.[70]

Many refugees found work in agriculture outside the city, though Americans involved in refugee support in Philadelphia rarely seemed satisfied with
this type of employment. At a task force meeting in 1980, a member of the
Logan Democratic Club's ad hoc committee on refugees "explained that the
Indochinese in Logan are being transported by bus to New Jersey to work"
on farms. In addition to "complaints that the bus driver drives too fast and
doesn't respond to complaints," he worried that "the refugees are being exploited pay wise. They are paid by the box, not by the hour and it's little pay
for hard work." A representative of the Farm Labor Services Center noted that
her "organization is very concerned about Asian workers." She cited "community relation problems, some farm workers perceive that Southeast Asians
are 'taking over' . . . willing to work at below minimum wage, thus jeopardiz-
ing the salary benefits earned by other farm workers."[71]

Responding to such tensions, resettlement agencies cast their clients as good
for America and its economy and the media developed a narrative of refugees
as uncomplaining, hard workers.[72] As early as 1980, Jewish Employment and
Vocational Service (JEVS) promoted the Cambodian participants in its English
language program in the *Main Line Times*, the newspaper of the region's
wealthiest suburbs. Staff labeled them as "tremendously motivated," with perfect attendance records, and "happy to start at an entry level job and do routine, repetitive work. Some suitable occupations would be lawn care and
maintenance, packaging, assembly line work, industrial or office cleaning, dishwashing, bussing tables and sewing machine operation."[73] The national press
pushed this narrative too, in stories like "Off the Boat and Ready to Work" in
*Industry Week*, which touted their "high productivity, and an inclination toward
teamwork."[74] Much of this narrative of passive, willing, productive workers
echoed the "model minority myth" that Americans had already developed
about Chinese and Asian Americans more generally.[75]

Dissatisfied with the Volags' job placement record in Philadelphia, though,
in 1982 state welfare officials stripped NSC of the contract for leading Southeast Asian refugee employment services in the city.[76] They awarded it instead
to JEVS, which had run English and occupational programs for European refugees since the 1930s.[77] JEVS had recently built a large training and placement center in Northeast Philadelphia, a half-hour bus ride from Logan and
Olney.

"The Vietnamese were more like the Russians," remembered Elinor Hewitt,
who designed JEVS' refugee training programs. "They weren't country

people," and many had gone to college. Hundreds of Vietnamese men trained at JEVS in plumbing, heating, electrical, and other mechanical trades, and most were placed in steady employment with decent wages in construction, building maintenance, auto mechanic shops, and manufacturing. Programs for a smaller number of women focused on clerical and accounting jobs, also with good results in attaining office and retail jobs. Vietnamese women most commonly found work as hairdressers and nail technicians.[78] By the twenty-first century, they would come to dominate the ownership and workforce of nail salons and the wholesalers that supplied them in the city and nation at large.

However, with Cambodians and Laotians, especially the Hmong, "language was difficult," Hewitt said, and the "kinds of jobs they could do were limited." Many "second wave" refugees were illiterate in their own languages, and Hmong was basically an unwritten language. For Southeast Asians from rural backgrounds and less educated refugees more generally, JEVS and the Volags helped adults find jobs as meat packers, maids in hotels, and aides in day care centers. A special six-month program training some Hmong men in machine tool operation was "a disaster," though, yielding no job placements.[79]

The region's labor market remained dismal in the 1980s. A study of "boat people" who were resettled in Boston, Chicago, Houston, Seattle, and Southern California found that two-thirds were employed by 1985. But the economies of those regions were far healthier than deindustrializing Philadelphia; the Bronx; Lowell, Massachusetts; or Oakland or Richmond, California, all of which were major centers of resettlement and poverty.[80] One particularly hopeless feature in the *Philadelphia Inquirer* concluded that "many of the [resettlement] agencies . . . could do little more than find them houses, pay the first month's rent and point to the welfare office."[81]

## Housing

If there were few available jobs in Philadelphia, the opposite was true of housing. The city's population dropped by about 370,000 residents between 1970 and 1990. But the condition of housing that was made available and affordable to refugees was often dangerous and owned by abusive landlords. These problems mounted as the Volags resettled large numbers of people in the "second wave."

As Thoai Nguyen remembered, "In 1975, we were probably the only Vietnamese family to have settled in that immediate area" of South Philadelphia. That changed after 1978. "Even [though] only two or three years separated our coming to their coming, it was a huge gulf," in their distinct backgrounds and greater challenges integrating in the city. Thoai had already faced intense pressure to assimilate. "It was not apparent to me that I had a connection with these people" from Southeast Asia. His Italian American friends referred to "the newcomers as 'chinks' and 'gooks' in my presence," and "when I protested that those people were me, they would say that I was not those people, that I was one of them," an American. "The realization of this contradiction among my closest white friends had a profound impact on my understanding of the complexity of my own identity and compelled me to build friendships with the newer Southeast Asian refugees in my school and in my neighborhood."[82]

His political identity further solidified in spring 1983 when an ESL teacher at South Philadelphia High School, Debbie Wei, asked Thoai, who was then in eleventh grade, to go on what she told him was a "picnic." Instead, it was "a community organizing thing where we were in West Philly and I was knee-deep in mud in a . . . housing area [where] mostly Laotians and Cambodians lived," a building called Admiral Court. "The landlord was just totally taking advantage of them. I think that was the first time that my eyes were kind of opened to the connection between how I got here and how they got here." The same forces had displaced them, and the same resettlement system had dumped them in declining city neighborhoods.[83]

Admiral Court was the most famous case of housing abuse, though it was by no means unique. Around the corner was Stoneleigh Court, another building where Wei and fellow advocates protested at the same time. It was part of an area of some forty city blocks in West Philadelphia where Southeast Asians were resettled, commonly in households of six to eight people, in rundown apartments and aging brick row houses. Volags sometimes filled row houses with a mix of Vietnamese, Cambodian, Laotian, Cuban, and Haitian refugees together, people who did not even speak each other's languages. Wei, a former community organizer and housing activist in Chinatown who lived in this area, began to organize her Southeast Asian neighbors.[84]

Refugees experienced varying housing conditions in other neighborhoods. In Logan, they lived mainly in old apartments like those in West Philadelphia, with peeling lead paint; faulty elevators and electric, plumbing, and heating systems; and sometimes asbestos. Housing conditions in Olney and South Philadelphia were generally better, as one or two families typically lived in two- and three-story brick row houses.[85] A 1981 article in the *South Philly Review* called the area's experience with Southeast Asians "an almost unqualified success story."[86]

But the large number of refugees in more precarious housing situations constantly faced threats of displacement. The landlord of Stoneleigh Court also owned a 106-unit apartment building in Logan called Bennett Hall, which likewise lacked heat, hot water, and in some units, even locks on the doors. In

December 1979, its 266 Southeast Asian tenants fled when a fire broke out in the fifth through seventh stories. Without other available housing options, they promptly returned.[87] At a meeting of the Refugee Task Force eight months later, caseworkers called attention to this building and another apartment building in Logan where the electricity was scheduled to be turned off in three days "and the gas disconnected a month later. Until the buildings are condemned, the tenants can't move out," they noted, and the city would only "condemn the buildings . . . when the electricity is disconnected. Forty-five families have to be moved," and they "will have to go to Community Legal Service to . . . file suit against . . . the owner."[88]

The story of Admiral Court illuminates the longer arc of such buildings' history and the greater range of stakeholders implicated in refugee housing. An investment property built in the early twentieth century, it was repeatedly sold to a string of investors. After World War II, its tenant population changed from white to Black, like most of the neighborhood around it. In 1981, the city declared the seventy-six-unit building unfit for habitation. One wing of the building had been badly damaged by fire a year prior. It had numerous code violations. Housing activists and leaders of a local community development corporation persuaded its mostly African American tenants to hold their rent in escrow. They used the money to repair "leaky plumbing, collapsing ceilings and fire alarm systems." But only "a handful of American tenants continue[d] to withhold their rent" and stay there, given that heat and hot water were "sporadic at best," as one resident described it.[89]

Most of the residents were replaced the next year by new tenants from Southeast Asia. The landlords approached a resettlement agency that was overwhelmed by the sudden increase in arrivals, in this case NSC, and offered a large group of apartments. In November 1982 it housed thirty-four families, including thirty from Laos, Vietnam, and Cambodia. The *Philadelphia Daily News* reported that the manager "told them the building was 'fit,' and threatened to evict them if they didn't pay their rent." The owners were "two of the city's most notorious tax delinquents." One had fled to Florida to avoid arrest.[90] The development corporation's director, Ellyn Sapper, found that the language barrier "made it impossible to organize the Asian tenants to fight for their rights."[91]

City authorities placed the building in receivership in late 1982. Responding to bad press about refugees' living conditions there and elsewhere, the City Managing Director's Office took over leadership of the Refugee Task Force.[92] The city auctioned Admiral Court at the sheriff's sale for tax-delinquent properties, closing the sale in 1984. This compensated the city for back taxes. But for the tenants and their neighbors, Sapper averred, "Selling the building to another speculator, who will milk it to death just like these two, is not the answer."[93]

In July 1985 the city again declared Admiral Court "unfit for human habitation," yet this time it was thanks to what a *Daily News* reporter called "the first organized protest by East Asian refugees since they arrived in Philadelphia." In response to "more than 100 housing and code violations" and no hot water, most of the 190 tenants from Southeast Asia put their rent in escrow that month. The new landlord had done "nothing to alleviate the situation," Debbie Wei told the reporter. "It's basically being slummed out." The eight families who began withholding rent a month earlier—"about $270 a month for a one-bedroom apartment—have been sent eviction notices," the reporter wrote, "and all but three who failed to pay rent this month have been notified by mail to vacate the building." One Cambodian mother of three said the Southeast Asian tenants were afraid of going to court.[94] But unlike earlier efforts, they kept up the protest.

Wei realized that teenagers were key to organizing Southeast Asians against housing abuses. They were learning English, unlike many adults, and showed up at one institution nearly every day. Before the school district transferred her to South Philadelphia, she got a job teaching at University City High, where teens from Admiral Court and Stoneleigh Court were in her class.[95]

She adapted the standard ESL curriculum to her students' housing problems. In a vocabulary lesson, they listed all the broken fixtures in their apartments. For a math unit, they calculated the costs of needed repairs, establishing the basis to withhold their rent in escrow. In a letter-writing lesson, they sent the city solicitor formal complaints about their living conditions. In the end, the city took the buildings from their owners (a second time for Admiral Court) and turned them into affordable housing, repaired and managed by a Quaker nonprofit. Out of this experience, Wei and her allies established the advocacy organization Asian Americans United.[96]

While the organizing at Admiral and Stoneleigh Court ended well for the tenants who remained, refugees' overall experiences of housing pointed up the inadequacy of the resettlement system for rebuilding lives and communities and promoting self-sufficiency. As one case worker for Catholic Social Services put it, "The refugees are moved from one ripoff place to another." Michael Blum of NSC complained that the Volags were afforded neither time nor funding to plan for refugee arrivals and housing. "We only get a day or two notice they are coming."[97] Especially at the height of refugee arrivals in the early 1980s, this left the agencies and the people they resettled vulnerable to unscrupulous landlords. The Volags were at the same time duped, unprepared to be good housing agencies, and negligent in settling people in hazardous homes with bad landlords. Those landlords saw refugees as tenants whose rent was guaranteed and who were unlikely to complain, since they did not know the laws and came from countries where questioning authority was dangerous.[98]

Refugees were not the only people to bear the costs of all this. As the November 1984 minutes of the Refugee Task Force acknowledged, some of those landlords had "Blacks moved out forcibly from housing where Asians were later placed," including at Stoneleigh Court and other buildings in West Philadelphia and Logan. In some cases, this undermined Blacks' own advocacy against housing abuses, as it did at Admiral Court.[99]

One the most scandalous things about Southeast Asians' experiences of housing abuse is that it did not stop. In 1989, after a fire displaced twenty families from two apartment buildings in West Philadelphia, the *Daily News* reported that for "most refugees . . . dependent on public assistance, home is wherever they can afford the rent. Most often," that meant indecent, unsafe housing. The reporter found "leaks and gaping holes in the ceilings go unrepaired. So do worn-out stoves and refrigerators. Floors are quilts of linoleum and carpet remnants, or rotting, sagging wood. Some apartments have plywood front doors, with a latch and padlock as the only lock." Few refugees complained to their landlords for fear of eviction, and those who did were often rebuffed.[100] A 1992 *Philadelphia Inquirer* story about a South Philadelphia row house expressed a similar mix of injustice and hopelessness: a water bill for $712, "so high . . . because the pipes in the basement leak. The pipes leak . . . because the landlord hasn't repaired them." Once the basement "flooded with half a foot of water. The landlord fixed the hole by jamming a stick into the pipe." Regrettably, the story concluded, the city lacked translators to help with this, as it remained fiscally strapped.[101] And while city agencies and activists paid attention to housing problems, they were more preoccupied with violence against Southeast Asians.

## Violence

The location of refugees' housing placed them in the midst of existing racial conflicts and created new ones. The particular parts of West Philadelphia, Logan, Olney, and some sections of South Philadelphia where Southeast Asian resettlement was concentrated were areas in between white and African American neighbors, some of whom fought over turf as the color line shifted, due largely to white flight.[102] On top of the systemic violence of the resettlement and welfare system and refugees' economic and housing experiences, Southeast Asians became targets of intimidation and physical violence by Black and white neighbors.

A front-page feature in the *Philadelphia Inquirer* in 1983 offered relatively tame but typical examples of interactions on the streets: "In South Philadelphia, a neighbor of Cambodian refugee Vanny Prak told him he did not have the right to park his car in front of his house on South Fifth Street because he was only a tenant and not a homeowner. Vanny moved it rather than argue. In West Philadelphia, Bee Xiong, another Southeast Asian from the primitive H'mong hill tribe of Laos, was accused by community people of taking work from poor blacks. Out of fear, Bee quit his newspaper delivery job."[103] The *New York Times* related more brutal incidents in 1984, especially involving Hmong people in West Philadelphia. "He say 'don't come down this street no more,'" said Ger Vang, "referring to an attacker who had thrown him to the ground and battered his face. 'I must walk this street,' Ger Vang said. 'I live here.'" Others "were beaten and robbed, apartment windows were hit by rifle bullets and homes and cars were stoned." Ger Vang's cousin "was beaten . . . with a steel rod and rocks on a street corner and left with a brain injury and both legs broken."[104] Similar scenes were repeated in other regions too. The US Commission on Civil Rights and the Justice Department launched investigations, holding hearings in Philadelphia, Sacramento, California, and other cities.[105]

Schools were another key site of violence. Southeast Asian students met everyday intimidation and occasional acts of severe brutality, especially at University City High, Olney High, and some of the schools in South Philadelphia. They were "jostled in bathrooms and taunted daily with slurs such as 'chink' and 'gook'" and were regularly assaulted on their way to and from school. In 1981, University City High experienced two stabbings and a series of brawls between Black and Southeast Asian students. When a brutal beating two years later left Do Manh, a student from Vietnam, with a broken neck, Debbie Wei "found out from his classmates that no student had even been suspended for that assault." After she went to the newspapers, the school district investigated, though leaders at the school declined to cooperate.[106]

"I feel not happy about going back to school," said one Cambodian boy after being attacked outside Olney High in 1986. "We want peace, but the guys just want to beat us up. We don't know why. . . . When I go to school, I'm not feeling safe, like my heart is going boom." This obstructed refugees' ability to escape poverty and violence in their neighborhoods. "Our future is to go to school and to get into college. The trouble is, how can I study? . . . If I am rich . . . I am going to move to another state. The place we want to go is peace."[107]

Violence begat a mix of nonviolent and violent responses. The president of the Cambodian Association of Greater Philadelphia encouraged students who were afraid to go to school to "join in a group and walk together."[108] Given their experiences of constant violence, though, it came as no surprise to many Southeast Asian parents, their children's teachers, and neighbors when young people formed gangs increasingly in the later 1980s.[109] As Naroen Chhin, a Cambodian refugee, explained, "'Gangs' started because kids wanted to protect themselves and they were being abandoned by their schools. I remember my uncle walking me and his kids to school, and he himself was attacked and knocked out."[110]

This changed Southeast Asian communities. "Once violence started" and gangs formed, Chhin recalled, "kids started using drugs" and selling them. "The focus of the community shifted from taking care of each other, to attacking each other and even killing each other. We escaped the Killing Fields in Cambodia, only to be resettled in the Killing Fields here in America."[111]

Like Southeast Asian community leaders, African Americans also mobilized to combat the violence against their Asian neighbors. Mary Cousar, a Democratic ward leader, helped form the Logan Multi-Cultural Task Force around 1984, after 900 residents signed petitions and eighty staged a street-corner protest expressing outrage after "several young black men attacked members of a Vietnamese family and bombarded their home with bricks" and bottles.[112] Two years later, they got the police to patrol a "safe corridor" for Cambodian students en route to Olney High.[113] In West Philadelphia, clergy and community leaders, including city councilman Lucien Blackwell and his wife and aide, Jannie, met with residents and organized a march on the local police station demanding more protection for Southeast Asians and their neighbors.[114] Some of the peacemakers became targets of threats and violence as a result.[115]

The resettlement agencies and others sought out the city's human relations commission to investigate the violence. The commission held four hearings in the fall of 1984.[116] In explaining the violence, people who testified cited cultural differences, scapegoating for economic troubles, resentment of support that refugees received, maladjusted youth, and criminal motives unrelated to race.[117]

Some Southeast Asians and their neighbors blamed the Volags for failing to prepare either refugees or receiving communities for resettlement. Instead, they had "dumped" a "'new, strange people' . . . by the thousands into poor, old neighborhoods . . . most of them rural people who had never ridden a bus."[118] One Volag administrator replied that the $560 provided at that time for a refugee's first thirty days in the United States "does not begin to cover" the costs of everything people needed. Following the recent funding cuts, there was nothing left for cultural orientation, she explained.[119]

Blum pointed out that "the history of racial tension in our community . . . pre-existed the resettling of refugees." Moreover, the "conditions being faced by our new Asian/refugee residents are conditions that are faced by many Philadelphians in similar economic and social circumstances." Surely no one should expect the Volags to solve these larger problems. Indeed, he stressed, "considering the number of new refugee persons that have moved into our neighborhoods, people have gotten along fairly well and have been support-ive of one another."[120] Though in many ways accurate, this narrative of rela-tive peace and success was drowned out by depressing media reports and the persistence of violence.

The human relations commission issued a report a year later, concluding, "The recent rapid swell in the number of Asians in the Philadelphia area has greatly increased intergroup tensions and magnified anti-Asian feeling in the population around them."[121] It detailed the struggles of thousands of Asian immigrants and refugees with poverty, language barriers, racism, crime, and "lack of preparation for urban life." Its recommendations included clarifying the city government's responsibilities toward refugees; increasing services for neighborhoods of resettlement, such as classes in legal rights, English, and us-ing city services; establishing neighborhood crime watches; and hiring bilin-gual staff in city agencies.[122]

However, as one *Daily News* reporter observed, "Now that the report is out . . . no one seems to know what to do with it." The report failed to say who should be responsible for implementing its recommendations. Members of the newly formed group Asian Americans United added that the school district, with close to 5,000 Asian students, had few Asian teachers and no Asian coun-selors. It had recently hired a Vietnamese-speaking man for its homework hot-line, but the district's "Asian liaison" was deemed ineffective, and he himself recognized that Asian students did not approach him "because I'm not Asian."[123] The hearings and the report made little difference, activists and the local media concluded, as violence toward Southeast Asians continued. In the late 1980s, close to one-quarter of the victims of interracial violence in the city were Asians, despite accounting for just 3 to 5 percent of the population.[124]

For African American communities, Southeast Asian resettlement posed more complex issues than the reasons cited at the hearings. It went far beyond undermining Blacks' housing activism and tenure at buildings like Admiral Court. Many Blacks had fought in the Vietnam War, usually having been con-scripted in the draft, and they continued to suffer psychological and physical trauma. The support they saw for their new refugee neighbors and mostly false rumors of its generosity pointed up their own lack of effective support and continued oppression, including housing and job discrimination and racial vio-lence, as whites and institutional racism enforced the color line.

The situation in West Philadelphia was especially complicated. Researchers at the University of Pennsylvania had played a role in developing the tactical herbicide Agent Orange for the military. Their laboratory was in the University City Science Center, a complex of office buildings next to University City High School on the edge of an area where many Hmong were settled.[125] This had been an African American neighborhood, called the Black Bottom, which the university demolished with urban renewal funds in the 1960s. In this context, the notion that the Volags could prepare receiving communities for the arrival of new neighbors from Vietnam, Cambodia, and Laos was naive at best.

Ultimately, in Philadelphia and other cities, resettlement faced numerous challenges and fundamental inadequacies, many of which compounded one another. The fact that the Volags and their staffs were asked to do virtually everything for refugees almost inevitably exposed their limits. They generally lacked expertise in housing and employment; their strengths were in social work and linking people to health, education, and other social services. Their generosity rarely overcame, and never should have been expected to make up for, the insufficiency of resources that the public sector devoted to resettlement. As Blum wrote in 1989, there remained "an unrealistic expectation by the Federal government that refugees should be self-sufficient economically and socially" within a year or two.[126] Nor was the city, which was reeling from decline and fiscal crisis, prepared to meet their needs, despite installing translators in the courts, police department, and health clinics and working with the Volags to support refugees' access to services.[127]

More critically, these institutions were all part of a system that reproduced violence and injustice in multiple forms. To community organizers and many refugees, not only the landlords but also some of the Volags and their contractors looked, if not downright corrupt, at least like "poverty pimps." They reaped public funds to do incompetent work that yielded abuse for their clients at home, work, and school, as well as other parts of their lives.[128] The welfare state and the resettlement system that became part of it largely determined these outcomes.

As the story of Admiral Court signaled, action by Southeast Asians and their allies was necessary to overcome many of the greatest problems they faced. Southeast Asians working with the nonprofit Education Law Center of Philadelphia won a class-action suit (1985–1988) against the school district for systematically violating the rights of Southeast Asian students. The ruling mandated investment in English instruction.[129] But ultimately, it would take the migration of Southeast Asians to new neighborhoods and formation of Southeast Asians' own community organizations to achieve more effective protection and support than refugees initially experienced in the 1970s and 1980s.[130]

# Secondary Migration

The resettlement system has struggled with the urban dimensions of its work, including housing, neighborhoods, and rural people's adaptation to life in American cities, since shortly after the Vietnam War. By the early 1980s, federal authorities, Volag staff, and the media openly expressed concern about the impacts of resettlement on cities and neighborhoods and about certain refugees' fit for urban living. Others wondered if migration to other places would help refugees and the resettlement program meet their needs and goals. At a meeting in June 1981, staff from Philadelphia's resettlement agencies and Southeast Asian community leaders agreed: "The goal of the refugee resettlement program is to help the refugees become self-sufficient. Jobs are difficult to get in the cities, so in order to survive, the refugees go on welfare. This is alien to the policy of self-sufficiency. . . . We should research areas where there are jobs and get the information to the refugees."[131] "Relocation is sometimes necessary for employment," a case worker from LCFS pointed out.[132]

However, federal authorities opposed secondary migration. This seemed to threaten their ability to manage resettlement and its impacts on receiving communities. The Volags and the State Department should outwardly seek to limit "undesirable and uncontrolled secondary migration," stated the federal Voluntary Agency Placement Policies issued that November.[133] These policies identified "impacted areas" and "areas of special concern," meaning cities and neighborhoods where large numbers of refugees appeared to stress community relations and localities' capacity to absorb newcomers. They laid out a set of criteria including availability of jobs, affordable housing, and health and social services; "community attitudes toward refugees"; "long-term welfare dependency situation among refugees in area"; and "degree of secondary migrants among the existing refugee population."[134] Impacted areas in 1981 included Honolulu; Providence, Rhode Island; St. Paul, Minnesota; and a handful of cities in California. Philadelphia made the list of "areas of concern which need to be treated with special sensitivity," along with Los Angeles, Chicago, New Orleans, Seattle, and several other cities. The Volags agreed to limit further placement of Southeast Asian refugees in these places when possible.[135]

This agreement notwithstanding, all these cities remained major centers of resettlement, with the Volags forced to defend their work on yet another front. They subsequently had to report the impacts of resettlement on cities and neighborhoods. Blum disputed the "developing opinion that Philadelphia is an impacted area" in late 1981: "Considering our decline in population, one could easily argue that refugees are bringing a new vitality and income base to this region."[136] NSC's site visitor from Washington, DC, reported important changes in 1983: case workers "no longer settle S.E.A. refugees in West Phila. . . . Will no longer use large volume realtors; the effort now is to use private houses, small apartments, so that better quality and control can be maintained." Under "General Impressions," she concluded, "Mechanisms for service provision are systematic and thorough. A policy of fostering client self-reliance and self-sufficiency is adhered to." Still, she rated NSC's "Agency Impact Status" as "SENSITIVE," just like the year before, given refugees' record of housing and employment problems in the city.[137]

By and large, Southeast Asians addressed the greatest problems arising from resettlement by resettling themselves again around the region and the nation through secondary migrations. Families and communities managed this process, with little or no involvement from the Volags. Their motivations ranged from seeking jobs and economic stability to promoting family and community reunification and responding to violence and school quality.[138]

From the mid-1980s through the 1990s, Southeast Asians left West Philadelphia for Southwest and South Philadelphia. Gentrification in the 1990s and 2000s played a part in pushing out families that remained in West Philadelphia longer. Some Cambodians and Vietnamese reunited with extended family in Massachusetts, Virginia, and other states. Some sought out places where they could resume old occupations and ways of life, including fishing and shrimping regions of Louisiana, Texas, and California.[139] But community leaders encouraged people to preserve and build enclaves in Philadelphia too, since living together in communities remained an important cultural practice, which was critical to the health of all, especially elders.[140]

In South and Southwest Philadelphia, Cambodians remained overwhelmingly working class, with high unemployment and high school dropout rates. But these neighborhoods had housing that was affordable enough for many to purchase homes, typically $30,000 to $40,000 in South Philadelphia and less in Southwest Philadelphia during the 2000s.[141] They built Buddhist temples in both neighborhoods and developed a vibrant district of small grocery stores, restaurants, and home-based kitchens where people cooked food for sale along 7th Street in South Philadelphia. Many also stayed in Logan and Olney, which became the city's most culturally diverse section in the 1980s and 1990s. While this, too, remained a working-class area that was not free of violence, Southeast Asians did not abandon it, thanks partly to interracial organizing (see figure 2.1).[142]

Vietnamese refugees and their children, who were more diverse in terms of class and background, more often moved to suburbs around the region in the later 1980s and 1990s. They rented and bought homes in working-class

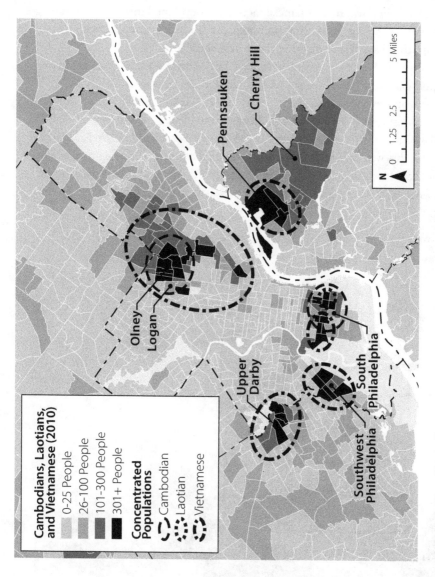

**FIGURE 2.1.** Map of Cambodian, Laotian, and Vietnamese settlement in Philadelphia and its suburbs in 2010. (Source: US Census; map by Danielle Dong.)

Upper Darby, just beyond West Philadelphia, and in working-class Pennsauken and middle-class Cherry Hill in New Jersey. Like other residents of the region, they sought safer neighborhoods, better schools, and communities where they knew people.[143] On weekends many returned to Washington Avenue in South Philadelphia, where Vietnamese merchants developed three large shopping centers with supermarkets, restaurants, cafes, wholesale suppliers for nail salons, travel agencies, and other shops (see figure 2.2).

Overall, Southeast Asians who stayed in or moved to the Philadelphia region gained in economic status, though with increasing inequality between more affluent Vietnamese and persistently poor Cambodians and Laotians. Southeast Asians' median household income in the region rose from $13,855 in 1980, most of it from welfare, to $25,238 in 1990, $42,400 in 2000, and $51,000 in 2010; this was still much lower than the median income among native-born households ($72,000). Over the same three decades, Southeast Asians' home-ownership rate rose from 31 percent in 1980 to 58 percent in 1990, 68 percent

**FIGURE 2.2.**   The entrance to New World Plaza shopping center on Washington Avenue in South Philadelphia, which flies the flags of the United States and South Vietnam. (Photo by Domenic Vitiello, 2021.)

in 2000, and 75 percent in 2010, surpassing the region's native-born households (73 percent).[144] These high homeownership figures reflect the affordability of housing in the region, where rents were often higher than mortgage payments. Most of these numbers would presumably be lower had people of the Hmong ethnic group stayed.

Hmong people left Philadelphia and other cities en masse. The president of the local Hmong Association, Bee Xiong, told a *New York Times* reporter that "as many as 5,000 Hmong moved to" the city by 1980 but only about 650 remained by September 1984. Other estimates put the figures at 3,000 and 800, respectively, but the trend was the same.[145] Most Hmong people followed their clan leaders to Minnesota, Wisconsin, and California.[146] But reunification was one of several factors in their decisions to leave Philadelphia. Resettlement agency leaders also quietly informed their Hmong clients that welfare was more generous in those states. Still, the most powerful push factors in their departure were their experiences of violence and struggles to get work and adapt to the city.[147]

Urban resettlement was a bad idea for Hmong people. "There was culture shock on both sides," noted one *Philadelphia Inquirer* reporter. "When the Hmong . . . first arrived in West Philadelphia, some of the men hunted the streets with their crossbows, shooting down pigeons for dinner."[148] As some of the most acutely disoriented and isolated refugees, Hmong adults in Philadelphia and other cities experienced a spate of suicides and mysterious deaths.[149] As frequent targets for mugging, "afraid of their neighbors, unable to find work and on the verge of exhausting their welfare payments," the reporter concluded, "the only recourse for many was to flee."[150]

The Hmong exodus from cities, which was "done against the strong wishes of US government officials," he wrote, "highlighted and quite inadvertently laid bare, the hollowness of American promises to these former allies." State Department officials overseeing resettlement "knew that the Hmong were different from the other Southeast Asian refugees—that they knew little of the modern world—and that they should be treated differently." Still, they "tried to 'mainstream' them—to the Hmong's immense sorrow." Resettlement separated their clans (the core Hmong social unit) and scattered them around the nation like other refugees. Most were sent to cities and separated from the land, which was virtually the only source of sustenance they knew. State Department officials cited the great number of refugees they resettled at the time as a reason why they made no special provisions for Hmong people. But even after federal resettlement authorities recognized Hmong people's resettlement as a disaster and increased aid to them, they used this new funding to try to keep them in their city homes.[151]

After a series of attacks in summer 1984, the US Attorney's Community Relations Division sought out Hmong leaders and residents in Philadelphia's Powelton neighborhood to "help keep the Hmong in Philadelphia." But Hmong elders decided their people should move, and family units ranging in size from ten to thirty people left daily.[152] Even on their way out, the *Daily News* reported, as one family left Powelton on a late summer evening, "their departure was noted by neighborhood youths who tossed stones at their U-Haul truck."[153]

Secondary migration away from cities saved Hmong families and communities, partly since it allowed for the reconstitution of their clan groups and preservation of their culture. They were "in near constant motion," wrote the *Philadelphia Inquirer* reporter in 1984. "Sometimes in large groups of up to 100, sometimes in the middle of the night, the Hmong have simply disappeared from many cities, usually without a word to those few Americans who knew them."[154] While they would remain in poverty according to any American standard, they largely succeeded in reunifying clan and family units and gaining some measure of self-sufficiency as small farmers in the Midwest and West.

By the second half of the 1980s, refugees also became the most influential actors shaping resettlement from Southeast Asia, in terms of both who was admitted and where they lived. Since refugees became permanent residents with green cards after five years and could then sponsor their family members, the Volags began doing more "anchor relative resettlement," which involved filing Affidavits of Relationship.[155] This became a large part of refugee arrivals, such that much of the US refugee system, like most of the nation's immigration system, was dedicated to family reunification. This as much as anything improved the process and experiences of resettlement overall, as many people now had preestablished family support networks when they arrived.

## Refugee Civil Society

For Southeast Asians who remained in Philadelphia, the growth of an increasingly Southeast Asian-led civil society addressed a variety of evolving challenges. The Volags helped develop Southeast Asian leadership and organizations in the 1980s, but they and their funders initially limited the work that those organizations did. By the 2000s, though, Southeast Asian community organizations in Philadelphia engaged in a wide range of social service, cultural, educational, interracial organizing, and refugee rights work. This reflected the persistence of some problems, such as poverty, violence, and trauma, and the emergence of new ones ranging from intergenerational relations to deportation.

Asian Americans United continued to play an important role in Southeast
Asian communities, confronting violence that persisted in the neighborhoods
where most lived, as they underwent racial transition in the 1980s and 1990s.
At McCreesh Playground in Southwest Philadelphia in 1991, a group of young
white men, some of whom belonged to a neo-Nazi group called the White
Power Boys, threatened some Southeast Asian youth. In the knife fight that
ensued, one of the white men died. Authorities charged a twenty-four-year-
old Vietnamese man who was not even present, after one of the white men
identified him as "one of the mother fucking gooks." They later charged seven
other Southeast Asian men with first-degree murder. District Attorney Lynne
Abraham's office cast them as a "gang" and, in the words of scholar Scott
Kurashige, pursued "a highly publicized trial stained by . . . thinly-veiled race
baiting." Local media repeated the same story and further enflamed racial tensions in the city and the neighborhood.[156]

This prompted Thoai Nguyen, Debbie Wei, who had taught five of the men
who were charged, and others in Asian Americans United to organize Asian
communities against violence and institutional racism in the criminal justice
system. "Due to the lack of Asian inmates" in the city's jail "to facilitate proper
lineups," Thoai "was one of the volunteers to go into the prison, put on prison
garb and [stand] in the lineups for the 'White Power Boys' witnesses. I was
told by our defense attorneys," he remembered, "that 6 of the 7 'witnesses'
selected me as the perp wielding the murder weapon . . . they could not even
pick out the people who were there."[157] Still, the members of Asian Americans United could not change the trial's outcome.

But their organizing, as Kurashige wrote, "validated the concerns of Asian
Americans in Southwest Philadelphia and others whose everyday lives were
structured by a climate of racism and hostility." Further, they set a precedent
showing "that Asian Americans in Philadelphia would organize, fight, and resist when threatened or attacked and that the Asian community's passivity
could not be taken for granted." They also inspired many Asian Americans to
activism and organizing, including advocacy for their right to space in the city,
its neighborhoods and institutions, often in collaboration with other immigrants and communities of color (see figure 2.3).[158]

Through his experiences in community organizing, "by the time I gradu-
ated high school," Thoai reflected, "my politics . . . was increasingly sympa-
thetic to the struggles of my people in overthrowing our colonial oppressors."
This clashed with the politics of many older refugees like his father. "After the
INS, my dad worked for the Philadelphia Police Department as a Community
Liaison and we found ourselves sitting across the table from each other as

**FIGURE 2.3.** Thoai Nguyen and other AAU members picket in support of a farmworkers' union drive in Kennett Square, Pennsylvania, outside Philadelphia, in 1993. The mushroom industry's farmworkers included mostly people from Mexico as well as some from Southeast Asia. (Photo courtesy of Thoai Nguyen.)

I was an organizer for Asian Americans United demanding accountability from the police while he was representing the police."[159]

Like the work of Asian Americans United, civil society organizations led by Southeast Asians in Philadelphia emerged in tension, if also in collaboration, with the resettlement system. Thoai's father's work for HIAS-PA signaled one of the most important things the Volags did for their own programs and for the growth of Southeast Asian civil society, namely, hiring refugees on their staff. By 1983, NSC's four resettlement case workers included two Khmer (the largest Cambodian ethnic group), a Hmong, and an Afghan.[160] Some of the Southeast Asian staff at Volags helped develop mutual assistance associations (MAAs), which the federal Office of Refugee Resettlement encouraged beginning in the early 1980s to provide social services in refugee communities, especially post-resettlement. The Pennsylvania department of welfare's refugee program office funded one of the Volags to support MAAs in the state.[161]

Both the Volags and the MAAs thought they were the better choice to meet the needs of Southeast Asians, even as the Volags had much greater influence and access to resources. In 1981, the state refugee program director acknowledged that the MAAs "play a part in the adjustment process for refugees and . . .

encourage[d] their cooperation with existing community efforts." But the state remained wary of the MAAs' capacity to deliver effective services, a stance the Volags reinforced in appeals to public and philanthropic funders. With separate MAAs for Philadelphia's Vietnamese, Cambodian, Laotian, Hmong, ethnic Chinese from Vietnam, and smaller ethnic or social groups within those communities, they remained small organizations, usually without paid staff. In the early 1980s, the state declined to contract with them "for direct services due to [the MAAs'] limited resources." The Volags would successfully defend their control of resettlement. The only late-twentieth-century refugee group that the State Department designated as an official resettlement agency was the Ethiopian Community Development Council, which was based in the Washington, DC, region. Southeast Asian MAAs would be social service, educational, and cultural organizations, with limited roles in housing or employment, at least formally and initially.[162]

As a compromise to gain funding from the William Penn Foundation, one of the region's largest philanthropies, and the national Ford Foundation, Philadelphia's principal MAAs united in 1984 to form the Southeast Asian Mutual Assistance Associations Coalition (SEAMAAC).[163] Led by first-generation refugees, including its director, Samien Nol, from Cambodia, SEAMAAC developed educational, health, and social service programs. Its ESL, after school, heritage, truancy prevention, senior services, and wellness programs addressed persistent challenges among working-class Southeast Asians. Outreach workers helped people apply for citizenship, handle utility cutoff notices, meet with school officials, deal with domestic violence, and, most commonly, access welfare, food stamps, medical insurance, and health care.[164]

In the 1990s and 2000s, SEAMAAC's geography and constituencies shifted. As Southeast Asians migrated to different parts of the region and the country, the organization remained in West Philadelphia and ran satellite offices in other neighborhoods for a time. When Liberians were resettled in West and Southwest Philadelphia in the late 1990s, SEAMAAC extended some of its services to them, hired Liberian staff, and in the early 2000s helped Liberians establish their own organizations. In 2005, Thoai Nguyen became SEAMAAC's chief executive officer, after graduating from Bates College, pursuing an anthropology degree in Southeast Asia, and working three years at the Committee Against Anti-Asian Violence in New York City, eight years at the American Friends Service Committee, and a short stint at LCFS.[165]

In 2006, SEAMAAC changed its mission to "serving immigrants and refugees" at large. In 2008 it moved to South Philadelphia, the biggest Southeast Asian neighborhood in the city but also a fast-diversifying immigrant gateway of Mexican, Central American, Indonesian, Chinese, North African, and other immigrants. "It doesn't do any good if you are only trying to work with one group of people," said Thoai. "Southeast Asians work and live in a larger context and neighborhood, and need to connect to those other populations if we are going to make a good society or neighborhood."[166] SEAMAAC's hip-hop heritage classes, youth leadership programs with Cambodian and African American teens, and community organizing with Mexican, Black, and Asian parents at South Philadelphia schools proactively sought to improve race relations, even if violence, especially against Asians, persisted in schools and neighborhoods.[167]

The one MAA that became a bigger service organization, the Cambodian Association of Greater Philadelphia, addressed the challenges of genocide survival and continued disadvantage faced by Cambodians. Coming to the United States with "nothing but suffering," and often no education, they needed all sorts of support, stressed Rorng Sorn, the association's director from 2008 to 2014, who later became director of immigrant, refugee, and language access services at the city's department of behavioral health. Like other grassroots groups in working-class immigrant communities, the association's staff and board members sought to help people with any problem they brought in the door, despite receiving funding for only their "formal" programs.[168]

Formed in 1979, like other MAAs the Cambodian Association helped with resettlement and post-resettlement, initially on a volunteer basis, distributing groceries and clothing donated through churches and helping people find new housing. With a core mission to preserve and share culture, help people thrive, and enable them to "become self-sufficient," it developed ESL, Khmer dance, and other education and social support programs especially for elders and diverse youth in South Philadelphia, Logan, and Olney. The association's staff and volunteers aided thousands of people with doctors' appointments and applications for public benefits, jobs, and citizenship.[169] With Asian Americans United and other allies, they advocated for Khmer-speaking staff in the city's schools, district attorney's office, workforce agencies, and human relations commission.[170]

The 1990s and 2000s brought multiple economic dislocations for working-class Southeast Asians in the region. Many were laid off as factories closed, prompting the Cambodian Association to start a job development program. In 1996, Congress passed welfare reform that cut support for over 52,000 disabled and elderly immigrants in Pennsylvania and New Jersey, including many Southeast Asians. Feelings of anger and betrayal returned.[171] Seniors and teens on break from school sought day labor. They boarded white vans that traversed South Philadelphia en route to suburban warehouses to pack boxes of food and other goods, making money under the table to supplement inadequate public benefits and family wages.[172] Others worked in fast food restaurants or did seasonal work in greenhouses, while some better-off families ran their own fruit salad and sandwich trucks downtown and on college campuses. In 2010, 41 percent of Cambodians and 31 percent of Vietnamese lived in poverty in Philadelphia, which was the big city with the highest poverty rate in the nation (25 percent). Many people lacked money to pay insurance and other bills, and many faced foreclosure and eviction. This led the Cambodian Association and SEAMAAC to teach financial literacy and connect people to mortgage refinance programs.[173]

Nationally, Southeast Asian MAAs declined in the 1990s to 2010s. SEAMAAC supported and collaborated with its constituent MAAs through the early 2000s, but most became less active as their founding generation aged and passed away.[174] By 2013, the Cambodian Association was one of fewer than fifteen surviving Cambodian MAAs around the country, down from over one hundred.[175] A former South Vietnamese soldier still broadcast Radio Free Vietnam from his split-level home in Pennsauken, and many Vietnamese family patriarchs had their own associations, though membership often included no more than extended family.[176]

But Philadelphia also gained new Southeast Asian organizations. In 2001, the national group Boat People SOS (BPSOS) established offices in South Philadelphia and Pennsauken, in response to "a need for community engagement for Vietnamese" people, according to Nancy Nguyen, who became the regional director of BPSOS in 2010. "There are very few Vietnamese organizations around the country which are nonprofit organizations . . . [and] not churches or temples," she observed. In her view, many MAAs struggled and faded in this era partly because they lacked "a vision beyond resettlement and survival," which diminished their reasons for being as time went on and older generations passed away.[177]

The region's chapter of BPSOS underwent a generational change much like other Southeast Asian social service groups. Like the Cambodian Association and SEAMAAC, its staff helped people with anything: "You walked in, they would help you," Nancy Nguyen said. They ran ESL, computer, and citizenship classes, after-school and summer camps, and translation and "health patient navigation" services. However, beginning in 2010 they expanded their work to include community organizing, advocacy, intergenerational, and interracial programs. They started youth-led festivals, voter engagement drives, and a community farm near their Pennsauken office in East Camden, a working-class Vietnamese, Latin American, and Black neighborhood in the nation's poorest city.[178] In 2015, the staff who ran the programs focused on social justice split from BPSOS to form a group called VietLead. No longer running social service programs, they represented a new generation of Southeast Asian American community organizing, advocacy, and power building and were closely aligned with other immigrant and refugee rights movements.[179]

More than four decades after the end of the Vietnam War, Southeast Asian civil society in Philadelphia continued to grapple with the disorientation, inadequacies, and injustices of resettlement. Community organizations continued to help first-generation refugees subsist. But they also engaged second-generation, intergenerational, interracial, and transnational constituencies in organizing and advocacy in the face of new political realities.

# From Refuge to Sanctuary

The deportation of Cambodian refugees beginning in 2002 helped shift the politics and geography of Southeast Asian American civil society. Congress's 1996 immigration act retroactively authorized the deportation of permanent residents who had committed an "aggravated felony," which the law broadened to include offenses ranging from public indecency and shoplifting to homicide.[180] Six years later, the United States secretly signed a repatriation agreement with Cambodia. This rendered the politics and practices of sanctuary suddenly relevant for people who had always viewed themselves, and were viewed by others, as permanent refugees, who were entitled to become US citizens and unlikely to return to the countries they fled.

Since two-thirds of Cambodian refugees had not applied for citizenship, which would have shielded them from deportation, and since many had been convicted of crimes that now qualified as aggravated felonies, they became targets for deportation. Many "lacked access to the legal support necessary to navigate the complex intersection between the criminal justice and immigration legal systems," noted Mia-lia Boua Kiernan, who worked at the Cambodian Association. Most had been represented by public defenders with limited knowledge of the intricacies of immigration law, and many had made plea agreements with no knowledge—and before 1996 no ability to know—that this could expose them to deportation.[181] Close to 16,000 Southeast Asian Americans received final orders of removal between 1998 and 2018, 78 percent of which were based on past criminal convictions.[182]

For virtually all "returnees" who were deported to Cambodia, the country was a place they hardly remembered and found extremely disorienting. In fact, many were born in refugee camps in Thailand and had never set foot in Cambodia before. Their American culture and tattoos made "them pariahs in this poor, hierarchical, Buddhist nation," wrote one *Philadelphia Inquirer* reporter describing two men who were deported from Philadelphia in 2003. On their arrival, authorities in the capital, Phnom Penh, immediately jailed them until they paid bribes. Living in the countryside with relatives who were subsistence farmers, they were "as unprepared for those conditions as their parents were for the United States." Moving to Phnom Penh, one went to work in a center for drug addicts while the other found a job with a program supporting returnees. Relatives sending American dollars kept them relatively comfortable compared to most Cambodians, a third of whom lived on less than fifty cents per day. But many remained depressed, jobless, and homeless, feeling betrayed by a nation that had once granted them refuge and victimized by a nation where their families had fled from genocide. The reporters concluded, "The returnees' odyssey also underscores just how unprepared everyone here—the Cambodian government, nongovernmental aid organizations, and the returnees themselves—was for this new reality."[183]

In 2002, the first deportations of men from Philadelphia who had served time for gun and drug crimes occasioned a small protest outside the federal immigration office in the city.[184] The Cambodian Association assisted families of deportees in dealing with their trauma and grief. Its staff also helped them stay connected with their brothers, sons, and fathers who were deported to Cambodia and made them aware of a halfway house and other services in Phnom Penh.[185]

Younger Southeast Asian American activists in Philadelphia, led by Kiernan and AZI Fellas, a group of Cambodian American hip-hop artists, subsequently started a movement to end the separation of Cambodian families through deportation. They saw this "as yet another cycle of displacement a generation after resettlement," as Kiernan put it.[186] When the United States sought an identical repatriation agreement with Vietnam in 2007, they and other Southeast Asians in the United States mobilized and convinced the administration of George W. Bush to add a clause that prevented the deportation of people who had experienced persecution or violence in Southeast Asia. In 2010, Kiernan and her colleagues established 1Love Movement, which initially fought, although unsuccessfully, to stop the detention of Cambodians.[187] Rorng Sorn served on its board.[188]

The leaders and members of 1Love and VietLead collaborated with other groups in Philadelphia in sanctuary city and immigrant rights activism, and against police brutality. After 2002, whether local police and prisons turned people over to ICE mattered at least as much to Southeast Asians as to any other people. Indeed, it was these activists in 1Love Movement who convinced their allies in the New Sanctuary Movement to advocate in 2014 for Philadelphia's sanctuary policy to cover everyone, including people convicted of the most serious crimes. People who had done their time in prison and paid their debts to society, they argued, should not be doubly punished and denied a second chance, separated from their families and communities and deported to places where in so many ways they did not belong.[189]

A key moment in this organizing came on the twentieth anniversary of the 1996 immigration law, when these activists held hearings in Philadelphia's city council on its impacts. They detailed how this law fostered a "school-to-prison-to-deportation pipeline" for Black, Southeast Asian, and Latin American immigrants. Council members Jannie Blackwell and Helen Gym, former board chair of Asian Americans United, presided. The mother of one deportee testified in Khmer, through an interpreter, "I still don't understand the laws that deported my son. . . . I know he was in a fight with other teens his age. . . . He came out of prison in his 20s. . . . Seven years after he came home, he was deported. . . . It's like a knife cutting through my heart. . . . Without him here, it's like I have no soul."[190]

Via Skype from Cambodia, another deportee, Chally Dang, told of how he was arrested for assault and gun possession in Philadelphia in 1997 at age fifteen, tried as an adult, spent five and a half years in prison, and then "released into society as a rehabilitated young man. I worked, bought a home, had kids, and created a good life for my family." But all that, including his marriage, ended with his deportation. "I've watched from afar as [Philadelphia] has taken stands to defend the rights of immigrant families and formerly incarcerated people," he said. "I hope the city keeps on this path, and works to change laws so people like me will have a chance to return home."[191] Council members subsequently petitioned Congress to repeal the 1996 law, echoing similar appeals from an earlier era of sanctuary activism in the 1980s.[192]

In 2015, 1Love's leaders launched a national campaign with partners in the Southeast Asian Freedom Network (SEAFN), including groups in New York, Rhode Island, New Orleans, California, and the Midwest. They organized Southeast Asians in support of a federal policy platform to extend the US agreement not to deport refugees to Vietnam to cover Laos and, retroactively, Cambodia. VietLead, Asian Americans United, and the Cambodian Association of Greater Philadelphia all participated, as did many other groups around the country.[193]

SEAFN members from Philadelphia; Providence, Rhode Island; and the Bronx, including Naroen Chhin, traveled to Geneva, Switzerland, for the United Nations' Universal Periodic Review of the United States' "human rights performance" in March 2015. They cited violations starting with "8 years of illegal US bombing of the Cambodian countryside beginning in 1965, to the secret signing of the US-Cambodia Repatriation Agreement that began the deportation crisis in the Cambodian-American community." They called for "an immediate suspension of all US deportations to Cambodia, an open review" of that agreement, "and the right to return." As Chanravy Proeung, the delegate from Providence, testified, "We have been rooted in an intergenerational struggle over the last five decades to keep our families together against unjust forces of US militarism, war, systemic poverty, education inequity, imprisonment, institutionalized racism, discrimination." And now, "with over 500 Cambodian-American families broken apart since 2002, and over 4000 more awaiting the same fate, our human rights fight today, is deportation."[194]

Leaders of SEAFN and 1Love also took their work to Cambodia. They assisted returnees there with cultural orientation led by Southeast Asians, beyond the assistance they received from the mostly white American ministers and psychologists working for charities or on contract with the US Agency for International Development. Also, the SEAFN's organizers supported returnees' own human rights advocacy aimed at the Cambodian government.[195]

Out of this work, returnees organized 1Love Cambodia. In their Khmer New Year message to families and communities in the United States in April 2016, activists in 1Love Cambodia wrote, "We were . . . resettled with a history of trauma into unjust systems and surroundings that led us to make mistakes that would forever label us 'Criminal Aliens' by the US government. . . . We are not perfect," they noted; rather, "we are human. We recognize the harm we have caused, and we live to amend that harm everyday because we believe in healing and accountability for our actions. We also believe in our human ability to change and be better people in the world for ourselves, our families, and our communities."[196]

In urging their allies in the United States to continue fighting to change unjust deportation policies, they acknowledged, "We know it brings us stress to fight against a system that seems unbreakable," but their struggle was not simply for their own right to return. "We are fighting for all of our Khmer people who have endured family separation and destruction too many times in one lifetime." This included their "spouses who are battling against all odds to live normal lives, . . . our children who are struggling to believe in a world that takes their parents away from them, . . . our parents and grandparents who want us to take care of them in their old age and pass them on to the next life with dignity and family unity."[197] However, the work of 1Love Cambodia has "since been severely challenged," Kiernan related, "due to lack of resources, and coming up against multiplying levels of deportation through the Trump years."[198]

In 2017 the administration of Donald Trump abandoned the policy of not deporting Vietnamese refugees who arrived before 1995.[199] In that year, the

Philadelphia-based tristate office of ICE increased its arrests at the fastest rate of any ICE region in the nation.[200] At VietLead's annual Tet (Vietnamese New Year) celebration in a high school gym in South Philadelphia in February 2018, people wore stickers that read "ICE-free zone." Posters on the wall offered a checklist of what to do if federal agents came to the door. Staff and volunteers from VietLead ran an immigration information booth educating people about changes in federal enforcement practices that raised the threat of deportation for an ever-wider range of people.[201] Even after Trump's exit from the White House, while the administration of President Joe Biden stepped back from some Trump-era deportation policies in early 2021, it continued to deport Southeast Asian refugees.[202]

The fact that sanctuary mattered for anyone with refugee status was brutally ironic, perhaps especially so for people whose displacement derived so directly from US actions overseas. Decades later, the nation's leaders decided that the permanence of settlement and absorption promised in the 1980 Refugee Act no longer applied to Cambodians or other Southeast Asians, at least those who had not acquired the protections of citizenship.

## Twenty-First-Century Resettlement

While Southeast Asians continued to face displacement and injustice, the resettlement system exhibited unfortunate continuities, too. While refugee admission and resettlement had changed in important ways since the 1980s, the basic problems of the system persisted. New groups of refugees and the communities where they settled continued to bear most of the costs of these failures.

Refugee admission to the United States underwent dramatic changes after the 1980s. The breakup of the Soviet Union in 1991 removed the Cold War logic of US refugee policy, though the United States expanded its resettlement of Russian Jews in the 1990s. In the 1990s and 2000s, the US resettled people from Bosnia, Liberia, Somalia, and Burma. The yearly number fluctuated, never reaching the highs of 1975 (over 140,000 people) or 1980 (over 200,000), but stayed over 100,000 from 1989 to 1994 and between 50,000 and 100,000 for most of the period from 1995 to 2015.[203]

These changes transformed the United States' political relationship with refugees and the scale of resettlement, though the practices of resettlement and refugees' experiences of it changed rather little. The basic set of services and things given to refugees were much the same. Their work experiences and often their neighborhoods, schools, and relationships with receiving communities repeated much of Southeast Asians' experiences in the 1980s. The re-settlement system and the resources devoted to it remained insufficient to produce much better results.

The landscape of Volags in Philadelphia shifted in ways that reflected the diminished refugee admissions as well as federal authorities' still-critical view of the city as a place for resettlement. When Catholic Social Services aban-doned its local resettlement program in 2008, only three agencies remained, down from six.[204] The remaining three, HIAS-PA, LCFS, and NSC, continued with reduced staffs.[205] The State Department had recently restored NSC's au-thorization to resettle "free cases," meaning people without relatives in the United States, after some years as an "agency in concern" since officials lacked faith in NSC's ability to find safe, high-quality, affordable housing and decent jobs for refugees in Philadelphia.[206] Since NSC had almost always resettled the most "free cases," this essentially amounted to a rejection of the city as a site of large-scale resettlement.

In regaining its status as a "free case" agency, NSC staff relearned how to resettle people, recalled its new director of resettlement at the time, Juliane Ramic.[207] "I felt like I had to recreate everything" in the program.[208] After a trial resettling Meskhetian Turks amid other Russian speakers in Northeast Philadelphia in 2004, NSC resettled people from Bhutan, Burma, Liberia, Iraq, Syria, and other parts of Africa and Asia in the later 2000s and 2010s.[209] The agency resettled roughly 450 people a year in in this period, while HIAS and LCFS resettled smaller numbers, all a fraction of the thousands of people in the late 1970s and 1980s.[210] As they had in that era, the agencies worked with other organizations to support the people they resettled, including a strong network providing health care for refugees.[211]

Public assistance remained crucial for most refugees in their early months and years of settlement, though the resettlement system sought to make them less dependent on welfare. A matching grant fund established in the 1980s to keep Cuban and Soviet refugees off welfare expanded over the years, though it still covered a minority of refugees. This turned resettlement into a more competitive industry, forcing agencies to vie for federal and philanthropic fund-ing.[212] For refugees who were still on welfare, the Philadelphia welfare office formed a central refugee unit where caseworkers included several refugees. On their first business day in the United States, refugees could walk out of the office with a debit card for welfare and food stamp payments and within twenty-four hours food stamps and Medicaid would be activated. "That doesn't happen anywhere else in the country," said Ramic, and it was critical for speed-ing people's integration and meeting immediate needs. By contrast, NSC had some bad experiences with suburban county welfare offices losing or taking weeks to process refugees' applications.[213] This is one of the factors that kept most resettlement in the Philadelphia region inside the city.

Refugees' experiences of housing generally improved in the twenty-first century but repeated key patterns of the past. The resettlement agencies vetted rental properties more carefully and navigated the rental market more successfully than in the 1980s.[214] Arguably the greatest factor in refugees' improved housing, however, was Philadelphia's revitalization in the 1990s and 2000s, which reduced the city's stock of hazardous, deteriorating homes. People still complained of landlords who failed to make repairs, but overall conditions were better.[215]

Refugees' neighborhood experiences were likewise mixed. People found more community organizations to support them post-resettlement in some neighborhoods, including South Philadelphia, where SEAMAAC, the new Bhutanese American Organization, congregations, and other groups assisted newcomers.[216] The need to find affordable rents still meant that refugees continued to live in areas undergoing racial transition, particularly in South and Lower Northeast Philadelphia, with attendant tensions, including over race, religion, and, in South Philadelphia, also gentrification.

Ideas about "impacted areas," secondary migration, and criteria for selecting neighborhoods that formalized in the early 1980s still influenced how people working in resettlement understood the relationships between refugees and cities. Countering that narrative, HIAS-PA's leaders cast resettlement as part of the city's revitalization in the twenty-first century.[217] Philadelphia was initially a destination for Bhutanese secondary migration within the United States, but by 2015 people were leaving. Many went to smaller cities and rural areas of Ohio where they could find affordable land to farm. Push factors cited by people leaving included difficulties with employment, long commutes, violence (mostly muggings), and "congestion" in row house neighborhoods without open land.[218]

Employment remained challenging for most refugees in the Philadelphia region. With a labor market now dominated by service jobs, the largest number of which were dispersed in the suburbs, it was still tough for people from rural origins and others who spoke little English or lacked driver's licenses. Job training and search services operated much as in the past, pushing refugees to quickly find and stay in "entry-level" jobs without opportunities to advance. Many worked in meat and other types of food packing and light manufacturing, stocking shelves in grocery stores, and washing dishes in restaurants.[219] The largest single employer of refugees since the 1990s, Northeast Philadelphia–based auto parts maker Cardone Industries, in 2016 began to cut its local workforce from 2,500 to 1,000 as it moved a major division to Mexico.[220]

LCFS closed its resettlement program in the region in 2015 as the program had run up a $4.5 million debt to its parent organization. The staff acknowledged that federal funding covered just a fraction of the actual costs of resettling people in ways they considered sufficient.[221] This pointed up not just the challenges of Philadelphia but also the failures of the larger resettlement system.

Ultimately, the resettlement system's core contradictions and injustices endured into the twenty-first century. The system remained fundamentally committed to self-sufficiency, but with insufficient resources to help many people attain it, reflecting the nation's continued ambivalence toward refugees. As NSC's caseworkers oriented new arrivals to their government benefits and the things they would have to figure out for themselves, Juliane Ramic came to realize, "you're also subtly telling them that the federal government doesn't believe in the program enough." HIAS-PA's director Judith Bernstein-Baker stressed that refugees' children integrated and achieved upward mobility, even if many of their parents could not.[222]

The city also remained a challenging destination for resettlement, despite its increasingly welcoming stance toward newcomers in the twenty-first century. "The economic structure in Philadelphia," particularly refugees' job outcomes, remained poorer than in other regions of the country, Ramic observed.[223] "Refugees come, and feel . . . this immediate sense of protection . . . welcomed, wanted," she remarked, "you can find somebody that looks like you," and a place to worship. But then many people move away since they cannot make enough money to survive. Mayor Jim Kenney's statements about upholding the city's sanctuary policy "resonated, made them feel good," even if most refugees did not need its specific protections. But other forms of sanctuary proved lacking, including protection from everyday violence and assistance in overcoming the structural violence of persistent poverty and inequality. As Ramic concluded, "We don't move beyond this, from safety to quality of life. . . . After we welcome you, we don't figure out what you need."[224] These shortcomings were not new, though they played out differently for different groups of refugees, including people from Africa and the Middle East whose histories are explored in the next two chapters.

# CHAPTER 3

# African Diasporas

## Liberians and Black America

"My natural parents were from the interior. And then my foster family are Americo-Liberian," says Rev. Dr. John K. Jallah. "So that gave me a unique connection and advantage."[1] It also gave him, like Liberians in general, a more complicated relationship with the United States than most peoples of the world. For Liberia was America's first colony.

From his birth in 1946, Jallah was "groomed to succeed my father," a Grand Poro Zoe (priest) of the Loma tribe in rural Western Province, near Liberia's border with Guinea. But around age nine, he converted to Christianity thanks to Swedish Pentecostal missionaries visiting their village and took the name John. At age twelve, in 1958, he realized, "If I continued living in the tribe, I would not be able to continue in school. . . . So, I decided, like some were doing," to go stay with his brother, who worked and lived at the Firestone Tire Plantation some three hundred miles away.[2]

A logical destination for a boy who wanted to remain in school, Firestone was the centerpiece of America's second colonization of Liberia.[3] In 1926, at a time of expanding US influence in Africa, the company offered the nation's government a five-million-dollar loan to pay off its crippling debt to Britain. In exchange, it got a ninety-nine-year lease on one million acres (about 10 percent of the country's arable land) for six cents an acre. By the 1980s, the plantation supplied some 40 percent of the US demand for latex and 10 percent of global demand.[4] As a correspondent for The Atlantic wrote in the 1970s, the company "became such a dominant factor in the Liberian economy and so great a source of public services such as roads and schools that cynics enjoyed joking for years that, while most of Africa was colonized by Britain or France, Liberia was colonized by Firestone."[5]

After two days of walking, to his surprise John found his brother in another town, Fissibu. "That evening we boarded the Raymond Concrete Pile employee bus for Zorzor," catching a ride with people who worked for this company based in New York City "that had the contract from the government to construct the road" from Liberia's capital Monrovia to Western Province.[6] Later named Lofa County, this corner of the country was one of the last areas to recognize the nation's central government, in the 1930s. One man on the bus was a manager for the company. "So, he asked my brother, 'who is this boy?'" He replied that John, the son of their father's third wife, had come looking for him so he could go to school. The stranger said, "No, I am adopting him right now." His brother "resisted a little bit," but soon gave in to the man's demand.[7]

The manager, Horatio George Hutchins, "was one of the pioneer's children," descended from the free-born American Blacks and emancipated slaves who had initially colonized Liberia.[8] Beginning in the 1820s, the American Colonization Society, an institution with deep ties to Philadelphia, settled thirteen thousand Black people there.[9] In 1847, these colonists severed ties with the colonization society and made Liberia the first independent republic in Africa. US leaders refused to recognize the nation until the American Civil War in the 1860s, since they did not want Black diplomats in Washington.[10]

Americo-Liberian colonists and their descendants controlled the nation's wealth and its government until 1980, exploiting indigenous populations much like Europeans in the rest of Africa. However, as *The Atlantic* correspondent observed, "Unlike most white ruling minorities in Africa," Americo-Liberians had "a system of drawing tribal people into their culture."[11] They commonly took in native children to educate and raise in return for their labor as domestic servants, especially the children of second and third wives, like John Jallah. They called this the ward system.[12]

John moved to Monrovia with the Hutchins family, gaining a new family and access to the privileges of Americo-Liberian society, especially education. Hutchins "educated me throughout high school" and "in time he became my sponsor. He was my parent. . . . Called me as his son. All his children, we are brothers and sisters." In high school, John trained at the Bible School for Ministry. He also studied electrical engineering at the Liberian/Swedish Vocational Training Center in Yekepa, Nimba County, the iron-mining town of the Liberian-American-Swedish Mining Company (LAMCO). "Then I went to teacher's college to teach in vocational schools, then went back to regular teacher's college."[13]

With this training, he landed a position as supervisor at the largest hospital in Liberia. Then under construction, the John F. Kennedy Memorial Medical Center in Monrovia was a project supported by the US Agency for International Development (USAID).[14] This was the third era of America's imperial relationship with Liberia, a key Cold War ally, with attendant aid, mining contracts, and military support.[15]

In September 1969, through the Liberian Ministry of Health, John "got a World Health Organization fellowship grant that took me to England, West Germany, Holland, and then in Milwaukee to specialize in medical equipment." He trained at General Electric in Milwaukee and then in Washington, DC. He spent spare time with two "school mates from Liberia" in DC, one in the same fellowship program, specializing in hospital administration, the other a physician.[16] Migration to the United States for higher education, training, and professional jobs had become common for the sons of Americo-Liberians in the 1960s, as for Ghanaian, Nigerian, and other West African sons from families with means. US scholarships also funded some students from more modest backgrounds in newly independent African nations in this period.

In 1971, John returned to his position at the JFK Hospital in Monrovia, which officially opened that year. USAID assisted its start-up—"every department had an American consultant"—for a few years after that. Then he took "a short break" from 1974 to 1978, working as the chief hospital technician for LAMCO in Yekepa and teaching electricity at his alma mater.[17]

In 1980, Samuel Doe, a career military officer trained by US Green Berets, staged a coup with seventeen fellow soldiers from the Krahn tribe, executing Liberia's president and thirteen cabinet members. Doe became the nation's first native premier, but his regime would prove to be as corrupt and abusive as those of the Americo-Liberians before him.[18] The administration of president Ronald Reagan ignored this in return for permission to station US military broadcasting and navigation infrastructure in Liberia.[19]

Following the coup, the People's Redemption Council, Doe's initial governing body, "requested that I go back to the [JFK] hospital and take over the engineering department," Reverend Jallah explained. The council included people who had been adopted by Americo-Liberians and had trained in Europe and the United States, like himself. "A lot of people ran away from the country, the hospital was down, they were looking for people who were experienced" to revive it. He remained there until the First Liberian Civil War (1989–1997), "the Charles Taylor war" as he put it, broke out a decade later.[20]

Taylor, whose father was Americo-Liberian and whose mother was from the Gola tribe, graduated with a BA in economics from Bentley College, outside Boston. He headed the General Services Agency in Doe's government before his removal in 1983, based on accusations that he had embezzled nearly one million dollars. He fled to the United States, was arrested in Boston, escaped from jail, and found his way to Libya, where he trained as a guerilla fighter. In December 1989, he led forces of the National Patriotic Front of Liberia (NPFL), backed by Libya, Burkina Faso, and Ivory Coast, over the Ivoirian border into Nimba County. On their way to Monrovia, they ransacked the Firestone plantation. But Taylor soon made the plantation his base of operations and the company negotiated with him to restart production. Firestone's "taxes" paid to Taylor would fund the NPFL for the rest of the war, including its battles with government and West African forces protecting Monrovia and with rebel factions around the country; its training of child soldiers; and its genocidal extermination of the Krahn and Mandinka tribes, among other atrocities.[21]

"It took them six months or so to get to the suburbs" of the capital, a distance of a few hundred miles, remembered Reverend Jallah. "I finally gave up and left Monrovia in June" 1990 with his wife, their younger daughter and son, and two grandchildren. Their two older daughters were already out of the country, one studying social work in New York, the other specializing in early childhood education in Germany. The family walked to Tubmanburg (named for Harriet Tubman), in Bomi County, western Liberia, near Sierra Leone. "We stayed there until the area had fallen to Charles Taylor." Departing in early September, "there were checkpoints everywhere, so traveling was not easy. . . . Some places we negotiated with the rebels," who "had commandeered people's cars," and who "could execute you" on a whim.[22]

Taylor controlled most of the country by this point, even as West African forces intervened, landing in Monrovia. They would defend the capital throughout the conflict. But on his way to greet them on September 9, Samuel Doe was captured by former Taylor ally Prince Johnson and his splinter rebel group, who executed him live on international television.[23]

Meanwhile, the Jallah family "partly rode, partly walked from Bomi to Lofa. That's about two hundred miles or so." It took two weeks. "I went to my village," Reverend Jallah recalled, a big smile coming over his face. "When things were normal [before the war], we had built a residence in the village. And we lived there for almost a year." Tragically, though, during their time spent in the villages, without access to medical care, his wife became blind from glaucoma.[24]

"So, we came back to Monrovia" in 1991, crossing rebel territory. He went to work at the JFK hospital again for two years, all the while "doing the church work" too. Then, in 1993, he "retired" and went into full-time ministry at a church he had established in the city. Two years later, in August 1995, the main rebel factions agreed to a cease-fire and formed a unity government. Its civilian head invited Reverend Jallah to serve as deputy minister for internal affairs. He was responsible for county and local government properties, indigenous agriculture, community economic development, and local security in the country.[25] But in April 1996, heavy fighting broke out in Monrovia between rebels and forces of the Economic Community of West African States (ECOWAS) trying to enforce peace, which further destroyed much of the city.

"So, when there was [this] mass disturbance, we went across to the Ivory Coast as refugees." The government there "didn't allow the refugees to establish a camp there," as it feared refugee camps could breed further violence. "So, you go and rent from the citizens. They used it as a way of generating income," and some families and churches hosted and fed Liberians for free. In November 1997, after eighteen months of interviews, employees of the International Organization for Migration refugee program put Reverend Jallah, his wife, and four of their grandchildren on a plane to Brussels with a connection to JFK Airport in New York.[26]

The Jallahs' two eldest daughters and some friends picked them up in two cars. "They had a whole group to meet us, a big event." Their daughter in New York had moved to Philadelphia, got a job, applied for a green card, and "filed for us" through the Lutheran resettlement agency. Their son and youngest daughter, who had been cut off from them as they fled Monrovia, arrived some months later.[27]

They came at what turned out to be just past the midpoint in Liberia's civil wars. The first civil war ended when Charles Taylor was elected president in summer 1997. But his large margin of victory resulted from voter intimidation and his troops continued to terrorize their enemies. In April 1999, a dissident force of largely Krahn and Mandinka fighters invaded from Guinea, beginning the Second Liberian Civil War, which lasted until 2003. By war's end more than 250,000 Liberians had died, in a nation of about 3.3 million prior to the wars. Some 1.5 million people fled, mostly to neighboring countries, where they lived in camps or among the local population and often experienced displacement again as the civil wars spread.[28]

Liberians' neighbors shared their civil wars and experiences of displacement. Taylor's NPFL allied with rebels in Sierra Leone at the start of its eleven-year civil war (1991–2002). This group was notorious for recruiting child soldiers and severing the limbs of their victims as they fought to control the export of "blood diamonds" from Sierra Leone's mines. The NPFL then supported rebels in Ivory Coast in 2002–2004. Two decades on, as the Philadelphia Ivoirian community leader Eric Edi observed, "The region is still burning and unstable," with enduring violence and tensions, even if the wars are officially long over.[29]

The Jallah family's story of multiple displacements was typical for Liberians during the wars, and the ways in which its members got to the United States reflect some of the broad diversity of Liberians' migration.[30] Their prior experiences and links to people in the United States were the norm for people with Americo-Liberian family ties. These relationships often helped people leave, often as permanent family refugees like much of the Jallah family. Many other Liberians came to the United States during and after the wars via tourist or other temporary visas and were granted Temporary Protected Status (TPS), allowing them to stay. This variety of statuses was just one of the ways in which Liberians were diverse. They came from urban and rural backgrounds, Christian and Muslim and indigenous religions, and different ethnic groups, which meant different sides in the civil wars.

Liberians had diverse ties to America, too. While some were descended from the African Americans who colonized Liberia, many came from tribes that had been exploited by Americo-Liberians. Some had close ties to American businesses and institutions, and others were descended from people who had sold fellow Africans into slavery. "It's history that we ought to face," says Reverend Jallah.[31]

## American Family

Liberians' experiences of protection and support in the United States reflected old patterns of ambivalence about the place of African people and their descendants as members of American society whose lives matter. The colonization movement grew largely from slaveholders' concern that free Blacks could lead slaves to rebel and from white Americans' broader hostility toward free Blacks. Nearly two centuries later, Liberians could virtually all claim a well-founded fear of persecution based on their membership in a social group, given the interethnic violence of the civil wars. Under UN and US law, this should qualify them for permanent refuge. Yet close to one-quarter of all Liberians who came to the United States during the civil wars and more than 40 percent of those with refugee, asylum, or other protected status received TPS instead. Liberians' place in the American family became even more complicated when they settled themselves—and were resettled by agencies—in the Black neighborhoods of Philadelphia and other US cities.

As with Southeast Asians, sanctuary is a concept seldom associated with Liberians and other Africans. In Philadelphia, Liberians rarely participated in sanctuary movements, though they supported the city's sanctuary policies. Instead, they built other networks and civil society institutions, often with other Black people. They only occasionally called this work "sanctuary." However, the often temporary and disputed legal status of many Liberians, the interpersonal and structural violence they faced in the United States and Africa, and the protections and assistance they sought and provided for one another make sanctuary a fitting framework for grappling with their experiences and position in US cities and society and their postwar reconstruction of Liberia.

The United States played a leading part in the long history that produced Liberia's civil wars and people's displacement. The Liberian Truth and Reconciliation Commission concluded that the atrocities of the wars, counting thousands of human rights violations by all sides, "were the result of complex historical and geopolitical factors." These included the "slave trade, US efforts to return slaves and free African Americans to Africa, the abuse of the indigenous population by" Americo-Liberians, "looting of the country's substantial natural resources by its own corrupt government and by foreign interests" (largely from the United States), and "political ambitions of other African leaders."[32] The commission called out US leaders who "failed to take effective action to limit the bloodshed."[33] They had not stopped Firestone and Liberians in the United States from funding Taylor and other warlords whose forces raped, murdered, and burned the villages of rival groups. During the final rebel siege of Monrovia in 2003, Liberians piled bodies of civilians killed in the bombing in front of the US embassy, upset that the roughly 200 US Marines stationed on three warships off the coast came ashore only briefly.[34]

The question of what the United States owed Liberians was clearer to Africans than to Americans. As a Liberian woman at a reception center in Abidjan, Ivory Coast, in 2004, succinctly put it, "Our parents went into slavery in America. They helped America develop. The United States has a moral debt to us."[35] But lawmakers in Washington, DC, like US citizens at large, knew little to nothing about Liberia's history. Moreover, the United States did not participate in Liberia's civil wars in the same way it did in Vietnam, and the Cold War ended around the time the first war began, removing the old logic that had determined which peoples the United States accepted as refugees. Still, while a few thousand Liberians went to Europe, the United States took in most of the people who were resettled.

Americans often cast Liberians' refuge as temporary, and their experience of the US immigration system proved especially complicated. President George H. W. Bush first granted Liberians TPS in March 1991. President Bill

Clinton allowed that to expire in 1999 but transferred Liberians on TPS to the status of Deferred Enforced Departure (DED), a category newly created by the 1996 immigration law. Under TPS and DED people received work permits, but under DED they were not eligible for federal financial aid for college and could not leave the country and return. The Patriot Act, passed after the terrorist attacks of September 11, 2001, blocked the admission of anyone who had materially aided groups that were trying to overthrow their government. As a result, Liberians who had been forced at gunpoint to do laundry, cook, and other noncombat tasks for rebel troops could no longer come as refugees.

In 2002, during the second civil war, George W. Bush redesignated Liberians for TPS, which was extended until 2007, when people on TPS went back on DED. In 2006, the United States removed Liberia from the list of countries eligible for family-based refugee resettlement. The administration of Barack Obama extended DED several times, and with the outbreak of Ebola in West Africa in 2014, it again granted TPS to Liberians, Guineans, and Sierra Leoneans (who also had had TPS from 1997 to 2004).[36] The Trump administration announced the end of DED for Liberians in 2018.

In explaining why some Liberians did not merit permanent protection, US officials spoke of war and Ebola as temporary crises that would ultimately abate, making it safe to return home. Many Liberians, however, cried foul. They pointed to other groups to whom the United States granted permanent refugee status amid civil wars and "ethnic cleansing," including people fleeing the Balkans at the same time in the 1990s. Why were they given the right to stay permanently while so many Liberians and Sierra Leoneans received only temporary protection? Many Africans charged that these decisions were simply racist.[37]

The US media often presented Liberians as a people broadly on TPS, but most were not. Between 1989 and 2004, almost 21,000 Liberians were resettled as permanent refugees in the United States, many through family. Just over 6,000 were granted asylum. The figures for TPS are not well documented, but by 2004 an estimated 20,000 Liberians in the United States had signed up for it. Still, the largest number of Liberians in this period, over 27,000 people, came as immigrants, usually through family reunification visas, rather than refugee or other protected status. Such family-based visas accounted for close to two-thirds of all immigration to the United States in this era.[38] However, TPS and its ultimate promise of forced departure hung over the Liberian diaspora in the United States at large. Nearly every Liberian in the country was "family" with someone who was on TPS or DED.

As the life story of Reverend Jallah suggests, Liberians' definition and experiences of family are far more expansive and inclusive than the nuclear family categories recognized in US law. Uncles and aunts are legitimate parents, with specific obligations to care for nephews and nieces as their own. Children of first, second, and third wives are direct siblings, as with adoptive Americo-Liberian extended families. A broader definition of family like this is typical of many West African societies. "US immigration has not been fair in trying to understand this cultural dynamic," charged Voffee Jabateh, another Liberian community leader in Philadelphia. Knowing they could not trust people's claims about parenthood, authorities resorted to DNA testing before approving family refugee or immigration applications for Liberian and other African children.[39]

Like the federal government, Liberians did not treat their own status as static. Most people on TPS actively sought more stable status and many got it. Some married people with green cards. Some "played the lottery," as another Liberian community leader in Philadelphia put it, by applying for the Diversity Visa Lottery. Many of those who won the lottery, as well as others with green cards, used family reunification visas for immigrants to bring or change the status of as many family members as they could.[40] This diminished the number of people on DED to about 3,600 by the time the Trump administration declared an end to that protection.[41]

Liberians had a different relationship with the resettlement system from Southeast Asians and other refugees who had no coethnic receiving community when they first arrived. Liberians' diversity of immigration status and social class made them less tied to welfare than most refugee groups. Liberians on TPS received resettlement support services just like permanent refugees, such as job seeking and ESL. But more than most refugee groups, Liberians resettled themselves.

Liberians founded and adapted preexisting community organizations that built their own support networks, both locally and transnationally. The Volags and other receiving community groups provided key support. But Liberian civil society grew its own services partly, and quickly, out of preexisting associations established by Liberian migrants in the 1970s and 1980s. The most prominent were the Liberian Associations of different states; their national umbrella organization, the Union of Liberian Associations in the Americas (ULAA); and county associations.

More than most other immigrants, Liberians participated in rebuilding their homeland after the wars. The diaspora also played a greater role in the truth and reconciliation process than refugees from other civil wars. The ULAA and other groups supported the formation of state and civil society institutions in Liberia. The county associations invested in education, health, telecom, and other infrastructure and community development in each of its fifteen counties.[42]

Even the most transnationally active Liberian organizations in Philadelphia and the United States, though, remained focused on the welfare of the diaspora first. In addition to helping people reunite families and stabilize their status, Liberian civil society addressed a host of social issues, from trauma among children who had experienced and sometimes fought in the wars to the isolation that elders faced in the city. Community leaders, including Reverend Jallah, established social service organizations that grew to serve a wider range of African immigrants and refugees, and often also African Americans and other immigrants. Liberians played central roles in forming a set of Pan-African institutions in the region. In these and other ways, Liberian Philadelphia illuminates the experiences of a broad set of African diasporas.

Philadelphia's Pan-African civil society reflected the city and region's importance as a center of African and Caribbean immigration, along with a welcoming politics of many African Americans, including key city leaders. It also grew partly in response to tensions and violence between Black immigrant and receiving communities in the 1990s and 2000s. In some ways, this and other patterns resembled the experiences of Southeast Asian refugees in the 1980s.

Liberians settled and were resettled in majority–African American neighborhoods, especially Southwest and West Philadelphia and adjacent suburbs, with other people from Africa, the Caribbean, Southeast Asia, and other regions. Liberians and other immigrants helped revive these areas, which revitalized largely without gentrifying. However, Liberians and other African and Caribbean immigrants shared African Americans' residential segregation and many of their experiences of economic discrimination, disadvantage, and racism. In the city neighborhoods where they settled, violence remained high, especially compared to other US cities, where violence diminished significantly at the end of the twentieth century.[43]

Intergroup relations among African and Caribbean immigrants and African Americans were of an entirely different character, being often more intimate, more complicated, and more productive than those between African Americans and Southeast Asians. Philadelphia's diverse Black communities came from distinct histories, with different relationships to slavery and to the United States. But more successfully than some centers of African and Caribbean immigration, foreign- and native-born Blacks in Philadelphia developed a politics and practices of mutual protection and assistance on both local and transnational scales.

# Little Africa

Philadelphia has been a prominent center of Black life for centuries, making African and Caribbean immigrants' experiences distinct from those of many other newcomers. In 1790, one in seven city residents was of African descent.[44] In the nineteenth century, the city had the largest Black population in the North. In the twentieth it was a major destination of the First and Second Great Migrations of African Americans from the South, during and after the two world wars. In the 1960s and 1970s, some Liberian, Nigerian, Ghanaian, and other African university students and professionals came to Philadelphia, drawn by its many institutions of higher education. By the 1980s it was a minority-majority city, due also to white flight.

Since then, Philadelphia has been an important center of immigrant settlement from dozens of countries in Africa and the Caribbean. Nigerians, Ethiopians, Jamaicans, and Haitians have been among the largest groups.[45] By 2010, Liberians were the largest group of foreign-born Blacks in the city and region. The US Census counted some 13,000 Liberians in the city and suburbs, among over 60,000 African immigrants, though community leaders estimated much higher figures.[46]

Philadelphia became the number one destination for Liberians in the late 1990s and early 2000s. Many people relocated from New York or Washington, DC, as the *Philadelphia Inquirer* reported, "drawn by word among fellow Liberians of cheaper homes, more jobs and safer neighborhoods" than many could afford in those more expensive regions.[47] Another factor in choosing Philadelphia was the help they could expect from community organizations run by other Liberians. West and Southwest Philadelphia had been home to several Liberians attending universities in the 1980s, who started one of the first chapters of the ULAA and hosted the meeting at which leaders formed the national organization. In 2003, the second annual Miss Liberia USA pageant took place in the city.[48] By 2006, more Liberians lived there than in any other metropolitan region of the United States.[49]

The 1990s and 2000s marked a change in the character of the Liberian population in the United States. As journalist and social worker Sam Togba Slewion noted, by the 1990s it was no longer "only college kids."[50] Now Liberians in the United States included people of varied ages, from both urban and rural origins, and with a range of personal and family problems resulting from the wars. Most were fleeing the wars, no matter their diverse visa categories. Virtually all had family dispersed across West Africa, the United States, and sometimes the United Kingdom, many of whom they were obligated to support.

The resettlement of Liberians followed the same logic of self-sufficiency applied to other refugees, yet crucially, their preponderance of family-based resettlement and preexisting community ties made that a more realistic goal than for some other groups. When Reverend Jallah, his wife, and their grandchildren arrived toward the end of 1997, their daughter and her husband "had their house prepared for us. We had a room there, all of those things. Then they notified Lutheran Children and Family Services that we were here. They, too," came to meet the family. The next week, they attended a one-day orientation class. "Then we started looking for a job."[51]

To illustrate just how different Liberians often were from many other refugees, staff at the Volags liked to tell stories such as the one about waiting at the airport to welcome a couple: When they arrived, the husband informed them that his wife, a famous singer, had booked tour dates around the United States and had a connecting flight. They were sorry, but they could not accompany the caseworkers to the apartment they had arranged for them.[52]

Like other West African immigrants, and like other refugees, Liberians came with a wide range of education and work histories, from people with advanced degrees and international experience to people who had hardly ever been outside their village. In 2010, 13 percent of Liberian adults in the United States had not finished high school. Yet more than two-thirds had attended college, one indication of how privileged people were more often able to flee overseas.[53] Still, like many other immigrants and refugees, even Liberians with the highest credentials and notable experience, like Rev. Dr. John Jallah, typically started near the bottom rung of the US labor market. Some sought new training and some moved up the occupational ladder, often in public and nonprofit roles where they helped other people. Reverend Jallah's story reflects these patterns and trends, too.

The most common first job in Philadelphia for Liberian men, young and old, was as an attendant at a parking lot or garage, either downtown or at one of the hospitals scattered around the region. Reverend Jallah got a job with the Colonial Parking company at the Healthplex hospital in suburban Media, about a twenty-minute car ride from Southwest Philadelphia. The problem was, though, that he was an inexperienced and lousy driver, even at age fifty-one. Back in Liberia, like other prominent employees of major companies, institutions, and government, he usually had a chauffeur. Consequently, rather than have him move cars, his boss at the parking lot assigned him the role of cashier on the night shift.[54]

While many Liberian men with little education remained parking attendants, Reverend Jallah quickly pursued other opportunities. "Then I got a second job in the day," he explained, as therapeutic support staff, a "wraparound" employee assisting an African American student with learning disabilities at University City High School. "Then I went back to school, to Philadelphia Biblical College, did some other . . . training at Temple [University], micro-business training with [Lutheran Children and Family Services], participated in several workshops." In the LCFS program, he drafted a business plan for a cleaning company, which he started in 2000. Employing other Liberian men and women, they cleaned mainly offices in the city and suburbs, mostly at night. This would be Reverend Jallah's source of income.[55]

The nonprofit workshop at Temple "led me to open the Agape Senior Center," also in 2000, one of various social service organizations founded by Liberians around the same time.[56] All the founders were college-educated men and women. Many, including Rev. John Gblah, Voffee Jabateh, Portia Kamara, and Sam Togba Slewion, earned master of social work degrees at Temple and worked at the city's Department of Human Services (DHS). By one account, sixteen Liberians worked at DHS in the late 1990s and early 2000s and others worked in counseling and similar positions in schools and nonprofits around the city. A few Liberians became university faculty, teaching staff, and administrators.[57]

The largest number of Liberian women worked as home health aides or in nursing homes, joining the ranks of women from the Caribbean, Philippines, and Latin America in "caring sector" positions largely staffed by immigrant women. Others worked in retail and fast food. Many Liberian women and men arrived in Philadelphia in the 1990s and 2000s saying they wanted to be a Certified Nurse's Assistant, even if they had no related experience, remembered Juliane Ramic from NSC.[58] They were already attuned to this occupational niche and the pathway it offered. As they gained training, including at the Jewish Employment and Vocational Service Center for New Americans, many attained higher-level nursing positions in hospitals and rehab centers. The growth of the region's service economy from the 1990s opened more doors for work as certified nurses, in child care, and other parts of the health and care sectors. These occupations often had greater "ladders" that enabled people to move up than other sorts of jobs.[59] By the 2010s, though, the second generation—their daughters—more often went to social work school, aiming to work in Liberia and the United States.[60]

Like work opportunities, housing conditions in West and Southwest Philadelphia improved in the 1990s and 2000s. To be sure, with a century-old housing stock and a mix of more and less responsible landlords, old problems persisted. But the city and local nonprofits targeted vacant properties for demolition and rehabilitation in these decades, and immigration offset the city's loss of older working-class white and African American populations.

Yet even as immigration helped stabilize the housing market in sections of West and Southwest Philadelphia such as Cobbs Creek and Elmwood, these areas where Liberians and other Blacks lived remained relatively poor and segregated. African American and Black immigrant residents experienced greater rates of eviction, foreclosure, and violence than residents in the gentrified neighborhoods of West Philadelphia near the University of Pennsylvania and downtown. In 2010, more than half of all Liberians in the United States were "cost-burdened," spending more than 30 percent of their household income for rent or mortgage payments.[61]

Like Southeast Asians, many Liberians lived in multigenerational households—grandparents with their children and grandchildren, even if elders often experienced isolation. Many people lived with extended family, and those who lost relatives in the wars lived with surrogate families. These two categories made up 20 percent of all people in Liberian-headed households in the United States in 2010.[62] Also like Southeast Asians, some Liberians lived in apartments before moving to row houses in the city and nearby suburbs. Many moved to Upper Darby and nearby towns in Delaware County, just across the city line, where immigrants and African Americans hoped to find better schools and safer, quieter neighborhoods.[63]

Southwest Philadelphia remained the center of Liberian Philadelphia, however. Other immigrants in the area included Malians, Haitians, Jamaicans, and many other people from West and East Africa and the Caribbean, along with Southeast Asians and later, Central Americans. The Jallah family lived just off Woodland Avenue, with "two other Liberian families on the same block," as well as Nigerian, West Indian, and African American neighbors.[64]

Liberians opened a growing number of groceries, restaurants, cafes, hairbraiding, and other shops along Woodland Avenue, where West African foods such as cassava leaf and fufu, a root porridge, became widely available.[65] Local residents and journalists dubbed the area, alternately, "Little Monrovia," "Little Liberia," and "Little Africa."[66] Other African and Caribbean merchants on the avenue opened shops too, as did Southeast Asians. Black people remained largely absent from America's popular and scholarly narratives about immigrants' contributions to economic development. But places like Woodland Avenue and other corridors in Southwest Philadelphia, Upper Darby, and African and Caribbean immigrant neighborhoods in the cities and suburbs of New York; Washington, DC; Atlanta; Minneapolis–St. Paul; Denver; and other metropolitan regions, showed they also belong at the center of our understanding of America's urban revival (see figure 3.1).[67]

The biggest way in which Liberians' housing and neighborhood experiences differed from those of most other refugees was their reception and support,

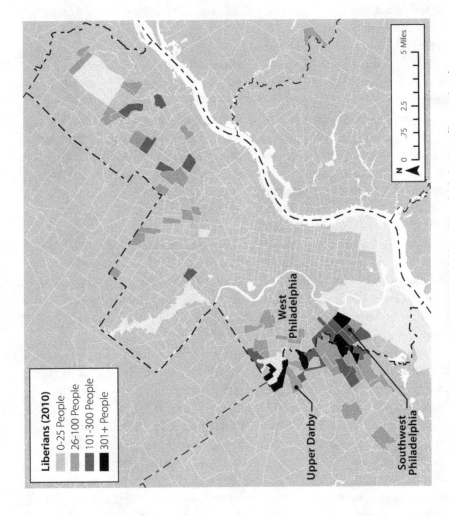

**Figure 3.1.** Map of Liberian settlement in Philadelphia and its suburbs in 2010. (Source: American Community Survey; map by Danielle Dong.)

from the start, from extended families and fellow members of community associations. "You can go anywhere and sleep," said Portia Kamara, "two or
three families [sometimes live] in one home, working together and raising families." If they lost their housing, people in the Liberian community always
offered them a place to stay. Their experiences of displacement during the civil
wars were one thing that made people so accommodating, Kamara explained.[68]
But these informal support networks rendered people's housing problems
largely invisible to authorities. Indeed, Liberians' and other West Africans'
common practice of staying temporarily with a string of extended family and
friends was a form of what housing experts call "hidden homelessness."[69]

Resettlement agency staff marveled at the strength of Liberians' preexisting networks. At the meetings and banquets of county associations and the
Liberian Association of Pennsylvania, they witnessed how these groups' leaders and members assisted one another with landlord disputes, housing and
job searches, access to health care, children's problems in school, and myriad
other issues. Association leaders were regularly called to their constituents'
homes and places of work to help with all manner of things as well, including
sometimes to diffuse tense situations with police.[70]

Some Liberians found Philadelphia utterly disorienting. As Reverend Gblah
recounted, people who had never been on a plane flew into the airport at night,
seeing the lights of the city, and having come from a country at war, they
thought the lights were fires and the city was burning.[71] Many, he said, were
surprised to "find the same vegetables year-round in the store."[72] Reverend Jallah often told the story of an elderly couple who left their West Philadelphia
row house for the grocery store a few blocks away but on their return became
disoriented since all of the streets and houses looked the same. Being from a
rural village, they were not used to reading street signs or house numbers. For-
tunately, school was letting out and their grandson came running past as they
wandered down the block. They hurried after him and found their way home.
The isolation of elders like these, including many whose command of English
and whose accents were such that they had difficulty communicating with
Americans, inspired Reverend Jallah to start the Agape Center.[73]

Children also experienced isolation, leading to problems with neighbors and
the city. In Liberia, Portia Kamara observed, by age twelve children are expected to help manage the household, cooking, watching siblings, and so on.
In the United States, parents left children alone when they worked, often for
long hours in multiple jobs to support dispersed extended family. Sometimes
kids would go outside and get in trouble, occasionally hit by a car but more
often just seen alone on the sidewalk or street. In response, neighbors called
the Department of Human Services and the police, accusing parents of neglect.

These conditions inspired Kamara and other Liberians to pursue social work, as they and other parents and community leaders intervened to "save families and save our community." They sought to save their children from prison, which claimed many of their African American neighbors, and to save them from deteriorating relations with those neighbors and schoolmates.[74]

On October 31, 2005, at 60th Street and Woodland Avenue, three African American teens teased and then beat unconscious a thirteen-year-old Liberian boy named Jacob Gray, who was on his way home from school. Gray's jaw was fractured, and a blood clot formed in his brain. He told police he did not even know why the teens had attacked him. The event made international news.[75] Suddenly, Philadelphians at large became aware of the Liberian community and of its tensions with African Americans.

*Front Page Africa* in Monrovia reported that the "vicious beating . . . exposed a larger problem of animosity between African Americans and African immigrants," as community and school leaders noted that "the attack fits a widespread pattern." It had "been going on for quite a while," said a twenty-five-year-old Liberian student at Temple University who ran a music and video store in Philadelphia. "It's just the first time we've seen it in the newspapers." Sam Togba Slewion estimated that he heard complaints about "fights and near-fights between native-born and immigrant Blacks several times a week," some that became cases in municipal court, in family court, and before the human relations commission.[76] "The kids talk about being called African chimps, African monkeys, sometimes being told to go back to Africa," and were often mocked and bullied for their accents and clothes, noted Portia Kamara.[77] This harassment exceeded normal adolescent teasing.

Relations between Africans and African Americans suffered from unfamiliarity and stereotypes. They often knew little of each other's histories of slavery, colonization, exploitation, civil war, freedom struggles, Jim Crow, and mass incarceration. As one West African noted, some immigrants were shocked to hear African Americans "blame Africans for selling them into slavery."[78] Many Africans who came to the United States in the 1960s and 1970s "don't relate" to the Civil Rights Movement, observed Voffee Jabateh, as most were "isolated" with other international students on college campuses, even as some supported the movement. But African Americans' "problems have become our problems. Their segregation has become our segregation."[79]

Among adults, "the perception here is that Africans come and take jobs," said Konah Mitchell, another Liberian social worker. "And for Africans it's that you've been here, so what have you achieved?" As Jabateh explained, in Africa "we had no government assistance. No welfare. No housing assistance." Many African immigrants thought American Blacks who lived in poverty had it easy thanks to entitlement programs. "I work hard for everything I got," was their attitude, "I'm not like you, who get things free."[80]

By 2010, the median household income among Liberians in the region was $51,000, well below the native-born average ($72,000) but well above that of African Americans ($35,000).[81] Many American Blacks were unaware of Africans' diversity of social class. Some saw African neighbors getting good jobs and buying homes and wondered how they achieved that so quickly, while African Americans continued to experience entrenched poverty and discrimination.[82]

Like other groups before them, young African immigrants in Southwest and West Philadelphia sought protection by traveling to school in groups. Many families pulled their children out of Philadelphia public schools, instead choosing charter or parochial schools or moving to the suburbs.[83] Some teens formed gangs, including at Bartram High in Southwest Philadelphia and Upper Darby High, where a gang called Liberians in Blood (L.I.B.), was featured on National Public Radio in 2008.[84] As Portia Kamara related, one youth who was involved explained to her that these gangs were for self-defense: "We are not forming gangs to go out and rob people, but it is a way of protecting ourselves against African Americans who think they can hurt us."[85]

Young Liberians' problems in school extended beyond bullying and fights. As the *Philadelphia Inquirer* reported in 2003, "Schools have struggled to cope with the recent spike in African students, who often need language help even though they are considered to be English speakers." Many had missed schooling during the wars, "so they either must struggle in class with Americans their own age, or suffer the stigma of being put with younger students." Initially counted as African American by the School District of Philadelphia, some "battle-scarred children" lacked counseling or language support, and some "retreated into a stoic silence." Community activists, organizations, and school officials responded by developing programs in and out of school, working through children's trauma and "teaching everything from English to cultural cues."[86]

Tensions within the Liberian community perpetuated people's trauma as well. People from the nation's fifteen counties and sixteen ethnic groups, which were associated with different sides and events in the wars, lived in Philadelphia and its suburbs. Some would be accused of war crimes. In the supermarket and on the street, Liberians encountered people from their home country who were either directly or indirectly responsible for the deaths, displacements, or rapes of their family members during the wars—not unlike Guatemalans and Salvadorans in bigger centers of Central American population. As lawyers working with the Liberian Truth and Reconciliation Commission wrote in

2009, six years after the wars ended, "the peace remains fragile. The conflict's impact is evident in the streets of Monrovia, the homes of villagers in the Liberian countryside, and Liberian gathering places in London, Philadelphia, Staten Island, and elsewhere."[87] Ivoirian, Sierra Leonean, and other immigrants in Philadelphia experienced similar tensions among themselves and with Liberians.[88]

The beating of Jacob Gray in 2005 sparked widespread attention to the problems of violence and trauma, yet it also revealed that Liberians and their allies had already built an extensive civil society focused on these and other issues. Community groups, city agencies, and Philadelphia's Liberian consul, Teta Banks, held town hall meetings in response to the beating. Officials from the police, school district, district attorney, human relations commission, city council, and numerous churches, civic and community organizations attended, including from the new Mayor's Commission for African and Caribbean Immigrant Affairs.[89]

This last organization had been created that summer by Mayor John Street. Its founding press release "reaffirmed to the world Philadelphia's historic commitment to tolerance, freedom and democracy," and recognized African and Caribbean immigrants' contributions to the city. As the commission's secretary, Sam Togba Slewion, noted, Black immigrant advocates had long stressed to city officials that inner-city "communities would have died without immigrants."[90] The commission held its first official meeting in response to Jacob Gray's beating. Its members, however, had been working for some years on the commission's "main functions . . . to encourage the development and implementation of policies and practices intended to improve conditions affecting the cultural, social economic, political, educational, health and general well-being of the African and Caribbean immigrants, refugees, and asylees residing in Philadelphia."[91]

## Liberian and Pan-African Civil Society

Liberian associations in America represented a preexisting infrastructure for supporting the diaspora and families back in Liberia. But the civil wars inspired dramatic shifts in their membership, missions, and work. In the 1980s, the ULAA and county associations helped families cover funeral expenses and organized birthday parties and other social events. In the 1990s and 2000s, as Reverend Jallah put it, these organizations "took on new meaning and new roles," rebuilding families, communities, and institutions in Liberia and the United States.[92] Interethnic tensions among Liberians and other West Africans persisted from the civil wars, but much of this abated as community leaders worked to build peace among Africans and between them and their neighbors.[93] In Philadelphia, this work took increasingly Pan-African and multicultural forms.

The long list of organizations in which Reverend Jallah has engaged reveals a diverse ecosystem of civil society supported by active networks of leaders in Liberian and Pan-African Philadelphia. He has chaired the Liberian Association of Pennsylvania, the Liberian Ministers Association of the Delaware Valley, and the national Union of Liberian Ministers in the Americas. The ministers' groups play vital roles in supporting Liberians when family members die and in resolving family and community conflicts, among other crises. Reverend Jallah's Agape Senior Center has offered English classes and other basic supports and orientation to elderly Africans, building their survival skills and promoting dignity and self-esteem (see figure 3.2). This drew him into collaboration with the Philadelphia Corporation for the Aging, the city's largest service agency for seniors, whose advisory board he joined. In two of his many evening and weekend commitments, he has served on the boards of the region's most prominent Pan-African institutions, the Mayor's Commission for African and Caribbean Immigrant Affairs and the Coalition of African and Caribbean Communities in Philadelphia (AFRICOM), where he has led the Conflict Resolution Committee.[94]

**FIGURE 3.2.**    Rev. Dr. John K. Jallah (standing third from the left) with elders at the Agape Seniors Center in West Philadelphia in 2006. (Photo courtesy of Rev. Dr. John K. Jallah.)

The variety of local work in which he engaged reflects an effort to "do everything I can to help my people."[95] "Some of us, we see our responsibility" toward others, and therefore get "integrated and educate ourselves" as much as possible and "join as many organizations as we can." Reverend Jallah joined African American churches in order to understand Black Americans better, to put himself in a better position to help immigrants and native-born Blacks live together in peace. "You cannot help me to settle in Philadelphia if you are not part of Philadelphia," he acknowledged.[96]

In his sentiments and the variety of his organizational affiliations, he was representative of a large group of Liberian and other Black leaders in Philadelphia. Some of the earliest included Rufus Mendin and his colleagues at Liberian Redevelopment, which they founded in 1994 to assist Liberians and other "Africans in adapting to life in their new home." They offered help with conflict resolution, food for the elderly, housing and temporary shelter, and other support services, addressing almost any problem people wanted help with.[97] Others included the group of social workers who went to Temple, worked at DHS, and often went on to found and lead nonprofit organizations.

Voffee Jabateh was the second Liberian to graduate from Temple with a master's degree in social work, after Portia Kamara. Adopted and educated by an Americo-Liberian family in Monrovia, who renamed him Joseph, Voffee later took back his African name. He ran an import-export company and a used car business that employed twenty-five people in Liberia. His Americo-Liberian mother helped him leave in 1990 when the civil war broke out. The United States granted him asylum.[98]

In Philadelphia, he first worked washing dishes at a fast-food restaurant, but after a couple of weeks found work as a mental health counselor since he had a degree in sociology. Five years later, he went to work at DHS, and later went to Temple for his master's. He too became a prominent leader of the Liberian Association of Pennsylvania, ULAA, and other organizations. With help from SEAMAAC and Alphonso Kawah, the Liberian case worker it hired, Jabateh and his colleagues and relatives, including Reverend Gblah, pooled enough money in 1999 to found the African Cultural Alliance of North America (ACANA).[99]

Established by a group of performing artists and social workers, ACANA's mission and programs focused on arts and culture, human services, and community development. They used cultural programming to draw Africans, who were often wary of government-supported programs, into social services. They bought a former crack house, a laundromat where people used to sell drugs, and soon purchased other properties along Chester Avenue in Southwest Philadelphia, converting them into offices, classrooms, and performance spaces. When the sun set and the avenue's merchants pulled down the metal grates over their storefronts, ACANA's doors stayed open and the lights stayed on.[100] Jabateh and his colleagues imagined turning the area into an arts and culture corridor, a "sanctuary where people can walk down the street" without fear.[101]

With funding from the city, ACANA quickly became the largest African social service nonprofit in Philadelphia, running youth antiviolence, adult literacy, job readiness, after-school, food assistance, and other programs. Its founders were already well integrated and connected to city leaders and agencies. Their district councilwoman, Jannie Blackwell, was a strong supporter, as was her ally, council president John Street, who won the mayoral election the year they established ACANA. The organization's first music festival in 2000 attracted several thousand people to Bartram High's track and football stadium. The crowd overflowed for blocks all around. The festival moved to a larger venue downtown at Penn's Landing on the Delaware River in 2008.[102]

Across the 2000s, ACANA's constituency changed, shifting its mission and much of its work. From an initial aim "to help refugee and immigrant families," especially from Liberia and Sierra Leone, it quickly incorporated African Americans and other immigrants into its programs. Some attended its drumming and dance classes, which also employed African American instructors. This helped ease some initial tensions between Liberian and Sierra Leonean immigrants and African Americans who identified more with different West African cultural traditions, mainly from Ghana and Nigeria.[103]

After the beating of Jacob Gray, and as more and more African Americans and diverse immigrants knocked on its doors, ACANA's leaders recast their mission as "bridging the gaps"—in people's access to employment and services and between immigrants and their African American neighbors. In 2006, Jabateh reported that African Americans made up 25 percent of their clients. "We being Black people, we cannot" turn them away, he said. One year later, that figure climbed to more than one-third, and by the 2010s it was roughly half.[104]

ACANA's leaders formed close relationships with Black American and Caribbean community leaders, including the colloquial "mayor of Chester Avenue," Josephine Blow, an African American who was born in North Carolina to parents from Jamaica. The longtime leader of the avenue's merchants association, she began to literally pull African Americans into ACANA's computer, entrepreneurship, and youth programs. Both she and the organization's staff recruited people by presenting these services as a way in which African Americans and Africans alike could benefit from the advantages that each group perceived the other as having.[105]

Parts of ACANA's work remained focused on Liberians, Sierra Leoneans, and Guineans, such as Project Tamaa, which was run in partnership with the Liberian staff member at the Children's Crisis Treatment Center. This behavioral health program worked with former child soldiers and other traumatized youth and their parents and teachers. Project Tamaa employed the Sanctuary Model of recovery developed by psychiatrist Sandra Bloom in Philadelphia in the 1980s, an approach that recognizes the pervasiveness of trauma in people's experiences and seeks to build a broader "trauma-informed community" promoting safety and care.[106]

ACANA's multiple petitions to the State Department to become a resettlement agency were rebuffed. But the organization developed its own immigration services department, which employed two attorneys by the 2010s. They served some 1,400 clients in 2013. Like the lawyers at resettlement agencies, they helped Liberians and other immigrants gain permanent status.[107]

ACANA weathered steep funding cuts to its social programs during the Great Recession that began in 2008, partly thanks to its immigration services division and also since it had bought properties and did not pay rent on Chester Avenue, where it had begun to support a diverse group of Black and Asian shopkeepers. In 2016, it became the commercial corridor manager for the larger Woodland Avenue, expanding its neighborhood revitalization work with festivals, streetscaping, including a mural titled "Bridging the Gaps," and facade improvements and funding for small businesses, among other types of support (see figure 3.3). ACANA's staff assisted several groups of immigrant merchants who formed what Africans call *susu* lending networks, in which members' dues underwrite each other's business investments and expansion on a revolving basis. When several African Americans spread rumors about the organization "taking over" and "making it just for Africans," they hired them as community organizers.[108]

Similar but even more multicultural patterns characterized the organization that Portia Kamara and her husband, Gore, founded in Upper Darby in 2003, named Multicultural Community Family Services (MCFS). Like ACANA, their constituency quickly expanded from Liberians to West Africans more broadly, and by 2008 to people of all backgrounds. Initially, they ran counseling and support groups for immigrant teens and connected West Africans to health and educational services. They soon expanded to GED degree and job placement programs for young people who lacked a high school diploma. Like immigrant organizations generally, they assisted people with almost any manner of problem they brought through the door.[109]

What started as crisis intervention with immigrant families developed into more formal tutoring, including for the SAT college entrance exam, and a sup-

**FIGURE 3.3.** *Bridging the Gap* mural along Woodland Avenue in Southwest Philadelphia, by artist Willis "Nomo" Humphrey. The mural was produced in 2008 through community meetings organized by ACANA and the Philadelphia Mural Arts Program, a project funded by the Philadelphia Department of Behavioral Health to address community relations. The figures at the top are African American civil rights activist Nina Gomer DuBois and her husband, sociologist W. E. B. DuBois; nineteenth century cleric and founder of West Africa's Wassoulou Empire Samory Touré; and Liberia's postwar president Ellen Johnson Sirleaf. At the bottom left is a depiction of a colonial-era image of Africans packed into a slave ship. (Photo by Domenic Vitiello, 2020.)

port network for youth. In the organization's first or second year, Portia Kamara remembered, two teens who had been in their counseling program and were part of a "core group of students [who] shaped the focus and activities of MCFS" knocked on her door one night to ask if they could form a soccer team. From about thirty players at first, the MCFS soccer club grew to include more than two hundred boys and girls by the 2010s. Thousands of teens participated in MCFS programs over the years, which helped to stabilize their lives. Many went to college and some pursued PhDs. "With ongoing support and encouragement, immigrant youths will do well," Portia observed, "but they need that support, continuing support." With the group, "they had the support of each other, which was critical."[110]

Founded out of the Kamaras' living room and back porch after they moved from West Philadelphia to Upper Darby, they soon moved MCFS to its own office in the town's central business district. "The first time I ever felt unwelcome was in Upper Darby," Portia recalled, adding that it was the first place she "was ever called a n——." When she phoned a local councilman, he spent ten minutes railing against Africans, whom he claimed were all living twenty-five people to a house. Portia replied that Africans are hard-working and well educated. "As I pushed back, his voice became smaller."[111] This signaled larger trends in the area's population and intergroup relations.

In the 2000s, Upper Darby and nearby working-class suburbs became one of the two most diverse parts of the region, along with Lower Northeast Philadelphia. Like most immigrant suburbs, civil society and assistance for newcomers in these areas consisted almost exclusively of religious congregations and their largely informal supports. In Upper Darby and adjacent Millbourne, these included Sikh temples, mosques, and churches. The Irish Pastoral Center served largely undocumented Irish immigrants out of a Catholic church. One other immigrant support organization, the Welcoming Center for New Pennsylvanians, which helped people find jobs, was also established in Upper Darby in 2003 but soon moved to downtown Philadelphia. The township's own Welcome Center started the same year, helping immigrants and sometimes nonimmigrants access public services, employment, ESL classes, citizenship applications, health insurance, legal and homeowner assistance—some of this in partnership with MCFS.[112]

MCFS became a multicultural organization in virtually every way. Its staff and leadership reflected the area's diversity, with people from Liberia, India, Costa Rica, and the United States. By 2011, 40 percent of the people they served came from Asia and Latin America and 60 percent came from African, African American, and Caribbean communities. The soccer club included boys and girls from around the world. Their families came out to watch practices and games, producing multicultural community gatherings on a regular basis. A similarly diverse range of youth and adults participated in MCFS's ESL, behavioral health case management for children and families, and "friendship building" programs that engaged young people in and outside schools and with their caregivers at home. The only program for a single group was its Liberian Elders Circle, which combated social isolation among seniors with weekly activities.[113]

Like ACANA and other groups in Philadelphia, MCFS focused much of its work on building healthy relationships between immigrants and African Americans, occasionally framing them explicitly as "sanctuary." Portia Kamara and her colleagues played key roles in responding to bullying, fights, and the chapter of L.I.B. that formed at Upper Darby High School. Their advocacy and programs helped immigrant students learn to navigate schools, neighborhoods, and American culture and society. They helped Upper Darby's teachers, school staff, and social workers understand, serve, and integrate immigrants and children of immigrants more effectively, especially in the mid-2000s "when many first-generation youth were enrolled at the high school and facing significant challenges," Portia related. In 2016, the school board passed a resolution to welcome and protect undocumented students, becoming a "sanctuary district."[114]

MCFS and other Liberian organizations also influenced police-community relations in Upper Darby and nearby suburbs, where officers remained overwhelmingly white. In one instance, as a Liberian boy walked home from MCFS soccer practice, officers pulled up in a car and began questioning him about a robbery that had just happened. He led them back to the soccer field, where a diverse group of teammates attested to his being at practice a few minutes before.[115] Liberian community leaders in Upper Darby and neighboring townships actively built close relations with the police, so much that the police chiefs from various Delaware County towns attended the inaugural ceremonies of the president of the Liberian Association of Pennsylvania.[116]

Yet Upper Darby, like most suburbs, remained a place with less government and philanthropic funding available for social service programs than in big cities like Philadelphia. This meant that MCFS, like other nonprofits before it, would have a difficult time surviving just by operating social programs. Its leaders' decision to develop not only a training program for older youth to become home care aides but also a social enterprise providing home health and support services enabled the organization to sustain its other programs for youth, elders, and families.[117]

With its training program and business, Attentive Home Care, MCFS provided pathways to decent jobs for women, in its own business and others, as the health and allied caring industries grew in response to the baby boomer generation reaching retirement age in the early twenty-first century. By the mid-2010s, Attentive Home Care employed over seventy-five women at a time, almost all of whom were immigrants. They helped many longtime residents of Upper Darby and nearby city and suburban neighborhoods stay in their homes as they aged.[118]

Inside Philadelphia, city government and philanthropies supported a larger civil society, but immigrant and receiving communities still had to fight for resources and services. West Africans played key roles in getting immigrants and African Americans access to health care and other services, partly by pushing city departments to accommodate people with limited English and those without legal status or insurance. No one was more instrumental in this than Tiguida Kaba, a restaurant owner and activist from Senegal who was employed by the health department as an outreach coordinator from 2001 to 2007. She also cofounded an African women's group at the AIDS Care Group, a Delaware County nonprofit that provided medical care and social services to people living with HIV/AIDS and other diseases around Southeast Pennsylvania.[119]

In 2002, Kaba started the African Family and Health Organization (AFAHO), inspired by a friend who bled to death from a ruptured fibroid tumor because she was too scared to go to the hospital since she lacked legal status in the country. Kaba initially ran AFAHO out of her home, helping people with her own funds, her knowledge of a half-dozen languages, and certification as a medical and legal interpreter and HIV counselor. AFAHO conducted the first needs assessments of African and Caribbean populations' health in the city. The Family Planning Council in Philadelphia gave AFAHO an office and Liberian Alphonso Kawah helped Kaba reach English-speaking immigrants and African Americans. The organization grew in the 2010s under Kaba's successor, Liberian immigrant Oni Richards, who became its director in 2012.[120]

"Addressing and advocating for health equity is the foundation of AFAHO's work," Richards explained. AFAHO's staff sought out the most marginalized African and Caribbean immigrants and refugees in Philadelphia and Delaware County and connected them with care. They formed ties with churches, mosques, hair-braiding salons, women's groups, stores, restaurants, and community organizations to reach people and cultivated a wide network of medical, educational, and human service providers. The organization offered diverse kinds of support, from medical escorts, translation and interpretation, and bilingual health education materials to training for health professionals. Some of its work targeted specific health issues such as obesity, breast cancer, domestic violence, "culturally and linguistically appropriate sexual and reproductive health programs," and a "medical and supportive program for women impacted by female [genital] cutting." Among other outcomes, Richards reported, "maternal and infant mortality is nearly absent among AFAHO's clients," who numbered some 2,000 people each year. The organization also developed its own social services, including case management; ESL, financial and computer literacy classes; food and housing assistance; and a youth after-school program.[121]

In Philadelphia and Delaware County, Liberians and other Africans started and joined churches, mosques, and ethnic associations that furthered their networks of mutual aid. Reverend Gblah opened a church on Elmwood Avenue in Southwest Philadelphia in 2006, which ran a food pantry, helped people find jobs, and gave neighbors and congregants rides to the doctor and "to where the bus doesn't go," as he said.[122] Churches like his offered people a mix of regular and ad hoc support in ways that resembled ethnic and home associations formed by many immigrants from West Africa. Tiguida Kaba led the Benkomah (Mandingo) Women's Association, with members from Liberia, Guinea, Sierra Leone, Burkina Faso, Mali, Senegal, and Gambia, as people of Mandingo ethnicity live in a large area of West Africa.[123] Like other associations, its main activities involved mutual aid for members and their families and social events at which they helped people with their immediate needs. Members of ethnic associations, which also included groups like the Sierra Leone Women's Club and the Cote d'Ivoire Association, helped each other with child care and sometimes with temporary housing. They supported families financially at times of major life events such as births, weddings, and deaths by raising money and catering receptions. They also raised funds to bail immigrants and their children out of jail.[124]

Liberian and other leaders from these and many more organizations in the region were active members of AFRICOM, which was formed in 2001 after a group of Nigerians, including Dr. Bernadine Ahonkhai and Dr. Jude Iheoma, invited other African community leaders to form a Pan-African coalition. AFRICOM's founders and early members included Voffee Jabateh and others from the Liberian Association of Pennsylvania, as well as community leaders from Cote d'Ivoire, Eritrea, Mali, Senegal, Sierra Leone, and Sudan, and human relations commission employee Ernie Greenwood, an African American.[125] Over the years, it became even more Pan-African, with concerted efforts to involve more immigrants from the Caribbean. Liberians like Reverend Jallah and Vera Tolbert served for many years on its board and committees.

AFRICOM did not have a full-time staff in its first decade. But working with ACANA its members helped organize an annual health fair coordinated by Tiguida Kaba, along with the African and Caribbean Soccer Tournament that she ran and the Echoes of Africa cultural festival that she cofounded with Councilwoman Blackwell. The festival took place at the Philadelphia Zoo, and the health fair and tournament, which AFRICOM later took over, were usually held at a city recreation center in Southwest Philadelphia. Hundreds of people attended these events. At the health fair, staff from hospitals, clinics, and other organizations offered free screenings and information and signed up children and adults who were eligible for health insurance benefits. The soccer tournament attracted teams and fans from across Africa and the Caribbean. AFRICOM leaders, occasionally with funding but more often as volunteers, also engaged in regular health referrals and advocacy, conducted outreach for the US Census, and ran a food access program with the Greater Philadelphia Coalition Against Hunger, enrolling people for food stamp benefits and other food programs.[126]

AFRICOM's monthly membership meetings were at least as important for building peaceful relations among African and Caribbean immigrants and African Americans and connecting them to services. These meetings were a forum for networking, raising constituents' issues, and finding them support with everything from navigating public school bureaucracy to job fairs and social programs. Leaders of organizations ranging from ethnic associations to African American community development corporations (CDCs) joined and attended. The Partnership CDC in West Philadelphia hosted AFRICOM's meetings and rented an office to the organization from 2007 to 2011.[127] Radio Tam Tam and Radio Xalaat, two stations established by AFRICOM members from Senegal, regularly hosted colleagues from other communities and broadcast news and information to local and international audiences.

In its early years, AFRICOM's most active committee was its Conflict Resolution Committee, which sent leaders to schools and neighborhoods where people experienced conflict within and between different groups. By the 2010s, this committee's work diminished, even if it did not disappear entirely, as community relations improved. Women leaders of AFRICOM, such as Dr. Bernadine Ahonkhai, Tiguida Kaba, Vera Tolbert, and others, started volunteer-led cooking classes and a food cupboard serving immigrant and American families in West Philadelphia. Starting in 2016, AFRICOM had a small, part-time staff led by executive director Eric Edi, from Cote d'Ivoire, which started to do more outreach and community organizing.[128] Still, AFRICOM's greatest impacts lay in supporting a strong network of Pan-African community leaders (and many non-Black partners) who promoted a politics and practices of peacemaking and mutual interest, support, and well-being among immigrant and receiving communities.

The Mayor's Commission for African and Caribbean Immigrant Affairs played similar roles and included many AFRICOM leaders, growing out of and reinforcing these networks and this politics. Chaired by Stanley Straughter, an African American and honorary consul for Guinea, and by Councilwoman Blackwell, its monthly meetings likewise served as forums for exchanging information, including about changes in immigration policy and issues and events in various communities. Leaders of the commission convinced the Philadelphia Police Department to provide uniforms for the police in Liberia in 2007 as a gesture of goodwill toward the country's rebuilding.[129] Blackwell and the Street administration arranged for the commission to open an office in City Hall, where it aided immigrants in accessing public services until it fell victim to budget cuts under Mayor Street's successor, Michael Nutter, during the Great Recession.

In the mid-2000s, however, especially following the beating of Jacob Gray, Black immigrant-native relations attracted much attention as well as public and philanthropic investment. In addition to antiviolence and other social programs, some of the most visible work took place on the commercial corridors of West and Southwest Philadelphia. The Welcoming Center for New Pennsylvanians partnered with the African American-led 52nd Street Business

Association to start Welcoming Center West. Its two-person staff, an African American and an immigrant, helped bring together African, African American, Caribbean, and Asian merchants who had experienced tensions with customers and one another. They trained them in cross-cultural communication and customer service and organized events celebrating the cultures of merchants and area residents with food, music, and crafts activities for youth. Among other physical improvements, Welcoming Center West helped transform a Cambodian-run beer store, which neighbors had previously considered a nuisance. With the Welcoming Center's support, its owners removed the bulletproof glass at the counter, installed live plants, and hung pictures of customers and their kids on the walls.[130]

The Partnership CDC did similar diversity training with merchants on the 60th Street corridor. Like other African American-led organizations in West and Southwest Philadelphia, it hired an African immigrant, Lansana Koroma, an activist from Sierra Leone. His outreach to African immigrant families helped incorporate them into the CDC's financial literacy and homeownership programs. In 2006, when some one hundred West Africans, mostly Muslims who had overstayed their visas, were detained by ICE in the immigration prison in York, Pennsylvania, he visited their families and helped them access services to stay in their homes or find new ones.[131]

Much of the funding for these projects dried up at the end of the decade, and The Partnership CDC closed in the 2010s. But this community building and development work had lasting effects on intercultural relations and on the capacity of organizations like ACANA and the Welcoming Center, helping them expand commercial corridor support in subsequent years. The Welcoming Center would become an internationally known leader in local immigrant integration.

Another Pan-African nonprofit, the African and Caribbean Business Council, formed in 2006 with a similar mission: to "promote and preserve the business interests of African and Caribbean entrepreneurs in the Greater Philadelphia area while bridging the cultural divide between member countries and the larger community through education and mutual tolerance."[132] Its attempts to develop a credit union fizzled but its business capacity–building and networking programs lived on, growing a mutually supportive community of African, Caribbean, and African American entrepreneurs.[133]

Like other immigrant groups from highly educated backgrounds, Liberians also organized professional and alumni associations, some of which did community work and all of which strengthened their networks. These included the Association of Liberian Journalists, Association of University of Liberia Alumni in the USA, and Monrovia College Alumni Association in the

Americas, which all raised scholarship funds for Liberians and their children in Africa and America. The Philadelphia Folklore Project, based in Southwest Philadelphia, assisted Liberian dancers and musicians in sustaining their art, as did ACANA. The Philadelphia Folklore Project helped former members of Liberia's National Cultural Troupe establish the Liberian Women's Chorus for Change, which spread awareness of Liberia in the United States and raised support for postwar peace-building efforts.

Finally, the oldest organizations of the Liberian diaspora, the ULAA and county associations, continued to play crucial roles in aiding families in Philadelphia and other centers of Liberian settlement. Their leaders assisted people largely ad hoc at social events or by calling and visiting families at home, hospitals, and funeral homes. The chapters collaborated with local health and human service providers, including ACANA, MCFS, the Agape Center, and resettlement agencies, to connect their constituents to various resources. As with other African home associations in the United States and Europe, the welfare of the diaspora remained the first priority of the state chapters of the county associations and ULAA. The national bodies, meanwhile, focused principally on transnational community development, investing in the postwar stabilization and rebuilding of Liberia.[134]

## Reconstructing Liberia

Living as transnational families and communities, Liberian civil society leaders logically worked in America and West Africa at the same time. The county associations played the central roles in community and economic development in Liberia, though the diaspora also began to form smaller hometown associations. The ULAA engaged more in political affairs, from the truth and reconciliation process to re-forming public and civil institutions after the wars. Some of the other organizations discussed in this chapter worked in West Africa too, whether more or less formally. For most Liberian community leaders, this diverse and geographically dispersed work was interrelated, a single broad project of rebuilding lives, families, communities, and institutions in the places where Liberians had come to live. This was mainly Liberians' own project, though it sometimes involved others in Pan-African Philadelphia as well.[135]

Reverend Jallah's organizational life again reflected the diversity of Liberian transnational civil society, and the intense and extensive engagement of many community leaders like him. He served on the national board of the ULAA; chaired the Federation of Lofa Associations in the Americas, the national body for Lofa County associations; and was a member of the Loma University Alumni Association. He continued to serve as a minister to his church in Monrovia and helped lead church associations in Liberia. His church in Liberia ran a school, for which he raised funds in Philadelphia. He also coordinated a farm collective in Lofa County, traveling to Liberia periodically but mainly doing this work from Philadelphia, before training its managers and taking a less active role. This was just some of his transnational community work, the broad extent of which was fairly typical among the most active Liberian community leaders of his generation.

Although the ULAA established a social service council in 2004, it remained a largely political organization.[136] Its leaders were deeply involved in the reconstruction of Liberia's national government and civil society, supporting democratic elections and reforms that promoted transparency, including in communication with the diaspora. As Sam Togba Slewion put it, they "stay involved in the government to make sure that government is treating people fairly."[137]

The administrations of Ellen Johnson Sirleaf, the first woman elected president in Africa, and her successor, George Weah, sent emissaries to consult diaspora community leaders in Philadelphia; Staten Island, New York; Providence, Rhode Island; Baltimore, Maryland; Columbus, Ohio; and Atlanta. They constantly appealed to members of the diaspora to return home, Slewion related. "One of the things that the Liberian government knows is that the middle class is in the States . . . the professional community is in the States," he said. The remittances they sent home were one reason "the Liberian government talks to them, keeps them in the loop . . . engages professionals in the government because they know that they have power."[138] Slewion himself would return to live and work in Liberia in the 2010s.

The ULAA and its leaders helped ensure that Liberia's was the first Truth and Reconciliation Commission to involve the diaspora in the entire truth-seeking process, among more than thirty nations that have implemented such commissions.[139] In Philadelphia, they partnered with the University of Pennsylvania's Transnational Law Clinic to take testimony from members of the diaspora. No residents of the region were tried for war crimes per se. Only Charles Taylor's son, US-born Chuckie Taylor, was convicted by a US court for crimes committed during the war. However, in the late 2010s the United States charged and convicted three men living in the Philadelphia suburbs for failing to disclose in their asylum applications or lying in other court cases about their responsibility for massacres and other atrocities during the wars.[140]

The county associations became the diaspora's main vehicles for supporting community and economic development in Liberia. Like other county associations, the Lofa County Association began as a student group in the 1970s, organized mainly for social purposes. After the war, people in the United States "wanted to get in touch with family members, with the village, and everyone who had been uprooted from the village wanted to get in touch with each other," Reverend Jallah related. They "sent delegates once the war started to end. . . . [We] sent people to see what had happened and see how the village was." Ultimately, "the crisis really caused the county associations to take a little more [of a] role in keeping track of what was going on and the rebuilding effort."[141]

The county associations, one for each of the nation's fifteen counties, raised funds in the United States for various programs and projects. The state chapters provided scholarships for school and university students in Liberia and sent medical and school supplies, typically through annual drives. Scholarships for students in the sciences, health, teaching, and agriculture targeted sectors of need in each county, requiring recipients to work there for two or three years after graduating.[142]

The national boards of the county associations usually took on the development projects, financing, planning, and building schools, medical clinics, and other facilities. Sometimes they helped launch agricultural and other enterprises. In the late 2000s and 2010s, many county association leaders, who were also often active in the ULAA, began to collaborate with the Liberian government and other partners on larger regional projects such as roads, telecommunications, air and seaports, and agricultural infrastructure.[143]

The Sinoe County Association was among the most active county associations in Philadelphia, with leaders including Sam Togba Slewion and Rev. John Gblah. When Slewion was president of the national board, it was the first county association to establish life insurance policies for its membership. In 2010 it acquired thirty acres in one of Sinoe County's largest cities, in partnership with Taylor University in Indiana. The association built and operated the $150,000 Samuel Morris Center for Global Engagement, with offices, conference rooms, and a library and media center to promote reading and internet access. The university was an early tenant. Development partners also included the county and national governments.[144]

During an "assessment tour" of the county in 2010, delegates from the Sinoe County Association observed that the lack of money transfer services in the county presented a barrier for people displaced by the war to return, as many who came back relied on support from family overseas. The association recruited Moneygram to open in partnership with the local First Financial Bank, establishing the first postwar money wiring service in a county with

100,000 residents. Liberian nonprofits also sent representatives to the United States to seek the association's assistance, including a builder of low-cost housing for teachers in rural areas that gained the association's financial and political support.[145]

Other county associations pursued projects of similar types and scales. The Grand Gedeh Association also invested in telecommunications, building an Internet café in the county seat.[146] When a multinational firm established a mine in Nimba, Liberia's largest and most resource-rich county, the county association, the United Nimba Citizens' Council (UNICCO), set up a committee of geologists who submitted a proposal to President Sirleaf for a development fund. In the resulting community benefits agreement, the mining company underwrote development funds for the governments of Nimba and neighboring Bong and Grand Bassa Counties. UNICCO's larger project was a 12,000 square foot Women's Empowerment Center, which trained women in prenatal and postnatal care and small business development. The association also helped Nimba County University College establish and build an electronic library system.[147]

Still, like other immigrants who invest in their homelands, Liberians who were active in county associations experienced tensions with people in Liberia. "They reject us," explained UNICCO's president, Dahn Dennis, who also served at various times as executive director of the Tappita District Development Association, president of the Liberian Association of Pennsylvania, founder and director of the Nimba Youth Organization, and board chair of the Kou Yorway Foundation, a faith-based organization investing in schools and training teachers and principals in Liberia. People who became American citizens "are not considered citizens of Liberia," and Liberians rejected a bill proposed by diaspora members to allow for dual citizenship. "In as much as we are advocating on their behalf, and meeting their needs daily, they still don't consider us to be Liberians." Even as Liberians in the United States "send money all the time" and association leaders visit annually to listen and learn which projects people in the counties want them to support, many "look at us as though we are strangers" and "don't want us to participate in any discussions" about governance and development.[148]

Some of these tensions stemmed from real and perceived inequality, as people in Liberia "feel that we have money, that we have a better life," said Dennis. Members of the diaspora "are sponsoring their kids in colleges here [in the United States], in Morocco, some in China, some in India, and some in South Africa. But yet still they look at us as outsiders. 'They are not one of us. . . . They are Americans, they are settled, they got their education, their kids are having three meals a day, and we are not,'" said critics in Liberia. Even for people who return to Liberia, "they consider us to be job takers. We come here, get education, go back and take jobs."[149]

This all made it more challenging to involve the diaspora in the county associations. "Other Liberians, other Nimbains, decide not to be a part of the organization," Dennis reported. "'Why should we continue to assist people who are continuously rejecting us,'" some say. But people dedicated to the work of county, district, and other transnational associations, "we say 'no.' . . . We have to continue this, because we think it is our call[ing], to help them, no matter what." Much as Liberians have worked to keep families and communities together in America, he concluded, "we are fighting . . . for peace, and oneness, and we want to continue to provide and meet their needs." Ultimately, "we try to overcome it professionally."[150]

Notwithstanding these and other challenges, county association leaders played key roles in state building and the oversight of development. Some of their work came from the diaspora's recognition that the postwar interim government and international organizations were not focused on local reconstruction, but rather on immediate national goals like security. They pushed county governments to perform and helped boost their capacity for development.[151] The associations' national boards often sent representatives to Africa on a monthly basis. Some, like UNICCO, maintained partner groups or employees in Liberia to assist with projects and communicate with leaders in the United States.[152] During the course of a large project, the national and county agencies in charge might call and send meeting minutes to association leaders in Philadelphia, Providence, and other US regions every week. Despite the tensions noted previously, for many Liberians in Africa and the United States this lent further legitimacy to reconstruction and development projects.[153] County associations and their leaders also sometimes backed political candidates, though, provoking tensions in Liberia and the United States.[154]

The more recently established hometown associations served smaller communities, usually first with mutual aid to members and their families and later via larger economic development and place-based projects. The Tallah Families Association began in 1993 as an effort of the roughly 200 migrants in the United States from the township of Tallah, Grand Cape Mount County, to remain connected and help fund extended family members' schooling and other needs in both North America and West Africa. In 2009 leaders renamed it the Tallah Development Corporation, reflecting their increased focus on infrastructure and building projects. This included wells that brought drinking water to six of the township's ten boroughs and a $10,000 investment to repair and upgrade Tallah Junior School, which they raised in collaboration with the school's alumni association. Like the state chapters of the county associations and of the ULAA, however, the corporation also remained focused on the immediate needs of its members and their families in Philadelphia and Africa.[155]

Similarly, Liberian and other West African ethnic associations and churches in Philadelphia raised funds for school fees and supplies for children in Africa. They commonly funded repatriation of deceased members' bodies to be buried in Africa, which cost over $10,000 by the 2000s, and more later. They sent money to departed members' families in Africa and to people deported by ICE to help make up for remittances and wages they no longer received.[156]

The staff of social service organizations run by Liberians in the Philadelphia region, including MCFS and the Agape Center, played largely informal, ad hoc roles helping constituents with transnational family problems.[157] However, ACANA established a more formal, largely independent satellite office in Monrovia. With partners in Freetown, Sierra Leone, and Accra, Ghana, its staff helped refugees and internally displaced people with reintegration services, largely education, mental health, and access to jobs for people returning to Liberia or staying in neighboring countries. The Liberia and Sierra Leone offices also distributed computers to classrooms around the two countries and supported small business development.[158]

Some of Philadelphia's Pan-African organizations engaged in transnational economic and community development, too. The Mayor's Commission for African and Caribbean Immigrant Affairs and the African and Caribbean Business Council together organized trade missions to Africa; their members traveled to Liberia and other nations along with local politicians and officials from Philadelphia's port authority and commerce department. In collaboration with AFRICOM, they hosted trade missions of dignitaries and business leaders from Liberia and other African countries. These efforts mostly promoted import-export ventures for companies of all sizes.

Two other Pan-African organizations established by West Africans in Philadelphia grew up in the 2000s to provide training, technical assistance, and networking for Black entrepreneurs and communities that were interested in transnational development, including Liberians. A Sierra Leonean, Agatha Johnson, who founded the Afri-Caribe Micro-Enterprise Network (AMEN), and an Ivoirian, Jean Marie Kouassi, who founded Palms Solutions, had both worked for the World Bank and other development agencies. They were critical of traditional approaches to development and they sought to involve diaspora community members more meaningfully in planning and owning their work. They also recognized the imperative to address social needs that must be met for diaspora communities to engage effectively in development. AMEN remained a business support group, operating between Philadelphia, Atlanta, and West and South Africa.[159]

But Palms Solutions became a more local organization, mainly since its constituents chose to focus on local rather than transnational projects. Working with youth and teachers, Kouassi became one of the chief advocates for immigrant children in city schools.[160] In 2012, he worked with other African community leaders to start what became the Philadelphia African and Caribbean Cup of Nations for Peace. "More than a soccer tournament, it [was] a diplomatic tool used to bring our communities together to address pressing local and international issues" through "sports diplomacy," commemorating the United Nations' International Day of Peace in September. Its annual themes included US-Africa relations, fund-raising to combat the Ebola epidemic in Liberia, and public health in Philadelphia and Africa, including a drive for immigrants to get flu shots. The *Philadelphia Inquirer* called its summer school program one of the best facilitators of immigrant integration into the city's school system.[161]

In 2016, Mayor Jim Kenney adopted the tournament, turning it into the Philadelphia International Unity Cup. It lost its international diplomatic, peace, health, and educational missions but continued to exert positive influence locally. The tournament expanded to teams representing countries around the world, though anyone could join any country's team. With its final held at the region's professional soccer stadium, it generated more excitement and about as much goodwill toward city government among diverse immigrants, especially men, as the city's sanctuary policies did. All games were free for spectators, and West African teams dominated. The Liberian team lost the final 1-0 to Ivory Coast in 2016 but won the tournament the next three years, defeating Sierra Leone 3-1 in the 2017 final, Ivory Coast 4-3 in the following year's final, and a United States team 3-0 in the final in 2019.[162]

Philadelphia's diverse set of Liberian and Pan-African civil society organizations, through both their transnational and their local work, reveal the multiple meanings and dispersed geography of Liberian reconstruction. To rebuild Liberia and its neighbors required repairing families. This extended not only to what Americans considered distant and adopted family in West Africa but also to promoting peace and mutual support among the larger family of Black people and sometimes even more multicultural communities where Liberians lived in America. As scholars of West African home associations in Britain have observed, it is important not "to overstate the distinction between 'development at home' and 'welfare in the diaspora.'"[163] In Philadelphia, Liberian and Pan-African civil society tied the work of community revitalization in the United States to that of rebuilding Liberia, Nigeria, Haiti, and other parts of Africa and the Caribbean.

# Deferred Enforced Departure

Liberian and Pan-African civil society mobilized successfully to promote peace and help diverse people with myriad needs. Still, Liberia remained one of the poorest nations on earth, and Southwest Philadelphia was among the region's poorest neighborhoods. Almost one-third of all Liberians in the United States attained American citizenship by 2010.[164] Yet in other ways Liberians' place in America was still tenuous, especially for those on TPS or DED. What protections and assistance they required became increasingly contested as Liberia stabilized politically and immigration debates in the United States became further polarized with the election of Donald Trump.

In Liberia, despite substantial investment from abroad, in 2012 more than half the population lived in extreme poverty, on less than fifty cents a day, and more than 60 percent were illiterate. The UN ranked Liberia 182nd out of 187 countries on its Human Development Index. Transparency International put it near the bottom in its Global Corruption Barometer. In 2011, President Sirleaf won the Nobel Peace Prize. That year, the nation received $765 million in development aid and an estimated $523 million in remittances from the diaspora; and the United Nations spent over $500 million on a peacekeeping force of 7,500 troops that remained in the country.[165]

Critics in the development industry charged that Liberia had become dependent on foreign aid and that development agencies had drawn Liberian professionals away from government and local civil society.[166] Many young Liberian Americans in Philadelphia, like their parents, sent remittances to extended family, but they were reluctant to invest in the country's development beyond that, due to corruption and concerns that their money would not be used wisely by government or civil society. The county associations continued to organize projects, though they were still run by Reverend Jallah's generation and mostly had not yet incorporated younger Liberian Americans.[167]

In Philadelphia and other US regions, Liberians remained, on average, wealthier than African Americans. But they shared the segregation and much of the discrimination and disadvantage that Black people in general experienced in US society, including in housing and labor markets. On Woodland Avenue, ACANA developed plans in the late 2010s to build an arch and market the corridor as a district worthy of cultural tourism akin to Chinatown and Little Italy. African Americans came to embrace the food, hair-braiding, and other businesses on the avenue.[168] But it remained an open question whether more than a small number of non-Black people would consider African culture desirable to consume and Southwest Philadelphia safe or attractive to visit. Notwithstanding the remarkable accomplishments in community building of Liberians and their allies, racism and inequality remained intractable in America.

Through the administrations of Bill Clinton, George W. Bush, and Barack Obama, Liberian community leaders in Philadelphia and their allies in city council and the region's state and congressional delegations lobbied for renewing TPS and DED.[169] They mobilized support with their counterparts in Georgia, Maryland, Minnesota, New York, Ohio, and Rhode Island.[170] The number of people on DED decreased to roughly 3,600 by 2018, out of some 60,000 or more Liberians in the United States. Still, virtually every Liberian in these regions knew, and most were close to, someone with that status.[171] People on DED could work, renew their driver's licenses, and access health benefits; but they could not get student financial aid, leave the country, or know when they might be told to leave.[172]

On March 27, 2018, President Trump announced that "conditions in Liberia no longer warrant a further extension of DED," which would be terminated effective March 31, 2019.[173] This decision came shortly after Trump enraged Liberian and other communities with remarks about "shithole countries" in Africa and the Caribbean.[174] At the same time, he ended TPS for people from El Salvador, Haiti, Honduras, Nicaragua, and Sudan. Like Liberians, many of these people had been in the United States for decades.

The lack of opportunity in Liberia meant that most people who were forced to return would lose their ability to support their family in Africa and America. The few thousand people who were repatriated to Liberia when Ghana closed its refugee camps in the prior decade had struggled to survive.[175] Some Liberians in the United States still feared violence from old rivals and people who had claimed their property. "To see that Liberians in the United States have stabilized their lives—and I think that's part of the American Dream and the pursuit of happiness—and still uproot us and send us back to Liberia will force us to become refugees all over again," one DED recipient protested.[176]

The Trump administration's stance was not new. Back in 2009, the president of the Federation for American Immigration Reform, one of the chief architects of Trump's later immigration agenda, declared as Liberians' DED was up for renewal, "It is time for people to go back and rebuild their country." For Liberians to stay after their country's wars were over would make "a mockery of the concept of short-term temporary humanitarian protection." Liberians were the only group ever to receive DED, which critics cast as an overly generous concession to a group that no longer needed protection.[177]

Uncharacteristically, three days before the March 2019 deadline, Trump extended it by a year. "The overall situation in West Africa remains concerning," his executive order stated. "The reintegration of DED beneficiaries into

Liberian civil and political life will be a complex task, and an unsuccessful transition could strain United States–Liberian relations and undermine Liberia's post-civil war strides toward democracy and political stability."[178] It was unclear if this decision responded to a lawsuit on behalf of fifteen Liberians challenging the end of DED.[179]

But two weeks later, in April 2019, the Trump administration announced a plan for ICE to target people from Liberia, Sierra Leone, Nigeria, Eritrea, and Chad who had overstayed their visas. The administration threatened these countries with restrictions on future visas. Under Trump, ICE significantly expanded the deportation of Black immigrants.[180]

Then, in December 2019, senators from Rhode Island and Minnesota, who had long supported their Liberian constituents, succeeded in inserting a section for Liberian Refugee Immigration Fairness into the National Defense Authorization Act for 2020. This gave Liberians without legal status access to green cards as long as they had not committed serious crimes or, under another new Trump administration rule issued two months later, as long as they and their family members were unlikely to use public benefits.[181] As many as 10,000 Liberians without permanent status were eligible, more than the several thousand people on DED.[182] Anti-immigration advocates cried foul, arguing that this "amnesty" set a terrible precedent, violated the principles of TPS and DED, and had nothing to do with national defense.[183] Liberians, on the other hand, asked why it took decades for the United States to grant them permanent legal status. Voffee Jabateh offered a simple answer, which was echoed by many advocates: "Historically, Black lives have never mattered to America."[184]

Still, thousands of Liberians' status remained unresolved. In Trump's last year in the White House, his administration botched the processing of people's applications under the new program. A computer glitch initially rejected them all. His successor, Joe Biden, reinstated DED for Liberians on his first day in office, giving more time for people to apply for green cards.[185] Yet ICE continued to deport Black immigrants at a substantial rate during Biden's first months in office. Changing the agency's culture and operations would take more than a new president.[186]

Black immigrants' experiences as targets of a racialized, exclusionary politics overlapped in some ways with the experiences of Muslim immigrants in the United States. Many African immigrants, including some Liberians, were Muslim, as were many African Americans and other immigrants in Philadelphia. Some Black immigrants were also affected by the United States and its allies and adversaries in the War on Terror that spread around Africa and Asia in the early twenty-first century. The next chapter relates the experiences of other people who were caught in the midst of this and related wars in the Middle East.

# CHAPTER 4

# Muslim Town

## Iraqis, Syrians, and Palestinians in Arab and Muslim America

The US invasion of Iraq in 2003 "changed my life for the better," at least for a while, remarked Mohammed Al Juboori, who was sixteen at the time. "Not a lot of Iraqis actually liked Saddam [Hussein]," the dictator who had been in power for three decades, "but they couldn't discuss this because they would execute you." Old and young people alike reveled in their new freedom of speech and expression. They burned Saddam's picture, tore down his statues, and destroyed his palaces. Like many Iraqis, Mohammed initially saw the invasion in a positive light. He recognized, however, that many people in his neighborhood, in the Al-Rusafa district of central Baghdad, lost their jobs and were forced to move, particularly those affiliated with Saddam's Ba'ath Party, some of whom were murdered while the rest lived under constant threat.[1]

When the United States began bombing the city on April 3, the Al Juboori family left for Anbar Province, with thousands of other people. "Anyone who had money fled to the West," which was much safer, Mohammed recalled. This interruption notwithstanding, his parents' jobs went relatively unaffected by the invasion. His father worked as a mechanical engineer, his mother as a chemical engineer, both for the Ministry of Industry and Minerals. This was a vital institution for the oil industry, which the United States quickly revived and parceled out to ExxonMobil, British Petroleum, Royal Dutch Shell, and other American and European corporations that had been shut out of Iraq for thirty years.[2]

But then conditions deteriorated rapidly, and people's attitudes changed. US forces failed to find weapons of mass destruction, which was their pretext for invading Iraq along with the claim, also discredited, that Saddam was supporting Osama bin Laden's Al-Qaeda terrorist network.[3] In reality, terrorism in Iraq flourished only after Saddam's defeat. The United States installed a new government that, with American forces, continued to fight a fragmented set of insurgencies with various religious and political ties but similar practices of guerilla warfare. Mohammed recalled that the Iraqi army would put bombs between people's houses for storage, creating further threats to their safety.[4]

One day in 2005, as US Marines went along Mohammed's street in Baghdad, knocking on doors and searching homes for weapons, they found out that his family spoke English. They offered his father a job as an interpreter. He refused, but Mohammed took up the offer instead. He had just graduated from The Baghdad College, one of the most prestigious high schools in the Middle East, and all his coursework since primary school had been in English. He wanted to participate in changing his country.[5]

He was part of this combat unit for the next two years, officially employed by an American defense contractor. The unit lived at Camp Habbaniyah in central Iraq, a former British air force base established in the 1930s where Saddam's regime later made chemical weapons, next to a tourist village on the banks of the Euphrates River.[6] He underwent military training and received the same uniform and weapons carried by his unit mates. He felt part of a family. "You are one of us; whatever rights and responsibilities we have, you have," they told him.[7]

Mohammed loved the job because it was exciting and never routine. His favorite part was the training sessions, in which the US advisory team prepared officers of the Iraqi army to fight terrorist and insurgent groups like Al-Qaeda and the Iraqi cleric Muqtada al-Sadr's Mahdi Army. He also accompanied the Marines on raids and interpreted during interrogations. But living at the base was "constant terror." Enemies launched mortar attacks at them every day, and during his tenure he saw some fifteen or twenty comrades die right in front of him.[8]

Eventually, insurgent groups found out Mohammed was working as an interpreter for the Americans. After escalating threats to his life, and fearing reprisals against his family, he was forced to quit and flee in early 2007. He took a bus to Damascus, the capital of Syria, along with other young Iraqi men. His mother accompanied him to help get settled but she returned home two weeks later. They did not need a visa to get into Syria. Iraqis called the country "Om el Khair," or "mother of good," for its economic opportunities, and now for security, too. But Mohammed left after a year since the universities there taught in Arabic and he had grown up learning everything in English. He moved to Jordan, acquiring a student visa at the border.[9]

After a year in the capital Amman studying civil engineering, he went to the US embassy and applied for a Special Immigrant Visa (SIV). This miscellaneous category consisted of immigrants with special relationships to the United States, who usually required special attention to their protection. Eligible categories included religious workers, employees of the North Atlantic Treaty Organization (NATO) and other international organizations, broadcasters, physicians doing work of national interest, and members of the armed forces. The National Defense Authorization Act of 2006 declared that Afghan and Iraqi translators who served the US military were entitled to SIVs, and the 2008 act added other Iraqis who worked for the US government. Special immigrants were permitted to bring immediate family—spouses and children under age twenty-one. State Department employees at the embassy processed Mohammed's visa application in 2010. He had kept in touch with a few officers and generals, who wrote letters of support. It would take until 2014 to be approved.[10]

He stayed in Jordan until 2011 and then returned to Baghdad, where he married a young Iraqi woman who was also from a middle-class family. They later had a baby daughter. Meanwhile, Mohammed continued his studies, pursuing an expedited associate's degree in aviation offered through Serco, an American company. He got a job with a British construction company that built Baghdad's new UK embassy.[11] Like other government, military, and corporate compounds, it was in the city's heavily fortified area known as the Green Zone. Then he went to work at Baghdad International Airport as an air traffic controller. Though his employer was a local authority, Mohammed was responsible for controlling air traffic for the US Navy as well as US Army helicopters. Insurgents found out about this work, too, and made further threats on his life. "I was threatened many times," he said. "I couldn't stay there because it was dangerous for me and my family."[12]

This entire time, Mohammed, his wife, and their daughter were confined to the Green Zone, where they lived, or the heavily guarded highway to the airport, where he worked. "People who used to work for the US administration were constantly receiving threats from political or religious groups and radical terrorist organizations who viewed them as traitors," he remembered. "I left and they burned my house down" a few years later.[13] On December 3, 2014, Mohammed, his wife, and their one-year-old daughter exited the Green

Zone, traveling the highway to the airport with their visas approved and tickets to New York. Touching down at JFK Airport, he felt "excited and grateful" for having left the dangers of Iraq.[14]

Mohammed was a special kind of immigrant in a few ways yet typical in others. Iraqis who fled to neighboring countries generally lived in cities, as he did, not in refugee camps.[15] By 2009, one in every six Iraqis had been displaced, including some 2.7 million in different parts of the country and over 2 million who fled across borders, mostly to Syria and Jordan.[16] Like Mohammed, most Iraqis who made it to the United States came from middle- and upper-class backgrounds, often with higher education, commonly from Baghdad or other major cities, and usually via Syria, whose civil war displaced many of them again.

The Al Juboori family came at the height of Iraqi resettlement in the United States. Iraqis made up more than one-quarter of all refugees to the country in 2013 and 2014, amounting to almost 20,000 in each of these years.[17] Only seventy-seven interpreters came with Special Immigrant Visas from Iraq and Afghanistan combined in these two years, though, along with 211 members of their families. More came through the SIV program for other US government employees. Overall, between 2007 and 2017, the United States resettled over 8,500 Iraqis with SIVs, with some 13,500 family members, along with roughly 143,000 refugees from Iraq.[18] This made special immigrants and their families about 13 percent of all Iraqis resettled in the United States during this period. Like refugees, they received resettlement services from the Volags.

The United States considered special immigrants from Iraq and Afghanistan a critical part of the War on Terror. At the outset, this was the nation's international response to Al-Qaeda's attacks on September 11, 2001, which killed close to three thousand people in New York and Washington. This war, explained vice president Dick Cheney, "may never end. At least, not in our lifetimes."[19] Its geography was fluid, too, extending wherever the United States identified an Islamic jihadist threat. Much of that threat grew and evolved in response to the United States' own actions in the Middle East.

The Iraq War that began in 2003 morphed into a broader conflict that involved multiple local factions and nations within and outside the region. The United States ceded increasing power in Iraq to postwar Prime Minister Iyad Allawi, a Shiite Muslim whom the CIA had supported in a coup attempt in the 1990s.[20] Al-Qaeda in Iraq and its leader, Abu al-Zarkawi, took advantage of disaffection among Sunni Muslims who had lost the favored status they enjoyed under Saddam, and recruited a growing army of followers. After American special forces killed Osama bin Laden in 2011, the group split with Al-Qaeda in 2014 and renamed itself the Islamic State of Iraq and the Levant.

Its leaders took a more violent path, particularly against Muslims who were not Sunnis, broadcasting their beheadings to the world through online video.[21] In 2014, Islamic State forces swept across Syria and Iraq. Its leaders declared this territory a new caliphate, meaning that it was under Islamic rule. By the time Mohammed Al Juboori got to the United States in December, the Islamic State had conquered roughly one-third of each country, amounting to an area as large as Belgium or Jordan.[22]

The fight against Islamic State drew the United States formally into the civil war in Syria in 2014. This war began in 2011, after President Bashar al-Assad violently suppressed protests pushing for democracy in the Arab Spring of that year, which toppled authoritarian regimes in Tunisia, Egypt, Libya, and Yemen. The war quickly spread into a conflict in which Assad's forces fought Islamic State and other jihadists as well as moderate rebel groups, including the Kurds. The United States trained, armed, and provided operational support to some of these latter groups.[23] Assad earned international condemnation for bombing civilian neighborhoods in Aleppo and other cities, sometimes with chemical weapons.

Between 2011 and 2019, of a prewar population around 22 million, 6.6 million Syrians fled the country and another 6.1 million were internally displaced to other parts of Syria. Some 3.5 million Syrians stayed in Turkey, and most of the rest ended up in Lebanon, Jordan, Germany, Iraq, Egypt, and Sweden.[24] Many people tried to reach Western Europe, taking treacherous journeys across the Aegean Sea on small boats to Greece, then walking and riding trains and buses through an increasingly militarized and anti-immigrant set of Eastern European nations, if they got that far. The limited number of refugee slots for them in America and the oceans between them presented greater barriers. The United States resettled just over 16,000 Syrians by the end of 2016.[25]

Iraqis and Syrians were part of a larger refugee crisis arising from the War on Terror, and in a deeper historical context they were part of a series of interrelated refugee crises in the Middle East. These stemmed from long-standing US intervention together with displacement at the hands of Arab dictatorships, revolutions, insurgencies, fanatical terrorists, and Israel. Much of this history of conflict centered on oil and on Israel and the Palestinians, which were the central political flashpoints in the region. The Anglo-American Petroleum Agreement of 1944 determined, as President Franklin D. Roosevelt told the Brits, that "Persian oil . . . is yours. We share the oil of Iraq and Kuwait. As for Saudi Arabian oil, it's ours."[26] The United States supported Israel since its founding in 1948, sending more military aid to Israel than to any other country and helping to underwrite a half-dozen major Arab-Israeli military conflicts. By 2015 over five million Palestinians were registered as refugees with the United Nations; they were dispersed mainly in the occupied territories of Gaza and the West Bank and in Jordan, Lebanon, and Syria.[27]

US relations with Iraq and Syria historically fluctuated between extremes, from military support to attempted coups and wars. Arab-Israeli wars and other events severed US diplomatic ties with Iraq and Syria periodically across the decades since World War II. Iraq allied itself with the Soviets through the 1970s, but the Islamic Revolution in Iran and the Soviet invasion of Afghanistan, both in 1979, brought the United States closer to Saddam, who claimed the presidency that year. The United States supported Iraq in its war against Iran from 1980 to 1988, selling Saddam millions of dollars of "dual-use technologies" that could be used to make chemical and biological weapons, some of which he used against the Kurds.[28]

Despite Syria's state sponsorship of Palestinian resistance groups that the United States considered terrorists, American authorities collaborated closely with the nation's leaders, sometimes against Iraq.[29] In 1990, under President Hafez al-Assad, Syria joined the US-led military coalition in the Gulf War, which quickly beat back Saddam's forces after Iraq invaded Kuwait. After September 11, 2001, his son and successor, Bashar al-Assad, partnered with the United States in the War on Terror. For a short time, Syria became one of the main destinations for the US military and CIA to send captives, mostly from the US-led war in Afghanistan, for interrogation and torture.[30] But Syria opposed the 2003 invasion of Iraq and relations worsened. In 2004, President George W. Bush authorized covert CIA and military operations against Al-Qaeda within Syrian territory, a decade before its Iraqi affiliate became the Islamic State and the United States entered the Syrian civil war.[31]

Some events in this dizzying history of geopolitical relations and conflicts did more than others to destabilize Middle Eastern societies and displace people. Mohammed Al Juboori was just three years old during the Gulf War in 1990. All he remembered was "hearing the sirens" of air raid warnings in Baghdad. Yet US forces bombed only a few targets in the city and declined to occupy the country and remove Saddam. Mohammed's family continued to live comfortably, unaffected by that war, even as the conflict produced three million refugees, including Kurds and 300,000 Palestinians who were resettled from Iraq to Jordan.[32]

Some of Mohammed's family left the country in the 1990s. His uncle went to Philadelphia to study electrical engineering at the University of Pennsylvania.[33] He was part of a longer history of middle-class Iraqis, Syrians, Palestinians, and other Arabs moving to the United States for education, work, and to find greater safety and stability since the founding of Israel in 1948 and revolutions in Egypt and Iraq in the 1950s. While most were not officially refugees, they often had similar reasons for leaving.[34] The wider bombing of Baghdad in 2003 and the violence thereafter displaced more Iraqis as refugees, especially middle-class city residents like the Al Jubooris.

With a Special Immigrant Visa, Mohammed had greater agency than most refugees in choosing where to be resettled. He selected Philadelphia, where the father of a friend had settled after fleeing Iraq several decades earlier. Like other special immigrants, the family received resettlement services from the Hebrew Immigrant Aid Society—Pennsylvania (HIAS-PA), but his friend's father was his official sponsor. He picked the family up at JFK Airport, found them a house to rent in a growing Middle Eastern community in Northeast Philadelphia, and "helped me get on my feet." Having grown up speaking English and having "heard so much about life in the United States" from his comrades in the Marines, he "felt the transition was easy." He was already "familiar with the society and the system."[35]

## Arab America

The history of Middle Eastern migration to the United States has been plagued by a sharp disconnect between political rhetoric and the reality of who Arab immigrants and refugees are. Most are Muslim but many are Christian, even if many Americans mistakenly believe that all Arabs are Muslim. Most are not special immigrants, who took risks and made sacrifices for the United States that most Americans would never sign up for. But most are like Mohammed Al Juboori in many other ways. They are fleeing countries destabilized by wars and terrorism, often fueled by US intervention. They are generally middle-class people with high rates of education, entrepreneurship, and involvement in community organizations, who value America's diversity and social freedoms— like Mohammed, people who are well positioned to succeed in US social and economic systems and institutions. Like Arabs in the Middle East, who typically dislike their despotic leaders, they overwhelmingly embrace democracy.[36]

This, of course, all contradicts the charges of Islamophobic Americans that Arab and Muslim immigrants and refugees pose a violent fundamentalist threat and thus should have no place in US society. To them, "Arab America" is a contradiction in terms.[37] "People think refugees are terrorists," observed a therapist working with Iraqis and Syrians in Philadelphia in 2015. But actually, "They are escaping terrorism."[38]

Since the vast majority of immigrants and refugees from the Middle East have legal status in the United States, they have little connection to the narrower meanings of sanctuary. Yet so many are seeking sanctuary in its broader senses, especially protections from terrorism and instability, which have often resulted from US actions in their homelands. In the twenty-first-century United States, Arabs and Muslims were increasingly targets of hate, discrimination, and violence. Many valued Philadelphia and other cities' sanctuary policies as gestures of inclusion and protection from Islamophobia. Arab and Muslim civil society, too, focused largely on promoting safety and providing support, which they sometimes cast explicitly as "sanctuary," in the face of these threats.

In Mohammed's first year in the country, a debate erupted over whether the United States should continue to admit refugees from Syria and, ultimately, any Muslims. After terrorist attacks on civilians in Paris by young men tied to the Islamic State in November 2015, the governors of twenty-four states, from Alabama to Massachusetts to Wisconsin, issued executive orders or requests to the State Department seeking to prevent the resettlement of Syrians in their states. The risk of resettling Islamic State sympathizers who might commit acts of terrorism in the United States was too great, they argued. The governors of twenty-one other states, including Pennsylvania, declared support for Syrians' resettlement, acknowledging that the UN and the State Department thoroughly vetted people before accepting them as refugees.[39] In December, presidential candidate Donald Trump weighed in, calling for a "total and complete shutdown" of US borders to Muslims, which he would go on to attempt in one of his earliest acts as president thirteen months later.[40]

These were only the latest chapters in Americans' long-standing disputes over whether Arabs and Muslims from the Middle East belonged in the United States, and in the case of refugees, whether they deserved protection and assistance. Most early Arab immigrants were Christians who came from the area of Lebanon and Syria, known as the Levant, in the late nineteenth century. Many had to fight for citizenship in the courts, including to debunk the assumption that all Arabs were Muslims. Under the Naturalization Act of 1790, which was in force until 1952, only immigrants who were considered white could gain US citizenship. American courts, politicians, and social scientists consistently classified Muslims as nonwhite. Christians from the Levant convinced judges in the Jim Crow South that they were white since they were from the land of Jesus and southern whites refused to believe that he had been anything but white.[41] But popular and political discourse cast Islam as un-American, increasingly since the 1980s after Palestinian airplane hijackings, and especially after terrorist attacks in the United States and Europe in the twenty-first century.[42] Special immigrants like Mohammed have occupied a different, somewhat more sympathetic place in American immigration debates compared to other refugees from the Middle East and Muslim-majority countries in Africa and Asia. Yet they have been caught up in some of the same opposition to Muslims, especially Arabs, that grew since 9/11.

The seven countries listed in President Trump's initial "Muslim ban" in January 2017 were Iran, Iraq, Libya, Somalia, Sudan, Syria, and Yemen. He ordered a ninety-day halt to immigration or travelers from these countries and an indefinite ban on Syrian refugees. In March, after lobbying from the Iraqi government and American intelligence officials, the second version of this order dropped Iraq from the list. "Iraq is an important ally in the fight to defeat" Islamic State, explained Trump's first secretary of state, former ExxonMobil chief Rex Tillerson, "with their brave soldiers fighting in close coordination with America's men and women in uniform."[43] However, in practice, the Trump administration effectively ended resettlement from Iraq as well as other Muslim countries, including SIVs.[44]

Although refugees who had already been resettled from Syria and Iraq had permanent residency and some had become citizens, some Americans contested their presence in the country in other ways. Some opposed the establishment of mosques in neighborhoods from California and Tennessee to New York City and suburban Philadelphia. More often, Iraqis, Syrians, and other newcomers from the Middle East, North Africa, and the wider Muslim world found comparatively welcoming, peaceful receiving communities in US cities. Still, Islamophobia remained constantly present at the local, national, and international levels, even if it manifested most publicly and violently in particular moments. This forced Arabs to constantly "counter the narrative by telling their story," as Nora Elmarzouky, an Egyptian American who worked with refugees in Philadelphia, put it.[45]

Iraqi and Syrian refugees differed significantly from one another in their backgrounds and their experiences of resettlement. Iraqis more often enjoyed help from family and friends who were already settled in the United States. Coming mainly from middle-class, urban backgrounds, some would soon return or travel back and forth to the Middle East for business. Departing somewhat from the predominant pattern of Arabs in the United States, Syrians came from more mixed class and geographic backgrounds, including a large proportion of poor and rural people from small, agricultural villages. As Nasr Saradar, a Syrian refugee in Philadelphia, explained in 2019, "Baghdad fell, so all the rich moved out. However, Damascus never fell and that is where all the merchants, upper-class and capital are in Syria. They remain there until today."[46]

Syrians from rural villages needed more help from the resettlement agencies and other civil society organizations. Most lacked family or community ties in America, and the few middle-class Syrians who had settled in prior decades in the Philadelphia suburbs did little to help them, unlike Syrians in other parts of the United States. Some community leaders speculated that this may have been due to class distinctions or old-timers' political allegiance to the Assad regime.[47] Hence Syrian refugees' ties with other Arabs and Muslims proved critical for their support.

In Philadelphia and other cities, immigrants and refugees from the Middle East formed organizations and networks of mutual support that were largely Pan-Arab, Muslim, or interfaith. In this they resembled African immigrants, and their social networks overlapped with Africans, African Americans, and South Asians, especially in mosques (*masjids* in Arabic), which commonly included community centers and schools and almost all held community gatherings. This, together with the diverse populations of the neighborhoods they inhabited, brought many Arab immigrants and their children into frequent contact with Black Americans and other Black and brown immigrants, even as Arabs identified variously as white or as people of color.

Much of the social politics that drove Arab immigrants to multicultural organizations came from a Pan-Arab worldview adopted widely among the middle classes of the Middle East decades ago. It also grew from a tradition in Islam of valuing diversity and promoting fellowship among cultures. Arabs in Philadelphia and the United States were diverse in terms of nationality and somewhat diverse in class and religion. But like their relatives in the Middle East and North Africa, to a great extent they recognized their experiences of displacement and of confronting discrimination as a shared history.[48]

The arrival of Iraqis and especially Syrians in the twenty-first century inspired Arabs in Philadelphia to mobilize support in ways that were not entirely new. The city was already home to a small Palestinian community, which collaborated with the resettlement agencies to orient and assist newcomers. Old and new masjids, cultural organizations, and mostly volunteer-led support networks helped Syrians, Iraqis, and other new immigrants from the Middle East navigate the housing and labor markets, as well as social and cultural challenges of settlement. Transnational civil society remained limited, even if some Arab immigrants and refugees traveled back and forth regularly, following seasonal work patterns or for businesses they maintained in Egypt or Jordan, and many sent remittances to family in the Middle East.

Repeating an established pattern of refugee community members who were employed in the resettlement system, Mohammed Al Juboori first volunteered and then got a job with the Jewish Employment and Vocational Service (JEVS), aiding fellow Arabs and other newcomers in gaining employment. Other organizations helped refugees from the Middle East deal with trauma from wars and displacement as well as new violence in the city and its schools. While some of this was familiar to other refugee communities, for Arabs and other Muslim immigrants, much of the violence and threats they faced took the particular form of Islamophobia. This, in turn, shaped the responses of civil society, including interfaith organizing and collaboration with law enforcement, as well as the everyday practices of newcomer and receiving communities working to live together in peace.

## Mecca of the West

Very few people from Iraq or Syria settled in Philadelphia before the end of the twentieth century, but the city had been home to Arabs for over a century and to Muslims for even longer. This mattered profoundly for twenty-first-century refugees from the Middle East. The first Muslims in America were slaves brought from Africa in the 1600s, and some Black people in colonial-era Philadelphia followed Islam. The Centennial Exposition of 1876 in the city attracted over 1,600 Arab traders. Some stayed, forming a Lebanese Christian community in South Philadelphia.[49]

In the twentieth century, thousands of African Americans in the city converted to various sects of Islam. Many joined the Nation of Islam in the 1950s and 1960s but most converted to Sunni Islam in the late 1960s and 1970s. With increased immigration from Africa, South Asia, and the Middle East in subsequent decades, by the early twenty-first century the Philadelphia region had the second-highest concentration of Muslims in America, behind only metropolitan Detroit.[50] In the twenty-first century, it had a Muslim police commissioner, city council member, and state senator.[51] In 2010, a *Philadelphia Daily News* columnist dubbed the city "Muslim Town."[52] Some Muslims in the region called it "the Mecca of the West."[53]

The largest Arab group among Philadelphia's diverse Muslims, the Palestinian community was a crucial receiving community for twenty-first-century refugees from the Middle East. Perhaps a few thousand Palestinians lived in the region by the mid-2000s. They are difficult to count since the US Census has historically not tracked them because they lack a nation of their own. The largest number of families in Philadelphia fled three villages near Hebron in the West Bank during the Yom Kippur War in 1973, which was the last full-scale Arab-Israeli war.[54] Others came as early as 1908 and more arrived after the establishment of Israel in 1948, as economic opportunities and social freedoms diminished in the occupied territories. Some came through the diversity visa lottery, some on student visas. Some came via South America, usually legally, and lived in New York and northern New Jersey before settling in Philadelphia. Some married American women, and many people later sponsored their relatives to migrate.[55]

Initially concentrated in the Lower North Philadelphia neighborhood of South Kensington, in the 1980s Palestinians began buying homes in the neighborhoods of Feltonville and Olney, three or four miles away in Upper North Philadelphia. These were still working-class row house neighborhoods, but had less industry, poverty, and violence than Kensington. In 1993, the Jalil family were the first Palestinians to purchase a house on Castor Avenue in Lower Northeast Philadelphia. Others soon followed, living in the neighborhoods of Oxford Circle, Rhawnhurst, and Lawncrest. The area's "large houses were necessary," said Aziz Jalil, because Palestinians generally lived with their extended families.[56]

Many of the Palestinian men who initially came alone had been farmers or construction laborers, but many people who came in the 1970s were college educated, often in engineering. Like other immigrants' degrees earned overseas, their professional credentials did not transfer. So, they opened small businesses, including corner stores, gas stations, food trucks, pharmacies, and the small chain of Cousin's Markets, the only supermarkets left in Eastern North Philadelphia by the 1990s. Palestinians came to own most of the ice cream trucks that fanned out across city and suburban neighborhoods in the summer. Some also bought, fixed up, and rented or resold homes in South Kensington, Feltonville, and neighborhoods in the Northeast, often renting them to more recently arrived Arab immigrants.[57]

In the late 1980s, a group of Palestinians, Egyptians, and Algerians formed the Al-Aqsa Islamic Society. They opened a mosque in an abandoned warehouse in South Kensington in 1992, where they later established a school, grocery store, emergency food pantry, and in 1997 the Arab American Development Corporation (AADC). By the 2000s, most of the students in Al-Aqsa's kindergarten-through–eighth grade school were African Americans, whose parents were looking to avoid the violence in the public schools and to expose their children to Islamic culture.[58] In 2000, a group of Palestinians formed the Masjid Al-Hidaya. They moved the mosque to a new building near Feltonville in 2007, where they started a school.[59] These businesses and institutions would become important for other immigrants and refugees from the Middle East, especially Syrians.

Iraqis and Syrians experienced a resettlement system that continued to promote self-sufficiency in mostly the ways it had since the 1980s, and many middle-class refugees achieved it reasonably quickly. Mohammed Al Juboori's case worker from HIAS-PA took him to the welfare office on his first full day in America. "The welfare office referred me to JEVS," he reminisced. He had hoped to work in air traffic control, but as with other refugees, the resettlement system expected him to take the first job he was offered. His counselor at the JEVS Center for New Americans helped him land a position as a sales associate at Walmart making eight dollars an hour, and since he was not content with the job, then as a machine operator at Weber Packaging. There he earned more money but faced "some racism and discrimination" from other employees. He also worked at a hotel, bouncing around between jobs.[60]

Though resettled officially by HIAS-PA, he "only used their services for one month," instead of the customary three. He benefited from the help of his friend's father, his uncle, and extended family in the country. Mohammed's exceptional language skills and deep knowledge about and experiences with Americans helped him adjust more quickly than other Iraqis to what he called "the hyper-capitalist economy" of the United States. After he volunteered at JEVS teaching English to other Arabic speakers, the agency hired him as an employment counselor, helping people from Syria, Afghanistan, Iraq, Egypt, Morocco, Congo, Ukraine, and other parts of the world to navigate the region's job market. He informally helped some of his Palestinian friends find jobs, too. After three years at JEVS, he took on a similar position at the Welcoming Center for New Pennsylvanians as a second job and at the same time enrolled at Community College of Philadelphia to study biology.[61] After earning his associate's degree with high honors, he enrolled for a bachelor's degree in biology at LaSalle University in the city and began studying for the test to attend medical school thereafter.[62]

"I love to help people," said Mohammed. "It's my job to help develop them so they can become contributing members of the community. I have countless success stories" of refugees getting jobs, better housing, and stabilizing their lives.[63] Pennsylvania Governor Tom Wolf recognized him in a set of "refugee success stories" for his work at JEVS and contributions to local communities.[64] Life was "pretty good" in the United States for Mohammed, he reflected, as he had "adjusted very well," which put him in a good position to help others.[65]

Like Mohammed, many of the roughly 1,150 Iraqis who were resettled in Philadelphia between 2002 and 2016 used resettlement services less than other refugees.[66] They did not need much "other than the basic services," such as being connected with welfare and cultural orientation classes, said a caseworker from HIAS-PA. At first, resettlement agencies struggled to find Iraqis who had lived in the region since the 1990s who were willing to help refugees in the 2000s, as some in the earlier generation had bravely spoken out against Saddam and did not wish to associate with these newcomers who had not. But many

Iraqis found ample support among relatives and friends who were already settled.[67]

The reticence of some Iraqis to accept much help from resettlement and other organizations also stemmed from a lack of trust in American institutions, which resulted largely from their experiences after the US invasion of their country. Unlike Mohammed Al Juboori and some other SIV holders, many Iraqis felt less grateful to the United States since the 2003 invasion had destroyed their livelihoods as well as their homes. For this, they believed, the United States owed them a better life than the resettlement and welfare systems provided, including the low-wage jobs available to them. For some, this contributed to social isolation and slow progress in finding stable work.[68]

In their expectations of employment, noted the case worker from HIAS-PA, "some Iraqis ask for a lot," making it difficult to "wean them off of welfare." Unlike Mohammed, many resisted working near the bottom of the US labor market, refusing to take blue-collar jobs that they considered beneath them. One of their greatest hurdles to overcome was pride. Some were used to being the boss in their own business, and many struggled to adjust in entry-level positions. Resettlement agency staff found it tough to get Iraqis to understand that their degrees did not transfer to America.[69] In this, they resembled refugees from the former Soviet Union, who were likewise "more educated and more demanding," as one HIAS-PA employee noted. Both groups also mainly lived in Northeast Philadelphia. When the agency organized a dinner to promote intergroup understanding among them, which was attended by Mohammed and others from Iraq and Russia who had been professional engineers, one of the Russians announced to the Iraqis, "You are a lot like us!"[70]

Among Iraqi women, more than one resettlement worker repeated, it was difficult for "people who were used to having maids to work as maids" or in other entry-level jobs. Moreover, some husbands did not want their wives to work. Tensions arose in these families, as many Iraqi women wanted to work. Some were enthusiastic to exercise the freedoms available in the United States and its labor market, compared to more restricted opportunities for women in much of the Middle East.[71]

Syrian refugees had different relationships with the United States and its resettlement system. The much smaller number of Syrians who were resettled in Philadelphia—fewer than 300 combined in the peak years of 2015 and 2016—were more grateful, warmer, and friendlier in their interactions with resettlement case workers. They had usually suffered more, came more often from poorer and rural backgrounds, lacked established family in the United States, and needed more assistance, including urgent medical care for children in many families. Crucially, they did not have as many negative memories associated with the United States and its military as did Iraqi refugees. Both groups, however, remained especially sensitive to issues of safety on the streets and in their homes.[72]

Iraqis and Syrians also found essentially the same job opportunities in Philadelphia, even if their educational, work, and class backgrounds and attitudes differed. The three months of resettlement support remained insufficient for training that could lead to more meaningful jobs.[73] For Iraqis, and especially Syrians who lacked family support, minimum wage or ten dollars per hour was not enough to cover rent, utilities, and other expenses, including their loans for travel to the United States, which like other refugees they had to repay to the International Organization for Migration. Thus, many initially preferred to remain on welfare, even if that was insufficient, too.[74]

Iraqis and Syrians found jobs mostly in packing plants, retail, restaurants, bakeries, housekeeping, and often at hotels or as security guards. Most of these jobs were in Philadelphia, with some in New Jersey, but virtually all required a forty-five-minute commute or more, as the neighborhoods of Northeast Philadelphia where the agencies resettled most of them were distant from major centers of employment. Like Mohammed in his first years in the region, most of them switched jobs often, looking for something better. Some with advanced degrees found office jobs, and some dentists worked to gain US credentials through the University of Pennsylvania's Dental School. Syrians from rural backgrounds had the toughest time getting stable work, as many were unfamiliar with the occupations and expectations of an urban labor market.[75] Many "suffered in silence in whatever minimum wage job until they found a stepping stool," said Sister Dana Mohamed, an Arab American psychologist.[76]

As Mohammed Al Juboori found in his factory job, discrimination also impacted Arabs' experiences in the labor market, so unlike him, many Iraqis and an even larger proportion of Syrians worked for Arab-owned businesses. Resettlement caseworkers reported that numerous white business owners whom they approached refused to employ Arabs. "I am not going to hire terrorists," some said.[77] Instead, Arab business owners and community organizations worked with the resettlement agencies and JEVS to help Iraqis and Syrians access jobs. The AADC played a central role connecting refugees to its large network of Arab small business owners, including Cousin's Markets and Jerusalem Furniture, as well as restaurants, pizza shops, and cell phone stores. The organization especially helped people for whom the resettlement agencies' employment teams failed to secure jobs.[78]

This gave Iraqi, and particularly Syrian, refugees a "cushion" and a "stepping-stone," as the AADC's associate director, Amnah Ahmad, put it. Working in an Arabic-speaking environment while taking English classes allowed them to build skills and experience while adjusting to their new home.[79] The network of Arab–owned businesses, mosques, and community organizations helped refugees understand the structures and expectations of the US labor market. Once they realized how difficult it was to get and keep a job, Syrians and Iraqis became more invested in getting integrated, said Nasr Saradar, who volunteered with Nationalities Service Center and then landed a job in its employment program helping other refugees. He was a linguist and had been a teacher in Syria, where he also had experience as an employment specialist.[80]

After working various entry-level jobs in their first years in Philadelphia, some Iraqis and many Syrians ended up driving for the ride-sharing company Uber. Like many immigrants before them who drove taxi cabs, they found this more rewarding work than most positions available to them, but safer and more stable than driving cabs. It brought them more income and the opportunity to become self-sufficient "on their own terms," without having to speak much English, related Aziz Jalil.[81] Those who were accustomed to running their own small businesses in the Middle East especially liked feeling that they were "their own boss" again, noted Saradar.[82] Some drove for Uber as a second job and worked in restaurants in the evening. Most leased or rented cars, starting their routes in Northeast Philadelphia but ending up downtown where ride-sharing services were in higher demand.[83]

The resettlement agencies chose Lower Northeast Philadelphia as the main area to house Iraqis and Syrians because of the preexisting Arab community, with its masjids and halal (Muslim kosher) food stores, and for its single-family homes and sidewalks, where elders could get around easily. They also placed Afghans in the neighborhood, as some people from Afghanistan who were resettled in the 1980s lived there. Some who owned franchises of the Crown Fried Chicken restaurant chain employed new refugees. The area's Palestinian community enabled Philadelphia to become one of few cities in the nation that resettled Palestinians from Iraq. Leaders of Al-Aqsa, the AADC, and others from the community wrote letters of support to the State Department for local resettlement agencies to receive them. Some Palestinian landlords rented to new Arab refugees, though they could not accommodate the majority.[84]

The agencies arranged housing in West Philadelphia for a small number of Syrians who were LGBTQ. They did not want these people and their families to be close to the Arab community of the Northeast due to the stigma they would likely experience. West Philadelphia was culturally diverse like the Northeast but generally more socially accepting, with many openly LGBTQ residents.[85]

In the Northeast, resettlement agency staff and Arab American advocates alike described much of the housing where Syrians and Iraqis first lived as "crappy." Some refugees, particularly from rural areas, were unaccustomed to attached homes or apartments and found them uncomfortable. Unlike in South Philadelphia, the Volags lacked a strong network of landlords in the area. One of the greatest challenges, as usual in refugee housing, was that many landlords refused to rent to people with no credit score or stable income, something the Palestinian landlords were willing to overlook. Other landlords in the area took advantage of refugee tenants, charging them illegal advance payments or failing to fix broken appliances, leaks, or pest control problems because they knew that they did not understand their rights as tenants and would not advocate for themselves.[86] The housing experiences of Iraqis and Syrians thus initially resembled those of many other refugees. However, like other Muslims in Philadelphia, they experienced greater discrimination from landlords who were unwilling to rent to them because of their faith.[87]

Still, people with family connections and middle-class backgrounds often improved their housing situations quickly. Some bought houses within just a couple of years and some moved to the suburbs. After a little more than four years in the city, Mohammed Al Juboori began looking for a house "somewhere more suburban." He sought out the townships just beyond Northeast Philadelphia, where Palestinians and other Arabs had moved, continuing their outward and upward housing trajectories characteristic of Americans at large. He ultimately settled in the Far Northeast, in a neighborhood of older Eastern European immigrants and longer-established Americans of European descent.[88]

Most Iraqis and Syrians remained in Lower Northeast Philadelphia, which like Upper Darby became what sociologists in the twenty-first century dubbed a "global neighborhood." As in other such neighborhoods, Asians and Latin Americans moved in first, followed by African Americans and African and Caribbean immigrants, as whites moved out to the suburbs. This produced a new form of diversity but ultimately reproduced Black-white segregation.[89] In the 1980s and 1990s, Cambodians, Vietnamese, Koreans, Colombians, and Puerto Ricans settled in Lower Northeast and adjacent Upper North Philadelphia neighborhoods. In the 1990s, the total population of the Lower Northeast grew by 15 percent; the proportion of whites dropped from more than half to just over one-quarter and the Black population grew 70 percent, to almost the size of the white population. In the 2000s, Haitians, Dominicans, Central Americans, Mexicans, Brazilians, Middle Easterners, and North and Sub-Saharan Africans further diversified the population. This rapid demographic change moved the color line further up into the Northeast, where the whiteness of its upper neighborhoods had been reinforced by Eastern European immigration and resettlement in the 1980s and 1990s (see figure 4.1).[90]

The politics of race and immigration in Northeast Philadelphia shared broad similarities with those of other white working-class neighborhoods in US cities and suburbs. When Philadelphia elected its first Black mayor in 1983, descendants of Irish, Italian, and other European immigrants launched a movement for the Northeast to secede from the city. These sentiments persisted in hostility toward nonwhite newcomers and affordable housing vouchers. "There exist pockets where people are very closed-minded and not very welcoming" in Philadelphia, acknowledged one Arab community leader, including a "lot of blatant racism" in the Northeast.[91]

However, compared to their Black and Latin American neighbors, through the 2000s Arabs drew relatively little attention from longer-tenured residents except other Arabs.[92] By the 2010s, when Syrians were resettled, they reported few issues with neighbors, getting along "just fine" in the Northeast, according to Saradar and other Arab staff of community organizations.[93] Likewise, Mohammed Al Juboori enjoyed good relations with his neighbors.[94]

Mohammed liked Philadelphia from the start because of its diversity, a sentiment echoed by many Arab immigrants and refugees who arrived in the twenty-first century.[95] Beyond Islam's teachings to value diversity, such feelings were often a reaction to the ethnic and racial diversity and relative peace they experienced in Northeast, West, and South Philadelphia and in other neighborhoods they frequented. Arab newcomers also expressed an appreciation that Philadelphia was a sanctuary city with welcoming policies, including the Mayor's Cup soccer tournament. Many cited the diversity of native and foreign-born Muslims in the city and the accommodation of halal diets, including the fact that national chain supermarkets in the Lower Northeast began selling halal meat and poultry. They also recognized the importance of the Arab communities that came before them and the support that newcomers received from the organizations they had built.[96]

The place where Arab immigrants, refugees, and particularly their children faced greatest hostility was in school. Iraqi and Syrian students were often bullied for not speaking English. Usually this took the form of verbal threats and taunting, being called "terrorists" or told to go back to their countries. In a few cases, high schoolers were beaten up or girls' hijabs were ripped off their heads.[97]

Like other refugees, including Southeast Asians and Liberians, they experienced the multiple traumas of recovering from their experiences of war and

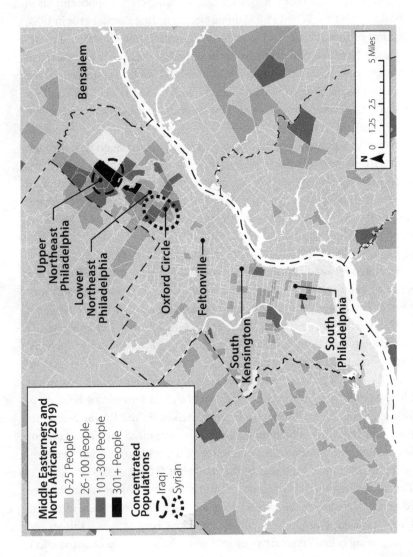

**Figure 4.1.** Map of Middle Eastern and North African settlement in Philadelphia and its suburbs in 2019. (Source: American Community Survey; map by Danielle Dong.)

terror in the Middle East and of disorientation and alienation while trying to adjust to life in the United States. In another repeated pattern, their parents often struggled to address these issues. Their fathers typically worked and few of their mothers could drive, making it difficult to monitor their children outside the home. Language barriers also limited parents' ability to engage with teachers and school administrators. And, again like some other newcomers, Arabs had to adjust to cultural expectations and laws about the verbal and physical treatment of children in the United States, particularly after neighbors or school staff leveled allegations of child abuse against some families.[98]

The city was not devoid of the Islamophobia and violence toward Arabs that grew in twenty-first-century America. Yet Muslims, Arabs, and others generally considered it far more welcoming than most of the country. The 2010 article in which the *Daily News* columnist dubbed Philadelphia "Muslim Town" detailed the fact that Muslims in the city experienced less Islamophobia than in other parts of the United States.[99] However, in 2015 incidents of violence increased after the Islamic State–affiliated attacks in Paris, debates raged over receiving Syrian refugees, and Donald Trump called for a ban on Muslim immigrants. In downtown Philadelphia, a group of young whites beat a Moroccan man after he addressed them with a friendly greeting in Arabic. A few blocks away, a white man outside a hamburger joint screamed at a Muslim woman to remove her head scarf until other restaurant-goers convinced him to leave. In December, someone tossed the severed head of a pig on the doorstep of the Al-Aqsa mosque.[100]

The city gained national attention the following month when an African American man claiming sympathy with the Islamic State fired shots at a police officer in West Philadelphia. Anti-Muslim politicians and pundits around the country responded with warnings about the threats of radical Islam and immigration. Two weeks later, Philadelphia City Council members introduced a measure for municipal government and public schools to recognize two major Muslim holidays, Eid al-Fitr and Eid al-Adha.[101]

When a *Washington Post* reporter visited the city the next summer, she found that 2017 was the fifth year in a row in which City Hall hosted a dinner breaking the daily fast to celebrate the Muslim holy month of Ramadan. "Philadelphia is a city that appears uniquely—or at least relatively—at ease with its long-standing Muslim community and identity," she concluded, "even as the United States grapples with a wave of anti-Muslim rhetoric and harassment."[102] The city's large African American Muslim population had a lot to do with this; so did the work of civil society.

## Arab American Civil Society

On September 11, 2001, even before the second plane hit the other World Trade Center tower in New York, Marwan Kreidie of the AADC was on the phone to Philadelphia's human relations commission. The two groups had collaborated since the Gulf War in 1990. On September 11, they "set up an Arab American 'control center'" to "monitor the needs of the community" and ensure that police protected local mosques. AADC's leaders gave them the names of mosques, St. Maron's Lebanese Church, and schools and neighborhoods with Arab populations. They met with officials from the local offices of the FBI and state attorney general, "offering assistance and making sure that Arab Americans weren't going to be targeted."[103]

In the hours and days that followed, national media reported vandalism of mosques and stores in various parts of the country as well as violence toward Arabs and people confused for being Arabs and Muslims, often Sikhs from India. Seeing this, Christians, Jews, Muslims, and others involved in Philadelphia's interfaith movements gathered at Al-Aqsa, the city's main Arab mosque. They set up lawn chairs on the sidewalk, picnicked, talked, and told stories.[104]

They were there to try to make sure nobody targeted Al-Aqsa with violence or hate and to show support and fellowship with a congregation that had long been involved in the city's robust interfaith networks. Five years later, the *Philadelphia Inquirer* reported, Al-Aqsa's leaders and congregants continued to host and participate in regular interfaith services, dialogue, and the annual Philadelphia Interfaith Walk for Peace and Reconciliation, which they played a leading role in establishing in 2004. These gatherings helped people grapple with the aftermath of 9/11, including fierce national debates about Islam, civil liberties, and the US invasions of Afghanistan and Iraq.[105] Al-Aqsa had been "in the forefront of interfaith efforts to stop hate crimes" before that time and since, the *Daily News* noted in 2007.[106]

The increased attention after 9/11 led to a public art project that remade the masjid's façade in 2004. People from diverse congregations and religious schools in the city and suburbs painted tiles and two "doorways to peace" with the word "peace" scripted in more than a dozen languages. What had been an inconspicuous, old stucco warehouse became a bright, ornate building, impossible for passersby to miss and the most visible sign of the Palestinian community that lived nearby (see figure 4.2). Al-Aqsa also acquired, paved, and fenced the adjacent vacant lot that it had long used for parking, especially during Friday prayers. This prevented any repeat of an incident in 2000 when the radical Kensington Welfare Rights Union occupied the lot, pitching tents where activists camped and launched protests against the Republican National Convention

**FIGURE 4.2.** Al-Aqsa Islamic Society, South Kensington, showing the tiles and paintings adorning its façade. (Photo by Domenic Vitiello, 2021.)

downtown. Besides the annoyance of having to park elsewhere, the mosque's leaders and constituents did not wish to be associated with this group's oppositional stance against the American establishment.[107] Indeed, before and especially after 9/11 they collaborated closely with the local police and FBI.[108]

Still, pundits and conspiracy theorists drew Al-Aqsa into national debates about Arabs and Islam in America. Daniel Pipes, a prominent anti-Muslim political activist, decried the mosque's collaboration with the FBI as "obstruction of counterterrorism."[109] His allies at the Militant Islam Monitor blog labeled its new façade, which received a small grant through the federal empowerment zone in Kensington, "a cynical exploitation of public funding for spreading Islam and free money (and labor) for their renovations." Though cast as radical by these critics, Al-Aqsa was a moderate mosque. But these attacks in the blogosphere intensified after the news that some of the six men living in New Jersey who were arrested for plotting to bomb the Fort Dix army base in 2007 had occasionally worshipped at Al-Aqsa.[110]

The masjid's religious and lay leaders responded to these challenges by continuing to inform their neighbors, public officials, and people of other religions about their moderate Sunni faith and their commitments to peace and counterterrorism.[111] They stressed Arabs' long-standing ties and contributions to the city and neighborhood. They wrote newspaper editorials, hosted and attended faith and cultural events, and partnered with organizations such as the national Arab American Anti-Discrimination League, National Association of Arab Professionals, and Council on American-Islamic Relations, which opened a Philadelphia branch in 2004.[112] After the pig's head landed on the mosque's doorstep in 2015, they held a barbeque attended by some five hundred people. As a local journalist related, "Designated captains from the masjid wearing pins showed guests around and answered any questions about Islam . . . to understand the religion straight from the source."[113]

The work of the Arab American Development Corporation, based at Al-Aqsa, changed after 9/11, too. Just four years old in 2001, the organization resembled many others in small immigrant communities. Sometimes it had the resources to hire staff, though usually just one person. At other times it was run entirely by volunteers, especially its longtime board chair Marwan Kreidie, an American-born chair of the Pennsylvania State Civil Service Commission and a university political science instructor of Lebanese heritage. The AADC partnered with other organizations, including nearby Puerto Rican groups, universities, and hospitals, to provide free English classes, tax filing, health screenings, job fairs, and enrollment in food stamps and other benefit programs. It assisted people in matters of immigration and citizenship and registered naturalized immigrants to vote. Al-Aqsa became a polling place for about half the voters in South Kensington.[114] After 9/11, the AADC increased its focus on interfaith and public relations, and it gained new constituencies as Iraqi and then Syrian refugees arrived in Philadelphia.

When Iraqis began arriving in 2006, the AADC's leaders formed close partnerships with HIAS-PA and Nationalities Service Center (NSC). They recognized the gaps left by the system of "underfunded, understaffed" resettlement agencies, as AADC's directors put it, especially in the "post-resettlement period." NSC began referring Iraqi and later Syrian refugees to the AADC for furniture and household items, employment, links to Arab physicians and therapists, and other services. A Palestinian family offered its spacious garage in Northeast Philadelphia to store donated furniture and supplies. The AADC's staff helped refugees seek new housing after their initial resettlement, understand their rights and duties as tenants, and navigate the school system. They also helped refugees, especially Iraqis, overcome their reticence to accept welfare, food stamps, and other sorts of assistance.[115]

The AADC's leaders and other Arabs who were established in the city sought to "create a sense of community" for Iraqis and Syrians. They held "welcome dinners" for newly arrived refugees, introducing them to Arabs and other neighbors. A group of women organized by the AADC went from house to house, visiting women and children who stayed at home and bringing them food and supplies they might need. This was especially important for community building, as these kinds of gatherings were a large part of social life and culture in Syria and Iraq, where women went to each other's homes with tea and pastries to pass the hours until their husbands returned from work. They also invited immigrant families to holiday celebrations at Al-Aqsa. In the AADC's ESL classes they met other immigrants living in Kensington, who were mostly from Latin America. Indeed, many of the organization's services, including its youth programs, sought to "provide a bridge," as AADC staff said, between the Arab community and its Latin and African American neighbors.[116]

Leaders of the AADC considering moving their office from Al-Aqsa to the Northeast but decided to remain in Kensington. They formed partnerships in the Northeast, including at Northeast High School, where, following 9/11, they helped establish intergenerational mentoring and cultural programs in partnership with Al-Bustan Seeds of Culture, an Arab cultural and educational organization. Staff from the two organizations helped mediate tensions between Arab teens and others at the school. In 2013, the AADC broke ground on forty-five units of affordable housing across the street from Al-Aqsa, named Tajdeed Residences, meaning "renewal" in Arabic.[117]

Al-Bustan, meaning "the garden," launched in 2002 as a space to learn Arabic language and culture in a secular environment. Much like the evolution of the AADC, its growth was unintentionally but profoundly shaped by 9/11 and the resettlement of Iraqi and Syrian refugees. Al-Bustan's programming focused largely on youth in its early years, initially a summer day camp. It also ran programs during school hours and after school at Northeast High and an elementary school in Kensington. These activities centered on art, identity, and culture, including the transnational lives of Palestinian youth, some who had attended elementary school in Gaza or the West Bank and others who spent summers with family there. They opened dialogues between Arab and other youth in the high school, seeking to ease tense relations in the wake of 9/11 and help Arabs "fit in," as Al-Bustan's founder and director Hazami Sayed noted. This work also coincided with the Second Intifada, the Palestinian uprising against Israeli occupation from 2000 to 2005, which created further stress and trauma, particularly for youth who traveled to the occupied territories. Al-Bustan also supported teens in the Arab Futures Club at Northeast High in creating self-expressive videos and in-school exhibitions on issues such as how young people could process their experiences of the intifada and discrimination they faced in America.[118]

When Iraqis arrived in Philadelphia in the later 2000s, teachers and administrators in the schools realized they did not have the resources to support them. ESL teachers turned to Al-Bustan for support. As membership in the

Muslim Student Association at Northeast High revealed, Philadelphia's Arab immigrant communities grew and diversified in the 2000s and 2010s, with Palestinian students joined by teens from Iraq, Egypt, Syria, and other parts of the Middle East and North Africa. Starting in 2016, Al-Bustan worked with a group of Muslim girls at the school, who sometimes experienced greater harassment than boys because they were more visibly identifiable as Muslims when they wore headscarves. That fall, Al-Bustan launched a project called "An Immigrant Alphabet" at Northeast High, working with eighteen students from around the world to reflect on immigration, identities, and xenophobia. The students produced large banners with photos and narratives that the city displayed as public art for eleven months at its Municipal Services Building downtown and then at the Cherry Street Pier, a new public space on the Delaware River.[119]

Al-Bustan offered programming for adults and the general public starting in 2009, and with the launch of its "(DIS)PLACED: Philadelphia" project in 2016, the organization positioned itself to support Syrian refugees in various ways. Like AADC, its staff partnered with NSC to help welcome them, providing meals, household and pantry items. Al-Bustan collaborated with various nonprofits, including the American Friends Service Committee and university student groups, to hold a series of "community meet and greets," and to raise funds and donations to support refugees. Most of these events focused on Arab arts and culture, including culinary traditions. They hired Syrian chefs to cater some of these meals.[120]

Based in West Philadelphia, Al-Bustan raised money to transport families from the Northeast to attend cultural events, meet other Arabs, and network with Philadelphia residents, professionals, and business owners. While Al-Bustan did not develop formal financial or employment assistance for refugees, these informal connections helped build newcomers' social networks, through which Syrian refugees and others could get better jobs. Al-Bustan's staff maintained relationships with many of the Syrian families they engaged, continuing to help them as most still struggled to make ends meet four or five years after their resettlement.[121]

Another collaboration that engaged Syrian and Iraqi refugees through arts and culture programming connected their resettlement to ideals and debates about sanctuary. The "Friends, Peace, and Sanctuary" project based at Swarthmore College ran from 2017 to 2019. "Driven by questions about displacement and refuge," wrote its leaders, their workshops, symposiums, and exhibitions held around the region explored "art's capacity to build empathy and create a deeper sense of belonging."[122] In an effort to bring "Arabic into the public realm," they projected images of some of the work they produced on the walls of City Hall, where they mounted an exhibit reflecting on what it meant for Syrians and Iraqis to find sanctuary in Philadelphia.[123] They asked, "What does it mean to resettle in a new country, where one's identity has already been defined by negative media portrayals and stereotypes? How might listening to resettled Syrians and Iraqis help policy-makers and residents realize our shared values as a Sanctuary City?" Signaling the intersectional politics of sanctuary in the twenty-first century, they asked, "What are the commonalities between the global refugee crisis and local issues like urban displacement, mass incarceration, education, and community economic development? How can we make Philadelphia a true place of sanctuary for all?"[124]

While mainly focused on literature and "book arts," the project's events also supported the work of Syrian and Iraqi chefs and artists working in other media and furthered refugees' integration and networks. The project's leaders sought to identify and elevate refugees' talents, especially ones they did not employ in more mundane day jobs, and to create a "space of trust and sanctuary" in which refugees and other residents of the region could connect and appreciate one another's cultures and experiences.[125] With artists from the People's Paper Co-Op, they "created a guide for new refugees based on their own experiences," which they shared with HIAS-PA and NSC.[126] The project also helped connect Syrian and Iraqi newcomers to a variety of cultural and community organizations, from the Free Library of Philadelphia and its Culinary Literacy Center to the Ladder 71 fire station in Northeast Philadelphia, where some firefighters had served in the Iraq War. As the series of events wrapped up, Arabs who had collaborated in them expressed a desire to stay in touch and continue to build understanding across cultures. This inspired two people who had worked on the project, Egyptian American Nora Elmarzouky and Iraqi refugee Yaroub Al-Obaidi, to establish the region's first Arab-language newspaper in over a century, titled the *Friends, Peace, and Sanctuary Journal*.[127]

Other Arabs in Philadelphia marshaled more material assistance for Syrian and Iraqi refugees, especially in 2015 and 2016, when the administration of Barack Obama increased the number of people resettled. Palestinians and other Arab Americans started a volunteer group called the Pennsylvania Refugee Task Force, which was a collaborative of the Muslim Youth Center of Philadelphia (MYCP), a youth-focused masjid in Northeast Philadelphia, and the Philadelphia chapter of the Islamic Circle of North America (ICNA) Relief. Like the AADC and Al-Bustan, they recognized that the resettlement agencies "are only nine-to-five and only offer three months of support" with core resettlement functions, said MYCP member Aziz Jalil, a cofounder of the Task Force who grew up in Northeast Philadelphia, went to Temple University, and then earned a PhD in chemistry at the University of Pennsylvania. In response, they organized to "pick up" where the agencies' assistance ended. Even if agency staff still helped with problems beyond their official programs and their employment and some other services extended beyond three months, many people had greater needs.[128]

Many Syrians' inability to afford basic necessities was a primary motivation for the Task Force's half-dozen organizers and larger network of volunteers. They collaborated with other Arab organizations and nonprofits around Pennsylvania, "who contributed in-kind donations such as kitchen items, bedding, furniture as well as . . . financially to help us to help the refugees," noted another cofounder of the Task Force, Sister Dana Mohamed, who was the program manager for ICNA Relief in Philadelphia.[129] Partnering with NSC and HIAS-PA, they learned about families that were coming before they arrived. With this knowledge, they lined up assistance from their sizable network of Arab, South Asian, and Muslim-convert professionals, including doctors, therapists, and pharmacists who volunteered their services. They communicated and mobilized support partly through groups on the social media platform WhatsApp, a fitting method as the Syrian refugee crisis was among the first in which refugees kept in touch largely via social media while they moved around the Middle East, Europe, and beyond. Task Force members offered ESL classes and planned cultural events for Arab refugees. But the Task Force stopped operating in 2017, after the Trump administration cut off resettlement of Syrians and Iraqis and the urgency to assist substantial numbers of recent arrivals diminished.[130]

More lasting support for Syrian and other refugees continued through ICNA Relief. Headquartered in Queens, New York, ICNA formed in the 1960s, and its charitable relief arm began in the 1970s. Most commonly, ICNA Relief assisted Syrians with mental health counseling, as many suffered from posttraumatic stress, especially the children. This work led ICNA Relief to open the Social Health and Medical Services (SHAMS) Clinic in the Mayfair neighborhood of Lower Northeast Philadelphia, offering free health care, including mental health services, especially, but not only, to Muslim refugees.[131] The word *shams* means "sun" in Arabic, a reference to the clinic's effort to "bring brightness to peoples' lives." More than half the approximately 75,000 Muslims living in Philadelphia, its founders estimated, lived in poverty, and a quarter lacked health insurance, figures that largely reflected the high poverty rate and prevalence of Islam among African Americans.[132]

But when white neighbors learned of plans for the clinic in summer 2017, some objected. People posted on social media and neighborhood blogs, and called the area's city councilman, saying Muslims should "go back to where they came from" and expressing concerns that the clinic would harbor "terrorists."[133] Many neighbors "had questions," reported the *Philadelphia Inquirer*. "Will the clinic be open to anyone, only Muslims? (Answer: Anyone.) Will doctors impose their religious beliefs on patients? (No.) Is this a front for extremism? (No.)"[134] Some people threatened the owner of the building where the clinic would be housed. He was frightened, and for a time he reconsidered giving them the space.[135]

"Initially we were all kind of shocked," said the clinic's director, Ammar Shahid, one of its ten original volunteer doctors and dentists. "We thought, we're just trying to do a good deed here." Rather than cry racism, they chalked it up to "miscommunication" about what they would be doing, and for whom.[136] Working with the area's Irish American city councilman, local civic associations, and other partners, they launched a concerted outreach effort. "We've reached out to the local churches, synagogues, local businesses and let them know that sure we're under a Muslim name and Muslim leaders, but we are open to everyone," said Shahid. "We're not discriminating based on race or culture, even where you're from. The whole community is helped, not just the Muslims here."[137] Like Arab Americans in Detroit and other regions, they drew on a "politics of respectability" rather than more confrontational pushback against Islamophobia.[138] Still, this experience echoed that of many Muslim communities across the United States, especially Arabs and immigrants, when they sought to build new mosques. In one such case, a Muslim congregation in the suburb of Bensalem next to Northeast Philadelphia had to sue the town in its effort to build a mosque in 2014.[139]

Beyond the medical care and social service referrals of the SHAMS Clinic, the staff at ICNA Relief continued to help Syrian and Iraqi refugees in many of the same ways that other organizations did. When Arab children were bullied at school, they hosted several teach-ins and dialogues at the schools. They helped refugees resolve issues with their landlords and find new housing when needed. They held special fund-raising drives for individuals in the community. One campaign paid for sewing machines for some Syrian women in the Northeast to start home-based businesses. In another case, Sister Dana and colleagues from the Task Force helped raise money for a single mother who had been a beautician in Syria, funding most of the equipment necessary for her to open an in-home hair salon.[140] ICNA Relief also aided refugees through its Muslim Family Services Program, "providing financial assistance, counseling and access to our specialty pantry which provides household, cleaning and hygiene products [appropriate for Muslims] at no charge," related Sister Dana. To reach Arabs and Muslims living in other parts of the region, they established a new facility with a food and "specialty pantry, refugee services office, case management, counseling, and more," in Norristown, a suburb northwest of Philadelphia where working-class Egyptians and other immigrants lived.[141]

Much of the most important, enduring, and everyday assistance that Muslim newcomers found in Philadelphia came through a largely preexisting set of masjids. Some newcomers attended the Al-Hidaya mosque on the edge of Feltonville, where the Muslim American Society Islamic Center ran a weekend school with some 200 students. Arabs made up about 90 percent of the people at prayer services and the school; they were mainly Palestinians, Iraqis, Egyptians, and later Syrians, with a small number of South Asians and others. The center's youth clubs hosted social gatherings to foster relationships among newly arrived refugees and people who had lived in the United States longer. As one of the center's leaders explained, most Arab refugees came from societies where transactions are usually relational. Consequently, she and her colleagues structured many of their programs so refugees and immigrants from different countries and generations could meet on a daily or weekly basis and help each other less formally with jobs, housing, and many other things.[142]

One way in which people in Al-Hidaya and the broader Palestinian community often assisted each another was by lending money to avoid taking loans from banks, as charging interest is forbidden in Islam. Iraqis in Philadelphia also developed a network of such lending, though it was not as large or established. Syrian refugees did not initially form such networks, mainly due to the community's greater proportion of poorer families and their recent arrival.[143]

When people asked Al-Hidaya and its center's staff about housing or jobs, the center would first put out a message through WhatsApp, which was their main mode of getting information to constituents. The staff maintained relationships with several Arab American attorneys who could help in matters of immigration and citizenship. They also kept a list of local businesses run by Arabs, mostly grocery stores and restaurants in the Northeast, referring people seeking jobs or announcing job openings on WhatsApp. This was a common practice in the WhatsApp groups at various mosques. Al-Hidaya and its center's staff sought work for teenagers too, to "keep them off the streets, drug-free and in communication with people from their culture and religion," explained one of the center's leaders. When nothing came of jobs or housing inquiries with their networks of employers and WhatsApp contacts, they referred people to Al-Aqsa and the AADC, which Arabs in the city considered the main source for help with those things. Again, members of the Task Force played key roles in facilitating these connections, especially before, but also after, they formally closed the Task Force.[144]

Like Al-Bustan and the AADC, Al-Hidaya and its center did the work of cultural preservation and integration simultaneously. Expanding out of the Arabic and Islamic studies lessons in its weekend school, the center started a cyber charter school, which attracted students from families who did not want their children in public schools for fears of bullying or corrupting influences like drugs or alcohol. It hired Iraqi and Syrian refugees, especially women with backgrounds in Arabic instruction and Islamic and social studies, who were unaccustomed to working in the Middle East but felt the need to bring in extra income beyond their husbands' earnings. The center offered family and marriage counseling, which helped constituents avoid going to court to settle matters (which sometimes proved an obstacle given the stigma of divorce in Arab societies). While not as engaged in interfaith movements as Al-Aqsa, Al-Hidaya also organized peace walks and food drives for refugees and homeless people. It hosted an annual breakfast with over one hundred local police officers, which helped Arabs who were distrustful of law enforcement and other officials form friendlier relationships with the area's police.[145]

Al-Hidaya's imam (a mosque's religious and prayer leader) used Friday prayers, the most important and well-attended service of the week, to address topics like adjusting to a new community and getting along with neighbors. He used examples from the Quran and the Prophet Mohammed's writings about how he and his followers migrated from Mecca to Medina, adapted to life in their new home, formed peaceful relations with their neighbors, and sought to show how Islam is a religion of peace. Imams at other masjids delivered similar messages, too.[146]

Masjids and their WhatsApp groups helped Iraqi and Syrian refugees find language classes, which were scattered around the city. Many women were especially eager to learn English so they could communicate with their children's teachers and more easily navigate regular tasks like grocery shopping.[147] The networks they built through Arab and Muslim civil society helped many immigrants to overcome challenges posed by resettlement in Northeast Philadelphia.

In the 2000s and early 2010s the Northeast lacked a substantial presence of community organizations besides congregations. As scholars who compared refugees' experiences in South and Northeast Philadelphia concluded, these neighborhoods were "disparately positioned to support new refugee populations through both the presence and flexibility of their refugee-serving institutions." Moreover, area residents did not enjoy easy access to downtown or other job centers via public transit, especially compared to other neighborhoods of resettlement like South and West Philadelphia. Some Iraqis and Syrians in the Northeast remained isolated, as an Iraqi man in his forties who worked at Walmart expressed: "I see that Iraqis really suffer. There is nowhere for them to go, even for something as simple as help with reading a piece of mail or filling out an application." The resettlement agencies received funding to open a satellite office in the Northeast but not enough to keep it open, and the main neighborhood-based nonprofit serving refugees in the area did not expand beyond its Eastern European constituency.[148]

Yet as diverse Muslim immigrants increasingly settled in the Northeast, more new masjids opened there, including Al-Furqan in 2008, located across the street from a donut shop popular with Arabs and Pakistanis in the area. Africans and African Americans also attended. Following the larger pattern of masjids, Al-Furqan started a weekend school, offered marriage counseling, and communicated with constituents through its WhatsApp group, where people shared job postings, housing vacancies, prayer times, event invitations, and problems that others in the network might be able to help solve. It ran occasional workshops to assist people in filling out applications for food stamps and other benefits. When Al-Furqan's leaders noticed many new faces showing up several years later, they built a kitchen and hosted meals for people to get to know each other, though they converted the space to an extended prayer area after Trump's "Muslim ban" reduced the arrival of new refugees.[149]

Iraqis, Syrians, and other Arab newcomers also attended other mosques around the city, which likewise served many of their needs. When driving for Uber or other work or appointments took people from the Northeast to different neighborhoods, they worshipped at old and new mosques with South Asians, African Americans, and North and Sub-Saharan Africans. This connected them to Algerians settled in South Philadelphia, Bangladeshis and Pakistanis in West Philadelphia, Malians and other West Africans in Southwest Philadelphia, people from all over the world in Upper Darby, and African Americans in all these neighborhoods and others. These connections expanded their social networks and sometimes led to jobs or customers for Uber and taxi drivers or people in other lines of business.[150]

In Al-Aqsa's building, next door to Al-Furqan and in the immediate vicinity of most other masjids, immigrant and native-born entrepreneurs opened stores catering to their constituents and other neighbors. They sometimes grew up after people from the masjids chased drug dealers away from the area, as at 45th and Walnut Streets in West Philadelphia. They carried halal meats, imported and prepared foods, kitchenware, clothing, and books in Arabic and often offered other goods and services, including barber shops and travel agencies. Some of the grocery stores doubled as small restaurants serving Middle Eastern dishes. These and other restaurants and cafes that located across the street from many mosques served as additional spaces of interaction and sociability for the city's diverse Muslims, especially before and after prayers. This clustering of commerce around masjids was a common pattern in other US cities and suburbs as well. It was one of the most visible ways in which Arab and other Muslim immigrant entrepreneurs and their customers contributed to neighborhood revitalization.[151]

In general, the civil society institutions experienced by Iraqis, Syrians, Palestinians, and other Middle Easterners in Philadelphia were Pan-Arab, Pan-Islamic, or more broadly multicultural. Together, they formed overlapping networks of usually small-scale, yet meaningful and sometimes intense, support and protection. For LGBTQ Syrians in West Philadelphia, instead of the mosques and other Muslim organizations, the William Way Center downtown in what Philadelphians called "the Gayborhood" provided more supportive social networks and help with health and other needs. For the largest group of Palestinians in the city, from the village of Mukhmas in the West Bank, Aziz Jalil created a website listing all heads of household in Pennsylvania and New Jersey and the few in other states so people could keep in touch with one another and with news from the village. The website was also a tool to make sure everyone got invited to weddings that took place in the United States. In 2018, Jalil and others established the Palestinian American Community of Greater Philadelphia, an association with the broad goal of bringing the region's Palestinian community together.[152] These hometown and home region-specific groups were relatively exceptional, though, within Philadelphia's more multicultural Arab and Muslim civil society.

## Transnational Lives

The transnational lives of Iraqi, Syrian, and other Arab communities in Philadelphia were rarely mediated through civil society. Compared to Central Americans and their allies in the 1990s or Liberians and Mexicans in the 2000s, the city's older and relatively small community of Palestinians was slow to develop transnational organizations. For Iraqis, Syrians, and Palestinians, ongoing conflict in their homelands limited their transnational activities and often directed them to other countries in the Middle East.

Palestinians in Philadelphia and other parts of the United States commonly traveled to the occupied territories, visiting in the summer and voting in elections. They sent money to relatives through Western Union. Their pattern of family migration over decades made these activities well established parts of their lives. Some of the ice cream truck owners spent only the summer season in Philadelphia and went to the West Bank for the winter. The work that Al-Bustan Seeds of Culture did with Palestinian youth at Northeast High

School helped them navigate their transnational identities and everyday experiences. Though based entirely in Philadelphia, this was some of the only formal civil society support that was focused transnationally.[153]

Only some Iraqis began to travel back to their home country, though many sent money to family in Iraq and neighboring countries. Mohammed Al Juboori and other people with specific threats to their lives could not return to Iraq, though his parents often traveled from Baghdad to visit him in Philadelphia. "If I was still in Iraq," Mohammed said in 2017, "life would be hell and I probably would've been killed or kidnapped."[154]

For Syrians, as one Arab in Philadelphia put it, "There is no hope to go back," and it was difficult to send money back home since that was blocked by the Syrian government. Many Syrians, however, transferred money to relatives in Lebanon, Egypt, Jordan, or Turkey, and sometimes those funds reached people in Syria. Like other migrants, Syrians as well as Iraqis and Palestinians used WhatsApp to communicate with their relatives and friends overseas and stay connected to news and events in their homelands.[155]

Some Palestinians and Iraqis sent the bodies of deceased family and community members to their homelands for burial. But the cost of sending bodies to the Middle East for interment in the 2010s (almost $15,000), together with ongoing war in Syria, made this impossible for Syrians. A group of Syrians in Philadelphia formed a committee to figure out where to bury deceased relatives and friends. They sought advice at Al-Aqsa, whose leaders, they learned, had purchased a plot of land for Muslims to bury their dead.[156]

Palestinians, Iraqis, and Syrians sometimes traveled, kept in touch, and wired money to the Middle East in support of their own businesses. Palestinians opened small shops and restaurants in their hometowns, some of which exported foods and other products to Philadelphia and other parts of the United States. Iraqis and some Syrians also maintained businesses in the Middle East, usually in Egypt or Jordan. A caseworker from HIAS-PA related the story of one man from Iraq who resettled his family in Philadelphia and even before getting his green card processed, traveled back to Jordan to take care of business. Some Iraqis had considerable capital abroad, she noted. And some did not really want to come to the United States, but felt it was the safest option for their families to reside in America and stabilize their lives, while the father worked mainly in the Middle East, hoping they could all return some day.[157]

Some of the relatively few middle-class Syrians in the Philadelphia region supported humanitarian relief during their homeland's civil war. In 2013, a retired limousine company owner and his wife started the Narenj Tree Foundation, named for a bittersweet orange that grows in Damascus. This charity collected and shipped containers of clothes, schoolbooks, medical and personal hygiene supplies to the Syrian port of Idlib, and to refugee camps in Turkey and Lebanon.[158] In March 2014, people formed a Philadelphia chapter of the Syrian American Medical Society, with about twenty members. They raised money for the work of this national organization, founded in 1998 as a social and educational association. It funded two dozen field hospitals, clinics for refugees at the borders of Jordan, Lebanon, and Turkey, and trained and paid medics and other health care providers in opposition-held areas of Syria that were off-limits to foreign medical missions. Members gathered medical equipment and supplies to send them and assisted doctors in Syria with unfamiliar surgeries via Skype.[159]

Solidarity with the occupied territories was the most established part of Arab transnational civil society in Philadelphia and the United States, but it was not always tied to Arab immigrant communities in the city. The organization Playgrounds for Palestine, based out of the home of its founder in a suburb outside of Northeast Philadelphia, drew supporters from diverse backgrounds around the United States. They raised funds and coordinated with partners in the occupied territories to build playgrounds, an act promoting peace and well-being among the often-traumatized children living in the West Bank and Gaza. More a part of larger movements in solidarity with the people of Palestine, it neither grew out of nor engaged in the affairs of Philadelphia's Palestinian or other Arab immigrant communities. Transnational advocacy for Palestinian rights came more from local communities through Arab American graduates of Northeast High, especially at Temple University in North Philadelphia, where they led the Muslim Student Association and an active chapter of Students for Justice in Palestine.[160]

## Post-Resettlement

After two years working its way through the courts, the US Supreme Court upheld President Trump's revised ban on refugees from majority-Muslim countries. In the meantime, his administration lowered the number of Muslim refugees being resettled in the United States from 38,555 (out of close to 85,000 total refugees resettled) in 2016 to 3,312 (out of almost 22,500) in 2018, a 91 percent drop in Muslims and 74 percent drop in refugees overall. The United States admitted just two interpreters from Iraq with SIVs in 2018. Between June 2017 and the end of 2020, it resettled only one Syrian family in Philadelphia, an elderly couple who arrived in 2019.[161]

Globally, displacement reached an all-time high of 68.5 million people by the end of 2017, a figure that kept growing. But in September 2019, Trump administration officials announced they were considering cutting resettlement to zero, closing the United States to refugees altogether. Apparently the only voice within the administration that favored some resettlement was the Pentagon, whose leaders advocated continuing to admit people with SIVs from Iraq.[162] The United States never offered SIVs to people who assisted the American military in Syria. These were mainly Kurds whom Trump abandoned in October 2019, making way for Turkish forces to massacre them and for the Assad regime to retake northeast Syria. This sparked new waves of displacement.[163]

While President Trump and many of his supporters imagined America without Muslims or refugees from the Middle East, this vision belied the realities of Philadelphia, Detroit, New York, New Jersey, Los Angeles, Houston, Chicago, Washington, DC, and other major centers of Arab and Muslim life. Some Arab families and communities had been established for generations. Others, like Mohammed Al Juboori, applied for US citizenship as soon as they became eligible, five years after getting a green card.[164] Mohammed found the citizenship test easy, and he received his US passport in summer 2020. He changed his name at the same time, to Ethan Aljuboori, in order "to have a new start" (see figure 4.3).[165]

North Africans, especially Algerians and Moroccans, became some of the fastest-growing foreign-born groups in Philadelphia in the second half of the 2010s. In total, by that decade community leaders estimated that between 30,000 and 50,000 Arab Americans and immigrants from the Middle East and North Africa lived in the region, though exact figures were difficult to ascertain. They lived in various parts of the city, in diverse neighborhoods where African American Muslims often resided, too, including South, West, North, and especially Lower Northeast Philadelphia, as well as a range of working- and middle-class suburbs.[166]

Like Central Americans, Southeast Asians, Africans, and Mexicans, Arabs played major roles in the revitalization of city neighborhoods. Their largely multicultural social networks and civil society formed a web of support that helped Arab and other newcomers find their way in the region, its job and housing markets, and its increasingly diverse communities. This was especially crucial in the post-resettlement phase after help from the refugee system came to an end. Sometimes they explicitly conceived of this work as sanctuary.

As recounted in this book's introduction, city solicitor Nelson Diaz, with his boss, mayor John Street, and police commissioner John Timoney, instituted a sanctuary policy in spring 2001, several months before September 11. Iraqi, Syrian, and Palestinian communities in Philadelphia had less need than many others for its immediate protections, as most people in these communities had

**FIGURE 4.3.** Ethan Aljuboori at a friend's wedding in New Jersey in 2020. (Photo courtesy of Ethan Aljuboori.)

permanent resident status or US citizenship. Moreover, the middle-class status of many people in these communities gave them other types of stability, including an ability to help other members of the community financially, especially the poorer Syrian refugees who were resettled in 2015 and 2016.

From 9/11 to the presidency of Donald Trump and beyond, Philadelphia was a sanctuary for Arab, Muslim, and other immigrants in many more ways beyond local police and prisons refusing to cooperate with federal authorities in detention and deportation. Protection from hate and violence remained of everyday relevance for Arabs and Muslims in America. Thanks partly to the work of civil society and local government, Philadelphia was a safer, more welcoming place for Arab and Muslim immigrants than much of the United States, most of the time. The meanings of sanctuary were also diverse for Mexicans, who likewise were the target of much of the xenophobia and anti-immigrant movements of early twenty-first-century America. But as the largest single group of new immigrants to Philadelphia in this period, most of whom lacked legal status in the country, for Mexicans the police protections of sanctuary mattered more.

# CHAPTER 5

# New Sanctuary

## Mexicans and the New Immigration Movements

The United States is "a country I never planned nor aspired to live in," said Carmen Guerrero. Her business in Mexico City was growing fast. "I would say to myself, 'I don't need the North,'" unlike other Mexicans who were leaving for the United States in record numbers in the 1990s, after the North American Free Trade Agreement (NAFTA) undercut their livelihoods. Instead, Carmen would flee another major, if underappreciated, driver of Mexican migration: violence.[1]

Born in Mexico City, the third of six daughters of indigenous parents, as a toddler Carmen moved with her mother and sister to their father's hometown in the countryside. Their mother farmed to feed the family—corn, many kinds of beans, grains, peppers, squash, chickens, cows, sheep. Their father stayed in the city to work as a carpenter, visiting on the weekends. "The entire community used one" primary school, so "when we were ready" for middle school, they returned to the city.[2]

"When we arrived in the city, we started doing many types of jobs," since their father's wages were insufficient to support the family. Their mother worked as a housekeeper, bringing home other families' clothes to wash and iron as well as piecework for manufacturers. The girls sowed buttons onto shirts and leather onto baseballs. "Every vacation or every weekend, we went to different places to plant seeds, to work on farms, to babysit, to clean houses" in middle-class neighborhoods of the metropolis.[3]

Carmen struggled in primary school. But "when I started middle school . . . optometrists came to the school," and "discovered that I needed glasses, and after that I was a really smart girl," she said, laughing. "I was very energetic." She excelled in chemistry and public speaking in high school, at the same time teaching adult literacy classes and working in a clothing store.[4]

"After high school, I enrolled in the university," studying political science. "But in those years," Carmen said, "it was very hard" for Mexicans to attend high school or college. Teacher strikes and youth gangs paid by political parties to attack educational institutions disrupted their learning. Sometimes professors held classes in the street. But ultimately, "I was enrolled just two years." Carmen left the university after giving birth to her first daughter in 1987.[5]

More intimate violence shaped her life and work thereafter. Three years later, when her second daughter "came I started having a job selling cars in an automobile dealer. I had pretty good money selling cars," she recalled. "But my daughters' father started being jealous." He quit his post in the army and left for California to stay with family there. When he returned to Mexico, Carmen left him and joined the navy herself, but he took their two daughters away to the state of Jalisco, where his parents lived. She was pregnant with their third daughter, so she followed him. But he "still abused me, domestically, physically," and she left him again.[6]

During her early twenties Carmen rarely held a job for long, usually due to sexual harassment in the workplace. In Jalisco, she worked government jobs in the Federal Electoral Institute, the National Institute of Statistics (Mexico's census bureau), and the state police. Then she took a post in a construction company working on highway projects, moving around with her daughters in tow. She worked as a machinery assistant, haulage assistant, and then assistant accountant. She observed, matter-of-factly, that "99.9 percent of women in Mexico experience sexual harassment" at work, even if official statistics say less. "I lost my jobs many times for that reason," after standing up for herself and arguing, "I have my job for my knowledge, not because I want to give my body."[7]

Then in 1994, "the economic crisis came to Mexico, and everybody lost their jobs." NAFTA went into effect on New Year's Day, stimulating increased foreign investment. But the economy crashed in the fall as investors pulled their capital after an establishment presidential candidate was murdered and peasants launched an armed insurrection in the southern state of Chiapas. Workers in construction and a wide range of sectors lost their jobs.[8]

The displacement of Mexican peasants owed more to NAFTA directly, which compounded a longer history of limited political support for rural development along with environmental shocks, usually droughts. American corporations flooded Mexico with heavily subsidized corn and other staples, which now moved freely. Prices suddenly fell so low that it became impossible for small farmers to make a living.[9] Mexican migration to the United States took off. From 1990 to 2007, the number of Mexicans in the United States increased from 4.3 million people to 12.6 million.[10]

The great majority of Mexicans crossed the border illegally, as most had since 1965, when the United States imposed its first quotas on immigration from the Western Hemisphere.[11] For most of the two nations' history before then, Mexicans traveled back and forth more freely across the border. They often worked seasonally in agriculture in the southwestern states between Texas and California (the territory the United States took from Mexico in the Mexican-American War of the 1840s), even if many lived in "virtually peonage," as the President's Commission on Migratory Labor wrote in 1951.[12] Many Mexicans also moved to Chicago for factory, railroad, and warehouse work.

The United States had a long history of recruiting Mexican labor but also of violently expelling Mexican people from the country. Most famously, the government began the Bracero Program in 1942 to address wartime labor shortages in agriculture. But starting in 1954, Operation Wetback rounded up and deported 3.8 million Mexicans, people who had entered with and without permission. The United States created seasonal work visas that would endure into the twenty-first century, though like the Bracero Program, these visas continued to legalize a fraction of the Mexican workers that farms, meat packers, and other employers demanded.[13] After passage of the new quotas in 1965, the US Border Patrol and Immigration and Naturalization Service (INS) increased deportation, expelling more than thirteen million people, mostly Mexicans, over the next twenty years. As historian Adam Goodman reported, "From the mid-1970s on, deportations averaged nearly 925,000 per year, or more than 2,500 each day."[14]

The Immigration Reform and Control Act of 1986 legalized the status of almost three million Mexicans in the United States.[15] But thereafter the act made it illegal for companies to knowingly hire people without papers, even if this usually went unenforced. Leaders in Washington increasingly militarized border enforcement with new weapons and surveillance technology.[16] Ironically, this had the effect of keeping Mexicans without legal status *in* the United States, not *out*, by dramatically reducing their historical practice of more fluid, "circular" migration.[17]

Even as the United States made it more illegal and dangerous for Mexicans to cross the border to work, the service and tech economy took off in the late twentieth century, boosting demand for low-wage workers in food and domestic service, construction, and other sectors. Agreements like NAFTA helped US corporations access foreign markets while reducing the cost of many goods

to US consumers, who now had more money to spend. But US politicians declined to extend the freedom of movement to Mexican people, meaning that
most Mexicans who moved in this era lived in the United States illegally, where
they were often exploited and had limited protections.

Under these conditions, even though Carmen was laid off from her construction job in 1995, she had no interest in migrating north. She had no family
or friends to join there. She moved to Mexico City and began working as a
secretary in an engineer's office. She made only 400 pesos (42 dollars) a week,
not enough to survive, but soon found a higher-paying job in the city's 810-
acre wholesale food market, the largest one in the Americas. Selling cilantro
there from five to seven a.m. for 700 pesos a week, she also had more time to
spend with her daughters.[18]

She was good at the job and soon started her own wholesale business. She
partnered with a growing number of small farmers, many from the state of
Puebla, just south of the city. Carmen paid for the seeds, fertilizer, and other
expenses; the farmers supplied the land and labor; and they divided the prof-
its from her sales of thousands of bunches of cilantro, radishes, onions, spin-
ach, and other vegetables. "It was like, wow, the money was growing." She
bought a car and a truck. Her workforce grew to twenty employees. The only
big downside was that she worked long hours and traveled a lot, so her oldest
daughter, age ten, "became like a mother to the others."[19]

In the early morning on December 24, 1999, after she "finished selling all
my stuff in the market" around 3:00 a.m., Carmen and one of her employees
got into the truck, headed for "planting lands in Puebla." They gave a ride to
another merchant's thirteen-year-old son since he was tired and his father still
had work to finish.[20] About an hour later, on a narrow country road, a big truck
passed them and then slowed to a stop. Fifteen armed men wearing masks
jumped out and surrounded their vehicle, pounding on it with the handles of
their guns and shooting into the air. They screamed threats at Carmen, her
driver, and their young passenger until they opened the doors. Then they pistol-
whipped the boy for not unlocking the door sooner. The men threw them
into their truck, tied them up, and put tape over their mouths and eyes as they
drove off, beating them with their pistols if they moved, while the boy's head
continued bleeding.[21]

Other wholesalers at the market had suffered violent robberies, but this was
different. The masked gang held Carmen hostage for a week, until one of her
colleagues paid 500,000 pesos ransom (over $50,000). "I cannot recount all the
violence of this tragedy; those were moments in which our lives hung by a
thread," she said. "I made it out alive of that terrorist attack," but it "marked my
life and my young daughters . . . with pain that to this day hasn't been erased."[22]

"I was completely destroyed," and "nobody supported me, nobody helped me, I was really frustrated . . . hopeless," and in overwhelming fear.[23] Her workers at the market needed to be paid, but she had no money. When they reported the crime, the police chief, a woman, refused to give her a copy of the crime report, instead asking Carmen, "Do you love your country?" The chief explained that if they filed the report, then the national crime statistics would get worse.[24]

Carmen could not imagine where in Mexico it might be safe to make a living and raise her family. "I felt like [the kidnappers] knew everything about me, and I can build again my dreams, and they're going to destroy it at any minute." She "felt like there is no other option, as violence was spreading all over" the country.[25] So she decided to seek safety in the United States. "My heart was torn apart because I had to be separated from my daughters. What a nightmare!"[26]

"When I decided to cross the border, I decided to come with people who knew people in the US . . . had relatives in the US . . . to come with people who had some experience," she said, in order "to feel safe." A family she knew from Puebla had a relative who had lived in the United States a long time. They invited her to come to New York City, which was the largest center of Poblano population in the country. "Many people from Puebla traveled in that time," leaving its small farming towns. A group of three women and five men, they flew from Mexico City to Hermosillo in the north, about three hours from Arizona, and traveled by bus through several towns along the border.[27]

"The man in charge, the father . . . told me . . . he knew the coyotes [smugglers] at the border. He was supposed to have everything arranged." But when they got off the bus in a small, dusty border town, Carmen learned he did not. The hotel had bed bugs, "the town was so uninhabitable . . . a very dangerous place; and also expensive." Her carefully planned budget was decimated by the inflated prices in towns whose economies ran on gouging migrants. "All my money went away," as they stayed about six weeks along the border, looking for a decent coyote.[28] It took so long that she lost track of time and did not even know what month it was by the time they crossed the border.[29]

Like many migrants, they made multiple attempts. The first coyote they hired was inexperienced and left them in the Sonora Desert after a day's walk, saying he was going to check for the border patrol and would be back. When he had not returned a day and a half later, the group retraced their steps, fortunate that they remembered the way and had enough water and food. Later, in Tijuana, they found a coyote who took them three hours east, where they crossed the border in the desert near Yuma, Arizona. The border patrol "immediately arrested us on the other side," took them to jail in Yuma, and put them on a bus back to Mexico the next day. The same coyote waited for them and took them to Arizona again eight days later.[30]

After three nights walking in the desert, sheltering themselves from the sun and authorities by day, the coyote's colleague picked them up in a van and drove them three hours west to Los Angeles. They stayed in a hotel where thirty people were waiting for rides to other parts of the country. The smugglers stuffed Carmen and her traveling companions into a van headed east, which was overfilled with people going to Colorado, Tennessee, New Jersey, New York, and Florida. After three days, hardly stopping, "just putting gasoline, eating a lot of hamburgers," they arrived at a rest stop on the New Jersey Turnpike.[31]

Most of the passengers piled out of the van and headed for the bathroom, leaving Carmen alone with the father from Puebla. "I had no money, and the guy in charge of the group started to sexually abuse me." He said he would pay the $2,500 for her coyote from Los Angeles to New York and she could stay with his family there but she had to sleep with him in return. She refused and told him she was fleeing sexual violence in Mexico. He threatened to call immigration authorities and have her deported. She ran out of the van into the cold winter air.[32]

She got back in for the ride to New York but refused to stay. The man demanded she repay him the $2,500 with interest. Two teenagers who were headed to Florida invited her to come with them and stay with their family there. She thanked them but instead called a phone number her sister had given her—a former neighbor of her sister in Mexico City, a single woman, who now lived in Norristown, Pennsylvania, outside of Philadelphia, to ask if she could go there. "For me it was so much better, because it was a woman who was going to give me a place to stay."[33]

The following year, Carmen made the arrangements and paid the coyote fees to have her daughters join her in Norristown; they arrived in October 2001. Her mother accompanied them on the journey, following the same route that Carmen had taken through the Sonora Desert. Her mother returned to Mexico a month later.[34]

## The New Latin American Migration

Eighteen years later, Carmen observed, "An immigrant in the United States is a slave, a slave to neoliberalism, a slave that is not seen as a human being, just as in the history of this country: The African American slaves were brought, and they were not seen as human beings with rights."[35] While Africans' bondage served European imperialism and early national expansion, Mexicans and other immigrants living illegally in the United States moved and worked under the terms of a newer political economy. Still, much as in the age of colonization, in this era of liberalized markets and free trade, pacts like NAFTA favored the interests of global capital over the freedoms of people, particularly if they were working-class and had black or brown skin. Similar dynamics characterized the last era of mass immigration, around the turn of the twentieth century, when Americans did not consider Italian immigrants fully white and passed "Exclusion Acts" for Asians.[36] Also echoing that era, a new—or in some ways new—set of movements grew up, alternately aimed at restricting and expelling or protecting and assisting working-class immigrants, especially people without legal status. These included the New Sanctuary Movement.

On the surface, the questions of why Mexicans migrated to the United States and what protections or assistance Americans might owe them recalled a history of economic interdependence among neighbors more than wars, at least in modern times.[37] Mexicans were not refugees, and cases of asylum for Mexicans were exceedingly rare. Americans found it quite logical to label them "economic immigrants," people simply seeking a better life in a wealthier country.

However, the history of US-Mexico relations, labor recruitment and demand, and border enforcement revealed clear patterns of structural violence that made sanctuary not only relevant but also justified and necessary in the eyes of its supporters. "We are neighbors of the most powerful, militarized country" in the world, Carmen remarked. The United States has long "abus[ed] the Mexican population through the governments that they handle like puppets." As in other parts of the Americas, the United States "imposed neoliberalism" through trade deals and the terms of foreign aid and loans, along with support for militaries and authoritarian regimes. "Free commerce means all the corporations came to Mexico and made the rules," eluding taxes and stealing wealth. Mexico is rich in natural resources—water, oil, mining. But US corporations like Coca-Cola and oil companies control much of those resources, while in 2010 one-third of Mexicans lived on less than five dollars a day.[38] Mexican politicians also enabled and profited from organized criminals' control of sectors ranging from narcotics to avocados. "The migration is a result," said Carmen.[39]

NAFTA and the US-supported drug war against Mexican cartels, which was launched in 2006, were just the latest chapters in this history. NAFTA "cut a wide path of destruction through Mexico," observed a director of the Center for International Policy, a thinktank in Washington, DC. It displaced some two million Mexican farmers in the two decades after 1994.[40] Compounding the effects of NAFTA, the drug war caused a spike in violence in an already violent nation.[41] Between 2006 and 2020, more than 73,000 Mexicans were reported "disappeared," with many more missing from official reports.[42] Violence toward women, which was already high, worsened, including rising rates of femicide.[43] The United Nations ranked Mexico among the world's most violent countries for women, along with its Central American neighbors.[44]

The border region between Mexico and the United States added another layer to the violence people faced, as human traffickers and drug cartels took advantage of migrants for their money, their bodies, and sometimes their lives.[45] Once in the United States, people's illegal status limited their rights and mobility—the types of work they could do, access to drivers' licenses, and a wide variety of police and social protections—and exposed them to further exploitation and physical violence. These were just some of the reasons how and why sanctuary mattered for Mexicans beyond the protections and access to services promised by the typical sanctuary city policy.

Carmen Guerrero and her daughters were increasingly the face of Mexican migration in the twenty-first century, and in some ways more generally the face of immigration in the United States and globally. First, they represented the broader feminization of migration, which was driven partly by interpersonal and structural violence and by shifting work opportunities. This included growing demand in wealthy countries for child and elder care, domestic service, and other work usually done by women. Children from Latin America crossing the border, with and without parents or guardians, likewise became more common.[46]

Carmen's settlement in Norristown reflected the new geography of Mexican migration and of immigration to the United States. As the American service economy boomed at the end of the twentieth century, immigrants, especially Mexicans, settled just about everywhere, well beyond the old gateways of Chicago, New York, and the Southwest. They went to places with no memorable history of immigrant settlement, such as North Carolina, Alabama, and Tennessee, or to places that had experienced little immigration for generations, like Philadelphia and most of the Rust Belt.[47]

In the other big geographic change, most immigrants since the 1990s settled in the suburbs, no longer primarily in central cities. One reason was that by the end of the twentieth century, most jobs in the United States were in the suburbs. Moreover, after 1965 the growing proportion of immigrants coming with wealth and for high-paying jobs typically settled in well-off suburbs. Poorer immigrants, including Mexicans, more often settled in working-class suburbs, many of which had declined as employers and prior residents left. These trends contributed to a broader suburbanization of poverty and people of color in places such as Norristown, Upper Darby, and other suburbs across the country.

While immigrants in the United States became more diverse in almost every way, Mexican migration dominated much of the nation's increasingly heated immigration debates. These debates focused ever more on the estimated thirteen million people living in the country illegally by the 2000s, more than half of whom came from Mexico. By 2002, Mexicans made up 30 percent of all immigrants in the United States, seven times as much as people from the Philippines, the second-largest group at the time.[48] An estimated 54 percent of Mexican immigrants in that year lived in the country illegally, and more than 80 percent of those who had come since 1990 lacked legal status, including most Mexicans in Philadelphia, which was a newer destination for Mexican migration.[49]

Twenty-first-century immigration debates in the United States focused largely on illegal immigration's costs and benefits for the nation and its receiving communities, and little on Mexicans' reasons for moving. Conservative talk radio, cable news pundits, and restrictionist thinktanks lamented this "alien invasion," its violation of the rule of law, and fiscal costs, which they deceptively claimed outweighed the benefits. More centrist, often corporate interests and many people on the left, embraced Mexicans' low-wage labor in essential sectors. They celebrated the people who provided their food, cared for their children, mowed their lawns, remodeled their kitchens, and opened shops and restaurants.[50] Advocates for immigrant rights, including immigrants themselves, more often recognized the structural violence against Mexicans and Mexico and were more aware of the extent of the physical violence and trauma they experienced.[51]

One of the biggest ironies and injustices of all, some immigrant rights activists noted, was that working-class immigrants, again especially Mexicans, increasingly did the hard work of creating and sustaining wealth in the United States. Their low wages made middle-class living comfortable and affordable. Through their labor, and by opening stores and repopulating neighborhoods, Mexicans played multiple roles in revitalizing US cities and towns in the late twentieth and early twenty-first centuries, and dramatically so in Philadelphia. For the most part, other people, both native-born people and wealthier immigrants, reaped the benefits, whether through home values, inexpensive services, or Social Security payments that many unauthorized immigrants supported by paying taxes with no hope they would ever get the retirement funds themselves.[52]

Mexican immigrants also played a central part in forcing Americans to confront what we owed immigrants and what sanctuary might mean in the twenty-first century. As detailed in the introductory chapter, a new immigrant rights movement erupted after the US House passed a bill at the end of 2005 that would have made illegal immigration a felony rather than a civil offense and made assisting unauthorized immigrants also a crime. Much of this soon coalesced in the New Sanctuary Movement. Even more than the movement of the 1980s, this was a decentralized set of local groups that only occasionally came together to share and coordinate their advocacy. It was always a multicultural movement, but at least in its early years worked especially with Mexican communities in Chicago, New York, and Philadelphia.

Compared to many other groups of immigrants in recent decades, Mexican immigrant civil society necessarily focused more on claiming rights and assisting people without legal status. Mexicans also organized a transnational civil society to address some of the conditions that drove their migration. Often their work resembled that of other migrant communities, such as Liberian county associations and Southeast Asian community organizing. Still, issues of legal status, people's position in the labor market, and generational changes in Mexican communities produced distinct patterns and histories.

## Mexadelphia

Mexicans settled first in rural parts of the Philadelphia region, in the early 1970s around the mushroom-growing capital of the world, Kennett Square, Pennsylvania, thirty miles west of the city. Most came from the state of Guanajuato and many gained legal status with the 1986 immigration law. By the early twenty-first century, several thousand Mexicans and thousands of their children lived around Kennett Square. Across the river in New Jersey, Mexicans settled in the agricultural centers of Vineland and Bridgeton, where they picked tomatoes and blueberries, finding work in food processing and other jobs in the winter. Many others passed through rural parts of the region, moving up and down the East Coast seasonally, from harvesting peaches in Georgia to picking apples in upstate New York.[53]

## The Suburbs

The post-NAFTA migration brought many Mexicans to the Philadelphia suburbs, with the largest number settling in Norristown. The origin story people tell is of a man of Italian descent who went to Acapulco on vacation and fell in love with a woman there, whom he brought back. She then invited family and friends, initiating a chain migration of people from central and southern

Mexico. Some came to work seasonally in landscaping and construction. Others stayed permanently, working year-round in janitorial, restaurant, and factory jobs. At least one landscaping firm that was employing people illegally got in trouble with the INS, which steered it and other area employers into the US guest worker program, recruiting men from Puebla. Many of these firms were owned by Italian Americans who had moved to nearby suburbs and rented their old homes to new arrivals. By 2000, the US Census reported that about 3,000 people of Latin American origin, mostly Mexicans but also Puerto Ricans, lived in Norristown, and almost 10,000 a decade later. Mexican immigration reversed population loss that the town had experienced since the 1970s as its textile mills and other factories shut down.[54]

People from Mexico also settled in other working-class, formerly industrial suburbs across the region, such as Upper Darby, Pottstown, and Lansdale. Michael Katz and Kenneth Ginsburg termed such places "reservations for low-wage labor." Migrants found affordable rents in these towns and worked in homes, malls, and office parks in affluent suburbs nearby.[55]

Most people found jobs through family and friends who had already settled. Carmen Guerrero had less help, but her experiences were otherwise typical of Mexicans in the suburbs. "Looking through the newspapers in the trash cans, I started looking for a job. I cut out an ad and I showed it to a taxi driver and asked him to take me to that address," she recalled. "I got to a hotel lobby and using my hands I signaled to the receptionist saying, 'Working, working yo' [me] as I pointed a finger to myself."[56] A Filipina woman approached "me and asked 'trabajo' [work]? . . . and helped me to fill in the application."[57] Carmen worked at this Best Western near the King of Prussia Mall, the largest shopping mall in the East, for the next three years. She cleaned twenty to twenty-five rooms in a seven-hour shift, for $7.25 an hour. "The first weeks, I'd fill my stomach with tiny cookies, cheeses and chocolates that we'd put in baskets for the hotel visitor, until I got my first paycheck and I could buy some Chinese food. Ohhhh, what a feast!"[58]

These wages were not enough to cover her expenses plus debts to family in Mexico for her ransom and coyote fees. So, like many Mexicans, she sought a second job. She met a woman on a bus who pointed her to a dishwashing post at a Bob Evans restaurant. She worked seven-to-eight hours at the hotel, then seven-to-ten at the restaurant, "sometimes more on weekends." Carmen justified her exhaustion since this allowed her to save money to bring her daughters to Norristown sooner.[59] Over the next several years, she worked her way up at Bob Evans to the food prep line, then cook, then manager. She also worked at the Cheesecake Factory and California Pizza eateries at the mall. She kept her jobs at Bob Evans and the Cheesecake Factory when she left the hotel in 2003, after a workplace injury that the hotel's managers refused to acknowledge.[60]

The apartment where Carmen first stayed "was so little . . . there was no room for" her daughters. Her host told her, "'You can stay here, but you have to look for a place to live.'" Knowing few people, she saw other Mexicans mainly at the laundromat, where one day a man referred her to a house nearby, where she rented a spot.[61] But so many people lived in this house, with mattresses and beds crammed into each room, that Carmen spent virtually all her waking hours elsewhere. She soon found a home to rent just across the river on the border between the small town of Bridgeport and King of Prussia, closer to the mall, where she and her daughters could have more space.[62]

But when the girls arrived, administrators in the school district there refused to enroll them. They threatened to report them to immigration authorities after Carmen could not show them a visa in her passport. She gave up the house and enrolled the girls in Norristown schools instead. They rented a small room in Norristown and later moved to a town house on a cul-de-sac in King of Prussia.[63]

Mexican immigrants generally had decent relations with their landlords, employers, and neighbors in Norristown and Bridgeport, but local governments varied in their responses to their settlement, from sanctuary to exclusion. In 2003, Norristown's city council passed an ordinance recognizing Mexicans' consular identification cards as valid to access local schools, libraries, and health clinics. Copied from the Detroit suburb of Pontiac, Michigan, this ordinance also aimed to combat payday robberies. Council members got local banks to recognize the card, so Mexicans without legal status could put their earnings in the bank rather than keep cash in their pockets and homes.[64] Though distinct from policies limiting police and prisons' cooperation in deportation, this offered a certain form of sanctuary, another limited act of protection and support.[65]

In addition to safety and access to services, Norristown officials, including the town's Kenyan economic development director, cited Mexicans' role in revitalization as impetus for the act. Mexicans had repopulated the town, reviving its housing market and the commercial district on West Marshall Street. This area housed only a small cluster of Mexican groceries when Carmen arrived in 2000, but in the next several years it transformed as Mexicans opened a large and diverse set of stores. People started calling it "Little Mexico."[66]

Bridgeport's council took an opposite stance in passing its Illegal Immigration Relief Act in October 2006. The act promised to fine and revoke the licenses of landlords and employers of people who were in the country illegally and declared English to be the town's official language. Mayor Jerry Nicola and the act's sponsor, Councilman John Pizza, cited the rule of law and Congress's failure to act on illegal immigration for their action, echoing Hazleton Mayor Lou Barletta, a fellow Italian American. Bridgeport leaders also expressed anxiety over their town's revitalization and a fear that new immigrants might dictate its course.[67] After the Pennsylvania Immigration and Citizenship Coalition advocacy group, which was based in Philadelphia, threatened to sue, they put the act's implementation on hold as challenges to Hazleton's law made their way through the courts.[68]

Yet Norristown's public response to people who were in the country illegally proved inconsistent, particularly in the actions of its police department. Initially, department leaders tried "to make a bridge between the Hispanic community and the police," recalled Carmen, who participated in community safety trainings that they ran.[69] As in other places, the police sought to build trust with immigrants so victims and witnesses of crimes would feel comfortable reporting them. As a union organizer who worked in the area noted, they did not want to make this new "part of the community ungovernable."[70]

But in the late 2000s, Norristown police began to set up checkpoints to verify that people had auto insurance, thus restricting unauthorized immigrants' movement.[71] One day in 2011, Carmen went to the police station to find the parking lot full of vehicles from ICE. "They had a big list of names." Thereafter, Norristown police and ICE began raids targeting the local Home Depot and 7-Eleven parking lots, where men waited to be picked up for day labor. A city councilman explained to Carmen the police needed to cooperate with ICE in order to receive federal funds.[72]

People who were in the country illegally navigated a fragmented landscape of policing and services in suburban Philadelphia and other regions, especially after 2005. This was a particular challenge for Mexicans and Central Americans, who were most often targeted by ICE. Riverside, New Jersey, also copied Hazleton's act in 2006, only to repeal it a few months later. A decade later, nearby Bensalem, Pennsylvania, explored a 287g agreement with ICE to deputize its police as immigration agents. This sort of partnership was used mainly by counties in the American South. Bensalem's mayor backed out in response to pressure from activists and the county's human relations council. In other suburbs, police departments and town governments were more or less accommodating to immigrants who lacked legal status, rarely as a matter of official policy. Their response often varied depending on the politics of individual officers and employees of other agencies, from schools to town halls.[73]

## The City

Philadelphia was a sanctuary city, though in most ways Mexicans' experiences of migration and settlement there closely resembled their experiences in the suburbs. As in the region at large, the greatest number of Mexicans came from rural origins, especially the state of Puebla. People from Puebla had settled in New York since the 1980s, and over time they found work and homes in the broader region from the Hudson Valley to southern New Jersey. A community from the town of San Lucas, Puebla, formed in the city of Camden, New Jersey, by the early 1990s.[74]

San Lucas sits in a valley between two snowcapped volcanoes, the dormant Iztaccihuatl ("white woman" in the Aztec language Nahuatl) and Popocatepetl ("smoking mountain"), Mexico's second-highest peak and most active volcano. An eruption in December 1994, spewing ash more than fifteen miles, prompted the evacuation of towns in the valley. This compounded farmers' growing struggles to survive off their harvests and drove migration to the United States.[75]

Efren Tellez, a farmer from the next town over, San Mateo Ozolco, abandoned his corn fields and plum orchards in early 1995. He traveled to Camden to stay with a friend from San Lucas. As he looked for work, one day he walked across the mile-long Ben Franklin Bridge to downtown Philadelphia. After wandering around for a few hours, he spotted a sign he could read: "Tequilas Restaurant." He walked in and got a job as a dishwasher in this upscale restaurant owned by Mexican chef David Suro. Tellez found a cheap room in a row house in South Philadelphia, close enough to walk or bike to work. He called home, encouraging family and friends to join him. A decade later, about half of San Mateo's roughly 4,000 residents had moved to South Philadelphia.[76]

Mexicans' housing and neighborhood experiences in South Philadelphia resembled those of Mexicans in Norristown and of Italians in both places a century earlier. They lived in brick row houses near old factories that were being converted to condos, renting largely from Asian and Italian American landlords. The first people to arrive were mostly men of working age, including many in their teens and twenties, who often traveled back and forth from Mexico before bringing or starting families and settling more permanently. They often lived together in large numbers so they could send more of their earnings home. All this echoed the earlier experiences of Italians.[77]

In the late 1990s and early 2000s, South Philadelphia's Mexican community was made up mostly of young men, who experienced considerable violence and trauma. Some people called it an "island of men," remembered Cristina

Perez from Women Organized Against Rape. Many had faced violence in their migration—abandoned in the desert, beaten by border patrol agents, robbed—even before cartel violence escalated in the mid-2000s. With fifteen to twenty people in a house, they experienced problems of theft, fights, and alcohol and sexual abuse among each other. When some of the first women arrived, including women in their teens and twenties living alone with multiple men, some suffered sexual harassment and rape, finding themselves effectively trapped by the men who had paid their coyote fees.[78] As Jaime Ventura from San Mateo recalled, "We were too young, a lot of people who came were just kids, unprepared to live on their own."[79]

Mexicans in South Philadelphia found a mix of more and less regular employment. Some worked for Italian family businesses that were still in the area, though more found jobs in downtown restaurants, to a lesser extent in construction, and when women came, in hotel and home housekeeping and child care. Some Mexicans also boarded the white vans that passed through the neighborhood in the early morning, picking up Southeast Asians, African Americans, and Latin Americans for day labor in suburban warehouses and chocolate factories. They spent long hours packing produce or cutting fruit salad and other prepared food sold at convenience stores like Wawa and 7-Eleven. Men from San Mateo most often took restaurant jobs because, as Ventura explained, "They would feed us, and we could eat well. This allowed us to save money on expenses, and to save more to send home." It was also more regular and safer work than most construction jobs, where wage theft was more common, especially in day labor.[80]

Mexicans did the most precarious jobs in construction, landscaping, warehouse packing, restaurants, and housekeeping. Their bosses and coworkers regularly subjected them to verbal abuse, calling them "dirty Mexicans" and worse. In some settings, especially construction, they kept Mexican laborers working long hours in tight spaces, unprotected from chemicals or dust, doing repetitive and exhausting tasks without breaks. Workplace injuries also occurred in restaurants and, especially in the late 1990s and early 2000s, young Mexican men and women working in restaurants were sexually harassed, abused, and sometimes raped. Some experienced verbal and sexual abuse from the drivers of vans taking people to day labor. Some men attained better construction jobs over time, including in a general contracting cooperative formed by Mexican carpenters who had been active in labor organizing. Many Mexicans opened their own restaurants and stores. But both structural and interpersonal violence at work persisted for many Mexicans who remained without legal status, insurance, or benefits, doing irregular and dangerous work.[81]

Outside of the workplace, while relations with most neighbors in South Philadelphia remained peaceful, violence affected Mexicans' everyday experiences. For restaurant workers, who were paid in cash and walked or biked home late at night from downtown, systematic muggings by African Americans and sometimes whites became routine. Italian, Irish, and African American neighbors sometimes harassed or threatened them. Mexicans learned to avoid the blocks where some of their neighbors sold drugs on the street. When some of the first teenagers living with their parents in the neighborhood went to South Philadelphia High School, they faced aggression from some of their classmates. A December 2009 attack by African American students who chased and beat up thirty teens recently settled in the area targeted mostly youth from China, but also a few Mexicans and a Dominican boy who suffered permanent hearing damage in one ear.[82]

In other ways, though, Mexicans' relationships with most of their neighbors were deeply symbiotic, driving revitalization in a large swath of the city. Their labor served a growing population of young white families and other affluent residents, visitors, and businesses downtown and in surrounding neighborhoods, including South Philadelphia. Mexican busboys, dishwashers, and cooks provided the cheap and expandable workforce behind an unprecedented boom in high-end restaurants across these neighborhoods, making downtown and South Philadelphia world-renowned restaurant destinations.[83] While poorer parts of the city continued to lose population, these areas grew enough starting in the 1990s that by 2007 the city was expanding again, thanks particularly to Mexican immigration. As one title in the *Daily News* in 2011 quipped, "Let's put it this way: Philadelphia gained more amigos."[84]

Mexican merchants reopened shuttered corner stores throughout South Philadelphia and revived the historic Italian Market on Ninth Street. Once a vital neighborhood shopping district and still a tourist attraction, the six-block-long market had declined as whites left for the suburbs. In 2001, the city's planning commission certified the southern half of the market as blighted, noting a preponderance of boarded-up storefronts. But by 2008, every storefront was reopened or under renovation, mostly by Mexican merchants. Within a five-block radius from the market, Mexicans had opened eighty-five shops and restaurants, and they would open more in coming years.[85]

Initially, they ran just two types of business: restaurants serving other Mexicans and some other customers and small general stores with an array of groceries, household goods, phone cards, sometimes prepared meals, and in the back, money wiring, package shipping, and travel agent services.[86] In the late 2000s a barber and a used bicycle shop opened, signaling that the community had grown enough to support specialized stores. Then Mexican merchants opened bakeries and shops selling clothing, soccer shoes and jerseys in youth and adult sizes, music and electronics, religious statues, and dresses and decorations for quinceñera celebrations, Mexican girls' coming-of-age religious services and parties held at age fifteen.[87] In just a few years it had become a fast-growing community of families, some of whom were starting to buy homes.

Many Mexicans left the New York region after the September 11 attacks and more came from Mexico, many from Puebla but also from all over the country. Between 2000 and 2010, the city's population of Mexican heritage, mostly people born in Mexico and their children, expanded from some 6,000 to over 15,000, according to the census. This was almost surely a substantial undercount, as demographers' models could not fully account for the recent growth, nor completely make up for Mexicans' low census response rates. By the later 2010s, Mexicans lived in neighborhoods all over the city and region, especially concentrated around Norristown, Bensalem, and Camden (see figure 5.1).[88]

South Philadelphia remained the center of Mexican Philadelphia, however. One local newspaper dubbed the neighborhood "Mexadelphia" in 2006. Credit for the moniker "Puebladelphia" went to Marcos Tlacopilco, who, with his wife, Alma Romero, first worked at an Italian-owned fish market on Ninth Street, then bought the shop when their boss retired and died, and later opened a restaurant specializing in breakfast for people on their way to work.[89]

People began to observe that the Italian Market had become just as much a Mexican market.[90] In its northern blocks, where Italian cheese shops and butchers remained, the unofficial historic markers erected by a local historian accentuated the impression that, like other Little Italy districts, this part of the market had become an "ethnic Disneyland," as another scholar averred. These and other signs on shops reminded visitors that Italians had been there longer, and their foods always "predominated." A three-story mural of Frank Rizzo, the city's notoriously racist police commissioner in the 1960s and mayor in the 1970s, also adorned this area. Mexican and Southeast Asian merchants, meanwhile, felt no need to defend their authenticity and claims to the area, since they largely served coethnic customers who lived in the neighborhood.[91]

Other Italian Americans reacted to their Mexican neighbors with more blatant racism and xenophobia. "*I AM MAD AS HELL! I WANT MY COUNTRY BACK!*" read a sign that Joey Vento, owner of Geno's Steaks, one of the city's landmark cheesesteak shops on Ninth Street, pasted on the window where people made their orders. The sign just below it portrayed a bald eagle and an American flag. It read, "This Is America. When Ordering Please 'Speak English.'"

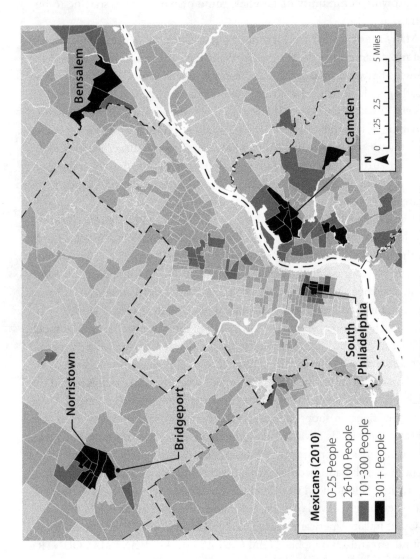

**Figure 5.1.** Map of Mexican settlement in Philadelphia and its suburbs in 2010. (Source: US Census; map by Danielle Dong.)

In interviews with local media, Vento lamented that a politics of multiculturalism had eclipsed the politics of Americanization that his own immigrant grandparents had endured. They had "tried" but "had a hard time" learning English, and rarely left South Philadelphia. "Go back to the 19th century, and play by those rules," he proposed. "I don't want somebody coming here to change my culture to their culture," he said. "They want us to adapt to these people. What do you mean, 'Press 1 for Spanish'? English, period. Case closed. End of discussion."[92] He seemed unaware that Mexicans were learning English at a faster rate than Italians and Poles had a century earlier.[93] And his critique of illegal immigration suggested his ignorance of the fact that the United States had virtually no restrictions on migration from Europe or the Americas in that era.

This rejection of new immigrants from Latin America and call for "English only" repeated much of the logic and rhetoric of nineteenth- and early twentieth-century nativism and assimilationism that had been directed toward Italians.[94] Italians "became white" in the twentieth century partly through violence against their own new neighbors of color: opposing civil rights and Black Power, school desegregation and public housing for Blacks, including in South Philadelphia.[95] Some turned this racism toward Mexicans in the twenty-first century.

Vento's "Speak English" sign gained national attention in early 2006, as debates over illegal immigration blew up. He appeared on Lou Dobbs's show on CNN, Fox News, and right-wing talk radio. Vento and his sign survived a discrimination charge by the city's human relations commission, and he continued to push anti-immigrant messages locally and nationally. On occasion, he drove his Hummer SUV around South Philadelphia with a loudspeaker, denouncing businesses that employed "illegals" before heading home to suburban New Jersey.[96] On New Year's Day 2009, he sponsored a skit in the city's annual Mummers parade, a century-old event that grew out of the racist tradition of minstrel shows. Titled "Aliens of an Illegal Kind," the *Philadelphia Inquirer* related, a grinning Vento popped "out of the top of a float . . . with a 'When ordering, speak English' sign." He tossed fake cheesesteaks into the crowd. Then an announcer cried out, "'Uh-oh, here comes the border patrol!'" Band "members wearing Texas-sized cowboy hats and brandishing wooden rifles pretended to hold back a rioting crowd of 'immigrants,'" white men in costumes that caricatured different cultures around the world, "from storming the" cardboard "border 'fences.' As the immigrants burst forth, they traded in their country's flag for an American flag, and a Mummer dressed as President-elect Barack Obama handed out Green Cards."[97]

Vento became the largest individual donor to the legal fund defending Hazleton's Illegal Immigration Relief Act and gave almost $67,000 to defend the state of Arizona's similar law. Hazleton mayor Lou Barletta and Pennsylvania state representative Daryl Metcalfe traveled to South Philadelphia to raise money for Arizona's legal defense fund with a talk radio show broadcast from under the neon lights of Geno's façade.[98] In the year before he died of a heart attack in 2011, Vento promoted Metcalfe's movement to enlist state legislatures to repeal the US Constitution's guarantee of birthright citizenship.[99] This was part of Metcalfe's nineteen-point platform to deny unauthorized immigrants and their US-born children everything from drivers' licenses to housing and public services and to strip sanctuary cities of state funding.[100]

# Mexican and New Latin American Civil Society

It was in this context that Mexican civil society in Philadelphia, Norristown, and other new immigrant destinations grew up, with a major focus on immigrant rights. At one of the protests held in front of Geno's, Carmen Guerrero barely dodged a punch from one of Vento's defenders, only pulled away from his swinging fist at the last moment by another activist.[101] Yet standing up to anti-immigrant rhetoric and violence was just one part of a larger set of protections and supports that Mexicans and other Latin American immigrants and their allies built in the early twenty-first century.

## South Philadelphia

Cristina Perez had worked just a few years at Women Organized Against Rape (WOAR), one of the first rape crisis centers in the United States, when she began to meet fellow Mexicans in South Philadelphia in 2000. While doing street outreach to find and support people who were experiencing abuse, she learned about the exploitation and violence that women and men faced at home and work. In 2002 she met Peter Bloom, who had taken time off from college along with a friend and recently begun holding volunteer English classes at St. Thomas Aquinas Catholic Church, which had started a mass in Spanish. As Bloom related, after class "there'd be a line of students with issues. They'd have pieces of paper that they needed translated . . . my boss didn't pay me, or I need to find childcare for my kids, or my husband is beating me, how do I get out?" Bloom and his friend had no expertise in these issues, "but we could at least understand what the letter said." They also had a space to "help the community . . . organize themselves."[102]

In the run-down room the church provided them to work with Mexican immigrants, Perez and Bloom agreed on how they would pursue what she called "sanctuary work." They embraced the critical pedagogy of Brazilian philosopher Paulo Friere, a method of supporting oppressed people in regaining their humanity and overcoming their problems. Its proponents integrated human rights topics into classes such as English lessons, as Debbie Wei had done with her Southeast Asian students (discussed in chapter 2). Friere's ideas deeply influenced South American liberation theology and consequently, the Sanctuary Movement. Perez had worked as a human rights activist in El Salvador and Nicaragua in the 1980s and recognized that "we needed to recreate the models of sanctuary that existed at the border" in that era. There in the room at St. Thomas Aquinas they "started to create a culture of sanctuary," she recalled, in which people could feel welcome, identify their capacities and skills, and do the work of "repair," addressing individual trauma and collective social problems.[103]

The early work of Perez, Bloom, and their partners focused on accessing services and confronting the violence that people experienced. Bloom recalled that Mexican people whom they met told them, "'Our community's growing really rapidly, and we've nowhere to go. . . . No one understands what our particular issues are, and all sorts of shit happens to us.'"[104] People slowly began to talk about the violence and exploitation they experienced. Perez formed a group called Hombres en Transicion ("men in transition"), who worked to identify and help others confront the abuses and rights violations that Mexican immigrants faced. They did outreach at restaurants, where they met with groups of men and women and discussed issues of mental health and the challenges of finding help. They "invited a lawyer to come to the church to give a workers' rights training," related Bloom. And they appealed to the Mexican consulate downtown to "really understand that there was a growing population, that they weren't getting the services they needed."[105]

The consular identification card was particularly valuable for people who were in the country illegally. As Bloom explained, "[US] society is pretty much based on having an identity . . . in a very real, who are you, where do you live" sense. Accordingly, the first community organizing campaign that Mexican migrants working with Bloom and Perez launched sought "to get the Mexican Consulate to come out to the community, and . . . [help people] understand how this card could help them." Like leaders in Norristown did around the same time, they spoke with "banks about accepting the card" so people could open accounts and avoid getting robbed of their cash. They also advocated for banks to hire Spanish-speaking tellers at branches in the neighborhood.[106]

When some of the women with whom Perez and Bloom were working, who had been raped crossing the border, decided to get abortions, it became time for them to leave the church. In January 2004, they opened Casa de los Soles ("house of the suns"), the first Latin American community center in South Philadelphia, in the ground floor and basement of a two-story rowhouse. There they incorporated the community-organizing and immigrant rights organization Juntos ("together"), which Bloom would direct. Along with English and computer classes, Casa de los Soles served as "a resource center and sanctuary for the community at large," as early member and later Juntos board chair Carlos Pascual Sanchez put it. Juntos's first two organizers, Mario Ramirez and Jaime Ventura, came from Mexico, though its constituency evolved from entirely Mexicans to also include Central and South Americans.[107]

Their next campaign came from the Safety Committee that Juntos formed, led by Carlos Rojas, a restaurant worker from Mexico City. They met with police at Casa de los Soles multiple times and organized a community meeting on safety at a church, which was attended by over one hundred people. There, committee members negotiated an agreement with South Philadelphia's police precincts to more actively patrol "safe corridors" where people returned home late at night from downtown jobs. The police also reaffirmed their commitment to protect the neighborhood's immigrant community without asking about people's legal status.[108]

In 2006, Perez moved WOAR's work with Mexican immigrants out of the row house it shared with Juntos, as they needed their own safe space for women and others experiencing abuse. WOAR continued to call the spaces it rented Casa de los Soles, and Perez expanded her work with Latin American women around the city. They adopted the community health promoters (*promotoras*) model of outreach, health education, and organizing by people in their own communities that is prevalent in Latin America. In the late 2000s, some 300 promotoras worked with WOAR, mainly in recent immigrant communities.[109] For a few years the organization rented a prominent space on Broad Street in South Philadelphia to work with an even wider range of people on labor violence, discrimination, mental health, and HIV/AIDS, as well as domestic violence and rape. Though it closed after 2015 due to a lack of funds, people in the neighborhood's Latin American communities spoke about Casa de los Soles as if it existed long afterward, Perez reflected. They saw it "in our hearts," as a sort of "sanctuary inside ourselves."[110]

Juntos continued to work with many of the same Mexican community leaders, organizing to address other areas of immigrant rights. In 2007, it moved to the Houston Community Center, not far from the row house it vacated.

Its Latin American constituents joined Asians and African Americans in the English and computer classes run by the center. While Juntos staff still helped people with any problem they brought in the door, its committees of community members took on more focused campaigns.[111] They recognized, organizer Zac Steele related, that "we needed to help people solve their individual social issues," including medical, legal, school, housing, and other needs, "in order to engage them in organizing."[112] However, he explained, "We do not want to be a service organization" because in that model "you are just helping somebody without changing the structure of inequality that produces the problem."[113]

As more children were born and grew up in South Philadelphia's Mexican community, people who were involved in Juntos formed an Education Committee. This group of mostly women, led by Irma Zamora and others, forced the school district to improve language access for parents and students in neighborhood schools. They organized Latin American parents to engage with teachers, administrators, and school programs. With partners around the city, they repeatedly fought proposed funding cuts to the district office that supported English language learners and their families, which Debbie Wei ran for a time. They collaborated with Asian communities and organizations in response to the violence at South Philadelphia High in 2009, and thereafter partnered with the Southeast Asian organization SEAMAAC and its Indonesian constituents to engage in parent organizing together. Some of their work helped improve the culture and sense of community at schools such that wealthier parents became more willing to send their children to neighborhood public schools. This was yet another way that Mexicans and other working-class immigrants enabled gentrification.[114]

Workers' rights remained a constant area of Juntos's work. Staff connected individuals to Community Legal Services, hospitals, and health clinics to redress wage theft and workplace injuries. In 2008, Mexican and Central American men from Northeast Philadelphia approached Juntos about abuses by contractors who hired them at a Home Depot parking lot. Twenty percent of the time they were not paid, and many experienced unsafe and illegal working conditions, sometimes even being abandoned at faraway work sites. Working with the Philadelphia Area Project on Occupational Safety and Health (PhilaPOSH), Juntos ran know-your-rights and safety trainings and organized these men to protect and advocate for themselves. With Community Legal Services they won an $18,000 judgment for ten workers who had been denied pay.[115] Juntos Labor Committee members and partners at PhilaPOSH, including labor organizer and later Juntos board chair Javier Garcia Hernandez, also did outreach and trainings with restaurant workers. Later, they supported the establishment of a chapter of the national Restaurant Opportunities Centers to carry forward this work.[116]

In US traditions of community organizing, organizers typically build non-profit organizations like Juntos, PhilaPOSH, and WOAR. But in Mexican and other Latin American traditions, people practice a great deal of community organizing and solidarity work outside formally incorporated institutions. Many of the leaders involved in Juntos and WOAR, such as Carlos Pascual Sanchez, Carlos Rojas, Maximino "Charro" Sandoval, Irma Zamora, and others, engaged in organizing and assisting other immigrants in numerous ways both in and outside organizations. According to Ricardo Diaz Soto, a doctoral student at the University of Pennsylvania who became involved with fellow Mexicans in South Philadelphia starting in 2004, the "natural leaders" in the community could be found among the women who were most involved in the churches, merchants such as the Tlacopilcos, and the captains of soccer teams, such as "Charro" Sandoval, a community leader from San Mateo Ozolco who served on Juntos's board.[117]

Diaz Soto began by hanging out at a soccer field in the neighborhood where Mexican men played, and soon some players asked him to help organize what became the Amistad Soccer League, based at another field at Fourth and Washington Avenue. As he recalled, it "was created as a place to offer social services and reach those that would not come out to church." At its peak in the mid-2000s, "every Sunday I met with near 600 people that came to watch the games. . . . Our immigration lawyer would sit at one corner of the field, the HIV testers by the basketball court, and the food vendors," who were coordinated by the Tlacopilcos, "took turns instead of competing for customers." They raised funds to refurbish the playground at Fourth Street but met resistance from neighbors when they tried to name it after Mexican American farm labor leader Cesar Chavez.[118]

After the US House of Representatives passed the bill further criminalizing illegal immigration in December 2005, Diaz Soto initiated the first "Day Without an Immigrant" protest in the nation. He engaged merchants, soccer players, people at churches, and Juntos and other groups to organize a rally downtown on Independence Mall. People from the short-lived Orgullo Azteca ("Aztec pride") association of Mexican merchants, led by its treasurer Marcos Tlacopilco, raised funds for the event.[119] Organized as a workers' strike on Valentine's Day 2006, one of the busiest days of the year for restaurants, it underlined the importance of undocumented workers in that industry which Americans increasingly saw as central to the economies and vitality of their cities.

Similar rallies and marches erupted in cities across the country that winter and spring, including more in Philadelphia. Immigrant rights groups launched campaigns targeting members of Congress and other politicians, and lobbied for sanctuary city policies after the passage of Hazleton's restrictive act that summer.[120] While Diaz Soto's Day Without an Immigrant coalition faded, Juntos and other organizations remained involved in similar advocacy.

In 2007, Juntos members and staff were among the first to join the New Sanctuary Movement of Philadelphia (NSM), which was initiated by Pastor Margaret Sawyer and Peter Pedemonti of the Catholic Workers house in North Philadelphia. Manuel Portillo was one of the only early members connected to the Sanctuary Movement of the 1980s, and he oriented others to some of that movement's pitfalls of paternalism and racism.[121] Like the movement of the 1980s, at the start this new interfaith coalition involved mainly white churches and synagogues, but later Black churches and sometimes mosques also joined. Initially, Juntos's Immigration Committee, including Carlos Pascual Sanchez and others, was its largest conduit for involving immigrants, who increasingly took leadership roles in NSM.[122]

In 2010, NSM and Juntos stepped up advocacy for a stronger sanctuary city policy, after the Obama administration expanded the Secure Communities program begun under George W. Bush to force local authorities' collaboration with ICE. As Juntos organizer and NSM board member Zac Steele averred, "The police-ICE relationship . . . is like a covenant of the old Sanctuary Movement, a government practice that is violating God's law that is objectionable."[123] They organized a community forum attended by over 400 Latin Americans and leaders of Haitian, West African, and other communities. There, Mayor Nutter's deputy for public safety announced that the city would stop sharing data on victims and witnesses of crime with ICE.[124]

Four years later, facing further pressure from NSM, Juntos, 1Love Movement, and fellow advocates organized as the Philadelphia Family Unity Network, the mayor signed the executive order creating one of the nation's strongest sanctuary policies. As Peter Pedemonti explained, it was their Southeast Asian allies in 1Love who inspired NSM and other partners to insist that even people convicted of the most serious felonies should be shielded from deportation after doing their time in prison. The leaders of 1Love made a compelling case that they were equally valued members of families and communities, who were just as deserving as anyone of sanctuary protections and of a second chance after their incarceration.[125]

In the 2010s, Juntos's director position passed to a number of Latin American women, including community organizer Erika Almiron, who was the daughter of immigrants from Paraguay. Their work focused ever more on youth. As issues of gender identity and LGBTQ rights gained prominence in the nation at large, Juntos's leaders helped Latinx young people advocate for themselves and navigate the challenges of growing up in communities with entrenched histories of machismo and traditional views of gender and sexuality. With the election of Donald Trump, Juntos's sanctuary work likewise intensified, the details of which are recounted in the final section of this chapter.

While Juntos, NSM, WOAR, and others made sanctuary and human rights a core focus of Mexican and Latin American civil society, people formed organizations in the 2000s to meet various educational, health, and social needs. In many ways they resembled civil society in other communities. Yet their work also underscored the barriers and injustices that Mexican immigrants faced and how they largely had to build support systems for themselves. One of the earliest was a bilingual Head Start program for some of the first young children born in or brought to Philadelphia by Mexican parents, which was run by Dalia O'Gorman, a woman from Mexico.

Beginning in 2002, Rosalva Ruth-Bull, who was born in Cancun and played for the Mexican women's national soccer team, ran soccer leagues for men, women, and children in South Philadelphia, leading as many as fifty-two teams.[126] Though not overtly focused on accessing services like the Amistad league, which faded later that decade, her women's league was an important venue for promoting women's empowerment. Women from Mexico, especially rural areas, rarely played soccer growing up. Therefore, this challenged traditional gender roles, and some of their husbands and boyfriends resisted their involvement in the league. Ruth-Bull confronted some women's partners about this, and Carlos Pascual Sanchez and other men helped watch their kids during practice and games, making their participation possible. The league also served as an informal setting for people to help each other with small and big problems, including connecting to services. Team captains like Irma Zamora became important mentors to other women.[127]

However, the soccer leagues also pointed up the precariousness of Mexicans' claims to space and the ironies of their roles in neighborhood revitalization. Ruth-Bull's teams initially played at Columbus Square Park, but neighbors complained. It was not the Italian American neighbors, who appreciated the sport and welcomed them. Rather, it was the "white, younger professionals, with a burgeoning gay community, and . . . tree-hugging families," said the assistant director of the women's league, a young American woman. They voiced concerns about property values and revitalization, which were laden with undertones of racism. "When it comes to money," she averred, "people are willing to turn in their values."[128] Similar opposition to immigrants' soccer games and gatherings was repeated in city and suburban parks across the country, whether in the name of property values, environmental protection, historic preservation, or less veiled racism.[129]

Ruth-Bull and her teams did much to improve the park, revitalizing a dusty patch of dirt into a well-manicured field. She used her own money for supplies at first, and later became a seasonal grounds worker for the city's Department of Recreation since she was already doing the job. Yet neighbors and city officials proposed moving the leagues to FDR Park, three miles away and tough for players to access between work, family, and other responsibilities. In the end, they moved to a closer recreation center, which had another dusty field that needed sprucing up.[130]

The organization formed out of South Philadelphia's Mexican community that developed the greatest set of services was Puentes de Salud ("bridges to health"). Started in 2003 by three physicians from the University of Pennsylvania, Steven Larson, Jack Ludmir, and Matthew O'Brien, along with nurse Rebecca Bixby, they sought to ensure access to good health care for people who lacked insurance. Ludmir grew up in South America and led the region's top maternity ward at Pennsylvania Hospital. He became the chief obstetrician for babies born to Mexican women, even as other hospitals' wards closed and struggled with the costs of serving people who were uninsured.[131] Larson, whose mother was Puerto Rican, had worked at a clinic serving Mexican farm-workers in Kennett Square. O'Brien and Bixby worked with Alma Romero Tlacopilco, Irma Zamora, and others in Juntos's Health Committee to form a promotoras team and its health education programs.[132]

The Puentes de Salud health clinic in South Philadelphia grew progressively over the years. From seeing patients one day a week at Casa de los Soles and the basements of churches, the Houston Center, or St. Agnes Hospital on Broad Street, they opened a new, full-service health and wellness center in a building donated by the university in 2015. It was funded partly by world-famous restauranteurs whose workforce Puentes served. In the new facility, Latin American immigrants came from nearby suburbs and states as well as Philadelphia. The clinic sometimes also served Africans, Iraqis, and other immigrants and refugees, related its administrator, Carlos Pascual Sanchez.[133]

Seeing that other organizations remained focused on immigrant rights, Puentes' leaders began a range of social and education programs. First they ran after-school tutoring for children of Mexican parents, with college student volunteers joining the medical students who helped staff the clinic. Over the years they expanded with the Puentes Hacia el Futuro ("bridges to the future") youth education program, Lanzando Lideres ("launching leaders") for teenagers, Puentes a las Artes ("bridges to the arts"), and yoga. These programs spanned a continuum from early childhood education and literacy to homework help, summer camp, and SAT and college prep for high schoolers.[134] Puentes also helped the Mighty Writers youth literacy program start a branch for children from Spanish-speaking families on Ninth Street, where Alma Romero Tlacopilco volunteered to prepare and deliver breakfasts five days a week for its students.[135]

As Juntos, Puentes, and other organizations served an increasingly diverse Latin American constituency, Mexicans in South Philadelphia established forums specifically for Mexican cultural expression. This was not just a matter of recreation but also of people's rights to space and to their own culture and identity. Community leaders from San Mateo, led by David Piña, started the San Mateo Carnavalero in 2007, a large annual parade and festival celebrating the Mexican army's defeat of the French in the Battle of Puebla on May 5, 1862. The event drew thousands of people from as far away as New York and Maryland.[136] People from San Mateo and other towns where people spoke Nahuatl started six Aztec dance troupes. While schools and other institutions in Mexico often suppressed indigenous traditions and identities, migration offered opportunities to get in touch with and express them more freely.[137]

In 2009, Dalia O'Gorman and Juntos board member Leticia Roa Nixon opened the Casa Monarca cultural center in a South Philadelphia row house. This was a community-based alternative to the Mexican Consulate's cultural center, whose events at places like the downtown symphony hall attracted more affluent audiences. In the next decade, after Casa Monarca closed, Carlos Pascual Sanchez helped the Fleisher Art Memorial, a free arts school founded in 1898 for Jewish immigrants in the neighborhood, to begin bilingual classes, engage more Mexican artists, and start an annual Day of the Dead celebration, an important holiday in Mexico on the day after Halloween. Its parade through the Italian Market ended with a Mariachi band and Aztec dance at Fleisher's Sanctuary, a former church where artists and community members adorned the altar with the customary blanket of flowers.[138]

Radio stations helped connect and assist people in Mexican Philadelphia from early on. Spanish-language radio mobilized support for the immigrant rights marches in 2006 and later years.[139] In 2013, Edgar Ramirez, a community leader from Oaxaca who was involved in Puentes, Juntos, the Carnavalero, Casa Monarca, and other groups, formed Philatinos Radio. It was a digital station and served myriad purposes, from information, entertainment, and cultural programming to helping people access services and promoting workers' rights.[140]

South Philadelphia Mexican restaurants and their owners also played key roles in civil society, as demonstrated in the work of the Tlacopilcos, and some attracted national attention to the community and its issues. In 2016, *Bon Appetit* magazine named South Philly Barbacoa one of America's best new restaurants. Its undocumented chef and owner, Cristina Martinez, received multiple nominations for the prestigious James Beard chef's award in subsequent years. The increased media attention gave her a national platform for her immigrant rights advocacy.[141] With her husband and coowner, Ben Miller, she formed a cooperative making masa corn meal, which Carmen Guerrero joined as a member.[142] When the coronavirus pandemic hit in 2020, they started the People's Kitchen, making 1,000 meals a week for people out of work.[143] The Tlacopilcos' restaurant Alma del Mar was featured on national television that summer with a makeover on the Netflix show *Queer Eye*.[144]

The most enduring institutions in many Mexican immigrants' lives were churches. "The church is the first place people go looking for services . . . the first place people come together," said Irma Zamora. Their basements were the most accessible "public spaces," noted Carlos Pascual Sanchez: they provided places to gather, talk, and launch projects together, including with Juntos, Puentes, and other groups. Almost always at least one priest or nun in each Catholic parish in South Philadelphia spoke Spanish.[145] They accompanied people to the doctor, translated, and connected them with a wide variety of social, legal, and health services, too.[146]

In 2013, St. Thomas Aquinas church opened the Aquinas Center in its shuttered convent. Its new programs included counseling for mental health, domestic violence, and parenting, as well as ESL classes, know-your-rights trainings, food-based micro-enterprises, and a Hispanic Leadership Institute promoting professional career paths. It ran cultural festivals, a community garden, and a bike-sharing station largely for people who worked in downtown restaurants. Some of these programs served specific constituencies but most promoted interaction among the neighborhood's diverse immigrant and African American communities.[147]

## Norristown and the Suburbs

In Norristown, as in the suburbs at large, Latin American civil society remained smaller than in the city, though it expanded in the twenty-first century. Latin American Community Action of Montgomery County (ACLAMO) in Norristown and Pottstown originated with the older Puerto Rican communities in these towns. Its constituency shifted with new immigration. However, after its director, a Cuban refugee, expressed his opposition to illegal immigration in the local newspaper, many new immigrants avoided the organization and its programs.[148]

However, other people formed programs and partnerships to support newcomers in the area. In 2011, Mexican artist and University of Pennsylvania lecturer Obed Arango opened the Centro de Cultura, Arte, Trabajo y Educación

(CCATE—"center of culture, art, work and education").[149] Initially serving a handful of families in after-school and computer classes, by the end of the decade its membership counted over 250 families. The center's long list of programs, which were initiated and taught by community members and volunteers, included arts, media and technology, environment, language and literacy, health, sports, and college and career development. CCATE structured much of this work as participatory action research in which members conducted research addressing social, economic, and environmental inequities they faced, using their findings to shape programs and make policy recommendations to different levels of government.[150]

Some of the new services and organizing among immigrants in Norristown and nearby suburbs gained traction via the Montgomery County Latino Collaborative. This network formed in the late 2000s through the work of Ludy Soderman, the liaison to community-based organizations at Family Services of Montgomery County, whose mother was Puerto Rican. Its meetings aided communication and service coordination among ACLAMO, CCATE, clergy, and school district officials in Norristown, among other public agencies and nonprofits in the county.[151] Carmen Guerrero was also a member.[152] The collaborative faded after Soderman left to direct the Philadelphia School District's Office of Multilingual Family Support.

But ACLAMO expanded and transformed its relationship with new immigrants, especially after 2015, when it hired a new director, Nelly Jiménez-Arévalo, a Venezuelan who had worked at Latin American organizations in Kennett Square and North Philadelphia. She and her colleagues rejected the notion that organizations serving Latin Americans could work with a single segment of the community. Recognizing that public funds often cannot be used to serve people without legal status, they raised money from private and philanthropic sources to bring services for people without papers up to the same level as those for people with papers. "Everything I do, I think of all my people the same," Jiménez-Arévalo asserted, "and I'm going to offer the same high-quality services to everybody."[153]

From relatively modest social service and ESL programs, ACLAMO developed a large set of new educational, health and wellness programs; housing counseling and assistance; a food pantry; a girls' empowerment group; a fatherhood program; and more. Its leaders pushed other agencies and health clinics in the county to improve access and services and stop discriminating against Latin Americans. ACLAMO opened a new office in Lansdale as the Latin American community grew in that part of the county. And like Puentes de Salud, it formed a group of community and health promoters, thus giving the community greater ownership and leadership of the organization and its work.[154]

In most suburbs, though, Catholic and Evangelical churches remained the chief, and often the only, formal community organizations assisting new Latin American immigrants. La Puerta Abierta's therapy and mentoring programs for Latin American youth (noted in chapter 1) were one exception. La Comunidad Hispana ran social and health programs in rural Kennett Square, while CATA—the Farmworkers Support Committee—promoted workers' rights in Kennett and Bridgeton, both organizations initially founded and sometimes still run by Puerto Ricans.[155]

Some people, however, pursued community work in the suburbs less formally, and probably no one more actively than Carmen Guerrero. In her first few years in the country, she "saw a lot of injustices," harassment and racism at work, school, on the bus. She heard people on the street and in the news say "so many negative things about me and other people from my country."[156] "When I spoke to other people from my country, they had the same" experiences and found no organizations that would help. "I decided to do something that would show us as people with values and culture in the face of a society blind with hate."[157] She started knocking on doors of people's homes and businesses in Norristown, "organizing each other like in Mexico." First, in 2003 they held a festival for Mexican Independence Day, September 16, which was attended by over 1,000 people in the town's largest park. They would continue to organize Mexican cultural events, sometimes with ACLAMO and area churches.[158]

The festival "marked an important point in my work in the community," Carmen noted, "as people sought to continue" the effects it yielded, especially to "help people in the community see us as Human Beings full of dignity and friendship."[159] Soon after the first event, a man named Jonathan Schmidt "arrived to my house," and "signaling with his hands, while I spoke a little bit of English . . . he invited me to be part of some community meetings" of his Southeast Pennsylvania First Suburbs Project. He said, "Come, there's no one who represents Hispanics here, you are a leader." But "I was afraid to open my heart to him, because he looked like a police officer," she recalled. Actually, he was an attorney at a big law firm in Philadelphia, and First Suburbs was his project outside work, uniting people to address the social and economic challenges of the region's working-class suburbs.[160]

Carmen began to attend the First Suburbs meetings. There, organizers from the Service Employees International Union invited her to help reach out to immigrant janitorial workers. She began to visit office buildings at night, across the suburbs and the city. "I [was] afraid to drive, to be in these places, because maybe the police [were] going to" pick her up, she recalled. But "I saw how little money people are making for their work. Not only people who are undocumented, but also people who had green cards. I couldn't believe that people who had papers were abused this way."[161]

At First Suburbs meetings, "all the time I brought my notebook . . . trying to catch the words in English," and "slowly, I had more connections." Her English improved, "and finally we started [being] more active in the community . . . and people started recognizing me as doing many things, like translating in hospitals, in police stations, and in the schools. It was exhausting work for me, because I also needed to do two jobs. This made me really, really tired. But I love it." In 2007, she began volunteering as a counselor and legal advocate at the nonprofit Women's Center of Montgomery County, helping victims of domestic violence. They gave her all the Spanish-speaking clients, whom she met after hours at the center's offices around the county.[162]

The escalation of immigration debates after 2005, and the expansion of deportation, changed Carmen's work. With the Pennsylvania Immigration and Citizenship Coalition and other groups she visited politicians in the region and in Washington, DC, advocating for the Dream Act to protect and support people who were brought to the United States illegally as children, like her daughters. Then came the first major ICE raids on janitorial and landscaping workers around King of Prussia, in 2007. Carmen and colleagues formed a women's group, supporting children and families of people who were deported. "I kept in my house four women with children after the raids, and three children because they didn't have parents after the raids." People from the nascent New Sanctuary Movement "came with so much food, and they gave money to the families . . . connected them with attorneys," and helped find homes for the children. This drew Carmen into work with NSM, Juntos, PhilaPOSH, and attorneys from HIAS-PA and Friends of Farmworkers (later renamed Justice at Work).[163]

Carmen and her partners in Norristown started a "Sunday school" in the parking lot of one of her employers, where attorneys and organizers provided know-your-rights trainings. They continued this work in people's homes, adding ESL classes and support for women who were experiencing domestic abuse. They organized groups of day laborers and students, mainly from Mexico, to address various human rights issues. They formed the Greater Norristown Association of Latino Businesses and held mobile consulate events in Norristown with Mexican, Guatemalan, Honduran, and Salvadoran consular staff from Philadelphia and New York. When bus companies refused her business, Juntos's leaders helped Carmen arrange buses to bring people to marches in Washington, DC. Carmen and her colleagues also joined other communities' campaigns, such as rallies for Palestinian rights and sovereignty. But following another set of ICE raids in 2011, the Norristown area became, for a time, the site of the second-most deportations in the country. Carmen and her allies won a partial victory, however, when they organized to stop police and ICE checkpoints in the town.[164]

In 2012, after Carmen experienced a debilitating bout of Lyme disease, "my daughters retired me" from her day jobs and became her partners in activism. That June, President Obama signed an executive order creating the Deferred Action for Childhood Arrivals (DACA) program, since Congress had repeatedly failed to pass the Dream Act. The following year Carmen's daughters began organizing other young women, in part to help one another take advantage of the protection from deportation and the authorization to work and attend college that DACA promised. Working with their mother, who took a growing leadership role in the group, they helped women to access child care and schooling, information about labor rights, and legal aid for family members detained by ICE. They also began meditating, knitting, and cooking together.[165]

As Carmen related, they would ask one another "'for what are you good? What is your power?' We empower . . . each other, because some would say 'I'm good for nothing.'" Thus, part of their work became identifying women's unrecognized capacities, "because we are vulnerable people . . . we don't have stability," due to legal status and abuse by employers, governments, and men in their lives. They organized monthly health workshops with doctors and an acupuncturist and started a community garden. This was "another way to grow," employing Mexican women's knowledge and skills from their largely rural and indigenous backgrounds. When men asked to join the group in 2016, they changed its name from Mujeres Luchadoras ("fighting women") to Coalición Fortaleza Latina ("coalition of Latina strength"). Their mission, Carmen explained, was to empower each other, educate themselves, "to be respected and to know our human rights," and to help themselves and others realize those rights.[166] As in many immigrant communities, this work was just as active in "informal," unincorporated groups and networks like theirs as it was among more institutionalized nonprofits—both locally and transnationally.

# Transnational Communities and Development

Mexican communities in the United States have a strong tradition of transnational community development and have always lived transnational lives. Older communities in California, Texas, Chicago, and New York had long-established hometown associations through which migrants organized to invest in schools, health clinics, churches, and even roads, parks, water and electrical infrastructure; and sometimes in agricultural and other enterprises as well. Some played large roles in cultural affairs and political and community organizing in their home regions. In these parts of the United States, they formed federations of hometown associations that gained significant political and economic influence in Mexico. Politicians in Mexico responded by developing the Tres-por-Uno (three-for-one) program in 2001, through which local, state, and federal government authorities matched migrants' investments in infrastructure projects.[167]

As a newer destination for Mexican migrants, Philadelphia lacked such institutionalized transnational development. But new migrants all sent remittances to family, and they formed hometown associations engaged in various organizing, advocacy, and community development. "Mexicans always help their communities in Mexico," said Edgar Ramirez. "Almost all towns raise money and send it, . . . they fix schools, purchase things people need, rebuild churches, etc."[168] Individuals sent much of their earnings to their families, especially, but not only, when the community consisted mainly of single people. These funds paid for basic necessities, building and expanding homes, keeping siblings in school longer, and subsidizing family businesses. Like countless other towns in Mexico with economies dependent on remittances, San Mateo Ozolco and other parts of rural Puebla developed a landscape of "remittance houses," which were larger and better furnished than their neighbors. Small shops dotted seemingly every corner, most of which lacked a sufficient customer base to survive without remittances (see figure 5.2).[169] These were some of the most important urban changes produced by Mexican migrants.[170]

Because their settlement coincided with a revolution in telecommunications, Mexican immigrants lived ever more "virtual" transnational lives. In the late 1990s, people in South Philadelphia could still find pay phones on street corners, Carlos Pascual Sanchez remembered. At the back of Mexican-run stores in the neighborhood, people paid to use computers to Skype with family and friends back home. For a time, one merchant opened an entire Skype parlor, as part of the short-lived rise of Internet cafes. But then everyone got a smartphone, joined social media platforms, and could communicate constantly with people across borders.[171]

As in other regions of the United States, Mexican communities with large numbers of people from specific towns sometimes formed their own leadership structures. These mirrored town governments but without the same authority or resources. They helped manage communication with leaders at home and gave newcomers from the town someone they could turn to for in-

**FIGURE 5.2.**  A "remittance house," shop, and bakery built by early migrant Efren Tellez's family in San Mateo Ozolco, Mexico. (Photo by Domenic Vitiello, 2007.)

formation and assistance with all sorts of issues, from problems with land-lords or housemates in Philadelphia to supporting family members in Mexico. People from San Mateo Ozolco elected Maximino "Charro" Sandoval as their leader for many years.[172]

The church was another venue for transnational connections. People imported statues of their hometowns' patron saints, including from San Mateo and nearby Domingo Arenas. They held formal ceremonies to install them in South Philadelphia Catholic churches and paraded the statues through the neighborhood on their saint's days and at the start of the Carnavalero festival.

In the 2000s, Juntos played a substantial role in supporting transnational organizing and development. Its first community organizer, Mario Ramirez, returned to Mexico City in the mid-2000s and incorporated "Juntos Mexico." He began holding *charlas* ("talks"), which were largely informal discussions counseling people who planned to migrate north. Like other service organizations and many priests in Mexico, he sought to debunk the myths they had heard about the United States being an easy place to live and make money and to otherwise prepare people for the realities of migration and life in the North. This included raising their awareness of issues of immigrant rights and know-your-rights training before crossing the border.[173]

With migrants from San Mateo Ozolco, Domingo Arenas, and the village of Oyometepec in another part of the state of Puebla, Juntos staff and board members in Philadelphia pursued other political work. They organized people in Philadelphia and Mexico to advocate against the privatization of these towns' water sources, which politicians threatened to sell to corporations. In Oyom-etepec they launched a reforestation campaign, in which people from San Ma-teo also helped. They reclaimed and planted *ejido* lands, which technically belonged to the village residents collectively but where local politicians had enriched themselves by allowing a logging company to clear the forest. Halt-ing the illegal taking of ejido lands, a widespread problem in Mexico, was an aim of Juntos's organizing in all three towns.[174]

The hometown association Grupo Ozolco, which was led by "Charro" San-doval, Juntos's second community organizer Jaime Ventura, and others from San Mateo, pursued the most active set of projects, usually in collaboration with Juntos. First, they raised enough money in Philadelphia to build a high school in San Mateo Ozolco, which had never had a high school before. Previ-ously, young people wishing to continue past middle school had to travel nearly an hour down the mountain to further their education. Members of Grupo Ozolco also raised funds to fix the town's main church. Some helped Tequilas Restaurant owner David Suro, a board member of Juntos and Puentes de Salud, organize visits to San Mateo with Lisa Nutter, the wife of Philadelphia's mayor, in the early 2010s. A Philadelphia-based artist who was originally from Mexico City came on the first trip and, along with students, teachers, and other people from the town, painted murals on the side of the new high school, de-picting migrants who had left. Suro's foundation donated funds to commu-nity art and education projects in the town. Grupo Ozolco's biggest project, though, came with Ventura's return to live with his mother, sister, niece, and nephew in San Mateo, where he wanted to see if he and others could survive as farmers again.[175]

As Ventura wrote in an essay on maize, under NAFTA, agriculture had be-come "incapable of generating either income or jobs for Mexico's rural resi-dents, and is even less capable of feeding the people." Indigenous farmers "are condemned to live in the margins of society . . . while their children take advan-tage of opportunities to migrate." Indigenous farming methods and seeds passed down for generations were further threatened by multinational corpora-tions' promotion of "industrialized flour" and genetically engineered seeds, and by "the cultural erosion of our indigenous towns," due partly to migration.[176]

Ventura and his colleagues in San Mateo formed a cooperative enterprise to revive organic production of indigenous blue corn in the town's ejido lands. They would toast the kernels over a wood fire on a traditional ceramic platter called a *comal*; take them down the mountain to be mixed with sugar and cinnamon and milled into a flour called *pinole*; and then ship it to Philadelphia. In their vision, in addition to preserving indigenous culture, this could pay at least some farmers in San Mateo enough to survive and perhaps make migration less attractive and necessary for some people. Ironically, they saw this as a way to take advantage of free trade under NAFTA, which was one of the main forces behind their displacement. This was also a chance to capitalize on migrants' relatively unfavorable position in the US labor market, selling pinole to the fancy restaurants that employed them.[177]

In the project's initial years, Peter Bloom, with the freedom of movement afforded by his American passport, traveled back and forth to San Mateo, carrying duffel bags of pinole on his return flights to Philadelphia. Ventura, Bloom, and their colleagues began working with product development and certification experts in Mexico. In Philadelphia, Juntos staff and members of Grupo Ozolco tried out different recipes using pinole, assisted by Carlos Rojas, who worked as the head pastry chef at a swanky Asian fusion restaurant downtown and whose wife was from San Mateo. They made pinole mousse, cheesecake, and muffins, among other desserts, and crafted a marketing plan with visions of creating an import cooperative owned by Grupo Ozolco members. A major grant from Hispanics in Philanthropy and the Packard Foundation supported this project, with a little more than half of the funds going to the work in Mexico.[178]

To some observers in the migrant community, this project was just crazy, and in Philadelphia its success remained limited. As one community leader in South Philadelphia opined, "JUNTOS runs this as a transnational project to resolve an economic and migration problem. If it was a cultural project, it would be better . . . but as an [economic] project it doesn't work."[179] Grupo Ozolco members did import some large batches of pinole and sold it to restaurants, cafes, and specialty food shops. But only one member continued to import and sell pinole, and at a small scale. Years later, though, "Charro" Sandoval opened a well-reviewed restaurant called Blue Corn in the Italian Market with his siblings, all of whom had worked at upscale restaurants downtown. They sourced pinole and unsweetened blue corn flour by the ton from the cooperative led by Ventura in San Mateo, making blue tortillas and huaraches and pinole cheesecake and cupcakes staples of their menu.[180]

Both Juntos and Hispanics in Philanthropy abandoned their transnational community development work in 2011. The Mexican women who made up most of Juntos's board of directors decided to focus the organization's work more on children growing up in South Philadelphia. People's mindset had changed from earlier years, in which most imagined they would soon return to Mexico, especially as they had children in Philadelphia. The philanthropy's leaders were so daunted by the complexity and limited economic returns of the projects they funded that they shut down the entire program supporting this sort of work after just one grant cycle and a few projects. Transnational community development indeed holds many challenges that make it difficult to succeed on traditional economic terms. Moreover, some critics argue that migrants should not be expected to solve their home countries' economic or political problems.[181]

But in San Mateo the cooperative flourished, a relatively rare example of economically successful transnational development and rural small enterprise in Mexico, with notable impacts on migration. With forty members by 2010 and more later, their big break came when they gained a contract selling pinole baked goods to the state of Puebla's indigenous school-meals program. This rough equivalent of the free school-meals program in the United States prioritized sourcing traditional foods from indigenous producers. Slow Food and other international artisan food organizations promoted the cooperative and its products and they shipped blue corn flour to customers in Guatemala and Costa Rica, though this all proved less important for their business than markets in central Mexico.[182]

Members of the cooperative in San Mateo grew blue corn on ejido and private land, converting some of it back to organic production after years of growing transgenic crops using chemical fertilizers. Farmers earned over 100 percent more for their organic blue corn than they could for other corn harvests. They also fermented *pulque*, a strong drink made from juice of the maguey cactus cultivated by many farmers in the area. In 2012 they started an annual pulque festival, which attracted thousands of people and became a venue for promoting their corn products, too.[183] By the end of the decade they ran four lines of business, selling blue and white corn, pulque, and fruits and vegetables.[184]

At least as important was the fact that the cooperative was based at San Mateo's new high school. Its members worked with students daily, contributing to environmental, cultural, business, and other areas of education. Migration to the United States slowed for multiple reasons in the 2010s. But young people who left San Mateo were generally older, more educated, and better prepared for life in the United States or Mexico City than Ventura's generation before them.[185]

While the transnational activities of Juntos and Grupo Ozolco faded in the 2010s, Mexicans in the Philadelphia region launched other work. In 2014, with the disappearance of forty-three students in Mexico, Carmen Guerrero "joined international groups dealing with my homeland's issues of violence, misery and wars," and femicide.[186] After Trump's election in 2016, she and her colleagues in Coalición Fortaleza Latina sought out attorneys who specialized in international family law to aid families that had been separated by deportation. Carmen and other advocates from the Philadelphia region became increasingly involved with the Border Angels and other cross-border networks. Members of Coalición Fortaleza Latina collaborated with people who had been deported from Pennsylvania, looking into the well-being of other people in Mexico. They helped people find and assist relatives who disappeared or became stuck without money or family in the border region of northern Mexico, as some cartels began kidnapping and recruiting people who were deported.[187] These constituted key transnational dimensions of an energized, but only in some ways new, sanctuary movement.

## What's New about Sanctuary?

While echoing older visions and practices of sanctuary, the politics, violence, and injustices of the twenty-first century rendered America's immigrant rights movements even broader projects of solidarity and human rights. After Trump came to power, "nothing changed regarding many hours working within the community" and supporting people, Carmen reflected. But she and her partners in Coalición Fortaleza Latina "started organizing immediately after the election," expanding their know-your-rights workshops and partnerships with university- and community-based advocates. This included the Shut Down Berks coalition, with Juntos and others, which sought to close the only immigrant family detention center in the Northeast United States, in nearby Berks County (see figure 5.3). They engaged attorneys to help Central Americans and Haitians in the Norristown area keep their Temporary Protected Status. Working with students from Bryn Mawr College, they started a "piggy bank" emergency fund for families of people detained by ICE. They supported people as far away as Kennett Square, almost an hour from Norristown, with clothing drives, donated beds, paying for dental care, and accompanying and interpreting for people in meetings with ICE. They helped churches in Norristown connect with NSM.[188]

The Trump administration ushered in a new, but not entirely new, era of immigration politics and of detention and deportation practice, spurring greater immigrant rights and sanctuary activism. Through his first three years in office, the United States deported fewer immigrants annually than under

**FIGURE 5.3.** Carmen Guerrero (right) and Blanca Pacheco, codirector of NSM, at a rally to end family detention in 2018. (Photo by and courtesy of Sabrina Vourvoulias, *Generocity*.)

Obama. But under Trump, ICE targeted a wider range of people, while under Obama it focused on people with criminal records, even if its raids also swept up others. The Trump administration detained more people in immigration prisons, for longer periods, including many more children and families.[189] Moreover, Trump took steps to dismantle the entire immigration, refugee, and asylum system, as detailed in prior chapters.

Trump's rhetoric escalated fears of detention and deportation among Mexican and other immigrants. He continually railed against immigrants and refugees in openly xenophobic and racist speeches and social media posts, starting with his campaign launch in June 2015. "When Mexico sends its people, they're not sending the best," he proclaimed. "They're sending people that have lots of problems and they're bringing those problems. . . . They're bringing drugs, they're bringing crime. They're rapists."[190] In the nation's immigration debates, facts mattered little, including criminologists' consistent finding that Mexican and other immigrants were less likely to commit crimes than native-born people and played a major part in the decline of violent crime in American cities in recent decades.[191] Trump promised to build a "big, beautiful wall" on the southern border, make Mexico pay for its construction, and form an expanded "deportation force" to expel some three million "illegal aliens."[192] As in Central American communities profiled in chapter 1, many Mexicans withdrew from public life to some extent during the Trump era. Organizers canceled the San Mateo Carnavalero in May 2017 out of fear that ICE would target the festival to detain and deport people.[193]

Yet well before Trump's election in 2016, Mexican migration to the United States had slowed and return migration to Mexico was increasing, even if Philadelphia's Mexican population continued to grow and the second generation expanded significantly. The recession that started in 2008 limited job opportunities in the United States, while opportunities in Mexico improved. By 2018, for the first time Mexicans accounted for fewer than half of all people living illegally in the country and China replaced Mexico as the top sending country of immigrants to the United States.[194] In Philadelphia, people's practice of inviting family and friends from Mexico to join them diminished. Trump's rhetoric along with stepped-up border enforcement and detention deterred new migration and made people without legal status more afraid to visit Mexico due to the risks involved in trying get back into the United States.[195]

The legal status of the great majority of recent Mexican immigrants remained an intractable issue, despite repeated proposals in Congress to give people a path to citizenship in the early twenty-first century. The Obama administration's DACA program granted only tenuous protections to a limited set of people, and courts quickly struck down Obama's attempt to give similar protections to unauthorized immigrant parents of children who were US citizens. As Peter Bloom noted back in 2008, "the dream" is "just to be legal, to be decriminalized, and to be able to live our lives with dignity." With the growth of the second generation, "part of the future has happened already . . . it's all about the kids, what happens with them . . . really determines what happens in the community."[196] But sanctuary remained relevant, especially for their parents and for millions of other families in Mexican and other communities across the country.

South Philadelphia's Mexican community was well established by the time of Trump's election, and in some ways it was more accepted than a decade earlier. Mexican merchants joined the Italian Market's 9th Street Business Association.[197] Members of the San Mateo Carnavalero participated in the Mummers Parade on New Year's Day in 2016.[198] In October that year, Geno Vento removed the "Speak English" sign that his now-deceased father had posted in the window of their cheesesteak shop.[199] In 2020, during nationwide protests over police violence and racial injustice, city officials painted over the mural of Frank Rizzo in the Italian Market. They vowed to replace it with a mural celebrating the area's many cultures.[200]

Philadelphia's city government increasingly supported immigrant communities, and sanctuary, in the later 2010s. After Mayor Nutter brought about a brief hiatus in the city's sanctuary policy in the weeks before he left office in January 2016, Mayor Kenney not only revived the policy on his first day, he also expanded the Mayor's Office of Immigrant Affairs, which Nutter had started. It soon became a permanent city department, coordinating services to newcomer communities and supporting immigrant advocates. In 2018 the city's new district attorney committed to do all he could to prevent the deportation of immigrants accused of nonviolent crimes.[201] After successfully defending its sanctuary policy against the Trump administration in court, the next year Mayor Kenney announced a pilot program in which the city would pay for the legal defense of some immigrants in detention. His administration also launched a municipal ID card to ease immigrants' access to city services.[202] Still, Pennsylvania's state capitol remained a hotbed of anti-immigrant legislators, and police in the suburbs continued to collaborate with ICE.[203]

These local and state dynamics were not all new, but Trump's rhetoric, his emboldening of anti-immigrant movements, and his administration's actions inspired a dramatic expansion of immigrant rights and sanctuary movements. Straightaway following his election, thousands of people flocked to the New Sanctuary Movement, including participants in the 1980s Sanctuary Movement who had been unaware or disinterested in joining the new group in its first decade.[204] More congregations expressed interest than NSM could accommodate.

Compared to the 1980s, NSM advanced a similar but expanded definition of sanctuary. NSM's geopolitical vision of global solidarity, as well as many of its practices, from legal and material aid to sanctuary in churches, closely resembled those of the Sanctuary Movement of the 1980s. So did its foundations in religious faith, for immigrant and receiving community members alike. But it was a broader human rights movement, embracing the most repeated slogan of twenty-first-century immigrant rights advocates, Holocaust survivor Elie Wiesel's observation that "no human being is illegal."[205] Most obviously, NSM was not just focused on Central Americans. It was not an antiwar movement, and its national political platform was much less specific than that of its predecessor's asylum and foreign policy demands. Yet its campaigns for city and state policies were more specific and mattered more to a much greater share of Philadelphia and other cities' residents.

People in the New Sanctuary Movement in Philadelphia and across the country expressed an intersectional critique of injustice much like, but perhaps even more than, activists did in the 1980s. Especially after the presidential election of 2016, this constituted a response to Trump and his allies' assault on immigrants, people of color, and LGBTQ rights. Since its start in 2007, NSM had always asserted that Black and brown lives mattered, whether immigrant or native born.[206] This all echoed, but usually went beyond, efforts to link the oppression of Central Americans, Haitians, Chileans, South Africans, and African Americans in the 1980s.

The practices of sanctuary activism took both old and new forms. The New Sanctuary Movement in Philadelphia and other parts of the United States had only occasionally harbored people in churches before 2016. Angela Navarro, who fled violence in Honduras, was the first immigrant on the East Coast to enter sanctuary in the twenty-first century, in NSM member church West Kensington Ministry in North Philadelphia on November 18, 2014. Fifty-eight days later she won her case against deportation in court and left the church.[207] But after Trump's election this older tradition of sanctuary revived.

By April 2018, at least forty-two people were living in sanctuary congregations in twenty-eight cities around the United States.[208] In Philadelphia, NSM counted thirty member congregations by 2020, including immigrant-led churches in Haitian, Indonesian, and Latin American communities. Several, including the historic African American Church of the Advocate, Germantown Mennonite Church, and the city's first two sanctuary congregations in the 1980s, Tabernacle United and First United Methodist Church of Germantown, harbored families who had fled violence in Honduras, Jamaica, and Mexico and had orders of deportation against them. The second family from Honduras that entered sanctuary in a Philadelphia church won its appeal to stay in the United States in 2020, as did the family from Jamaica.[209]

Unlike Central Americans in sanctuary in the 1980s, some of these families stayed many months or years inside the church itself, in arguably more public acts of civil disobedience. They held solidarity dinners and other events with no bandanas covering their faces. Their asylum and other legal claims still hinged on the details of their specific experiences, but their cases were not usually tied to broader claims that a much larger group of people from particular countries merited protection, as in the 1980s.

Like sanctuary workers in the 1980s, people in the New Sanctuary Movement pursued a variety of community-based organizing strategies, especially in Philadelphia, but again they supported immigrant communities more broadly. NSM's campaigns to gain Pennsylvania drivers' licenses for immigrants without legal status, and to end Philadelphia's practice of impounding cars driven by people without licenses, predated Trump's election. So did its continued sanctuary city campaigns, as well as opposition to bills in the state legislature that sought to end sanctuary city policies.[210] NSM and Juntos also provided material assistance to people who were in the country illegally, including those whose family members were detained. In 2019 NSM supported more than 225 new legal cases for immigrants who were fighting deportation. During the COVID pandemic in 2020, NSM issued "stimulus checks" to 400 families who were out of work and whose legal status meant they would not receive the stimulus payments from the government.[211]

Some of this work highlighted the more urban focus of twenty-first-century sanctuary activists, their greater promotion not only of sanctuary city policies but also of mobility, neighborhood safety, and other issues in the city. In late 2016, NSM launched its Sanctuary in the Streets campaign, which trained people to disrupt ICE raids when their neighbors were detained. In at least one case people succeeded in driving away ICE agents attempting a raid. Juntos started a similar Community Resistance Zones program in South Philadelphia, held protests blocking ICE vans from exiting the agency's local office, and, along with other advocates, protested plans for new "shelters" in the city and suburbs to detain unaccompanied migrant children.[212]

NSM, Juntos, and their allies celebrated their victories in convincing city leaders to strengthen sanctuary protections, but they continually pointed out the limits of sanctuary city policies. On the eve of Trump's inauguration in January 2017, Juntos issued a statement declaring, "Philadelphia is NOT and has never been a Sanctuary City." As long as "ICE continues to deport our loved ones by either getting people on the streets or by raiding their homes," genuine sanctuary remained unattainable. "What Philadelphia does do is abide by the fourth amendment in that it requires ICE to produce a warrant signed by a judge if they want the city to hold someone" for ICE. "That alone does not make us a Sanctuary City."[213]

Indeed, after Trump's election Mayor Kenney eschewed the term *sanctuary city.* "We do not use that term," declared his Office of Immigrant Affairs. Instead, his administration called Philadelphia first a "Fourth Amendment City" and then a "Welcoming City."[214]

The sanctuary city's limits were painfully obvious to immigrants. In October 2018, reporters publicized what immigrants and activists already knew: "On two dozen occasions, police, probation officers and even one of Kenney's top deputies have quietly provided tips to ICE about undocumented immigrants who were charged with crimes. Other forms of information-sharing still continue," as well. These were just the two dozen instances documented in court or acknowledged by city officials, which were part of a larger and longer pattern.[215] After ICE detained a pregnant Honduran woman who was dropping off her child at a

South Philadelphia elementary school in early 2020, Juntos launched a survey of teachers and administrators that found little awareness that the school district was bound to follow the city's sanctuary policy.[216] While officially a "sanctuary district," its leaders did not use that term and it meant little in practice.

Activists around the country made similar critiques of the limits of sanctuary cities, echoing 1980s sanctuary workers but again going further.[217] They argued that American cities could not be true sanctuaries without affordable housing, good schools, safety, and decent wages for all. They demanded an end to discriminatory policing, mass incarceration, and other injustices.[218] Juntos's leaders repeatedly railed against public school closures and gentrification in South Philadelphia, including the replacement of their own office to make way for a coffee shop. They likened the displacement of immigrants in the neighborhood to their displacement from their home countries, both of which resulted from a neoliberal world order with few protections for working-class people.[219] NSM's leaders and members decried the erosion of "labor protections . . . and social infrastructure," including welfare and public housing, with the Trump administration's "resurgence of white supremacy."[220] Amid the rallies for racial justice and threats of city budget cuts during the pandemic in 2020, they advocated for antieviction and renter protection policies; funding for parks, homeless services, libraries, public health, arts and culture; and defunding of the police.[221]

For activists in the twenty-first century, sanctuary came to mean something all-encompassing and never-ending. People involved in NSM often repeated, "*Sanctuary* is not a noun, but a *verb*."[222] At the same time it was, as expressed in NSM's 2017 Statement on Sanctuary, "a vision continuously created through . . . thousands of years of struggle . . . a vision of collective and personal transformation," of "collective liberation." All the movement's "work, campaigns and community building are part of a larger vision to build Sanctuaries within ourselves, our cities, and our world." Sanctuary was "the umbrella that covers all of us from the storm, and the womb to birth a new world."[223]

Ultimately, while intensely focused on assisting and protecting the human rights of vulnerable immigrants, sanctuary was not just about newcomers. Rather, as the reverend of one member congregation expressed in her sermon welcoming a Mexican mother and her children into sanctuary in her North Philadelphia church, "We benefit ourselves when we love radically" and "stand for and with each other to fight for justice."[224] As Carmen Guerrero said to her partners in NSM in 2018, "We're living a new global dis-order. The human rights situation in our own countries is serious." In the United States, "we've experienced abuses all the time." For her, "the most important work that" sanctuary activists "can do is one of unification, to accomplish the changes necessary to recognize everyone as one humanity."[225]

# Conclusion

## What Do We Owe Each Other?

> The bosom of America is open to receive not only the opulent & respectable Stranger, but the oppressed & persecuted of all Nations & Religions; whom we shall wellcome to a participation of all our rights & previleges, if by decency & propriety of conduct they appear to merit the enjoyment.
>
> —George Washington to the Irish "lately arrived" in New York City (December 2, 1783)

It is difficult to square the United States' history of enslavement, exclusion, oppression, and expulsion of foreign peoples with what has also been at times a deeply generous and humane experience of welcoming and assisting newcomers. Often, individual communities, cities, and states have taken different stances on who deserves protection and support. This is one reason why sanctuary is an appropriately complex and contested frame through which to understand our history of immigration.

America and its cities have not been open in the same ways to different groups of immigrants and refugees, especially "the oppressed and persecuted of all nations and religions" whom George Washington indicated. Nor have newcomers enjoyed the same sorts of welcome "to a participation of all our rights and privileges." The meanings of sanctuary—the protections and assistance people seek, receive, and build for themselves and one another—have therefore varied in different communities, places, and times.

The many chapters of our nation's history have made the question of what we might owe immigrants and refugees fragmented, complicated, and often disputed. The United States has had different relationships with different nations and peoples of the world. Throughout our history we have demanded foreign peoples' labor, but Americans and our leaders have been less willing to grant those people full membership in our society or full rights as human beings, especially, though not only, when they have black or brown skin.[1] The actions of our government, military, and corporations overseas have often played a part in displacing the people who come to the United States as immigrants and refugees. Most Americans are not taught to think of our nation as an imperial power in this way. However, this is crucial for grasping not just our relations with other nations but also the ways in which we have racialized, excluded, and oppressed, yet also assisted and sometimes helped save, some of their people through our actions abroad and at home.[2] This is one of the reasons why immigration and sanctuary must be understood in transnational perspective and at other scales simultaneously.

A sanctuary city is something that most Americans define narrowly, relating only to local governments that resist our federal laws. This is presumably not relevant to refugees or immigrants who are in the country legally. But sanctuary means far more than sanctuary city or state policies and procedures. Sometimes, for some people, sanctuary policies matter little if at all, even if at other times they matter greatly for people who are in the country illegally, and for their families and communities. Often the protections and assistance offered by individuals, communities, and civil society have been more enduring and more meaningful. Newcomer and receiving communities' experiences of comparatively mundane aspects of life—housing, employment, neighborhoods, and relations with neighbors—have influenced people's well-being and life trajectories, as individuals and groups, usually more profoundly than the sanctuary declarations of city halls or state capitols. Moreover, these things matter for far more people than only those among us who lack legal status.

Some of the newcomers discussed in this book experienced more comfortable, welcoming histories of settlement, work, and inter- and intragroup relations. They all fled violence and experienced various sorts of trauma. They came to the United States with different legal statuses, but those statuses were frequently contested and often changed. Some people, like most Iraqis and many Liberians, arrived with relative advantages of education, wealth, and extended families and coethnic receiving communities that were ready to help them. Others, including Cambodians, Central Americans, and Mexicans, usually came without wealth, often from places far different from urban America, and sometimes as children without parents or guardians. Those who came in the 1970s and 1980s settled in a city that was declining, while those arriving in the twenty-first century found improved housing, neighborhoods, and sometimes work conditions and opportunities in a revitalizing city. These and other details of their histories before, during, and after migration to the United States, including their subsequent migrations and transnational relationships, help explain their varied outcomes and trajectories over time.

These histories also help explain why civil society has taken diverse forms, with varying emphasis, aims, and challenges in different communities, at the local and national and transnational levels. Sanctuary movements have focused intense love and assistance on relatively small numbers of people, especially in the 1980s. But viewed in the perspective of more enduring solidarity and human rights work, the sanctuary movements of the late twentieth and early twenty-first centuries both had broader effects on communities and public policy. Meanwhile, the resettlement system was almost never sufficient in itself for refugees to attain self-sufficiency. This was essentially by design. Instead, to a great extent each group of refugees and immigrants resettled themselves, took control of their own protection and support, and over time moved beyond survival to repair and rebuild their lives and communities. They almost always had key allies in receiving communities, who were often prior immigrants and refugees themselves. Civil society, in its more and less formal configurations, offers a vital way to understand these dimensions of sanctuary.

Comparing immigrant and refugee groups has great pitfalls as well as possibilities. It can help us grasp the diversity of newcomer communities; but when done too casually, it can reproduce ignorance, racism, and injustice. Some Americans ask why many Southeast Asians, Mexicans, or Africans have not achieved the same upward mobility that many Koreans, Indians, or Chinese immigrants have enjoyed.[3] Others ask, like Joey Vento did, why today's immigrants cannot play by the same rules as their ancestors did. Many Americans of "old immigrant stock" have viewed newcomers through the lens of their memory, and often fictions, about their ancestors.[4] These lines of questioning repeat "model minority" myths and mask the class and ethnic diversity within many groups. They fail to sufficiently appreciate the distinct political, economic, and social contexts of immigration for different groups arriving at very different times in history. They also fail to grasp—and in doing so they help to reproduce—contemporary global and local structures of inequality, oppression, and advantage that shape the experiences of different groups.

Reflecting on sanctuary offers a way to grapple with the histories and complexities of immigration and newcomers' relationships to the places they settle, as well as the places they leave and often return. Sanctuary, as a way to think about migration and cities, enables us to transcend the limitations of seeing immigrants and refugees from the reductive perspective of costs and benefits. It lends a more critical perspective and points up some of the limits of even the more positive and multifaceted, but still sometimes fraught, terms of revitalization and integration.

The history of sanctuary, of the protections and assistance some human beings offer others, also reminds us that we all have choices in how we view and treat newcomers. To paraphrase Judith Bernstein-Baker, the longtime director of the Hebrew Immigrant Aid Society—Pennsylvania (HIAS-PA), in her response to Joey Vento's demands that Latin American immigrants assimilate in the same ways his Italian grandparents were forced, but struggled, to do: We can say, like he did, that our people suffered, so new immigrants should suffer, too. Or we can decide we do not want newcomers today to suffer like many of our ancestors did and we can help them experience a different America.[5] Or as Thoai Nguyen put it, "We must fight to keep the doors open for those who come after us."[6]

Ultimately, considering sanctuary forces us to confront what we owe one another as people, as neighbors in a local and global sense. Some people feel greater responsibility toward their neighbors than toward strangers who live farther away. Some nations operate this way, with borders that remain open, or more open, to people from countries nearby, often out of a recognition that they share labor markets, economies, histories, and cultures. Following this logic, the United States should treat people from Mexico, Central America, and the Caribbean quite differently than we have (US border and employment policy is generally friendlier toward Canadians, as they come from a wealthier country and usually have white skin).

However, if we perceive neighbors not just as people who live in physical proximity but also as people with close ties of different sorts, whether political, economic, or otherwise, then the United States has many "global neighbors."[7] Our long history from the slave trade to wars, colonial relationships, and economic interdependence, including dependence on foreign people's labor on their own soil and ours, renders many of these ties quite intimate. This history also suggests that we owe a great deal of our prosperity and freedoms to the hard work and oppression of our global neighbors. Recognizing this history and the fact that it is not all in the past has inspired much of America's sanctuary and other immigrant rights movements.

Each chapter in this book ends during or shortly after the presidency of Donald Trump, which was a particularly intense period of anti-immigrant nationalism. But practically all of US history, including the several prior decades explored in this book, has been a time of tension and conflict over immigration, including questions about who deserves protection, assistance, and membership in US society, cities and communities. Even the most sweeping changes to the US immigration system, including those legalizing the greatest number of people who were in the country without permission, as in 1986, never created a nation that was entirely without unauthorized immigrants. Nor did they do away with people's need for protections and assistance of other sorts.

President Joe Biden undid many of the immigration, refugee, and asylum policies of his predecessor, Donald Trump, through executive orders issued during his first days in office. Still, his administration continued to treat different groups of immigrants differently, casting some as deserving and others as not deserving. The country and the world remained bitterly divided over immigration, and anti-immigrant sentiment and movements persisted.

As the different chapters of this book reveal, sanctuary has taken on many meanings and is continually debated and redefined. "The competing meanings of sanctuary," writes Ann Deslandes—the ancient purpose "to preserve the lives of murderers; to create temporary safety for fugitives; to maintain basic well-being for people fleeing oppression; to guarantee human rights—may keep the global debate about our obligations to each other alive."[8] As the world confronts climate change and new waves of environmental refugees, the meanings and work of sanctuary promise to take new forms, even as their old forms persist in some fashion.

*Sanctuary* is both a noun and, for many people, a verb—a set of actions and processes. It is just as much a vision, a bundle of aspirations for a better, more peaceful world. Sanctuary is about more than immigrants and refugees, even if it is centrally about them. It is fundamentally about solidarity with other people, and in another sense it is about our relationships to the places that sustain us.

To many people, "sanctuary" evokes, first and foremost, a physical space, whether religious or secular space where people feel at peace with themselves and one another. As the communities explored in this book demonstrate, sanctuary spaces exist at multiple scales. From churches, synagogues, mosques, homes, or schools, sanctuary also operates—as a vision and practice—in larger geographies, including neighborhoods, cities, states, and transnational communities.

As members of the Chicago Religious Task Force on Central America and the Tucson Ecumenical Council Central America Task Force wrote in their manual on sanctuary in 1982, not only were violent regimes "profaning the human through torture and terror . . . , but the very sacredness of the earth is being violated. Whole areas must be officially designated as sanctuaries for birds and other wildlife to protect them from extinction," and from "the onslaught of private developers, bull-dozers, and strip-mining. All around us we find the need to sanctify spaces in order to protect the sacredness of the earth, its animals, and its people."[9] This warning and this vision remain even more prescient in the twenty-first century, with an unprecedented number of people around the world displaced by wars, persecution, climate change, and related disasters. The protection and support of the most vulnerable among us offers a chance to save not just some "other people," but also ourselves.

# NOTES

## Introduction

1. Cristobal Valencia, Testimony to Philadelphia City Council Committee on Public Safety, March 12, 2014, https://phlcouncil.com/sanchez-blackwell-kenney-call-for -end-to-philadelphias-cooperation-on-ice-holds/.

2. 1Love Movement, "Philly's New ICE Detainer Policy: Time for Celebration, Caution, and Culture Shift," accessed June 29, 2021, https://1lovemovement.word press.com/2014/04/.

3. Tamara Jimenez, "What Are ICE Holds," accessed June 28, 2021, http:// paimmigrant.org/wp-content/uploads/2014/03/Tamara-Jimenez.pdf.

4. Chioma Azi, Testimony to Philadelphia City Council Committee on Public Safety, March 12, 2014, https://phlcouncil.com/sanchez-blackwell-kenney-call-for -end-to-philadelphias-cooperation-on-ice-holds/.

5. Ryan Tack-Hooper and Jacob Bender, "Testimony Submitted by the Philadelphia Chapter of the Council on American-Islamic Relations to the Philadelphia City Council Committee on Public Safety Regarding ICE Detainers," March 12, 2014, http://paimmigrant.org/wp-content/uploads/2014/03/CAIR-Philadelphia -Testimony.pdf.

6. Naroen Chhin, Testimony to Philadelphia City Council Committee on Public Safety, "Hearing: Police and ICE Collaboration," March 12, 2014, https://1love movement.wordpress.com/2014/03/14/testimony-naroen-chhin.

7. A word about some of the terminology used in this book: I mainly use the phrase "people who are in the country illegally" and similar phrases to acknowledge that I am writing about people and that their presence or residence in the United States is illegal. I sometimes use the terms "unauthorized" or, rarely, "undocumented," though the latter term—and also the term "illegal immigrants"—appears mainly in quotes from various sources. I tend not to use the term "undocumented" since I find it inaccurate in most cases, as the great majority of people—even those who are in the country illegally—do have some form of documents and are often "documented" by various authorities. Perhaps most significantly, the term "undocumented" obscures the fact that the majority of people who were in the United States illegally when I wrote this book actually arrived (migrated) legally, and their entry to the country was documented by federal authorities. I use the term *illegal immigration* (without quotation marks) to refer to people crossing the border without authorization.

8. "Resolution for City Council Action Declaring Philadelphia a City of Sanctuary," 1986, Philadelphia Committee In Solidarity with the People of El Salvador

(CISPES) Records (DG 183, Box 9), Swarthmore College Peace Collection, Swarthmore, PA, https://www.swarthmore.edu/peace-collection.

9. "Resolution for City Council Action."

10. "Resolution for City Council Action."

11. Angela Berryman, interview by Domenic Vitiello, January 13, 2016.

12. Outreach letter, April 1986, Central America Network files, Swarthmore Peace Collection.

13. "New Mexico Is Declared Sanctuary for Refugees," *New York Times*, March 30, 1986.

14. Gordon Connell-Smith, "The Crisis in Central America: President Reagan's Options," *World Today* 39, no. 10 (October 1983): 385–392.

15. "Why Philadelphia Should Become a Sanctuary City," Central America Network files, Swarthmore Peace Collection.

16. Christian Smith, *Resisting Reagan: The U.S. Central America Peace Movement* (Chicago: University of Chicago Press, 1996), 185.

17. Philadelphia's City Council had already passed resolutions supporting the Sanctuary Movement before congregations in the city began hosting Central Americans, for example: Resolution No. 732 (*Journal of the City Council* [Philadelphia, 1982], 331–332, 351); Resolution No. 1156 (*Journal of the City Council* [Philadelphia, 1983], 737–738, 781); and later, Philadelphia City Council, Resolution 707 (Philadelphia, February 1, 1990); Philadelphia City Council Resolution (September 30, 1999), reprinted on *School of the Americas Watch—West*, http://www.peacehost.net/soaw-w/philareso.html. See also, Israel Colon, email to the author, January 5, 2017; Jorge Morales, interview by Domenic Vitiello, November 10, 2016.

18. David Funkhouser, "Some Thoughts on CAOP Direction, 1/13/86," Philadelphia Area Alliance for Central America Collection (PAACA DG181, Box 9), Swarthmore Peace Collection.

19. Handwritten notes on typewritten memo and list of contacts, Sanctuary City Campaign folder (PAACA DG181, Box 9), Philadelphia Area Alliance for Central America Collection, Swarthmore Peace Collection.

20. Ron Devlin, "Sanctuary for Refugees Spreads across U.S.," *Morning Call* (Allentown, PA), November 30, 1986; Morales, interview; Anne Ewing, interview by Daniel Schwartz, November 12, 2009.

21. Devlin, "Sanctuary for Refugees Spreads."

22. Jim Corbett, "Sanctuary, Basic Rights, and Humanity's Fault Lines: A Personal Essay," *Weber* 5, no. 1 (Spring–Summer 1988), https://weberstudies.weber.edu/archive/archive%20A%20%20Vol.%201-10.3/Vol.%205.1/5.1Corbet.htm.

23. Norma Stoltz Chinchilla, Nora Hamilton, and James Loucky, "The Sanctuary Movement and Central American Activism in Los Angeles," *Latin American Perspectives* 36, no. 6 (November 2009): 101–126; Amy Villarreal Garza, "Religious Revivalism and the Politics of Immigration in New Mexico" (PhD diss., University of California, Santa Cruz, 2014).

24. Jim Corbett, *Goatwalking: A Guide to Wildland Living—A Quest for the Peaceable Kingdom* (New York: Viking, 1991).

25. Manuel Portillo, interview by Domenic Vitiello, March 1, 2017; Morales, interview.

26. Devlin, "Sanctuary for Refugees Spreads."

27. Michael B. Katz, *The Undeserving Poor: From the War on Poverty to the War on Welfare* (New York: Pantheon, 1989), and *The Price of Citizenship: Redefining the American Welfare State* (New York: Holt, 2001); Lawrence J. Vale, *From the Puritans to the Projects: Public Housing and Public Neighbors* (Cambridge, MA: Harvard University Press, 2000).

28. Yen Le Espiritu, "Toward a Critical Refugee Study," *Journal of Vietnamese Studies* 1, nos. 1–2 (2006): 410–433; Yen Le Espiritu, *Body Counts: The Vietnam War and Militarized Refuge(es)* (Berkeley: University of California Press, 2014); Quan Tran, "Anchoring Boat People's History and Memory: Refugee Identity, Community, and Cultural Formations in the Vietnamese Diaspora" (PhD dissertation, Yale University, 2016); Mimi Thi Nguyen, *The Gift of Freedom: War, Debt, and Other Refugee Passages* (Durham, NC: Duke University Press, 2012); Eric Tang, *Unsettled: Cambodian Refugees in the New York City Hyperghetto* (Philadelphia: Temple University Press, 2015).

29. Leonie Sandercock, *Cosmopolis II: Mongrel Cities of the 21st Century* (New York: Continuum, 2003), 127; see also Michael Jones-Correa, "All Immigration Is Local: Receiving Communities and Their Role in Immigrant Integration," Center for American Progress, Washington, DC, September 20, 2011, https://www.americanprogress.org/issues/immigration/reports/2011/09/20/10342/all-immigration-is-local/.

30. Domenic Vitiello, "Sanctuary and the City," *Metropole*, March 6, 2019, https://themetropole.blog/2019/03/06/sanctuary-and-the-city.

31. "Why Philadelphia Should Become a Sanctuary City."

32. Robert J. Sampson, "Immigration and the New Social Transformation of the American City," in *Immigration and Metropolitan Revitalization in the United States*, ed. Domenic Vitiello and Thomas J. Sugrue, 11–24 (Philadelphia: University of Pennsylvania Press, 2017).

33. Jacques Derrida, *The Politics of Friendship* (1994; reprint, New York: Verso, 2006); Derrida, *On Cosmopolitanism and Forgiveness* (New York, Routledge, 2001); Jacques Derrida and Anne Dufourmantelle, *Of Hospitality* (Redwood City, CA: Stanford University Press, 2000); see also Ann Deslandes, "Sanctuary Cities Are as Old as the Bible," *JStor Daily*, March 22, 2017, https://daily.jstor.org/sanctuary-cities-as-old-as-bible/.

34. Peter Mancina, "The Birth of a Sanctuary City: A History of Governmental Sanctuary in San Francisco," in *Sanctuary Practices in International Perspectives: Migration, Citizenship and Social Movements*, 205–218, ed. R. K. Lippert and S. Rehaag (Abingdon, UK: Routledge, 2012), 205–218; Helen B. Marrow, "Deserving to a Point: Unauthorized Immigrants in San Francisco's Universal Access Healthcare Model," *Social Science & Medicine* 74 (2012): 846–854.

35. Jonathan Darling, "Forced Migration and the City: Irregularity, Informality, and the Politics of Presence," *Progress in Human Geography* 41, no. 2 (2017): 178–198 (quote on 184); see also Tanya Basok, "Counter-Hegemonic Human Rights Discourses and Migrant Rights Activism in the US and Canada," *International Journal of Comparative Sociology* 50, no. 2 (2009), 183–205; Monica Varsanyi, "Interrogating 'Urban Citizenship' vis-à-vis Undocumented Migration," *Citizenship Studies* 10, no. 2 (2006): 229–249; Amy Foerster, "Solidarity or Sanctuary? A Global Strategy for Migrant Rights," *Humanity & Society* 43, no. 1 (2019): 19–42; Vicki Squire, "From Community Cohesion to Mobile Solidarities: The *City of Sanctuary* Network and the *Strangers into Citizens* Campaign," *Political Studies* 59, no. 2 (2011): 290–307.

36. Patricia Ehrkamp and Caroline Nagel, "'Under the Radar': Undocumented Immigrants, Christian Faith Communities, and the Precarious Spaces of Welcome in the U.S. South," *Annals of the Association of American Geographers* 104 (2014): 319–328 (quote on 321; also Ehrkamp and Nagel, "Immigration, Places of Worship and the Politics of Citizenship in the U.S. South," *Transactions of the Institute of British Geographers* 37 (2012): 624–638; Jennifer Bagelman, "Sanctuary: A Politics of Ease?" *Alternatives: Global, Local, Political* 38, no. 1 (February 2013): 49–62.

37. Darling, "Forced Migration and the City," 185; see also Jonathan Darling, "Giving Space: Care, Generosity, and Belonging in a UK Asylum Drop-In Centre," *Geoforum* 42 (2011),:408–417; Karen Wren, "Supporting Asylum Seekers and Refugees in Glasgow: The Role of Multi-Agency Networks," *Journal of Refugee Studies* 20, no. 3 (2007): 391–413.

38. Els de Graauw, *Making Immigrant Rights Real: Nonprofits and the Politics of Integration in San Francisco* (Ithaca, NY: Cornell University Press, 2016).

39. Wanda Motley, "Church Ministers to Salvadorans," *Philadelphia Inquirer* (August 6, 1989).

40. "Why Philadelphia Should Become a Sanctuary City."

41. Linda Rabben, *Sanctuary and Asylum: A Social and Political History* (Seattle: University of Washington Press, 2016); Deslandes, "Sanctuary Cities Are as Old as the Bible."

42. Chicago Religious Task Force on Central America and Tucson Ecumenical Council Central America Task Force, "Sanctuary," September 1982, reprinted in *Central American Refugees: A Survey of the Current Situation,* comp. Angela Berryman, 35 (rev. ed., Philadelphia: Friends Service Committee, May 1983); see also Rabben, *Sanctuary and Asylum.*

43. Others include Sikh, Bahá'í, and secular humanist traditions. See Lev. (19:34); Deslandes, "Sanctuary Cities Are as Old as the Bible"; Rabben, *Sanctuary and Asylum*; UNHCR USA, "Welcoming the Stranger: Affirmations for Faith Leaders," 2013, https://www.unhcr.org/51b6de419.html; American Friends Service Committee (AFSC), "Texts on the Shared Value of Welcoming the Stranger," n.d., accessed January 3, 2021, https://www.afsc.org/document/texts-shared-value-welcoming-stranger.

44. Rabben, *Sanctuary and Asylum*, 95–121; Andrea Roberts, The Texas Freedom Colonies Project, accessed July 13, 2020, http://www.thetexasfreedomcolonies project.com.

45. Nelson Diaz, interview by Domenic Vitiello, January 14, 2021.

46. Diaz, interview.

47. John Timoney, "Memorandum (01–06): Departmental Policy Regarding Immigrants." May 17, 2001; see also Malcolm Burnley, "How Michael Nutter Changed Philadelphia's Immigration Status," *Next City* (March 30, 2015).

48. Timoney, "Memorandum (01–06)."

49. Diaz, interview.

50. Laura Sullivan, "Enforcing Nonenforcement: Countering the Threat Posed to Sanctuary Laws by the Inclusion of Immigration Records in the National Crime Information Center Database," *California Law Review* 97, no. 2 (2009), http://www.californialawreview.org/wp-content/uploads/2014/10/09Apr_Sullivan.pdf.

51. H.R.4437—Border Protection, Antiterrorism, and Illegal Immigration Control Act of 2005, passed the House of Representatives amended on December 16, 2005, https://www.congress.gov/bill/109th-congress/house-bill/4437.

52. Hazleton City Council, Illegal Immigration Relief Act Ordinance (2006-18).

53. Monica Varsanyi, ed., *Taking Local Control: Immigration Policy Activism in U.S. Cities and States* (Stanford, CA: Stanford University Press and Center for Comparative Immigration Studies, 2010); Kyle Walker and Helga Leitner, "The Variegated Landscape of Local Immigration Policies in the United States," *Urban Geography* 32, no. 2 (2011): 156–178; Domenic Vitiello, "The Politics of Immigration and Suburban Revitalization: Divergent Responses in Adjacent Pennsylvania Towns," *Journal of Urban Affairs* 36, no. 3 (August 2014): 519–533; Justin Steil and Jennifer Ridgley, "'Small-Town Defenders': The Production of Citizenship and Belonging in Hazleton, Pennsylvania," *Environment and Planning D: Society and Space*, 30 (2012): 1028–1045; Justin Steil and Ion Vasi, "The New Immigration Contestation: Social Movements and Local Immigration Policy Making in the United States, 2000–2011," *American Journal of Sociology* 119, no. 4 (January 2014): 1104–1155.

54. Maria-Teresa Vazquez-Castillo, "Anti-Immigrant, Sanctuary, and Repentance Cities," *Progressive Planning*, January 3, 2009, http://www.plannersnetwork.org/2009/01/anti-immigrant-sanctuary-and-repentance-cities/.

55. Sullivan, "Enforcing Nonenforcement"; see also Jennifer Ridgley, "Cities of Refuge: Immigration Enforcement, Police and the Insurgent Genealogies of Citizenship in U.S. Sanctuary Cities," *Urban Geography* 29, no.1 (2008): 53–77.

56. Emma Jacobs, "Philly Police Will No Longer Hold Immigrants on Behalf of ICE," *NewsWorks*, April 16, 2014, http://www.newsworks.org/index.php/politics/item/66969-philly-police-will-no-longer-hold-immigrants-on-behalf-of-ice?linktype=featured_articlepage.

57. Julia Terruso, "Kenney: Philadelphia Stays a 'Sanctuary City' Despite Trump," *Philadelphia Inquirer*, November 10, 2016, https://www.inquirer.com/philly/news/politics/20161111_Kenney__Philadelphia_stays_a__sanctuary_city__despite_Trump.html.

58. Executive Order 13767—Border Security and Immigration Enforcement Improvements, January 25, 2017, https://www.federalregister.gov/documents/2017/01/30/2017-02095/border-security-and-immigration-enforcement-improvements; Executive Order 13768—Enhancing Public Safety in the Interior of the United States, January 25, 2017, https://www.federalregister.gov/documents/2017/01/30/2017-02102/enhancing-public-safety-in-the-interior-of-the-united-states; Executive Order 13769—Protecting the Nation from Foreign Terrorist Entry into the United States, January 27, 2017, https://www.federalregister.gov/documents/2017/02/01/2017-02281/protecting-the-nation-from-foreign-terrorist-entry-into-the-united-states.

59. Maria Cristina Garcia, *The Refugee Challenge in Post-Cold War America* (New York: Oxford University Press, 2017).

60. Audrey Singer, Susan Hardwick, and Caroline Brettell, eds., *Twenty-First Century Gateways: Immigrant Incorporation in Suburban America* (Washington, DC: Brookings Institution Press, 2008).

61. Henry Messaros, "Other Areas Lure Immigrants from Phila.," *Philadelphia Evening Bulletin*, March 23, 1969.

62. Carmen Teresa Whalen, *From Puerto Rico to Philadelphia: Puerto Rican Workers and Postwar Economies* (Philadelphia: Temple University Press, 2001); Matthew Countryman, *Up South: Civil Rights and Black Power in Philadelphia* (Philadelphia: University of Pennsylvania Press, 2007).

63. Jake Blumgart, "Can Philadelphia Continue to Thrive without Immigration?" *WHYY—PlanPhilly*, February 7, 2018, https://whyy.org/articles/can-philadelphia-continue-to-thrive-without-immigration/; Domenic Vitiello, "What Does Unauthorized Immigration and Sanctuary Mean for Philly's Revival?" *PlanPhilly*, January 12, 2017.

64. Domenic Vitiello and Thomas J. Sugrue, "Introduction: Immigration and the New American Metropolis," in *Immigration and Metropolitan Revitalization in the United States*, ed. Vitiello and Sugrue, 1–8.

65. Vitiello, "What Does Unauthorized Immigration and Sanctuary Mean."

66. The term *Middle East* was coined by the imperial powers of Europe and the United States that defined the borders of countries in Southwest Asia mainly after World War I. I employ this term in this book since it is the most widely recognized name for this region.

## 1. Sanctuary in Solidarity

1. Joel Morales, eulogy for Jorge Morales, December 3, 2016; see also Jorge Morales, interview by Domenic Vitiello, November 10, 2016.

2. Lini S. Kadaba, "Given a 'Rare' Blessing of Asylum: Life in Limbo Ends for Two Guatemalan Refugees in City," *Philadelphia Inquirer*, November 24, 1986; see also Ted Loder, *No One But Us: Personal Reflections on Public Sanctuary* (San Diego, CA: Lura-Media, 1986); Anne Ewing, interview by Daniel Schwartz, November 12, 2009; Joel Morales, interview by Daniel Schwartz, November 15, 2009.

3. Joel Morales, interview by Domenic Vitiello, November 10, 2020; Ann Crittenden, *Sanctuary: A Story of American Conscience and Law in Collision* (New York: Weidenfeld and Nicolson, 1988), 291.

4. Joel Morales, interview by Schwartz; Crittenden, *Sanctuary*, 292.

5. Kadaba, "Given a 'Rare' Blessing."

6. Joel Morales, interview by Schwartz; see also Ewing, interview; Loder, *No One But Us*.

7. Joel Morales, interview by Schwartz; Ewing, interview; Crittenden, *Sanctuary*, 292.

8. Estimating the number of disappearances is challenging. Families of "disappeared" people give figures in the range of 50,000 to 70,000, while other estimates are as low as 40,000 for these years; and the disappearances also continued after this period. The 45,000 estimate is from the International Committee of the Red Cross, "Guatemala: Desaparicón," April 22, 2020, https://www.icrc.org/es/document/guatemala-desaparicion; see also Kadaba, "Given a 'Rare' Blessing"; Loder, *No One But Us*, 181.

9. Joel Morales, interview by Schwartz; Ewing, interview; Loder, *No One But Us*, 181.

10. Kadaba, "Given a 'Rare' Blessing"; Crittenden, *Sanctuary*, 292–293.

11. James Smith, "Guatemala: Economic Migrants Replace Political Refugees," Migration Policy Institute, April 1, 2006, http://www.migrationpolicy.org/article/guatemala-economic-migrants-replace-political-refugees.

12. Angela Berryman, "Response to All Refugees," in *Sanctuary: A Resource Guide for Understanding and Participating in the Central American Refugees' Struggle*, ed. Gary MacEoin, 156 (New York: Harper and Row, 1985).

13. Joel Morales, interview by Schwartz; Crittenden, *Sanctuary*, 293.

14. The links between the Eisenhower administration and United Fruit also included US ambassador to the UN Henry Cabot Lodge, a major owner of the company's stock, and the president's personal secretary, Ann Whitman, whose husband was the company's chief public relations officer. Stephen Schlesinger and Stephen Kinzer, *Bitter Fruit: The Untold Story of the American Coup in Guatemala* (New York: Anchor, 1982); Baltimore County History Labs, "Background on the Guatemalan Coup of 1954," n.d., accessed November 23, 2020, https://www.umbc.edu/che/tahlessons/pdf/historylabs/Guatemalan_Coup_student:RS01.pdf; Rich Cohen, *The Fish That Ate the Whale: The Life and Times of America's Banana King* (New York: Farrar, Straus and Giroux, 2012).

15. Both the United Nations–affiliated Truth Commission for Historical Clarification of Guatemala and the Catholic Church–sponsored Commission for the Recovery of Historical Memories concluded that Guatemala's state-sponsored violence amounted to genocide. Proyecto Interdiocesano Recuperación de la Memoria Histórica, *Guatemala, Never Again! REMHI, Recovery of Historical Memory Project* (Maryknoll, NY: Orbis, 1999); Daniel Rothenberg, ed., *Memory of Silence: The Guatemalan Truth Commission Report* (New York: Palgrave MacMillan, 2012); Kadaba, "Given a 'Rare' Blessing"; Loder, *No One But Us*; Maria Cristina Garcia, *Seeking Refuge: Central American Migration to Mexico, the United States, and Canada* (Berkeley: University of California Press, 2006); see also Renny Golden and Michael McConnell, *Sanctuary: The New Underground Railroad* (Maryknoll, NY: Orbis, 1986); Robert Tomsho, *American Sanctuary Movement* (Austin: Texas Monthly, 1987); Crittenden, *Sanctuary*; Rotem Bar, "'If You Knew the Truth, Then Surely You Would Help Us,'" *Philadelphia Inquirer Magazine*, June 2, 1985.

16. Crittenden, *Sanctuary*, 294.

17. Joel Morales, interview by Schwartz.

18. Ewing, interview; see also Angela Berryman, interview by Domenic Vitiello, January 13, 2016.

19. *United States v. Aguilar*, US Court of Appeals, Ninth Circuit (1989), http://openjurist.org/883/f2d/662/united-states-v-aguilar; "Alien Tells of Aid in Entering US," *New York Times*, February 10, 1986.

20. *United States v. Aguilar*, 20.

21. *United States v. Aguilar*, 18–21, 100; Scott McCartney, "Sanctuary: Unlikely Bunch Are Leaders in the Sanctuary Movement," *Lewiston Daily Sun* (Lewiston, ME), 12.

22. Kadaba, "Given a 'Rare' Blessing"; Joel Morales, interview by Vitiello.

23. Manuel Portillo, interview by Domenic Vitiello, March 1, 2017.

24. Most histories of the Sanctuary Movement have been written by its American participants, largely as stories about themselves, though some scholars have placed Central Americans at the center of accounts of the movement. See, for example, Norma Stoltz Chinchilla, Nora Hamilton, and James Loucky, "The Sanctuary Movement and Central American Activism in Los Angeles," *Latin American Perspectives* 36, no. 6 (November 2009): 101–126.

25. Chicago Religious Task Force on Central America and Tucson Ecumenical Council Central America Task Force, "Sanctuary," September 1982, reprinted in Angela Berryman, "Central American Refugees: A Survey of the Current Situation," American Friends Service Committee, May 1983.

26. Chicago Religious Task Force on Central America and Tucson Ecumenical Council Central America Task Force, "Sanctuary."

27. Berryman, interview.

28. Portillo, interview.

29. Jim Corbett, "Sanctuary, Basic Rights."

30. Jim Corbett, "Sanctuary, Basic Rights."

31. See for example Corbett, *Goatwalking*; Bar, "'If You Knew the Truth,'" 22; Garcia, *Seeking Refuge*.

32. Marlena Santoyo, interview by Daniel Schwartz, November 12, 2009.

33. Sister Margaret McKenna, interview by Daniel Schwartz, December 1, 2009.

34. Phillip Berryman, *Memento of the Living and the Dead: A First-Person Account of Church, Violence, and Resistance in Latin America* (Eugene, OR: Resource, 2019).

35. Chinchilla, Hamilton, and Loucky, "The Sanctuary Movement and Central American Activism in Los Angeles."

36. Corbett, *Goatwalking*; Golden and McConnell, *Sanctuary*.

37. Chicago Religious Task Force on Central America and Tucson Ecumenical Council Central America Task Force, "Sanctuary."

38. Molly Todd, "'We Were Part of the Revolutionary Movement There': Wisconsin Peace Progressives and Solidarity with El Salvador in the Reagan Era," *Journal of Civil and Human Rights* 3, no. 1 (2017): 1–56; Jessica Stites Mor, ed., *Human Rights and Transnational Solidarity in Cold War Latin America* (Madison: University of Wisconsin Press, 2013).

39. Mary Day Kent, interview by Domenic Vitiello, January 4, 2016.

40. David Funkhouser, interview by Domenic Vitiello, December 11, 2015.

41. Angela Berryman and Phillip Berryman, "I Was a Staff Member," *Peace Works: Century of Action*, American Friends Service Committee, 2015, http://peaceworks.afsc .org/angela-and-phillip-berryman/story/251; see also Berryman, interview; Berryman, *Memento of the Living and the Dead*.

42. Berryman, interview.

43. Phillip Berryman, *Inside Central America: The Essential Facts Past and Present on El Salvador, Nicaragua, Honduras, Guatemala, and Costa Rica* (New York: Pantheon, 1985); Phillip Berryman, *Liberation Theology* (Philadelphia: Temple University Press, 1987); Phillip Berryman, *Memento of the Living and the Dead*.

44. Berryman, interview.

45. Kent, interview.

46. Kent, interview.

47. Ewing, interview; Dick Cox, interview by Daniel Schwartz, October 30, 2009; Vic Compher, interview by Daniel Schwartz, November 3, 2009.

48. Bar, "'If You Knew the Truth'"; Daniel Schwartz, "Recruiting for Sanctuary: Explaining Involvement in the Original and New Sanctuary Movements of Philadelphia" (University of Pennsylvania, Urban Studies senior thesis, 2009); Funkhouser, interview.

49. Sanctuary Congregations and Related Congregations, Philadelphia Area Alliance for Central America Records (box 9), Swarthmore Peace Collection, Swarthmore, PA, https://www.swarthmore.edu/peace-collection.

50. Smith, *Resisting Reagan*, 185; Ron Devlin, "Sanctuary for Refugees Spreads across U.S.," *Morning Call* (Allentown, PA), November 30, 1986.

51. Marion Brown, interview by Daniel Schwartz, October 22, 2009; Marion Brown, correspondence with Domenic Vitiello, January 4, 2021; Marion Brown, correspondence with Domenic Vitiello, January 8, 2021.

52. Schwartz, *Recruiting for Sanctuary*.

53. Cox, interview; Ewing, interview; Loder, *No One But Us*.

54. Cox, interview; Ewing, interview; Loder, *No One But Us*.

55. Loder, *No One But Us*, 53.

56. Loder, *No One But Us*, 53; Joel Morales, interview by Schwartz; Jorge Morales, interview.

57. Chicago Religious Task Force on Central America and Tucson Ecumenical Council Central America Task Force, "Sanctuary."

58. Brown, correspondence, January 4, 2021.

59. Loder, *No One But Us*; Kristin Holmes, "A New Meaning for Sanctuary: Political Changes Have Redirected the Energies of Activists," *Philadelphia Inquirer*, September 16, 1993; Kadaba, "Given a 'Rare' Blessing."

60. Michele Bartlow, interview by Daniel Schwartz, October 8, 2009; see also Brown, interview; Brown, correspondence, January 4, 2021.

61. Ewing, interview.

62. Loder, *No One But Us*; Bar, "'If You Knew the Truth.'"

63. Joel Morales, interview by Schwartz; Ewing, interview; Portillo, interview.

64. Loder, *No One But Us*; Holmes, "New Meaning for Sanctuary"; Kadaba, "Given a 'Rare' Blessing"; *United States v. Aguilar*.

65. Kent, interview.

66. Jorge Morales, interview.

67. Bar, "'If You Knew the Truth,'" 24.

68. George Garretson, interview by Daniel Schwartz; Kent, interview.

69. Chestnut Hill Meeting Declaration of Sanctuary, February 10, 1985, Chestnut Hill Meeting Archives.

70. Chestnut Hill Meeting Declaration of Sanctuary.

71. Chestnut Hill Friends Meeting Sanctuary report, December 6, 1985, Chestnut Hill Friends Meeting Archives.

72. Chestnut Hill Friends Meeting Sanctuary report.

73. Chestnut Hill Friends Meeting Sanctuary report.

74. Mary Day Kent, correspondence with Domenic Vitiello, June 3, 2021.

75. Betsy Morgan, interview by Daniel Schwartz, November 17, 2009.

76. Bar, "'If You Knew the Truth,'" 20, 22.

77. Morgan, interview.

78. Linda Holtzman, interview by Daniel Schwartz, October 20, 2009.

79. McKenna, interview by Schwartz.

80. McKenna, interview by Schwartz; Sister Margaret McKenna, interview by Domenic Vitiello, March 24, 2021.

81. McKenna, interview by Schwartz.

82. Domenic Vitiello and Michael Nairn, "Community Gardening in Philadelphia: Harvest Report," October 2009.

83. Crittenden, *Sanctuary*, 300.

84. Loder, *No One But Us*, 59–64; Jorge Morales, interview; Brown, correspondence.

85. Loder, *No One But Us*, 59–64; Jorge Morales, interview; Brown, correspondence.

86. Loder, *No One But Us* (quotes are from 213; see also 201, 212); Crittenden, *Sanctuary*, 296.

87. Loder, *No One But Us*, 214.

88. Jorge Morales, interview; Cox, interview.

89. Jorge Morales, interview.

90. Bar, "'If You Knew the Truth,'" 31.

91. Berryman, interview.

92. Kent, interview.

93. Portillo, interview.

94. Kent, interview.

95. Mary Jane Fine, "An Issue for Swarthmore Council: Refugee Sanctuary," *Philadelphia Inquirer*, February 28, 1986; Devlin, "Sanctuary for Refugees."

96. Schwartz, *Recruiting for Sanctuary*, 40–41.

97. Corbett, *Goatwalking*; Sara Kennedy, "Local Sanctuary Group Vows to Go On: Germantown Members to Continue Aid to Latin Refugees," *Philadelphia Inquirer* (May 2, 1986); Howard Witt, "Sanctuary Activists Lose Conspiracy Trial: 8 Guilty in Refugee-smuggling Case," *Chicago Tribune* (May 2, 1986).

98. Kadaba, "Given a 'Rare' Blessing."

99. Loder, *No One But Us*, 97.

100. Kadaba, "Given a 'Rare' Blessing."

101. Jorge Morales, interview.

102. Smith, "Guatemala."

103. While accounts of the Sanctuary Movement commonly note the importance of refugees' testimony, as "living witnesses," in the movement, recognizing their involvement and leadership of this transnational work helps capture their broader impacts on peace and reconstruction in Central America. The quote is from Chinchilla et al., "The Sanctuary Movement," 112.

104. Funkhouser, interview; also Andrew Maykuth, "On the 'Gringo Trail' in Nicaragua: Foglietta among Those Opening U.S. Fact-finding Season," *Philadelphia Inquirer*, January 19, 1987.

105. Maykuth, "On the 'Gringo Trail.'"

106. Kent, interview; Ewing, interview; Funkhouser, interview; Loder, *No One But Us*, 53.

107. Wanda Motley, "Church Ministers to Salvadorans," *Philadelphia Inquirer*, August 6, 1989.

108. Morgan, interview.

109. Motley, "Church Ministers to Salvadorans."

110. Guatemala Urgent Actions and Guatemala Focus Group folders, PAACA (DG181, box 13), Philadelphia Area Alliance for Central America Collection, Swarthmore Peace Collection.

111. Jorge Morales, interview.

112. Holmes, "New Meaning for Sanctuary."

113. Holmes, "New Meaning for Sanctuary."

114. Cox, interview.

115. Schwartz, "Recruiting for Sanctuary," 11; see also Holmes, "New Meaning for Sanctuary."

116. Cox, interview; Ewing, interview.

117. Molly Todd, *Beyond Displacement: Campesinos, Refugees and Collective Action in the Salvadoran Civil War* (Madison: University of Wisconsin Press, 2010); Molly Todd, "Wisconsin's Cold War Citizen Diplomats, Sister Cities, and the Salvadoran Civil War," *Wisconsin Magazine of History* 101, no. 1 (2017): 28–41.

118. "Congressman Peter Kostmayer Reports Important News from Guatemala," summer 1990, Delaware County Pledge of Resistance Records (DG 242, box 3), Swarthmore College Peace Collection.

119. Guatemala Committee, "The Permanent Commissions of Guatemalan Refugees in Mexico," 1993, and "Taking Action on Guatemala," 1993, Delaware County Pledge of Resistance Records, Swarthmore College Peace Collection; see also, Molly Todd, "The Paradox of Transamerican Solidarity: Gender, Race, and Representation in the Guatemalan Refugee Camps of Mexico, 1980–1990," *Journal of Cold War Studies* 19, no. 4 (2017): 74–112.

120. Joel Morales, interview by Schwartz; Guatemala Conference folder, Delaware County Pledge of Resistance Records, Swarthmore College Peace Collection.

121. PEACE for Guatemala Annual Report, 1990, Delaware County Pledge of Resistance Records, Swarthmore College Peace Collection.

122. PEACE for Guatemala Newsletter, Spring–Summer 1991, Delaware County Pledge of Resistance Records, Swarthmore College Peace Collection.

123. "Join the Guatemala Committee," letters, and committee notes in Philadelphia Area Alliance for Central America Records (boxes 12 and 13), Swarthmore College Peace Collection.

124. Holmes, "New Meaning for Sanctuary."

125. Central Baptist Church, "El Salvador Partners Mission Group History," accessed February 14, 2017, http://salvadorpartnershistory.blogspot.com.

126. Romero Interfaith Center, "About Us," n.d., accessed May 17, 2021, https://romerointerfaithcenter.wordpress.com/about/; U.S.–El Salvador Sister Cities, n.d., accessed May 17, 2021, https://www.elsalvadorsolidarity.org.

127. Central American Sanctuary Alliance of Delaware County (CASA) Records, Swarthmore College Peace Collection.

128. Holmes, "New Meaning for Sanctuary."

129. Michael Norman, "Origins of St. Martin's Companion Relationship with Guatemala," St. Martin-in-the-Fields Church, accessed October 14, 2015, http://www.stmartinec.org/archives/000234.html; Terry Clattenburg, correspondence with Domenic Vitiello, July 5, 2021, and July 14, 2021.

130. Norman, "Origins of St. Martin's Companion Relationship with Guatemala."

131. Funkhouser, interview.

132. Funkhouser, interview.

133. "History of SHARE," accessed February 14, 2017, http://www.share-elsalvador.org/history.html.

134. Rights Action, "About Us," accessed June 1, 2018, http://rightsaction.org/about-us/; see also Carmen Morcos, "The History of Rights Action," Advocacy Project, accessed June 1, 2018, http://www.advocacynet.org/the_history_of_rights_action_ra/.

135. Corbett, *Goatwalking*, 182.

136. Holmes, "New Meaning for Sanctuary."

137. Berryman, interview.

138. Morgan, interview.

139. Steve Kettmann, "El Salvador's Endless Ordeal," *New York Times*, November 15, 2019.

140. Bartlow, interview.

141. "Latino Philadelphia at a Glance," Historical Society of Pennsylvania, n.d., accessed February 16, 2017, http://hsp.org/sites/default/files/legacy_files/migrated /latinophiladelphiaataglance.pdf; Migration Policy Institute, "Immigrants from El Salvador, Guatemala, and Honduras in U.S., 2009–2013," n.d., visited February 16, 2017, http://www.migrationpolicy.org/programs/data-hub/charts/immigrants-el-salva dor-guatemala-and-honduras-us-2009–2013.

142. Portillo, interview.

143. Domenic Vitiello and Thomas J. Sugrue, "Introduction," in *Immigration and Metropolitan Revitalization in the United States*, ed. Domenic Vitiello and Thomas J. Sugrue, 1–8 (Philadelphia: University of Pennsylvania Press, 2017).

144. Marcelo Rochabrun, "The Trump Administration Plans to End a Refugee Program for Children," *ProPublica*, September 4, 2017, https://www.propublica.org /article/the-trump-administration-to-end-a-refugee-program-for-central-america -children.

145. La Puerta Abierta, accessed July 7, 2020, https://lpa-theopendoor.org.

146. Portillo, interview; Smith, "Guatemala."

147. Allison O'Connor, Jeanne Batalova, and Jessica Bolter, "Central American Immigrants in the United States," *Migration Policy Institute*, August 15, 2019, https://www .migrationpolicy.org/print/16567#.XW6rUi2ZPOQ; D'Vera Cohn, Jeffrey Passel, and Kristen Bialik, "Many Immigrants with Temporary Protected Status Face Uncertain Future in U.S.," Pew Research Center, November 27, 2019, https://www.pewresearch .org/fact-tank/2019/11/27/immigrants-temporary-protected-status-in-us/.

## 2. Refugee Resettlement

1. Thoai Nguyen, interview by Amanda Miller and Tobin Rothlein, August 14, 2010, Mural Arts Program, accessed September 12, 2013, http://www.philaplace.org/pdf /Thoai_Nguyen.pdf.

2. Christopher Goscha, *Vietnam: A New History* (New York: Basic Books, 2016).

3. Thoai Nguyen, interview by Rachel Van Tosh, January 18, 2011; Nguyen, interview by Miller and Rothlein.

4. Nguyen, interview by Miller and Rothlein; see also Thoai Nguyen, correspondence with Domenic Vitiello, January 18, 2021.

5. Nguyen, interview by Miller and Rothlein.

6. Jennifer Lin, "In Philadelphia, Refugees Found New Life, New Challenges, New Pain," *Philadelphia Inquirer*, April 19, 2000, A1, A16.

7. Nguyen, interview by Miller and Rothlein. The date and discussion of the US Marines' evacuation from Can Tho are in George Ross Dunham and David A. Quinlan, *U.S. Marines in Vietnam: The Bitter End, 1973–1975* (Washington, DC: U.S. Marine Corps, 1990), 174.

8. Nguyen, interview by Miller and Rothlein.

9. Nguyen, interview by Miller and Rothlein.

10. Nguyen, interview by Miller and Rothlein.

11. Dunham and Quinlan, *U.S. Marines in Vietnam*, 174.

12. Quoted in Lin, "In Philadelphia, Refugees Found New Life," A16.

13. Nguyen, *The Gift of Freedom*; Tram Nguyen, "Unsettled Refugees: Southeast Asian Communities Confront the Problems of Resettlement," *Color Lines*, September 15, 2001; Aihwa Ong, *Buddha Is Hiding: Refugees, Citizenship, the New America* (Berkeley: University of California Press, 2003); Tang, *Unsettled*; for exceptional cases of key US allies being settled in more advantaged circumstances, see Andrew Friedman, *Covert Capital: Landscapes of Denial and the Making of U.S. Empire in the Suburbs of Northern Virginia* (Berkeley: University of California Press, 2013).

14. Nguyen, interview by Miller and Rothlein; Nguyen, correspondence, January 18, 2021.

15. Nguyen, interview by Miller and Rothlein.

16. Andrew H. Malcolm, "48,000 Refugees Jammed on Guam," *New York Times*, May 10, 1975, A1.

17. Larry Clinton Thompson, *Refugee Workers in the Indochina Refugee Exodus, 1975–1982* (Jefferson, NC: MacFarland, 2010), 92; Public Law 94-24, May 23, 1975, 89 Stat. 89, 94th Congress, https://www.gpo.gov/fdsys/pkg/STATUTE-89/pdf/STATUTE-89-Pg89.pdf.

18. Mong Palatino, "1975: The Start and End of Conflict in Southeast Asia," *Diplomat*, December 1, 2015, https://thediplomat.com/2015/12/1975-the-start-and-end-of-conflict-in-southeast-asia/; Taylor Owen and Ben Kiernan, "Bombs over Cambodia," *Walrus*, October 2006), https://gsp.yale.edu/sites/default/files/walrus_cambodiabombing_oct06.pdf.

19. Rorng Sorn, presentation to ASAM 104, Asian American Community, University of Pennsylvania, April 8, 2021.

20. W. Courtland Robinson, "The Comprehensive Plan of Action for Indochinese Refugees, 1989–1997: Sharing the Burden and Passing the Buck," *Journal of Refugee Studies* 17, no. 3 (2004): 319–333.

21. The United States received roughly 880,000 Vietnamese, 250,000 Laotians, and 150,00 Cambodians. W. Courtland Robinson, *Terms of Refuge* (United Nations High Commissioner for Refugees) (London: Zed Books, 1998), 270, 276, Appendix 2.

22. Nguyen, interview by Miller and Rothlein; Marc Kaufman, "Ten Years after Vietnam: A Reunion of Hope and Sorrow," *Philadelphia Inquirer*, April 28, 1985, A1.

23. Nguyen, interview, by Miller and Rothlein.

24. Nguyen, *Gift of Freedom*.

25. Public Law 96-212, March 17, 1980 ("Refugee Act of 1980"), 1, https://www.gpo.gov/fdsys/pkg/STATUTE-94/pdf/STATUTE-94-Pg102.pdf.

26. Public Law 96-212.

27. Melissa May Borja, "The Government Alone Cannot Do the Total Job: The Possibilities and Perils of Religious Organizations in Public-Private Refugee Care," in *Shaped by the State: Toward a New Political History of the Twentieth Century*, edited by Brent Cebul, Lily Geismer, and Mason Williams, 261–288 (Chicago: University of Chicago Press, 2018).

28. The quote is from Michael Blum, interview by Domenic Vitiello, July 24, 2006; see also Juliane Ramic, interview by Domenic Vitiello, May 30, 2018; Judith Bernstein-Baker, interview by Domenic Vitiello, October 23, 2007.

29. Ellen Somekawa, "On the Edge: Southeast Asians in Philadelphia and the Struggle for Space," in *ReViewing Asian America: Locating Diversity*, ed. Wendy L. Ng,

Soo-Young Chin, James S. Moy, and Gary Y. Okihiro, 33–47 (Pullman: Washington State University Press, 1995), 33–47; Nguyen, "Unsettled Refugees"; Ong, *Buddha Is Hiding*; Tang, *Unsettled*.

30. Nguyen, interview by Miller and Rothlein. See also Lin, "In Philadelphia," A16.

31. Somekawa, "On the Edge"; Nguyen, "Unsettled Refugees"; Tang, *Unsettled*.

32. Lin, "In Philadelphia," A16.

33. Michael D. Blum to Joseph Miller, November 10, 1978, NSC Collection, Temple University Urban Archives.

34. Michael D. Blum to Willie Groninger, July 21, 1979, NSC Collection; see also JFS Indo-Chinese Program, Home/Health Management curriculum, May 30, 1980, NSC Collection.

35. Michael D. Blum to Joseph Yarborough, February 7, 1980, NSC Collection; Michael D. Blum to Refugee Task Force Members, August 10, 1982, NSC Collection.

36. "Refugee Seminar," June 5, 1981, NSC Collection.

37. Bill Erat, interview by Hannah Wizman-Cartier, April 3, 2009.

38. Holmberg, "For Refugees"; see also Minutes of the Southeast Asian Task Force Meeting, January 4, 1980, NSC Collection; Minutes of the Refugee Task Force Meeting, August 8, 1980; September 5, 1980; February 6, 1981; March 6, 1981; September 11, 1981; all NSC Collection.

39. Minutes of the Refugee Task Force Meeting, February 6, 1981; Domenic Vitiello and Michael Nairn, *Community Gardening in Philadelphia: 2008 Harvest Report* (Philadelphia: University of Pennsylvania, 2009).

40. Robert Todd, interview by Domenic Vitiello, June 19, 2018.

41. Archdiocese of Philadelphia Nutritional Development Services, "Life Skills Education Services," 1981, NSC Collection.

42. David Holmberg, "For Refugees," *Philadelphia Daily News*, June 10, 1983.

43. "Committees Form to Aid Refugees," n.d. (c. 1980), NSC Collection.

44. Jody Kerssenbrock to Bill Rorie et al., "Indochinese Refugees' Programs/Problems in Logan/Germantown Area," NSC Collection.

45. Bernstein-Baker, interview, October 23, 2007; Blum, interview; Fernando Chang-Muy, interview by Domenic Vitiello, January 29, 2007; Bonnie L. Cook, "For Refugees," *Philadelphia Inquirer*, February 20, 1982, A1; Melissa Dribben, "Moving in Group Helps Immigrants," *Philadelphia Inquirer*, July 13, 1989, H3.

46. Marc Kaufman, "A Clash of Culture and Hunger: Rule May Block Lunches 'To Go' for Refugee Children," *Philadelphia Inquirer*, August 5, 1986, B1.

47. Pennsylvania Refugee Assistance Program, Annual Performance Report (fiscal year ending September 30, 1981), NSC Collection.

48. Vernon Loeb, "Culture Shocks Refugees—For Southeast Asians, Melting Pot Boils Over," *Philadelphia Inquirer*, September 6, 1982, B1.

49. Rod Nordland, "U.S. Opens the Door to Cambodians," *Philadelphia Inquirer*, March 15, 1981, A2; see also Marc Kaufman, "New World, Uncertain Future: After Years in Camps, 6 Cambodians Come to Philadelphia," *Philadelphia Inquirer*, September 24, 1983, B4.

50. Blum to Yarborough.

51. Minutes of Refugee Assistance Program Providers Meeting of August 26, 1981, September 2, 1981, NSC Collection, Temple University Urban Archives.

52. Minutes of Refugee Assistance Program Providers Meeting of August 26, 1981.

53. Minutes of the Socialization/Recreation Planning Meeting, January 4, 1979, NSC Collection.

54. Michael D. Blum to Gloria Guard, January 5, 1982, NSC Collection.

55. Minutes of the Socialization/Recreation Planning Meeting.

56. Marc Kaufman, "Asians' Quandary—Welfare Cuts Force Many to Leave School," *Philadelphia Inquirer*, November 9, 1983, B1.

57. Kaufman, "Asians' Quandary."

58. Kaufman, "Asians' Quandary"; see also Cynthia Hanson, "The Dream: Fleeing Oppression, Many Find Work at Philadelphia Hotel," *Philadelphia Inquirer*, August 23, 1985, B8.

59. Murray Dubin and Marc Kaufman, "Ten Years after Vietnam: For Many Refugees, Quiet Despair in a New Land," *Philadelphia Inquirer*, April 28, 1985, A1.

60. Dubin and Kaufman, "Ten Years after Vietnam."

61. Philip Scranton, "Large Firms and Industrial Restructuring: The Philadelphia Region, 1900–1980," *Pennsylvania Magazine of History and Biography* 116, no. 4 (October 1992): 419–465.

62. Rod Nordland, "Dreams Go Sour for Second Wave of Southeast Asians Here," *Philadelphia Inquirer*, March 28, 1983.

63. Minutes of the Refugee Task Force, March 5, 1982, NSC Collection.

64. Minutes of the Volag Employment Council Meeting, December 17, 1981, NSC Collection; Nazli Kibria, *Family Tightrope: The Changing Lives of Vietnamese Americans* (Princeton, NJ: Princeton University Press, 1993).

65. For example, Minutes of the Refugee Employment Council, August 21, 1980; August 28, 1980; September 4, 1980; September 11, 1980; September 18, 1980; September 25, 1980; October 30, 1980; Michael Blum to Bernice Abrams, September 11, 1981, NSC Collection.

66. Philip Jaisohn Memorial Center, "On-the-Job Training and Employment for the Refugees from Southeast Asia," 1980, NSC Collection.

67. Minutes of the Refugee Employment Council; Jesse Lofton, "Report to Managers," November 13, 1980, NSC Collection, Temple University Urban Archives.

68. Nguyen, interview by Miller and Rothlein; Nguyen, correspondence, January 18, 2021.

69. Nguyen, interview by Miller and Rothlein.

70. Kibria, *Family Tightrope*; see also Nguyen, "Unsettled Refugees."

71. Minutes of the Refugee Task Force meeting, September 15, 1980.

72. Thomas M. Rohan, "Off the Boat & Ready to Work," *Industry Week*, July 7, 1980; Julian L. Simon, "Adding Up the Costs of Our New Immigrants," *Wall Street Journal*, February 26, 1981.

73. "Cambodian Refugees Seek Employment Opportunities," *Main Line Times*, February 28, 1980, NSC Collection.

74. Rohan, "Off the Boat and Ready to Work."

75. Vilna Bashi Treitler, *The Ethnic Project: Transforming Racial Fiction into Ethnic Factions* (Stanford: Stanford University Press, 2013); Peter Kwong, *The New Chinatown* (New York: Hill and Wang, 1987).

76. Gloria Guard, interview by Domenic Vitiello, October 27, 2011; Blum, interview.

77. Elinor Hewitt, *JEVS 70th Anniversary History*, 2011, typescript in the author's possession.

78. Elinor Hewitt and Steve Applebaum, interview by Domenic Vitiello, September 30, 2015; also Catholic Social Services, "Vocational Training—1981 Contract" (1981), NSC Collection, Temple University Urban Archives.

79. Hewitt and Applebaum, interview; see also Jay Specter and Zoya Kravets, interview by Leah Whiteside, March 13, 2013; Loeb, "Culture Shocks Refugees"; Refugee Women's Program Development and Coordination Project, "Economic Development for Refugee Women," July 1982, NSC Collection.

80. Marc Rapport, "Indochinese Refugees Progressing in U.S., Study Shows," *Philadelphia Inquirer*, July 19, 1985, A8; Nathan Caplan, John Kremers Whitmore, and Marcella H. Choy, *The Boat People and Achievement in America: A Study of Family Life, Hard Work, and Cultural Values* (Ann Arbor: University of Michigan Press, 1989); Marc Kaufman, "Challenging Stereotypes of Asians in America," *Philadelphia Inquirer*, June 5, 1994, C1; Sucheng Chan, "Cambodians in the United States: Refugees, Immigrants, American Ethnic Minority," *Oxford Research Encyclopedia of American History* (2015), https://oxfordre.com/americanhistory/.

81. Nordland, "Dreams Go Sour."

82. Nguyen, interview by Miller and Rothlein; Nguyen, correspondence, January 18, 2021; Thoai Nguyen, correspondence with Domenic Vitiello, January 21, 2021.

83. Nguyen, interview by Miller and Rothlein; Nguyen, correspondence, January 18, 2021; Nguyen, correspondence, January 21, 2021.

84. Debbie Wei, interview by Domenic Vitiello, November 15, 2006; Rorng Sorn, interview by Leah Whiteside, February 6, 2013.

85. Housing abuses were inflicted not only on Southeast Asian refugees, but the other large group of refugees in this period, Soviet Jews, generally experienced better housing quality and more supportive landlords and coethnic neighbors. Jack Smyth, "Immigrant Tenants Unhappy," *Philadelphia Evening Bulletin*, October 16, 1981; Beth Gillin, "Vietnamese and Italians: Coexisting in South Philadelphia," *Philadelphia Inquirer*, July 16, 1982, B1.

86. "S. Phila's Newest Immigrants," *South Philly Review*, June 25, 1981, NSC Collection.

87. "Asian Refugees: Housing Biggest Problem," *Philadelphia Evening Bulletin*, November 26, 1979, 1; "Asian Refugees Flee Blaze in Apartments," *Philadelphia Evening Bulletin*, December 21, 1979.

88. Minutes of the Refugee Task Force Meeting, August 8, 1980, NSC Collection.

89. Earni Young, "Joint Owners: Two Tax Delinquents, One Shabby Building," *Philadelphia Daily News* (November 12, 1982)."

90. Young, "Joint Owners," *Philadelphia Daily News*, November 12, 1982; see also Earni Young, "Tax-Dodgers' Alliance Rent," *Philadelphia Daily News*, December 3, 1982.

91. Earni Young, "'Unfit Tag Will Stay at West Philadelphia Apartment, City Says," *Philadelphia Daily News*, November 15, 1982.

92. Michael Blum to Refugee Task Force Members.

93. Young, "'Unfit Tag"; see also Young, "Tax-Dodgers' Alliance Rent."

94. Julia Lawlor, "Refugees Withhold Rent: Asian Tenants Struck While the Water Wasn't Hot, Got Building Cited," *Philadelphia Daily News*, July 19, 1985.

95. Wei, interview.

96. Wei, interview; Blum, interview; Sparkman, interview; Nguyen, interview by Miller and Rothlein.

97. "Asian Refugees: Housing Biggest Problem."

98. Wei, interview; Blum, interview; Edward Sparkman, interview by Domenic Vitiello, June 29, 2007; see also Marianne Costantinou, "No New Lease on Life for Them, Housing's American Nightmare," *Philadelphia Daily News*, February 2, 1989; Somekawa, "On the Edge."

99. Minutes of the Meeting of the Refugee Task Force, November 3, 1984, NSC Collection; Wei, interview; Sparkman, interview.

100. Costantinou, "No New Lease on Life"; Marianne Costaninou and Paul Maryniak, "L&I Sets Inspections after Tenement Blaze," *Philadelphia Daily News*, January 31, 1989, 12.

101. Jennifer Lin, "Their Only Refuge, and It Leaks: Many Asian Refugees Are Living in Neglected Housing—But the City Lacks the Translators to Help Them," *Philadelphia Inquirer*, February 3, 1992, B1.

102. Somekawa, "On the Edge."

103. Nordland, "Dreams Go Sour."

104. William Robbins, "Violence Forces Hmong to Leave Philadelphia," *New York Times*, September 17, 1984; see also Marc Kaufman, "The Last Victims of Vietnam? Why the Hmong Are Fleeing America's Helping Hand," *Philadelphia Inquirer*, July 1, 1984, A1, A14.

105. Henry Goldman, "Second Suspect to Be Tried in Beating of Refugee," *Philadelphia Inquirer*, December 19, 1984, B3; Henry Goldman, "After Hmong Victim Testifies, Suspect Is Bound over for Trial in Beating," *Philadelphia Inquirer*, December 15, 1984; Marc Kaufman, "Hmong Refugee Testifies of Beating by Three Men on a W. Phila. Street," *Philadelphia Inquirer*, January 22, 1986), B8.

106. Gustavo Martinez Contreras, "Tepid Response to Attacks Against Asians Is Nothing New," *Philadelphia Public School Notebook*, February 2010, 4.

107. Ann O'Neill and Valeria Russ, "No Escape from Hatred: Asian Students Fall Victim to Brutal Assaults in City's Schools," *Philadelphia Daily News*, December 8, 1986.

108. O'Neill and Russ, "No Escape from Hatred"; see also Marc Kaufman, "Severe Beating of Asian Shakes School," *Philadelphia Inquirer*, November 6, 1983, B1; Marc Kaufman, "School Transfers Assault Victim: Vietnamese Student Objects to Leaving His Friends," *Philadelphia Inquirer*, December 8, 1983, B14.

109. Vanessa Williams and Edward Colimore, "Rise in Gang Activity Alarms Vietnamese Community," *Philadelphia Inquirer*, January 2, 1987, A1; Sorn, interview.

110. Naroen Chhin, Testimony to Philadelphia City Council Committee on Public Safety, March 12, 2014.

111. Chhin, Testimony to Philadelphia City Council Committee on Public Safety.

112. Alexander Reid and David Holmberg, "Neighbors Rally on Behalf of Victims," *Philadelphia Daily News*, September 14, 1984; see also O'Neill and Russ, "No Escape from Hatred."

113. O'Neill and Russ, "No Escape from Hatred."

114. David Gelsanliter, "Through Philadelphia's Open Door," *Philadelphia Inquirer: Today Magazine*, January 4, 1981, 10; Blum, interview; Wei, interview; Michael D. Blum, "Refugees and Community Tension," *Proceedings of the Social Welfare Forum*, 1981, 115–130.

115. Robbins, "Violence Forces Hmong to Leave Philadelphia."

116. Margaret Lonzetta, "To the Philadelphia Commission on Human Relations, re: Community Hearings on Neighborhood Tensions/Conflicts," October 27, 1984, NSC Collection.

117. Tom Infield, "'Dumping' of Asians Is at the Root of Tense Relations, Hearing Is Told," *Philadelphia Inquirer*, October 30, 1984, B7; see also David Holmberg, "Agencies Blamed for Asians' Plight," *Philadelphia Daily News*, October 30, 1984; Edward Colimore, "Reasons Cited for Attacks on Asians," *Philadelphia Inquirer*, November 2, 1984, B2; Marc Kaufman, "For Asians and Their Neighbors, A Forum," *Philadelphia Inquirer*, November 9, 1984, B1.

118. Infield, "'Dumping' of Asians."

119. Maria Gallagher, "Report Fails to Help Asians Despite Study of Problems: 100,000 in City Still Wait for Assistance," *Philadelphia Daily News*, November 14, 1985.

120. Michael D. Blum to Letters to the Editor, *Philadelphia Inquirer*, November 15, 1985, NSC Collection.

121. Marc Kaufman, "Rights Panel Urges City Action for Asian Immigrants," *Philadelphia Inquirer*, October 23, 1985, B6.

122. Gallagher, "Report Fails to Help Asians."

123. Gallagher, "Report Fails to Help Asians."

124. Marc Kaufman, "Despite Hearings, Anti-Asian Violence Continues," *Philadelphia Inquirer*, October 27, 1985, B1; O'Neill and Russ, "No Escape from Hatred"; Daniel Amsterdam and Domenic Vitiello, "Immigration to Philadelphia, c.1930–present," *Encyclopedia of Greater Philadelphia* (2013), https://philadelphiaencyclopedia.org/.

125. Margaret Pugh O'Mara, *Cities of Knowledge: Cold War Science and the Search for the Next Silicon Valley* (Princeton, NJ: Princeton University Press, 2005), 176.

126. Michael D. Blum, "Delivery of Public and Private Services to Immigrants and Refugees," 1989, NSC Collection.

127. Roger Cohn, "Where Asia's Refugees Find Help and Health," *Philadelphia Inquirer*, December 31, 1981, B3; Christopher Hepp, "They'll Serve as City's Link with Asians," *Philadelphia Inquirer*, December 24, 1987, B1; Susan Caba, "City Helping Asians Use Court System," *Philadelphia Inquirer*, September 17, 1992, B7.

128. Wei, interview.

129. Martha Woodall, "Suit: School District Aids Asians Inadequately," *Philadelphia Inquirer*, December 31, 1985, B4; Dale Mezzacappa, "Education for Asians to Be Altered," *Philadelphia Inquirer*, February 20, 1988, B2.

130. Somekawa, "On the Edge."

131. "Refugee Seminar."

132. "Refugee Seminar."

133. "Voluntary Agency Placement Policies: Impacted Areas and Areas of Special Concern," November 5, 1981, NSC Collection."

134. "Voluntary Agency Placement Policies."

135. "Voluntary Agency Placement Policies."

136. Michael Blum to Walter T. Darmopray, November 3, 1981, NSC Collection.

137. ACNS Site Visit Report, April 26, 1983, NSC Collection.

138. Nguyen, interview by Van Tosh; Nguyen, interview by Miller and Rothlein; Blum, interview.

139. Blum, interview; Nguyen, interview by Van Tosh.

140. "Refugee Seminar."

141. Domenic Vitiello and Arthur Acolin, "Institutional Ecosystems of Housing Support in Chinese, Southeast Asian, and African Philadelphia," *Journal of Planning Education and Research* 37, no. 2 (June 2017): 195–206; see also Chia Youyee Vang, "Making Ends Meet: Hmong Socioeconomic Trends in the U.S.," *Housing Studies Journal* 13, no. 2 (2012): 1–20; Sorn, interview.

142. Michael Ruane, "Arising from Decline: A Flower Blossoms in Logan," *Philadelphia Inquirer*, June 22, 1983, A1; Cynthia Burton, "Olney High's Melting Pot Foreign-Born Students Find a Common Bond," *Philadelphia Daily News*, November 3, 1989, 6; John Woestendiek, "Finding Common Ground in Logan, These Summer Programs Bring Together Youths of Different Cultures," *Philadelphia Inquirer*, August 10, 1993, B1.

143. Steve Stecklow, "Asians Finding Their Niche in Suburbs," *Philadelphia Inquirer*, October 12, 1986, D2.

144. Vitiello and Acolin, "Institutional Ecosystems."

145. Robbins, "Violence Forces Hmong"; Kaufman, "Last Victims."

146. Margaret Lonzetta to the Philadelphia Commission on Human Relations, Testimony, "Re: Community Hearings on Neighborhood Tensions / Conflicts," October 27, 1984, NSC Collection.

147. Blum, interview; Guard, interview; Janet Panning, interview by Domenic Vitiello, November 16, 2006.

148. Kaufman, "Last Victims."

149. Pat McKeown, "By Night, Mysterious Death Steals Their Men," *Philadelphia Daily News*, December 30, 1983, 10; Marc Kaufman, "New Year for Beleaguered People in West Philadelphia: The Hmong Come Together to Be Hmong," *Philadelphia Inquirer*, November 25, 1984, B2; Marc Kaufman, "A Fatal Collision of Old and New: Laotian Immigrant Finds a Final Refuge in Suicide," *Philadelphia Inquirer*, March 20, 1985, A1.

150. Kaufman, "Last Victims."

151. Kaufman, "Last Victims."

152. Kaufman, "Last Victims."

153. David Holmberg, "Despite Arrests and Aid, Peace Eludes Hmongs," *Philadelphia Daily News*, September 13, 1984.

154. Marc Kaufman, "U.S. Moves on Rights for Hmong: Attacks on Group Subject of Probe," *Philadelphia Inquirer*, September 8, 1984, B1. See also Marc Kaufman, "Embattled Hmong Plan to Leave City," *Philadelphia Inquirer*, September 7, 1984, A1; Holmberg, "Despite Arrests and Aid."

155. Erat, interview; see also Julie Shaw, "Asians, Hispanics Make a Life for Themselves in South Philadelphia," *Philadelphia Daily News*, May 4, 2011, 8.

156. Scott Kurashige, "Pan-Ethnicity and Community Organizing: Asian Americans United's Campaign against Anti-Asian Violence," *Journal of Asian American Studies* 3, no. 2 (June 2000): 163–190 (quote from 169).

157. Nguyen, correspondence, January 18, 2021.

158. Kurashige, "Pan-Ethnicity," 178.

159. Nguyen, correspondence, January 18, 2021; Nguyen, correspondence, January 21, 2021.

160. ACNS Site Visit Report; see also Michael D. Blum to Lary Groth, September 29, 1980, NSC Collection.

161. Erat, interview; Fellowship Commission, "Synopsis of Southeast Asian Project," n.d. (c.1982), NSC Collection; Minutes of the Refugee Task Force, February 5, 1982, NSC Collection.

162. The quotes are from Minutes of the Refugee Task Force meeting, March 6, 1981, NSC Collection. See also Blum, interview; Chang-Muy, interview; Cox, interview; Guard, interview.

163. Blum, interview; Chang-Muy, interview; Cox, interview; Guard, interview.

164. SEAMAAC website, accessed April 1, 2007, www.seamaac.org.

165. Nguyen, interview by Van Tosh; Nguyen, correspondence, January 18, 2021.

166. Nguyen, interview by Van Tosh.

167. Nguyen, interview by Van Tosh.

168. Sorn, interview; Sorn presentation.

169. Sorn, interview; Monica Rhor, "Changing World for Older Asians: A Growing Group of New Americans Confronts Problems Familiar to Some," *Philadelphia Inquirer*, June 30, 1999, B1.

170. Sorn, interview; Sorn presentation.

171. Karl Stark, "Impending Cuts in Benefits Will Hit Some Refugees," *Philadelphia Inquirer*, February 9, 1997, B1; Marc Meltzer, "Reform Efforts Reopen War Wounds for Region's Vietnamese Refugees," *Philadelphia Daily News*, October 24, 1996, 8; Shaun D. Mullen, "Immigrants under Attack: Plans for Massive Savings Incite 'Great Deal of Panic,'" *Philadelphia Daily News*, October 24, 1996, 8.

172. Quế Sơn, "The Coolies of Philadelphia," *DanchimViet.com*, accessed January 28, 2006, http://danchimviet.com/php/modules.php?name=News&file=article&sid=167.

173. Sorn, interview; see also Julie Shaw, "Report Dispels 'Model-Minority' Myth of Asian Americans," *Philadelphia Daily News*, February 6, 2014. Some Southeast Asians also participated in the Family Savings Account programs run by the Women's Opportunities Resource Center. People saved money to purchase cars so they could access better jobs in the suburbs, fund home purchases and renovations, pursue further education, plan for retirement, and start small businesses. Hani White, interview by Domenic Vitiello, July 25, 2006.

174. Nguyen, interview by Van Tosh.

175. Sorn, interview.

176. Edward Colimore, "Sending Freedom's Message to Vietnam," *Philadelphia Inquirer*, September 13, 2004, B1.

177. No relation to Thoai. Nguyen is the most common Vietnamese surname. Nancy Nguyen, interview by Domenic Vitiello, October 21, 2015.

178. Nancy Nguyen, interview. See also Will Van Sant, "Giving a Voice to the Vietnamese," *Philadelphia Inquirer*, Camden edition, April 26, 2001, B1; James Osborne, "Group Tries to Bridge Viet Families' Generational and Cultural Gap," *Philadelphia Inquirer*, May 26, 2011, B1.

179. Nguyen, interview by Van Tosh; Nancy Nguyen, interview.

180. The Illegal Immigration Reform and Immigrant Responsibility Act of 1996, Division C of Pub.L. 104-208, 110 Stat.; Mia-lia B. Kiernan, correspondence with Domenic Vitiello, May 31, 2021.

181. Kiernan, correspondence; Nancy Nguyen, interview; Sorn, interview; see also Troy Graham, "Adjusting to a Land Their People Once Fled," *Philadelphia Inquirer*, December 31, 2007, A1.

182. Jeff Gammage, "New Year, New Fear: Year of the Dog Begins with Deportation Concerns," *Philadelphia Inquirer*, February 12, 2018, B1, B5.

183. Graham, "Adjusting to a Land Their People Once Fled"; see also Kiernan, correspondence.

184. Thomas Ginsberg, "Philadelphia's Cambodian Refugees Protest Deportations," *Philadelphia Inquirer*, November 9, 2002, B1.

185. Sorn, interview.

186. Mia-lia B. Kiernan, correspondence with Domenic Vitiello, February 10, 2021; Kiernan, correspondence, May 31, 2021.

187. Katya Cengel, *Exiled: From the Killing Fields of Cambodia to California and Back* (Lincoln: University of Nebraska Press, 2018).

188. 1Love Movement, "Organizers," accessed July 2, 2021, https://1lovemovement .wordpress.com/about/organizers/.

189. Peter Pedemonti, interview by Domenic Vitiello, March 29, 2017; "One Love's Truth Forum," New Sanctuary Movement alert, July 24, 2012, in possession of the author.

190. Michael Matza, "Testifying before Council, Witnesses Slam 1996 Immigration Law," *Philadelphia Inquirer*, June 14, 2016, https://www.inquirer.com/philly/news /20160615_Testifying_at_Council__witnesses_slam_1996_immigration_law.html.

191. Matza, "Testifying before Council."

192. Kiernan, correspondence, February 10, 2021; 1Love Movement, "#Fix96 Philly City Council Hearing!" July 25, 2016, https://m.facebook.com/1LoveMovement /videos/969401026492053/?refsrc=https%3A%2F%2Fm.facebook.com%2Fwatch %2F&_rdr.

193. Nancy Nguyen, interview.

194. SEAFN, "Press Release: #SEAFN2Geneva fights deportation at the United Nations!," March 18, 2015, https://1lovemovement.wordpress.com/2015/03/18/press -release-seafn2geneva-fights-deportation-at-the-united-nations/; Kiernan, correspondence, February 10, 2021; Owen and Kiernan, "Bombs over Cambodia."

195. Nancy Nguyen, interview; Cengel, *Exiled*.

196. 1Love Cambodia, "Open Letter from Cambodian Deportees to Our Community in the United States," April 21, 2016, https://1lovemovement.wordpress .com/2016/04/21/statement-from-cambodian-deportees/.

197. 1Love Cambodia, "Open Letter from Cambodian Deportees."

198. Kiernan, correspondence, February 10, 2021.

199. Sam Levin, "Detained and Divided: How the US Turned on Vietnamese Refugees," *Guardian*, March 3, 2018.

200. Deborah Sontag and Dale Russakoff, "In Pennsylvania, It's Open Season on Undocumented Immigrants," *ProPublica*, April 12, 2018.

201. Gammage, "New Year, New Fear."

202. Jeff Gammage, "Deporting Asian Refugees, Activists Say, Is Anti-Asian Violence—And Removals Are Up," *Philadelphia Inquirer*, March 27, 2021; Sam Levin, "Deported by Biden: A Vietnamese Refugee Separated from his Family after Decades in US," *Guardian*, May 3, 2021, http://www.theguardian.com/us-news/2021/may/03 /biden-deportations-vietnamese-refugee-california-ice.

203. Jens Manuel Krogstad and Jynnah Radford, "Key Facts about Refugees to the U.S.," *Pew Research Center*, January 30, 2017, http://www.pewresearch.org/fact-tank

/2017/01/30/key-facts-about-refugees-to-the-u-s/; US Department of Homeland Security, Office of Immigration Statistics, "Annual Flow Report—Refugees and Asylees: 2017," March 2019, https://www.dhs.gov/sites/default/files/publications/Refugees _Asylees_2017.pdf.

204. Catherine Baggiano, interview by Mengyuan Bai, June 29, 2016.

205. The national office of HIAS and HIAS-Pennsylvania (HIAS-PA) are separate nonprofits. All discussion of HIAS in this and subsequent chapters refers to HIAS-PA and not its national parent organization.

206. Juliane Ramic, interview by Rachel Van Tosh, November 19, 2011.

207. Ramic, interview by Van Tosh.

208. Ramic, interview, May 30, 2018.

209. Thomas Ginsberg, "Philadelphia's Immigrants: Who They Are and How They Are Changing the City," Pew Charitable Trusts, 2018.

210. Ramic, interview by Van Tosh.

211. Ramic, interview, January 26, 2016.

212. US Department of Health and Human Services Office of Refugee Resettlement, "About the Voluntary Agencies Matching Grant Program," 2019, https:// www.acf.hhs.gov/orr/programs/matching-grants/about; Blum, interview.

213. Ramic, interview, January 26, 2016.

214. Ramic, interview by Van Tosh; Judith Bernstein-Baker, interview by Domenic Vitiello, October 19, 2012.

215. Leela Kuikel, interview by Mengyuan Bai, June 28, 2016.

216. Julia Ann McWilliams and Sally Wesley Bonet, "Refugees in the City: The Neighborhood Effects of Institutional Presence and Flexibility," *Journal of Immigrant & Refugee Studies* 13 (2015): 419–438; Ramic, interview, January 26, 2016.

217. Bernstein-Baker, interview, October 23, 2007; Judith Bernstein-Baker, correspondence with Domenic Vitiello, December 31, 2020.

218. Kuikel, interview; Ramic, interview, January 26, 2016.

219. Erat, interview; Kuikel, interview; Panning, interview; Javier Garcia Hernandez, interview by Domenic Vitiello, May 3, 2013; Kelli Myers-Gottemoller, interview by Mengyuan Bai, September 16, 2016; Juliane Ramic, interview by Domenic Vitiello, July 25, 2014; Juliane Ramic, interview, January 26, 2016.

220. Jared Shelly, "1,300 Layoffs for Northeast Philly's Cardone Industries," *Philadelphia Magazine*, January 20, 2016, https://www.phillymag.com/business/2016/01 /20/cardone-industries-layoffs/.

221. Christina Tatu, "PA's Largest Refugee Resettlement Program to Close Next Month," *Morning Call*, May 19, 2016, http://www.mcall.com/news/local/allentown /mc-refugee-services-20160519-story.html.

222. Ramic, interview, May 30, 2018; see also Bernstein-Baker, correspondence.

223. Ramic, interview, July 25, 2014.

224. Ramic, interview, May 30, 2018.

## 3. African Diasporas

1. John K. Jallah, interview by Domenic Vitiello, October 23, 2018.

2. John K. Jallah, interview by Domenic Vitiello, December 6, 2018; Jallah, interview, October 23, 2018.

3. Already in 1922, in an essay titled "Liberia and Negro Rule," Evans Lewin, the librarian of the Royal Colonial Institute in London, charged that "by obtaining a commercial foothold in Africa, the American people has entered upon the first step that leads to direct economic, if not political, control." Lewin, "Liberia and Negro Rule," *Atlantic*, September 1922.

4. T. Christian Miller and Jonathan Jones, "Firestone and the Warlord: The Untold Story of Firestone, Charles Taylor, and the Tragedy of Liberia," *ProPublica*, November 18, 2014. See also Frank Chalk, "Du Bois and Garvey Confront Liberia: Two Incidents of the Coolidge Years," *Canadian Journal of African Studies* 1, no. 2 (November 1967): 135–142; Frank Chalk, "The Anatomy of an Investment: Firestone's 1927 Loan to Liberia," *Canadian Journal of African Studies* 1 (March 1967): 12–32.

5. Stanley Meiser, "Liberia," quoted in "Our Liberian Legacy," *Atlantic*, March 2006, https://www.theatlantic.com/magazine/archive/2006/03/our-liberian-legacy /304821/. With the support of the US government, Firestone helped resist a colonial takeover by Britain in the 1930s, after a League of Nations investigation found that Liberia's government tolerated widespread unpaid labor and the continued trade of forced labor to Spanish cocoa plantations in Equatorial Guinea.

6. John Jallah, correspondence with Domenic Vitiello, May 4, 2021; Jallah, interview, October 23, 2018.

7. Jallah, interview, October 23, 2018.

8. Jallah, interview, October 23, 2018.

9. Domenic Vitiello, "Liberia and Liberians," *Encyclopedia of Greater Philadelphia* (2017), https://philadelphiaencyclopedia.org/archive/liberians-and-liberia/.

10. Katherine Harris, *African and American Values: Liberia and West Africa* (Lanham, MD: University Press of America, 1985); Robert P. Murray, "Whiteness in Africa: Americo-Liberians and the Transformative Geographies of Race" (PhD dissertation, University of Kentucky, 2013).

11. Meiser, "Liberia."

12. Meiser, "Liberia."

13. Jallah, interview, October 23, 2018.

14. Jallah, interview, October 23, 2018.

15. Elwood Dunn, *Liberia and the United States during the Cold War: Limits of Reciprocity* (New York: Palgrave MacMillan, 2009); Reed Kramer, "Liberia: A Casualty of the Cold War's End?," Center for Strategic and International Studies, July 1995, https://csis-website-prod.s3.amazonaws.com/s3fs-public/legacy_files/files /publication/anotes_0795.pdf.

16. Jallah, interview, October 23, 2018.

17. Jallah, interview, December 6, 2018.

18. Wolfgang Saxon, "Samuel Doe: 10-Year Reign in the Shadow of Brutality," *New York Times*, September 11, 1990.

19. The United States gave Liberia half a billion dollars in development and military aid in the first five years under Doe, whom President Reagan invited to the White House, as "there was concern that the young soldier and his populist backers might tilt toward Libya or even Moscow." Bill Berkeley, "Between Repression and Slaughter," *Atlantic*, December 1992.

20. Jallah, interview, December 6, 2018.

21. Miller and Jones, "Firestone and the Warlord."

22. Jallah, interview, December 6, 2018.

23. Many Liberians believe the Economic Community of West African States (ECOWAS), and the United States were complicit in luring Doe to the airport and allowing Johnson to capture him. However, their requests for a war crimes tribunal to investigate this allegation have been rebuffed. Jallah, interview, December 6, 2018; Miller and Jones, "Firestone and the Warlord"; Saxon, "Samuel Doe."

24. Jallah, interview, December 6, 2018.

25. Jallah, interview, December 6, 2018; David Harris, "From 'Warlord' to 'Democratic' President: How Charles Taylor Won the 1997 Liberian Elections," *Journal of Modern African Studies* 37, no. 3 (1999): 431–455; Mark Kukis, "Africa's New Pariah—Liberia's Charles Taylor," *National Journal* 35, no. 22 (2003).

26. Jallah, interview, December 6, 2018; see also Eric Edi, correspondence with Domenic Vitiello, March 6, 2021.

27. Jallah, interview, December 6, 2018.

28. Advocates for Human Rights, *A House with Two Rooms: Final Report of the Truth and Reconciliation Commission of Liberia Diaspora Project* (St. Paul, MN: DRI Press, 2009).

29. Edi, correspondence; see also, for example, "Ivory Coast and Burkina Faso: A Measured Reconciliation," *Stratfor Worldview*, August 12, 2016, https://worldview .stratfor.com/article/ivory-coast-and-burkina-faso-measured-reconciliation.

30. IRIN, "Guinea-Liberia: American Dream Keeps Refugees from Going Home," *ReliefWeb*, March 1, 2006, https://reliefweb.int/report/guinea/guinea-liberia-american -dream-keeps-refugees-going-home.

31. John K. Jallah, interview by Domenic Vitiello, February 27, 2008.

32. Republic of Liberia Truth and Reconciliation Commission, *Final Report* (2009), 232, http://www.trcofliberia.org/reports/final-report.html; Advocates for Human Rights, *House with Two Rooms*, 3.

33. Advocates for Human Rights, *House with Two Rooms*, 3.

34. Loucoumane Coulibaly, "Thousands of Liberian Refugees to Resettle in U.S.," *Reuters*, February 23, 2004; Miller and Jones, "Firestone and the Warlord."

35. Coulibaly, "Thousands of Liberian Refugees"; Miller and Jones, "Firestone and the Warlord."

36. Madeline Messick and Claire Bergeron, "Temporary Protected Status in the United States: A Grant of Humanitarian Relief That Is Less Than Permanent," Migration Policy Institute, Migration Information Service, July 2, 2014; Jill H. Wilson, "Temporary Protected Status: Overview and Current Issues," *Congressional Research Service* 7-5700, October 10, 2018; Janet Panning, interview by Domenic Vitiello, November 16, 2006.

37. Voffee Jabateh, interview by Domenic Vitiello, August 15, 2006; Samuel Slewion, interview by Rachel Van Tosh, September 3, 2010; Jallah, interview. December 6, 2018.

38. Convention Refugee data downloaded from *Refugee Processing Center*, http:// www.wrapsnet.org; Wilson, "Temporary Protected Status"; Eric Marrapodi and Chris Welch, "Liberians Facing Mass Deportation from U.S.," *CNN*, February 9, 2009, http:// www.cnn.com/2009/US/02/09/liberians.deportation/index.html; Ciata Victor, "Statistics on West African Immigrants in the United States," *TLC Africa*, visited January 14, 2019 at http://www.tlcafrica.com/Liberian_statistics1.htm.

39. Hamida Kinge, "Hotel ACANA," *Philadelphia City Paper*, March 3–9, 2005.

40. Portia Kamara, interview by Domenic Vitiello, February 22, 2018.

41. Conor Finnegan, "Trump Gives Liberian Immigrants 1 Year to Leave or Face Deportation," *ABC News*, March 27, 2018, https://abcnews.go.com/Politics/trump-liberian-immigrants-year-leave-face-deportation/story?id=54054555.

42. Parts of this chapter's account of Liberian civil society and transnational development are based on Domenic Vitiello and Rachel Van Tosh, "Liberian Reconstruction, Transnational Development, and Pan-African Community Revitalization," in *Immigration and Metropolitan Revitalization in the United States*, ed. Domenic Vitiello and Thomas J. Sugrue, 154–170 (Philadelphia: University of Pennsylvania Press), 2017.

43. Patrick Sharkey, *Uneasy Peace: The Great Crime Decline, the Renewal of City Life, and the Next War on Violence* (New York: Norton, 2018).

44. Gary Nash, *Forging Freedom: The Formation of Philadelphia's Black Community, 1720–1840* (Cambridge, MA: Harvard University Press, 1991).

45. Amsterdam and Vitiello, "Immigration to Philadelphia, c.1930-present"; Audrey Singer, Domenic Vitiello, Michael Katz, and David Park, *Recent Immigration to Philadelphia: Regional Change in a Re-emerging Gateway* (Washington, DC: Brookings Institution, 2008); Leigh Swigart, "Extended Lives: The African Immigrant Experience in Philadelphia," *Historical Society of Pennsylvania*, 2001, https://hsp.org/history-online/exhibits/extended-lives-the-african-immigrant-experience-in-philadelphia; Etenesh Worku, interview by Arthur Acolin, July 2009.

46. Figures are taken from the US Census. See also Vitiello, "Liberia and Liberians."

47. Thomas Ginsberg, "West Africans Strive to Make Philadelphia Home: Fleeing Strife, They Find New Challenges in America," *Philadelphia Inquirer*, January 30, 2003, A1.

48. Voffee Jabateh, interview by Domenic Vitiello, August 15, 2007; Massa Washington, interview by Leigh Swigart, Historical Society of Pennsylvania, June 18, 2000; Slewion, interview; Portia Kamara, interview by Rachel Van Tosh, November 30, 2011; Union of Liberian Associations in the Americas, *Souvenir Program of the 32nd National General Assembly Union of Liberian Associations in the Americas*, Philadelphia, September 22–24, 2006.

49. Singer et al., *Recent Immigration to Philadelphia: Regional Change in a Re-emerging Gateway*; Stephanie Farr, "Fleeing to Philly: Thousands of Liberians Seek Asylum Here," *Philadelphia Daily News*, February 18, 2009, 3.

50. Slewion, interview.

51. Jallah, interview, December 6, 2018.

52. Juliane Ramic, interview by Domenic Vitiello, January 26, 2016; this story is repeated in Vitiello, "Liberia and Liberians"; see also Panning, interview; Erat, interview.

53. "American Community Survey (2008–2010)," US Bureau of the Census, https://www.census.gov/programs-surveys/acs/data.html.

54. Jallah, interview, December 6, 2018; Jallah, interview, March 12, 2019.

55. Jallah, interview, December 6, 2018.

56. Jallah, interview, December 6, 2018.

57. Rev. John Gblah, interview by Domenic Vitiello, March 12, 2019; see also Slewion, interview; Joe Dayrell, interview by Leigh Swigart, February 8, 2001, Historical Society of Pennsylvania.

58. Ramic, interview.

59. Jay Specter and Zoya Kravets, interview by Leah Whiteside, March 13, 2013.

60. Ramic, interview.

61. *Housing for Equity: An Action Plan for Philadelphia* (City of Philadelphia, 2018); "American Community Survey (2008–2010)."

62. "American Community Survey (2008–2010)."

63. Slewion, interview; Kamara, interview by Van Tosh.

64. Jallah, interview, December 6, 2018.

65. Michael Matza, "Liberian Immigrants Transforming S.W. Phila." *Philadelphia Inquirer*, June 6, 2008, A1.

66. Vitiello, "Liberia and Liberians"; Ginsberg, "West Africans Strive."

67. Vitiello and Van Tosh, "Liberian Reconstruction."

68. Kamara, interview by Van Tosh.

69. Jabateh, interview, August 15, 2006; Jean Marie Kouassi, interview by Domenic Vitiello, (May 3, 2019); Domenic Vitiello and Arthur Acolin, "Institutional Ecosystems of Housing Support in Chinese, Southeast Asian, and African Philadelphia," *Journal of Planning Education and Research* 37, no. 2 (June 2017): 195–206; Thomas Carter and Domenic Vitiello, "Immigrants, Refugees and Housing," in *Immigrant Geographies of North American Cities*, ed. Carlos Teixeira, Wei Li, and Audrey Kobayashi, 91–111eds. (New York: Oxford University Press, 2011), 91–111.

70. Ramic, interview, January 26, 2016; Panning, interview; Erat, interview.

71. Gblah, interview.

72. Rev. John Gblah, interview by Domenic Vitiello, March 24, 2021.

73. John K. Jallah, interview by Rachel Van Tosh, April 11, 2011; Jallah, interview, December 6, 2018; Jallah, interview, March 12, 2019.

74. Kamara, interview by Domenic Vitiello, February 28, 2018.

75. Rosemary Traore and Robert Lukens, "'This Isn't the America I Thought I'd Find': African Students in the Urban U.S. High School," *FrontPageAfrica*, November 14, 2005.

76. Traore and Lukens, "'This Isn't the America.'"

77. Traore and Lukens, "'This Isn't the America.'"

78. Ginsberg, "West Africans Strive."

79. Jabateh, interview, August 15, 2007.

80. Matza, "Liberian Immigrants."

81. About 42 percent of Liberian households were homeowners, compared to over 70 percent of native-born households.

82. Alisa Orduna-Sneed and Lansana Koroma, interview by Domenic Vitiello, November 10, 2006.

83. Traore and Lukens, "'This Isn't the America.'"

84. Jennifer Ludden, "Liberian Youth in U.S. Find Threat from New Violence," *National Public Radio*, February 18, 2008), accessed March 31, 2019, at: https://www.npr.org/templates/story/story.php?storyId=19148453?storyId=19148453.

85. Traore and Lukens, "'This Isn't the America.'"

86. Ginsberg, "West Africans Strive."

87. Advocates for Human Rights, *House with Two Rooms*, 3; also Johnny Steinberg, *Little Liberia: An African Odyssey in New York City* (London: Cape, 2011).

88. Eric Edi, interview by Domenic Vitiello, December 19, 2006.

89. Traore and Lukens, "'This Isn't the America'"; Slewion, interview.

90. Slewion, interview.

91. "Mayor Street Announces Commission on African and Immigrant Affairs," Press Release, City of Philadelphia, Mayor's Office, June 30, 2005.

92. Jallah, interview by Van Tosh; Slewion, interview.

93. Washington, interview.

94. Jallah, interview by Van Tosh.

95. Jallah, interview by Van Tosh.

96. Jallah, interview, February 27, 2008.

97. Leigh Swigart, *Directory of African Community Resources* (Philadelphia: Historical Society of Pennsylvania, October 2001), 30.

98. Voffee Jabateh, interview by Domenic Vitiello, March 2, 2016; Kinge, "Hotel ACANA."

99. Gblah, interview; Kinge, "Hotel ACANA."

100. Matza, "Liberian Immigrants."

101. Jabateh, interview, August 15, 2007.

102. Jabateh, interview, August 15, 2007; Jabateh, interview with Domenic Vitiello, March 27, 2019.

103. Jabateh, interview, August 15, 2006.

104. Jabateh, interview, August 15, 2006; Jabateh, interview, October 30, 2006; Jabateh, interview, August 15, 2007; Jabateh, interview, March 2, 2016.

105. Voffee Jabateh and Josephine Blow, interview by Domenic Vitiello, August 15, 2007.

106. There was "no direct connection" between the Sanctuary Model and the Sanctuary Movement of the 1980s. Jabateh, interview, August 15, 2006; Sanctuary Institute, "The Sanctuary Model" (n.d.), accessed March 18, 2021, http://www.thesanctuaryinstitute.org/about-us/the-sanctuary-model/; Sandra Bloom, correspondence with Domenic Vitiello, March 22, 2021.

107. Jabateh, interview by Domenic Vitiello, November 28, 2008; Jabateh, interview by Domenic Vitiello, January 25, 2014; Jabateh, interview by Domenic Vitiello, March 27, 2019.

108. Jabateh, interview, March 27, 2019.

109. Kamara, interview by Van Tosh.

110. Kamara, interview by Van Tosh.

111. Portia Kamara, presentation at "Local Responses to Change in the Philadelphia Region: Race, Class and Immigration," Penn Center for the Study of Ethnicity, Race and Immigration, Philadelphia, November 8, 2019.

112. Raya Fagg, presentation at "Local Responses to Change"; Anne O'Callaghan, presentation to CPLN 628, University of Pennsylvania, Philadelphia, April 9, 2019; Kamara, February 28, 2018.

113. Kamara, interview by Van Tosh; Kamara, interview, February 28, 2018.

114. Kamara, interview by Van Tosh; Kamara, interview, February 28, 2018; Kamara, presentation; see also Portia Kamara, correspondence with Domenic Vitiello, January 12, 2021.

115. Kamara, interview, February 28, 2018.

116. Dahn Dennis, presentation to CPLN 628, University of Pennsylvania (March 2, 2021).

117. Kamara, interview by Van Tosh.

118. Kamara, interview by Van Tosh.

119. Tiguida Kaba, correspondence with Domenic Vitiello, July 12, 2021; E .E. Foley, "HIV/AIDS and African Immigrant Women in Philadelphia: Structural and

Cultural Barriers to Care," *AIDS Care: Psychological and Socio-Medical Aspects of AIDS/HIV* 17, no. 8 (2005): 1030–1043.

120. Tiguida Kaba, interview by Rachel Van Tosh, April 20, 2011; Kaba, correspondence; African Family and Health Organization, "About Us," accessed May 8, 2019, http://www.afaho.net/about-us/; Oni Richards, correspondence with Domenic Vitiello, May 3, 2021.

121. Richards, correspondence; Kaba, interview; African Family and Health Organization, "About Us."

122. Gblah, interview.

123. *Mandingo* and *Mandinka* are terms used interchangeably to describe ethnicity, language, and territory within the larger Mande group, which covers a large area of West Africa between Mali and Guinea.

124. Kaba, interview; Eric Edi, interview, December 19, 2006; Edi, interview by Domenic Vitiello, December 22, 2006; Edi, correspondence; Jabateh, interview, August 15, 2006; Jabateh, interview, November 28, 2008; Kamara, interview by Van Tosh; Angela Jengo, interview by Hannah Wizman-Cartier, summer 2008; Moussa Traore, interview by Hannah Wizman-Cartier, summer 2008; Rev. Robert Djiriga, interview by Hannah Wizman-Cartier, summer 2008; Siddiq Hadi, interview by Leigh Swigart, Historical Society of Pennsylvania, June 13, 2001.

125. Bernadine Ahonkhai, correspondence with Domenic Vitiello, March 7, 2021; Edi, correspondence.

126. Edi, correspondence; Kaba, correspondence; Tiguida Kaba, interview by Domenic Vitiello, July 14, 2021.

127. Edi, correspondence.

128. Edi, correspondence.

129. Domenic Vitiello, AFRICOM monthly meeting notes, January 13, 2007.

130. Domenic Vitiello, meeting notes from Welcoming Center for New Pennsylvanians meeting at Fatou and Fama Restaurant, Philadelphia, January 10, 2007; Fatima Muhammad, interview by Domenic Vitiello, August 29, 2007; Muhammad, interview by Domenic Vitiello, April 7, 2009.

131. Orduna-Sneed and Koroma, interview.

132. "African Caribbean Business Council," *Global Philadelphia*, 2021, http://globalphiladelphia.org/organizations/african-caribbean-business-council.

133. Azuka Anyiam, interview by Rachel Van Tosh, March 26, 2011.

134. Vitiello and Van Tosh, "Liberian Reconstruction"; Slewion, interview; John Jallah, interview by Van Tosh.

135. Vitiello and Van Tosh, "Liberian Reconstruction."

136. Arthur Acolin, meeting notes from Union of Liberian Associations in the Americas, First Regional Conference of the National Social Services Council, June 27, 2009; Union of Liberian Associations in the Americas, *Souvenir Program*.

137. Slewion, interview.

138. Slewion, interview.

139. Advocates for Human Rights, *House with Two Rooms*, 4.

140. Jeremy Roebuck, "Did Delco Man Order Massacre of 600 Liberians Hiding in a Church? He Says It's 'All Lies,'" *Philadelphia Inquirer*, February 12, 2018; Roebuck, "Held to Account? Past Attempts to Hold Leaders Accountable for Liberian Civil War

Atrocities," *Philadelphia Inquirer*, September 29, 2017; Prue Clarke, "'Jungle Jabbah' Was Accused of Cannibalism and other Horrors in Liberia. How a U.S. Court Brought Him to Justice," *Washington Post*, April 14, 2018.

141. Jallah, interview by Van Tosh; Slewion, interview.

142. Slewion, interview.

143. Slewion, interview.

144. Sinoe County Association in the Americas, 2021, https://scaausa.org/; Slewion, interview; Slewion, correspondence with Domenic Vitiello, August 10, 2020.

145. Slewion, interview; Slewion, correspondence.

146. Fred Gwyan, interview by Rachel Van Tosh, March 27, 2011.

147. Vitiello and Van Tosh, "Liberian Reconstruction"; Dahn Dennis, interview by Domenic Vitiello, March 24, 2021; UNICCO, "Nimba Women's Empowerment Center" (2016), http://www.unicconational.com/about-us.

148. Dennis, presentation.

149. Dennis, presentation.

150. Dennis, presentation.

151. Kla Brownell, interview by Rachel Van Tosh, April 19, 2011; Gwyan, interview; Slewion, interview.

152. Brownell, interview; John Etim, interview by Rachel Van Tosh, March 25, 2011; Gwyan, interview.

153. Jallah, interview by Van Tosh.

154. Slewion, interview.

155. Kamara, interview by Van Tosh.

156. Kaba, interview, April 20, 2011; Edi, interview, December 19, 2006; Edi, interview, December 22, 2006; Edi, correspondence; Jabateh, interview, August 15, 2006; Jabateh, interview, November 28, 2008; Kamara, interview by Rachel Van Tosh; Angela Jengo, interview by Hannah Wizman-Cartier, summer 2008; Moussa Traore, interview by Hannah Wizman-Cartier, summer 2008; Rev. Robert Djiriga, interview by Hannah Wizman-Cartier, summer 2008; Siddiq Hadi, interview by Leigh Swigart, Historical Society of Pennsylvania, June 13, 2001.

157. Kamara, interview by Van Tosh.

158. Jabateh, interview, August 15, 2006; Jabateh, interview, October 30, 2006; Jabateh, interview, November 28, 2008.

159. Agatha Johnson, interview by Domenic Vitiello, December 14, 2006; Jean Marie Kouassi, interview by Domenic Vitiello, March 29, 2011.

160. Kouassi, interview, March 29, 2011; Kouassi, interview, May 3, 2019; Philadelphia International Unity Cup, accessed June 10, 2020, https://unitycup.phila.gov.

161. Philadelphia African Caribbean Cup of Nations for Peace, accessed July 28, 2020, http://pacconp.org/index.php/our-history/.

162. Kouassi, interview, May 3, 2019; Philadelphia International Unity Cup.

163. Claire Mercer, Ben Page, and Martin Evans, "Unsettling Connections: Transnational Networks, Development and African Home Associations," *Global Networks* 9, no. 2 (2009): 141–161 (quote from 150).

164. "American Community Survey (2008–2010)."

165. World Bank, "Annual Remittances Data: Inflows" updated as of April 2019, http://www.worldbank.org/en/topic/migrationremittancesdiasporaissues/brief

/migration-remittances-data; Blair Glencorse, "A Decade of Aid Dependence in Liberia," *Devex.com*, August 19, 2013, devex.com/news/a-decade-of-aid-dependence-in-liberia-81634.

166. Glencorse, " Decade of Aid Dependence."

167. Cokie Mayenpu Nanka, "Remit: Remittance Stories from the Liberian Diaspora" (CPLN 628 class project), 2019, https://cnanka0.wixsite.com/remittancestories.

168. Jabateh, interview, March 27, 2019.

169. Jabateh, interview, August 15, 2006; Jabateh, interview, March 2, 2016; Slewion, interview; Kamara, interview, February 22, 2018; Marrapodi and Welch, "Liberians Facing Mass Deportation."

170. Slewion, interview.

171. Editorial Board, "Liberian Refugees Have Earned the Right to Stay in U.S.," *Star Tribune* (Minneapolis, MN), March 23, 2018, http://m.startribune.com/liberian-refugees-have-earned-the-right-to-stay-in-u-s/477794963/; Conor Finnegan, "Trump Gives Liberian Immigrants 1 Year to Leave or Face Deportation," *ABC News*, March 27, 2018, https://abcnews.go.com/Politics/trump-liberian-immigrants-year-leave-face-deportation/.

172. Slewion, interview.

173. Finnegan, "Trump Gives Liberian Immigrants 1 Year"; Wilson, "Temporary Protected Status"; Sam Brodey, "Permanently Temporary: Liberian Case Demonstrates Perils of Relying on U.S. Temporary Immigration Status," *MinnPost* (Minneapolis, MN), April 6, 2018, https://www.minnpost.com/politics-policy/2018/04/permanently-temporary-liberian-case-demonstrates-perils-relying-us-temporary.

174. See for example, Josh Dawsey, "Trump Derides Protections for Immigrants from 'Shithole' Countries," *Washington Post*, January 12, 2018, https://www.washingtonpost.com/politics/trump-attacks-protections-for-immigrants-from-shithole-countries-in-oval-office-meeting/2018/01/11/bfc0725c-f711-11e7-91af-31ac729add94_story.html.

175. Marrapodi and Welch, "Liberians Facing Mass Deportation."

176. Finnegan, "Trump Gives Liberian Immigrants 1 Year."

177. Marrapodi and Welch, "Liberians Facing Mass Deportation."

178. Donald J. Trump, "Memorandum on Extension of Deferred Enforced Departure for Liberians," Presidential Memoranda, March 28, 2019, https://www.whitehouse.gov/presidential-actions/memorandum-extension-deferred-enforced-departure-liberians/.

179. Trump, "Memorandum on Extension"; "Update on the Liberian DED Lawsuit," *UndocuBlack*, March 29, 2019, http://undocublack.org/press-releases/2019/3/29/statement-on-the-liberian-ded-lawsuit-african-communities-together-v-trump-hearing-on-preliminary-injunction.

180. Yomi Kareem, "Trump's Latest Immigration Plan Targets African Countries whose Citizens Overstay Visas," *Quartz Africa*, April 16, 2019, http://qz.com/africa/1596686/trump-immigration-clampdown-targets-nigeria-liberia-eritrea/amp/; Louise Radnofsky and Rebecca Ballhaus, "White House Weighs Broader Immigration Curbs," *Wall Street Journal*, April 14, 2019, https://www.wsj.com/articles/white-house-weighs-broader-immigration-curbs-1155528378; Daniel Gonzalez, "Black Immigrant Advocates Praise Biden for Reinstating Deportation Protections for Liberians who Fled

Civil War," *Arizona Republic*, February 19, 2021, https://www.azcentral.com/story
/news/politics/immigration/2021/02/14/biden-reinstates-liberian-deportation
-protections-deferred-enforced-departure/4363464001/.

181. US Citizenship and Immigration Services, "Liberian Refugee Immigration
Fairness," accessed March 11, 2020, https://www.uscis.gov/green-card/other-ways
-get-green-card/liberian-refugee-immigration-fairness.

182. Gonzalez, "Black Immigrant Advocates."

183. Andrew Arthur, "Liberian Amnesty Stuffed into NDAA 2020," *Center for
Immigration Studies*, December 20, 2019, https://cis.org/Arthur/Liberian-Amnesty
-Stuffed-NDAA-2020.

184. Voffee Jabateh, interview by Domenic Vitiello, December 4, 2020.

185. Gonzalez, "Black Immigrant Advocates."

186. Jose Munoz, "Amidst Mass Deportations, Expulsion of Black Immigrants, President Biden's Redesignation of TPS for Haiti is a Welcome Relief," *United We Dream*,
May 22, 2021, https://unitedwedream.org/2021/05/amidst-mass-deportations-expul
sion-of-black-immigrants-president-bidens-redesignation-of-tps-for-haiti-is-a-welcome
-relief/.

## 4. Muslim Town

1. Mohammed Al Juboori, interview by Menatallah Shanab, March 17, 2019.

2. Al Juboori, interview by Menatallah Shanab, January 4, 2019; Al Juboori, interview, March 17, 2019; Dahr Jamail, "Western Oil Firms Remain as U.S. Exits Iraq," *Al
Jazeera* (January 7, 2012), accessed May 28, 2019, at: https://www.aljazeera.com
/indepth/features/2011/12/2011122813134071641.html.

3. Jeffrey R. Smith, "Hussein's Prewar Ties to Al-Qaeda Discounted," *Washington
Post* (April 6, 2007).

4. Al Juboori, interview, March 17, 2019.

5. Al Juboori, interview, March 17, 2019.

6. Federation of American Scientists, "Iraqi Facilities at Habbaniya and Samarra"
(February 1991), accessed June 11, 2020, at: https://web.archive.org/web/20050213
210558/https://fas.org/irp/gulf/cia/960517/60886_01.htm.

7. Al Juboori, interview, March 17, 2019.

8. Al Juboori, interview, March 17, 2019.

9. Al Juboori, interview, January 4, 2019; Al Juboori, interview, March 17, 2019.

10. USCIS, "Special Immigrants" (last updated 2011), accessed May 21, 2019, at:
https://www.uscis.gov/humanitarian/special-immigrants; Al Juboori, interview,
January 4, 2019; Al Juboori, interview, March 17, 2019.

11. Al Juboori, interview, January 4, 2019; Al Juboori, interview, March 17, 2019.

12. Quoted in Liz Spikol, "JEVS Celebrates 75 Years of Breaking Down Barriers,"
*Jewish Exponent* (March 21, 2017), accessed May 21, 2019, at: http://jewishexponent
.com/2017/03/21/jevs-celebrates-75-years-breaking-barriers/

13. Al Juboori, interview, January 4, 2019.

14. Al Juboori, interview, January 4, 2019; Al Juboori, interview, March 17, 2019.

15. Sarah Kenyon Lischer, "Security and Displacement in Iraq: Responding to the
Forced Migration Crisis," *International Security* 33, no. 2 (2008): 95–115.

16. Joseph Sassoon, *The Iraqi Refugees* (London: Tauris, 2009), 1.

17. Nadwa Mossaad, "Annual Flow Report, Refugees and Asylees: 2014," US Department of Homeland Security, Office of Immigration Statistics, April 2016.

18. Congressional Research Service, "Iraqi and Afghan Special Immigrant Visa Programs," CRS R43725, updated March 29, 2019; Jynnah Radford and Jens Manuel Krogstad, "Afghans Who Worked for the U.S. Government Make Up Growing Share of Special Immigrant Visa Recipients," Pew Research Center, December 11, 2017, https://www.pewresearch.org/fact-tank/2017/12/11/afghans-who-worked-for-u-s-government-make-up-growing-share-of-special-immigrant-visa-recipients; US Department of State, Bureau of Population, Refugees, and Migration, "Refugee and Special Immigrant Visa (SIV) Arrivals," Oct. 1, 2006–June 3, 2019, downloaded June 3, 2019 from WRAPSnet, https://static1.squarespace.com/static/580e4274e58c624696efadc6/t/5cf51bc28be3fb00017c8143/1559567298626/Arrivals+by+State-Iraqi+6-3-19.xls.

19. Bob Woodward, "CIA Told to Do Whatever Necessary to Kill Bin Laden," *Washington Post*, October 21, 2001, A1.

20. The United States had supported Allawi back in the 1990s in an insurgency against Saddam that involved bombings and sabotage. Joel Brinkley, "The Reach of War: New Premier; Ex-CIA Aides Say Iraq Leader Helped Agency in 90's Attacks," *New York Times*, June 9, 2004.

21. Tricia Bacon and Elizabeth Grimm Arsenault, "Al Qaeda and the Islamic State's Break: Strategic Strife of Lackluster Leadership," *Studies in Conflict and Terrorism* 42, no. 3 (2018): 229–263.

22. Kathy Gilsinan, "The Many Ways to Map the Islamic 'State,'" *Atlantic*, August 27, 2014.

23. From 2013 to 2017, the CIA and the Defense Department trained and armed close to ten thousand rebel fighters in the Syrian Civil War, at a cost of about a billion dollars a year. Greg Miller and Karen DeYoung, "Secret CIA Effort in Syria Faces Large Funding Cut," *Washington Post*, June 12, 2015.

24. United Nations High Commissioner for Refugees, "Syria," 2019, https://www.unrefugees.org/emergencies/syria/.

25. Mattea Cumoletti and Jeanne Batalova, "Middle Eastern and North African Immigrants to the United States," Migration Policy Institute, January 10, 2018, https://www.migrationpolicy.org/article/middle-eastern-and-north-aftican-immigrants-united-states.

26. Quoted in Daniel Yergin, *The Prize: The Epic Quest for Oil, Money and Power* (New York: Simon and Schuster, 1991), 401.

27. In the 1990s, Senator Jesse Helms called Israel "America's aircraft carrier in the Middle East," a most strategic ally affording the US a military foothold in the region, even as America maintained ties on and off with its Arab rivals. Jesse Helms, "Jesse Helms: Setting the Record Straight," interview, *Middle East Quarterly*, March 1995, 71–73; "General Progress Report and Supplementary Report of the United States Conciliation Commission for Palestine, Covering the Period from 11 December 1949 to 23 October 1950," United Nations Conciliation Commission for Palestine, 1950; Jenny M. Sharp, "U.S. Foreign Aid to Israel," Congressional Research Service 7-5700, April 10, 2018; UNRWA, "In Figures," 2015, https://www.unrwa.org/sites/default/files/unrwa_in_figures_2015.pdf; Robert P.G. Bowker, *Palestinian Refugees: Mythology, Identity, and*

the *Search for Peace* (Boulder, CO: Lynne Rienner Publishers, 2003), 81; Rashid Khalidi, "The State of Middle East Studies" (WOCMES Speech, Sevilla, July 18, 2018), http://wocmes2018seville.org/images/doc/Rashid_Khalidi_Speech.pdf.

28. The United States removed Iraq from the list of state sponsors of terrorism, not because Iraq had ceased support for Palestinian revolutionary groups but rather because US authorities wanted Saddam to win his war with Iran. Douglas A. Borer, "Inverse Engagement: Lessons from U.S.-Iraq Relations, 1982–1990," *U.S. Army Professional Writing Collection* (2003), https://web.archive.org/web/20061011195656/http://www.army.mil/professionalwriting/volumes/volume1/july_2003/7_03_2v2.html; Peter Hahn, "A Century of U.S. Relations with Iraq," *Origins: Current Events in Historical Perspective* 5, no. 7 (April 2012), https://origins.osu.edu/article/century-us-relations-iraq.

29. US Department of State, *Country Reports on Terrorism 2009* (2010).

30. Ian Cobain, "CIA Rendition: More than a Quarter of Countries 'Offered Covert Support,'" *Guardian*, February 5, 2013.

31. Eric Schmitt and Mark Mazzetti, "Secret Order Lets U.S. Raid Al Qaeda in Many Countries Outside the War Zones: Authorized since 2004 to Hit across Borders of 15 to 20 Nations," *New York Times*, November 10, 2008, https://www.nytimes.com/2008/11/10/washington/10military.html.

32. Peter W. Galbraith, "Refugees from the War in Iraq: What Happened in 1991 and What May Happen in 2003," Policy Brief, Migration Policy Institute, 2003, https://www.migrationpolicy.org/research/refugees-war-iraq-what-happened-1991-and-what-may-happen-2003.

33. Al Juboori, interview, March 17, 2019.

34. Edmund Ghareeb, Donald Ranard, and Jenab Tutunji, "Refugees from Iraq: Their History, Cultures, and Background Experiences," COR Center, October 2008, http://culturalorientation.net/content/download/1340/7833/version/4/file/Refugees%2Bfrom%2BIraq.pdf; Cumoletti and Batalova, "Middle Eastern and North African Immigrants."

35. Al Juboori, interview, March 17, 2019.

36. Khalidi, "State of Middle East Studies."

37. Dan Kopf and Annalisa Merelli, "The Legalization of Islamophobia Is Underway in the United States," *Quartz*, September 14, 2017, https://qz.com/1074415/anti-sharia-bills-exploit-islamophobia-in-the-us-like-anti-catholic-politics-used-to/.

38. Quoted in Tony Abraham, "These Are the Daily Challenges Local Refugee Families Are Working to Overcome," *Generocity*, February 15, 2017, https://generocity.org/philly/2017/02/15/daily-challenges-local-refugee-families/.

39. Mary Troyan, "After Attacks in Paris, Governors Refuse to Accept Syrian Refugees," *USA Today*, November 16, 2015.

40. Ed Pilkington, "Donald Trump: Ban All Muslims Entering U.S.," *Guardian*, December 7, 2015.

41. Khaled Beydoun, "Between Muslim and White: The Legal Construction of Arab American Identity," *Annual Survey of American Law* (New York University) 29 (2013), https://annualsurveyofamericanlaw.org/wp-content/uploads/2014/10/69-1_beydoun.pdf.

42. Khaled Beydoun, "Islamophobia Has a Long History in the U.S.," *BBC*, September 29, 2015, https://www.bbc.com/news/magazine-34385051.

43. Kevin Liptak, "Why Iraq Was Removed from the Revised Travel Ban," *CNN*, March 6, 2017, https://edition.cnn.com/2017/03/06/politics/iraq-travel-ban/index.html.

44. Dan Deluce, "Only 2 Iraqi Translators Who Worked with U.S. Troops Got U.S. Visas Last Year," *NBC News*, August 23, 2019, https://www.nbcnews.com/news/world/only-2-iraqi-translators-who-worked-u-s-troops-got-n1035661.

45. Nora Elmarzouky, presentation to URBS 270, University of Pennsylvania, April 19, 2021.

46. Nasr Saradar, interview by Menatallah Shanab, April 27, 2019; see also Aziz Jalil, interview by Menatallah Shanab, February 12, 2019.

47. Aziz Jalil, correspondence with Domenic Vitiello, December 12, 2020.

48. Khalidi, "State of Middle East Studies."

49. David M. Krueger, "Islam," *Encyclopedia of Greater Philadelphia* (2019), https://philadelphiaencyclopedia.org/archive/islam/.

50. Heon Kim and Edward Curtis IV, "Philadelphia, Pennsylvania," in *Encyclopedia of Muslim-American History,* ed. Edward Curtis IV, 1:446–448 (New York: Infobase, 2010); Christopher Ellison, "Patterns of Religious Mobility among Black Americans," *Sociological Quarterly* 31 (1990): 551–568; Krueger, "Islam."

51. Abigail Hauslohner, "'Muslim Town': A Look inside Philadelphia's Thriving Muslim Culture," *Washington Post*, July 21, 2017.

52. Will Bunch, "Muslim Town," *Philadelphia Inquirer*, September 7, 2010, https://www.inquirer.com/philly/blogs/attytood/Muslim_Town.html.

53. Mark Dent, "What It's Like for Muslims in Philly, 'Mecca of the West,'" *BillyPenn*, January 29, 2016, https://billypenn.com/2016/01/29/what-its-like-for-muslims-in-philly-mecca-of-the-west/.

54. Marwan Kreidie, interview by Domenic Vitiello, June 2, 2005; Kreidie, interview by Domenic Vitiello, February 14, 2006; Zeina Halabi, interview by Arthur Acolin, November 7, 2011; Kathleen Christison "The American Experience: Palestinians in the U.S.," *Journal of Palestine Studies* 18, no. 4 (1988–1989): 18–36.

55. Amnah Ahmad, interview by Menatallah Shanab, March 26, 2019; Jalil, interview; Kreidie, interview, June 2, 2005; Kreidie, interview, February 14, 2006; Halabi, interview; Ribhi Mustapha, interview by Arthur Acolin, July 8, 2009; Joseph Slobodzian, "In Philadelphia, Expatriates Thrive But Feel Cut Off from Mukhmas," *Philadelphia Inquirer*, May 29, 2007.

56. Jalil, interview.

57. Ahmad, interview; Jalil, interview. Kreidie, interview, June 2, 2005; Kreidie, interview, February 14, 2006; Halabi, interview.

58. Ahmad, interview; Kreidie, interview, June 2, 2005; Kreidie, interview, February 14, 2006; Halabi, interview.

59. Mustapha, interview.

60. Al Juboori, interview, January 4, 2019; Al Juboori, interview, March 17, 2019; Spikol, "JEVS Celebrates"; Refugees in PA, "Success Stories: Mohammed Al Juboori" (n.d.), accessed June 28, 2019, http://www.refugeesinpa.org/successstories/index.htm.

61. Al Juboori, interview, January 4, 2019; Al Juboori, interview, March 17, 2019; Spikol, "JEVS Celebrates"; Al-Bustan Seeds of Culture, "Reflections on Syria," September 8, 2018, http://www.albustanseeds.org/past-events/reflections-on-syria/.

62. Ethan Aljuboori, interview by Domenic Vitiello, December 5, 2020.

63. Spikol, "JEVS Celebrates."

64. Refugees in PA, "Success Stories."

65. Al Juboori, interview, March 17, 2019.

66. Thomas Ginsberg, "Philadelphia's Immigrants: Who They Are and How They Are Changing the City," Pew Charitable Trusts, 2018.

67. Marina Merlin, interview by Menatallah Shanab, May 7, 2019; Juliane Ramic, interview by Rachel Van Tosh, November 19, 2011.

68. Merlin, interview; Ramic, interview.

69. Merlin, interview.

70. Bernstein-Baker, correspondence with Domenic Vitiello, December 31, 2020.

71. Merlin, interview; Nadia Barclaiy, interview by Benjamin Dubow, March 2008.

72. Hazami Sayed, interview by Menatallah Shanab, December 6, 2018; Merlin, interview; Ramic, interview.

73. Saradar, interview, April 27, 2019; Nasr Saradar, interview by Menatallah Shanab, May 10, 2019; Sayed, interview; Jalil, interview.

74. Jalil, interview; Merlin, interview.

75. Jalil, interview; Dana Mohamed, interview by Menatallah Shanab, January 26, 2019; Saradar, interview, April 27, 2019; Saradar, interview, May 10, 2019; Sayed, interview; Zoya Kravets and Jay Specter, interview by Leah Whiteside, March 13, 2013.

76. Mohamed, interview.

77. Merlin, interview; Ramic, interview, January 26, 2016; Ramic, interview by Domenic Vitiello, May 30, 2018.

78. Ahmad, interview; Halabi, interview; Jalil, interview; Merlin, interview; Mohamed, interview.

79. Ahmad, interview.

80. Saradar, interview, April 27, 2019; Saradar, interview, May 10, 2019; see also Jalil, interview.

81. Jalil, interview.

82. Saradar, interview, April 27, 2019; Saradar, interview, May 10, 2019.

83. Sayed, interview; Jalil, interview.

84. Ahmad, interview; Halabi, interview; Jalil, interview; Kreidie, interview, June 2, 2005; Kreidie, interview, February 14, 2006; Merlin, interview; Ramic, interview, November 19, 2011; Ramic, interview, January 26, 2016; Ramic, interview, May 30, 2018; Sayed, interview; Aaron Kase, "Iraq and a Hard Place: Parts of the Northeast Become a 'Little Baghdad' for Displaced Iraqis," *Philadelphia Weekly*, September 14, 2010.

85. Ramic, interview, January 26, 2016; Ramic, interview, May 30, 2018; Sayed, interview.

86. Ahmad, interview; Jalil, interview; Merlin, interview; Mohamed, interview.

87. Samantha Friedman, Joseph Gibbons, and Colleen Wynn, "Religion, Housing Discrimination, and Residential Attainment in Philadelphia: Are Muslims Disadvantaged?," typescript, September 25, 2015.

88. Mohamed, interview; Al Juboori, interview, March 17, 2019; Aljuboori, interview.

89. John Logan and Charles Zhang, "Global Neighborhoods: New Pathways to Diversity and Separation," *American Journal of Sociology* 115, no. 3 (2010): 1069–1109; Michael Matza and John Duchneskie, "Section of Lower Northeast Sees Money

Erosion," *Philadelphia Inquirer*, January 3, 2011; Julie Shaw, "The White Shift Out of Philly," *Philadelphia Inquirer*, June 2, 2011.

90. Domenic Vitiello, "The Politics of Place in Immigrant and Receiving Communities," in *What's New about the "New" Immigration to the United States?* ed. Marilyn Halter, Marilynn Johnson, Katheryn Veins, and Conrad Wright, 83–110 (New York: Palgrave, 2014); Analysis by Domenic Vitiello of 2000 US Census tracts 028900, 028800, and 028700, on the Penn Cartographic Modeling Lab's Neighborhood Information System, accessed February 27, 2011, http://cml.upenn.edu/nbase/.

91. Sayed, interview.

92. Marwan Kreidie and Zeina Halabi, interview by Domenic Vitiello, January 22, 2009; Halabi, interview; Mustapha, interview.

93. Saradar, interview, April 27, 2019; Saradar, interview, May 10, 2019.

94. Al Juboori, interview, March 17, 2019.

95. Al Juboori, interview, March 17, 2019.

96. Al Juboori, interview, March 17, 2019; anonymous, interview by Menatallah Shanab, November 20, 2018; Saradar, interview, April 27, 2019; Saradar, interview, May 10, 2019; Sayed, interview; Kreidie and Halabi, interview.

97. Sayed, interview; Mohamed, interview; Thea Renda Abu El-Haj, *Unsettled Belonging: Educating Palestinian American Youth after 9/11* (Chicago: University of Chicago Press, 2015).

98. Sayed, interview; Mohamed, interview.

99. Bunch, "Muslim Town."

100. Dent, "What It's Like"; Michael Matza, "Severed Pig's Head Left at North Philadelphia Mosque," *Philadelphia Inquirer*, December 8, 2015).

101. Dent, "What It's Like."

102. Hauslohner, "'Muslim Town.'"

103. Arab American Institute, "Healing the Nation: The Arab American Experience after September 11," 2002, 9, 17, https://www.aaiusa.org/library/aaif-healing-the-nation; see also Marwan Kreidie, interview with Philadelphia Folklore Project, August 6, 1998.

104. Kreidie, interview, June 2, 2005; Kreidie, interview, February 14, 2006.

105. Mohammad Aziz, Vic Compher, and Ayala Guy, "Walking the Talk on Interfaith Ties," *Philadelphia Inquirer*, June 2, 2006; Ram Cnaan, *The Other Philadelphia Story: How Local Congregations Support Quality of Life in Urban America* (Philadelphia: University of Pennsylvania Press, 2006).

106. Kitty Caparella and Gloria Campisi, "Terror Shock," *Philadelphia Daily News*, May 11, 2007; Krueger, "Islam."

107. Kreidie, interview, June 2, 2005; Kreidie, interview, February 14, 2006.

108. Alan Feuer, "Mosques Are Shaken by Ties to a Plot," *New York Times*, May 14, 2007.

109. Daniel Pipes, "Marwan Kreidie: More Obstruction of Counterterrorism, More Rewards," October 6, 2004, www.danielpipes.org/blog/2004/10/marwan-kreidie-more-obstruction-of; see also "The FBI Loses Its Way [with Marwan Kreidie]," *New York Sun*, July 6, 2004.

110. "Did Duka's Al Aqsa Mosque Get Federal & Saudi Funding for Façade Decoration via Philly Empowerment & Marwan Kreidie?," Weblog, *Militant Islam Monitor*, June 15, 2007. www.militantislammonitor.org/article/id/2978. Like many blog posts,

this references and embeds most of a set of earlier posts. Also see Feuer, "Mosques Are Shaken"; Kitty Caparella and Gloria Campisi, "Terror Shock," *Philadelphia Daily News*, May 11, 2007.

111. Alfred Lubrano, "Muslims Here Have Three Reasons to Rejoice," *Philadelphia Inquirer*, May 3, 2011.

112. Kreidie, interview, June 2, 2005; Kreidie, interview, February 14, 2006; Halabi, interview; Kreidie and Halabi, interview; Krueger, "Islam."

113. Dent, "What It's Like."

114. Kreidie, interview, June 2, 2005; Kreidie, interview, February 14, 2006; Kreidie and Halabi, interview; Halabi, interview.

115. Ahmad, interview; Halabi, interview; Merlin, interview.

116. Ahmad, interview; Halabi, interview; Mustapha, interview; Kreidie and Halabi, interview.

117. Halabi, interview; Kreidie and Halabi, interview; Sayed, interview.

118. Sayed, interview; also Elmarzouky, presentation.

119. Sayed, interview.

120. Sayed, interview; also Hazami Sayed, correspondence with Domenic Vitiello, January 27, 2021.

121. Sayed, interview; Sayed, correspondence.

122. Swarthmore College, "Friends, Peace, & Sanctuary," accessed January 1, 2021, https://fps.swarthmore.edu/about/.

123. Nora Elmarzouky, correspondence with Domenic Vitiello, February 1, 2021.

124. "Art, Connection, Refuge: A Trio of Center City Exhibitions Open Windows on the Immigrant Experience," press release, Swarthmore College, May 28, 2019, https://fps.swarthmore.edu/assets/FPS%20Philly%20Press%20Release_05-28-19_Final.pdf.

125. Swarthmore College Friends, Peace, and Sanctuary Project, "Searching for Sanctuary Symposium," accessed January 1, 2021, https://fps.swarthmore.edu/public%20events/searching-for-sanctuary-symposium/.

126. Elmarzouky, correspondence.

127. Elmarzouky, presentation); Ximena Conde, "Philly Gets First Arabic Newspaper in 118 Years Thanks to 'Friends, Peace, and Sanctuary,'" *WHYY*, July 5, 2020, https://whyy.org/articles/philly-gets-first-arabic-newspaper-in-118-years-thanks-to-friends-peace-and-sanctuary/?fbclid=IwAR0atrxssy8IsmiVmYt8-W1XnarC66I2Zs9OQzoqujUCzd4r3DU2-0bRaLc.

128. Jalil, interview; Mohamed, interview; Saradar, interview, April 27, 2019; Saradar, interview, May 10, 2019; Eyad Takiedine, interview by Menatallah Shanab, May 1, 2019.

129. Jalil, interview; Mohamed, interview; Saradar, interview, April 27, 2019; Saradar, interview, May 10, 2019; Takiedine, interview; also Dana Mohamed, correspondence with Domenic Vitiello, March 5, 2021.

130. Mohamed, interview.

131. Mohamed, interview.

132. Shai Ben-Yaacov, "Free Muslim-Run Health Clinic Opens to All in Northeast Philly," *WHYY News*, April 8, 2018, https://whyy.org/articles/free-muslim-run-health-clinic-opens-to-all-in-northeast-philly.

133. Cherri Gregg, "Free Clinic Run by Muslims Opening in Northeast Philly Despite Initial Backlash," *KYW News Radio*, April 5, 2018, https://kywnewsradio

.radio.com/articles/free-clinic-run-muslims-opening-northeast-philly-despite-initial
-backlash.

134. Michael Boren, "Fear of Islamic Health Clinic Stirs Debate in Northeast Philly," *Philadelphia Inquirer*, September 5, 2017, https://www.inquirer.com/philly/news/icna-relief-islamic-health-northeast-holmesburg-20170904.html.

135. Mohamed, interview.

136. Gregg, "Free Clinic."

137. Ben-Yaacov, "Free Muslim-Run Health Clinic"; see also Logan Krum, "SHAMS Clinic Grand Opening Is Saturday," *Northeast Times*, April 5, 2018, https://northeasttimes.com/2018/04/05/shams-clinic-grand-opening-is-saturday/.

138. Sally Howell, "Rights versus Respectability: The Politics of Muslim Visibility in Detroit's Northern Suburbs," in *Muslims and U.S. Politics Today: A Defining Moment*, ed. Mohammad Hassan Khalil, 149–168 (Cambridge, MA: Harvard University Press, 2019).

139. Sam Wood, "Muslim Congregation Sues Bensalem to Build Mosque," *Philadelphia Inquirer*, December 8, 2014.

140. Mohamed, interview.

141. Mohamed, correspondence.

142. Hanaa Jaber, interview by Menatallah Shanab, November 2018; see also Jalil, interview.

143. Ahmad, interview; Halabi, interview; Kreidie and Halabi, interview; Jalil, interview.

144. Jaber, interview; see also Sayed, interview.

145. Jaber, interview.

146. Jaber, interview.

147. Sayed, interview.

148. Julia Ann McWilliams and Sally Wesley Bonet, "Refugees in the City: The Neighborhood Effects of Institutional Presence and Flexibility," *Journal of Immigrant & Refugee Studies* 13 (2015): 419–438 (quotes from 420 and 427).

149. Anonymous, interview.

150. Tamir Hasan, interview by Arthur Acolin, July 9, 2009; Dr. Wissam, interview by Arthur Acolin, July 16, 2009; Mustapha, interview; anonymous, Al Jamia Mosque, interview by Arthur Acolin, July 16, 2009; Pacius Breton, interview by Arthur Acolin, July 3, 2009; Mohamed Silla, interview by Arthur Acolin, July 2009; Imam Sidiq, Salam Mosque, interview by Arthur Acolin, July 2009.

151. Kreidie, interview, June 2, 2005; Kreidie, interview, February 14, 2006; Kreidie and Halabi, interview; Halabi interview; Mustapha, interview; Silla, interview; Hasan, interview; Elizabeth Song, "How West Philly Was Won," *Daily Pennsylvanian*, October 25, 2007; Inga Saffron, "Philadelphia Muslims Make a Statement with Opening of New Mosque," *Philadelphia Inquirer*, November 30, 2018; Akel Ismail Kahera, "Urban Enclaves, Muslim Identity and the Urban Mosque in America," *Journal of Muslim Minority Affairs* 22, no. 2 (2002): 369–380.

152. Sayed, interview; Jalil, interview.

153. Ahmad, interview; Halabi, interview; Kreidie and Halabi, interview; Jalil, interview; El-Haj, *Unsettled Belonging*.

154. Spikol, "JEVS Celebrates."

155. Sayed, interview; Al Juboori, interview, January 4, 2019; Jalil, interview.

156. Saradar, interview, April 27, 2019; Saradar, interview, May 10, 2019.

157. Sayed, interview; Jalil, interview; Merlin, interview.

158. Michael Matza, "Bryn Mawr Couple Forms Group to Help Syrian Refugees," *Philadelphia Inquirer*, September 18, 2015.

159. Michael Matza, "Syrian Medical Society in Philadelphia Provides Help for War-Torn Home," *Philadelphia Inquirer*, August 24, 2014.

160. Menatallah Shanab, interview by Domenic Vitiello, February 19, 2019.

161. Melissa Cruz, "Iraqi Interpreters Who Risked Their Lives Working with US Military Shut Out by Trump Administration," *Immigration Impact*, September 3, 2019, http://immigrationimpact.com/2019/09/03/iraqi-interpreters-military-visa/#.XYfKxS2ZPOQ; David Bier, "Trump Cut Muslim Refugees 91%, Immigrants 30%, Visitors by 18%," *Cato at Liberty*, December 7, 2018, https://www.cato.org/blog/trump-cut-muslim-refugees-91-immigrants-30-visitors-18; Jalil, correspondence; Brittany Blizzard and Jeanne Batalova, "Refugees and Asylees in the United States," *Migration Information Source*, June 13, 2019, https://www.migrationpolicy.org/article/refugees-and-asylees-united-states.

162. Julie Hirschfeld Davis and Michael Shear, "Trump Administration Considers a Drastic Cut in Refugees Allowed to Enter U.S.," *New York Times*, September 6, 2019, https://www.nytimes.com/2019/09/06/us/politics/trump-refugees-united-states.html.

163. Robert Burns, Lolita Baldor, and Matthew Lee, "Trump Defends Decision to Abandon Kurdish Allies in Syria," *Associated Press*, October 8, 2019, https://apnews.com/article/ac3115b4eb564288a03a5b8be868d2e5; Eli Lake, "The Kurds Have Paid Dearly for Trump's Recklessness," *Bloomberg*, September 17, 2020, https://www.bloomberg.com/opinion/articles/2020-09-17/kurds-have-paid-dearly-for-trump-s-reckless-withdrawal-from-syria.

164. Al Juboori, interview, March 17, 2019.

165. Aljuboori, interview.

166. Krueger, "Islam."

## 5. New Sanctuary

1. Sabrina Vourvoulias, "Carmen Guerrero: From Survivor of Kidnapping to Philadelphia Immigrant Leader," *Generocity*, June 29, 2019, https://generocity.org/philly/2019/06/29/carmen-guerrero-from-survivor-of-kidnapping-to-philadelphia-immigrant-leader/.

2. Carmen Guerrero, interview by Domenic Vitiello, December 6, 2019; Carmen Guerrero, interview by Domenic Vitiello, January 31, 2020.

3. Guerrero, interview, December 6, 2019.

4. Guerrero, interview, December 6, 2019.

5. Guerrero, interview, December 6, 2019.

6. Guerrero, interview, December 6, 2019.

7. Guerrero, interview, December 6, 2019; see also Edwin Lopez Moya, "'Immigrants Are Slaves to Neoliberalism,'" *Al Dia*, April 16, 2018, https://aldianews.com/articles/leaders/immigrants-are-slaves-neoliberalism/52343.

8. Guerrero, interview, December 6, 2019; Aldo Musacchio, "Mexico's Financial Crisis of 1994–1995," *Harvard Business School Working Paper* no.12-101 (May 2012), https://dash.harvard.edu/bitstream/handle/1/9056792/12-101.pdf?sequence=1.

9. Guerrero, interview, December 6, 2019; Mark Weisbrot, Stephan Lefebvre, and Joseph Sammut, "Did NAFTA Help Mexico? An Assessment after 20 Years," Center for Economic and Policy Research, February 2014, https://web.archive.org/web/20170517162846/http://cepr.net/documents/nafta-20-years-2014-02.pdf; Ranko Shiraki Oliver, "In the Twelve Years of NAFTA, the Treaty Gave to Me . . . What, Exactly?: An Assessment of Economic, Social, and Political Developments in Mexico since 1994 and Their Impact on Mexican Immigration into the United States," *Harvard Latino Law Review* no.10 (2007): 53–133.

10. Jeffrey Passel, "Mexican Immigration to the U.S.: The Latest Estimates," Migration Policy Institute, 2004, https://www.migrationpolicy.org/article/mexican-immigration-us-latest-estimates; Jeffrey Passel, D'Vera Cohn, and Ana Gonzalez-Barrera, "Migration between the U.S. and Mexico," Pew Research Center, 2012, https://www.pewresearch.org/hispanic/2012/04/23/ii-migration-between-the-u-s-and-mexico/.

11. Jeffrey Passel and D'Vera Cohn, "Mexicans Decline to Less Than Half the U.S. Unauthorized Immigrant Population for the First Time," *FactTank* (Pew Research Center), June 12, 2019.

12. Caroline Mimbs Nyce and Chris Bodenner, "Looking Back at Amnesty under Reagan," *Atlantic*, May 23, 2016, https://www.theatlantic.com/notes/2016/05/thirty-years-after-the-immigration-reform-and-control-act/482364/.

13. Kelly Lytle Hernandez, *Migra! A History of the U.S. Border Patrol* (Berkeley: University of California Press, 2010).

14. Adam Goodman, *The Deportation Machine: America's Long History of Expelling Immigrants* (Princeton: Princeton University Press, 2020), 107.

15. Muzaffar Chishti, Doris Meissner, and Claire Bergeron, "At Its 25th Anniversary, IRCA's Legacy Lives On," Migration Policy Institute, 2011, https://www.migrationpolicy.org/article/its-25th-anniversary-ircas-legacy-lives.

16. Joseph Nevins, *Operation Gatekeeper and Beyond: The War on "Illegals" and the Remaking of the U.S.-Mexico Boundary*, 2nd ed. (New York: Routledge, 2010).

17. Douglas Massey, "Five Myths about Immigration: Common Misconceptions Underlying US Border-Enforcement Policy," *Immigration Policy in Focus*, 4, no. 6 (August 2005), https://www.americanimmigrationcouncil.org/sites/default/files/research/IPC%20five%20myths.pdf.

18. Guerrero, interview, December 6, 2019; also Moya, "'Immigrants Are Slaves.'"

19. Guerrero, interview, December 6, 2019.

20. Guerrero, interview, December 6, 2019.

21. Carmen Guerrero, correspondence with Domenic Vitiello, October 5, 2020.

22. Carmen Guerrero, correspondence with Domenic Vitiello, October 8, 2020; Vourvoulias, "Carmen Guerrero"; Moya, "'Immigrants Are Slaves.'"

23. Vourvoulias, "Carmen Guerrero"; Carmen Guerrero, interview by Domenic Vitiello, February 26, 2020.

24. Guerrero, interview, January 31, 2020.

25. Guerrero, interview, January 31, 2020.

26. Vourvoulias, "Carmen Guerrero."

27. Carmen Guerrero, interview by Domenic Vitiello, December 18, 2019.

28. Guerrero, interview, December 18, 2019.

29. Guerrero, interview, February 26, 2020.

30. Guerrero, interview, December 18, 2019.

31. Guerrero, interview, December 18, 2019.

32. Guerrero, interview, December 18, 2019.

33. Guerrero, interview, December 18, 2019.

34. Guerrero, interview, January 31, 2020.

35. Moya, "'Immigrants Are Slaves.'"

36. Mathew Frye Jacobson, *Barbarian Virtues: The United States Encounters Foreign Peoples at Home and Abroad, 1876–1917* (New York: Hill and Wang, 2000).

37. In addition to the Mexican-American war of the 1840s, the United States intervened in Mexico's civil war, but that ended in 1920.

38. "Mexico—New Global Poverty Estimates," World Bank, 2010, povertydata.worldbank.org/poverty/country/MEX.

39. Guerrero, interview, January 31, 2020.

40. Laura Carlsen, "Under NAFTA, Mexico Suffered, and the United States Felt Its Pain," *New York Times*, November 24, 2013, https://www.nytimes.com/roomfordebate/2013/11/24/what-weve-learned-from-nafta/under-nafta-mexico-suffered-and-the-united-states-felt-its-pain.

41. Viridiana Rios, "The Role of Drug-Related Violence and Extortion in Promoting Mexican Migration: Unexpected Consequences of a Drug War," *Latin American Research Review* 49, no. 3 (2014): 199–217.

42. Marina Franco, "El Horror de las Desaparaciones en Mexico: El Pais Suma Mas de 73,000 Personas No Localizadas," *Noticias Telemundo*, July 13, 2020, https://www.telemundo.com/noticias/2020/07/13/el-horror-de-las-desapariciones-en-mexico-el-pais-suma-mas-de-73000-personas-no-tmna3822108.

43. Michael Lettieri, "Violence against Women in Mexico," University of San Diego, Kroc School Trans-Border Initiative, December 2017; "Resultados de la Encuesta Nacional Sobre La Dinàmica de Las Relaciones en Los Hogares 2016," Instituto Nacional de Estadistica y Geografia, August 2017.

44. United Nations, "Violence against Women," *The World's Women 2010: Trends and Statistics* (2010), 127–139, https://unstats.un.org/unsd/demographic/products/Worldswomen/WW_full%20report_BW.pdf; Azam Ahmed, "Women Are Fleeing Death at Home. The U.S. Wants to Keep Them Out," *New York Times*, August 18, 2019, https://www.nytimes.com/2019/08/18/world/americas/guatemala-violence-women-asylum.html.

45. Manny Fernandez, "'You Have to Pay with Your Body': The Hidden Nightmare of Sexual Violence on the Border," *New York Times*, March 3, 2019, https://www.nytimes.com/2019/03/03/us/border-rapes-migrant-women.html.

46. Arlie Hochschild, "The Nanny Chain," *American Prospect*, December 19, 2001, https://prospect.org/features/nanny-chain/; Jeanne Batalova, "Immigrant Women and Girls in the United States," Migration Policy Institute, 2020, https://www.migrationpolicy.org/article/immigrant-women-and-girls-united-states-2018.

47. William Frey, *Diversity Spreads Out: Metropolitan Shifts in Hispanic, Asian, and Black Populations since 2000* (Washington, DC: Brookings Institution, 2006); Audrey Singer, Susan Hardwick, and Caroline Brettell, eds., *Twenty-First Century Gateways: Immigrant Incorporation in Suburban America* (Washington, DC: Brookings Institution Press, 2008); Douglas Massey, ed., *New Faces in New Places: The Changing Geography of American Immigration* (New York: Russell Sage Foundation, 2008); William Frey,

*Diversity Explosion: How New Racial Demographics Are Remaking America* (Washington, DC: Brookings Institution Press, 2015).

48. Passel, "Mexican Immigration."

49. Passel, "Mexican Immigration"; Passel and Cohn, "Mexicans Decline."

50. Jerry Kammer, "The Backstory of the Vocabulary War," *Center for Immigration Studies*, August 20, 2015, https://cis.org/kammer/backstory-vocabulary-war; Jerry Kammer, "Is It Really 'an Invasion'?" *Center for Immigration Studies*, August 21, 2015, https://cis.org/Kammer/It-Really-Invasion; Peter Schuck, "The Great Immigration Debate," *American Prospect*, December 5, 2000, https://prospect.org/justice/great-immigration-debate/; Philippe Legrain, *Immigrants: Your Country Needs Them* (Princeton, NJ: Princeton University Press, 2007).

51. Peter Bloom, "Immigrant Rights in a State of Xenophobia," *Progressive Planning* no. 170 (Winter 2007): 11–13.

52. Bloom, "Immigrant Rights"; Domenic Vitiello, "What Does Unauthorized Immigration and Sanctuary Mean for Philly's Revival?," *WHYY*, January 12, 2017, https://whyy.org/articles/what-does-unauthorized-immigration-and-sanctuary-mean-for-philly-s-revival/; A. K. Sandoval-Strausz, *Barrio America: How Latino Immigrants Saved the American City* (New York: Basic Books, 2019).

53. Domenic Vitiello, Hilary Parsons Dick, Danielle DiVerde, and Veronica Willig, "Mexicans and Mexico," *Encyclopedia of Greater Philadelphia* (2017), https://philadelphiaencyclopedia.org/archive/mexicans-and-mexico/; Debra Shutika, *Beyond the Borderlands: Migration and Belonging in the United States and Mexico* (Berkeley: University of California Press, 2011); Mark Lyons and August Tarrier, eds., *Mirrors and Windows: Oral Histories of Mexican Farmworkers and Their Families* (Philadelphia: New City Community Press, 2012).

54. Chris White, interview by Domenic Vitiello, July 24, 2009; Vitiello et al., "Mexicans and Mexico"; Domenic Vitiello, "The Politics of Immigration and Suburban Revitalization: Divergent Responses in Adjacent Pennsylvania Towns," *Journal of Urban Affairs* 36, no. 3 (August 2014): 519–533; Stanton Wortham, Katherin Mortimer, and Elaine Allard, "Mexicans as Model Minorities in the New Latino Diaspora," *Anthropology & Education Quarterly*, 40 (2009): 388–404.

55. Michael Katz and Kenneth Ginsburg, "Immigrant Cities as Reservations for Low-Wage Labor," *Contexts* 14, no. 1 (2015): 26–31.

56. Vourvoulias, "Carmen Guerrero."

57. Guerrero, interview, December 18, 2019.

58. Vourvoulias, "Carmen Guerrero."

59. Vourvoulias, "Carmen Guerrero."

60. Guerrero, interview, December 18, 2019.

61. Guerrero, interview, December 18, 2019; Guerrero, interview, January 31, 2020.

62. Guerrero, interview, February 26, 2020.

63. Guerrero, interview, February 26, 2020.

64. Vitiello, "Politics of Immigration."

65. Vitiello, "Politics of Immigration."

66. Vitiello, "Politics of Immigration"; Vitiello et al., "Mexicans and Mexico."

67. Vitiello, "Politics of Immigration."

68. White, interview.

69. Guerrero, interview, December 18, 2019.

70. White, interview.

71. White, interview.

72. Guerrero, interview, December 18, 2019.

73. Guerrero, interview, December 18, 2019; Garcia Hernandez, interview by Domenic Vitiello, May 3, 2013; White, interview; Bucks County Human Relations Council, "Press Release: Bensalem Police Not Participating in 287(g) Program," April 10, 2018; Laura Benshoff, "Bensalem Mayor, Public Safety Director Send Mixed Signals on Partnering with ICE," WHYY, May 2, 2018, https://whyy.org/articles/bensalem-mayor -public-safety-director-send-mixed-signals-on-partnering-with-ice/; Immigrant Legal Resource Center, "National Map of 287(g) Agreements," October 21, 2020, https://www .ilrc.org/national-map-287g-agreements.

74. Vitiello et al., "Mexicans and Mexico."

75. "Popoctépetl Volcano Eruptions," Volcano Discovery, accessed March 9, 2020, https://www.volcanodiscovery.com/popocatepetl-eruptions.html.

76. Antonio Tellez, interview by Domenic Vitiello, June 19, 2007; Kate Kilpatrick, "Mi Casa, Su Casa," Philadelphia Weekly, April 5, 2006, http://www.philadelphiaweekly .com/news/mi-casa-su-casa/article_71e73c21-647b-56de-99a0-000c193b5b6d.html; Allyn Gaestel, "Reform in the Back of the House," Next City 1, no. 63 (2013).

77. Domenic Vitiello, "The Politics of Place in Immigrant and Receiving Communities," in What's New about the "New" Immigration to the United States? ed. Marilyn Halter, Marilynn Johnson, Katheryn Veins, and Conrad Wright, 83–110 (New York: Palgrave, 2014).

78. Cristina Perez, interview by Domenic Vitiello, March 11, 2021.

79. Jaime Ventura, interview by Domenic Vitiello, February 26, 2019; see also Edgar Ramirez and Father Abel Osorio, interview by Juliana Pineda, May 3, 2010; Zac Steele, interview by Juliana Pineda, May 4, 2010.

80. Ventura, interview; Steele, interview; Carlos Pascual Sanchez, interview by Yary Muñoz and Natasha Menon, April 19, 2018; Garcia Hernandez, interview, May 3, 2013; Perez, interview.

81. Ventura, interview; Bloom, "Immigrant Rights"; Steele, interview; Natasha Iskander, Christine Riordan, and Nichola Lowe, "Learning in Place: Immigrants' Spatial and Temporal Strategies for Occupational Advancement," Economic Geography 89, no. 1 (2012): 53–75; Pascual Sanchez, interview; Garcia Hernandez, interview, May 3, 2013; Javier Garcia Hernandez, interview by Domenic Vitiello, March 24, 2021; Perez, interview.

82. Ramirez and Osorio, interview; Pascual Sanchez, interview; Steele, interview; Perez, interview.

83. Gaestel, "Reform"; Peter Bloom, interview with Mural Arts Program, November 10, 2008, in possession of the author.

84. Vitiello, "What Does Unauthorized Immigration and Sanctuary Mean"; Julie Shaw, "Let's Put It This Way: Philadelphia Gained More Amigos," Daily News, March 12, 2011.

85. Oscar Benitez, "Philadelphia as a Re-Emerging Immigrant Gateway: An Exploration of Mexican Entrepreneurship and Its Economic Value" (University of Pennsylvania Urban Studies Senior Thesis, 2009), available at SSRN, http://ssrn.com /abstract=1689748.

86. Vitiello et al., "Mexicans and Mexico"; Benitez, "Philadelphia as a Re-Emerging Immigrant Gateway"; Ramirez and Osorio, interview.

87. Vitiello et al., "Mexicans and Mexico"; Ben Bradlow, "Mexican Community Comes of Age in South Philadelphia," *WHYY It's Our City Blog*, February 4, 2009, http://whyy.org/blogs/itsourcity/2009/02/04/mexican-community-comes-of-age-in-south-hiladelphia/.

88. Shaw, "Let's Put It This Way"; Vitiello et al., "Mexicans and Mexico."

89. Alma Romero Tlacopilco and Marcos Tlacopilco, interview by Domenic Vitiello, June 1, 2021; Michael Klein, "Alma del Mar, a Restaurant Designed by the 'Queer Eye' Cast, Is a Family Affair in the Italian Market," *Philadelphia Inquirer*, July 14, 2020, https://www.inquirer.com/food/queer-eye-philadelphia-alma-del-mar-restaurant-italian-market-marcos-tlacopilco-20200714.html; "South Philadelphia: Hispanics Play an Important Role in the 'Italian' Market," *Philadelphia Neighborhoods*, October 3, 2011, https://philadelphianeighborhoods.com/2011/10/03/south-philadelphia-hispanics-play-an-important-role-in-the-italian-market/.

90. Vitiello et al., "Mexicans and Mexico."

91. Cassidy Hartmann, "Sign Language: The Italian Market Gets a New Plaque and an Old Name," *Philadelphia Weekly*, August 8, 2007; Caitlin Meals, "Sign of the Times," *South Philadelphia Review*, August 28, 2008; Rick Nichols, "Can the Italian Market Be Saved?" *Philadelphia Inquirer*, November 13, 2008; Stefano Luconi, *From Paesani to White Ethnics: The Italian Experience in Philadelphia* (Albany: State University of New York Press, 2001); Vitiello, "Politics of Place."

92. Gaiutra Bahadur, "An Old Struggle to Adapt to a New Country's Ways," *Philadelphia Inquirer*, May 30, 2006.

93. Michael Katz and Mark Stern, *One Nation Divisible: What America Was and What It Is Becoming* (New York: Russell Sage Foundation, 2008).

94. Mae Ngai, *Impossible Subjects: Illegal Aliens and the Making of Modern America* (Princeton, NJ: Princeton University Press, 2005); Aristide Zolberg, *A Nation by Design: Immigration Policy in the Fashioning of America* (New York: Russell Sage Foundation with Harvard University Press, 2006).

95. Luconi, *From Paesani to White Ethnics*.

96. Vitiello, "Politics of Place."

97. Wendy Ruderman, "Did Routine Cross Badtaste Border," *Philadelphia Inquirer*, January 3, 2009.

98. "The Big Talker WPHT Stands with Arizona," *Radio +Television Business Report*, July 12, 2010, https://www.rbr.com/the-big-talker-wpht-stands-with-arizona/.

99. Vitiello, "Politics of Place"; Uriel J. Garcia, "Donations Pour in to SB 1070 Defense Fund," *Tucson Sentinel*, October 29, 2011, http://www.tucsonsentinel.com/local/report/102811_sb1070_defense_fund/donations-pour-sb-1070-defense-fund/; Daniel Denvir, "Right Makes Might," *Philadelphia City Paper*, July 27, 2011, https://mycitypaper.com/Right-Makes-Might/.

100. PA State Representative Daryl Metcalfe, "Lawmakers Unveil 'No Sanctuary' Components to National Security Begins at Home Illegal Immigration Reform Package," press release, June 11, 2008, visited October 6, 2015,http://www.repmetcalfe.com/NewsItem.aspx?NewsID=1198.

101. Guerrero, interview, February 26, 2020.

102. Perez, interview, March 11, 2021; Cristine Perez, interview by Domenic Vitiello, March 18, 2021; Bloom, interview; see also Ramirez and Osorio, interview; Pascual Sanchez, interview; Steele, interview.

103. Perez, interview, March 11, 2021; Perez, interview, March 18, 2021; Leslie Bethell, "Politics in Brazil: From Elections without Democracy to Democracy without Citizenship," *Daedalus* 129, no. 2 (2000): 1–27; Paulo Friere, *Pedagogy of the Oppressed*, trans. Myra Bergman Ramos (1970; reprint, New York: Bloomsbury, 2017).

104. Bloom, interview; see also Pascual Sanchez, interview; Steele, interview.

105. Bloom, interview; see also Pascual Sanchez, interview; Steele, interview.

106. Bloom, interview; Michael Matza, "Attacks on Mexican Immigrants Often Go Unreported," *Philadelphia Inquirer*, June 15, 2009.

107. Juntos, grant application to the Hilles Foundation, 2007, in possession of the author; Bloom, interview; Pascual Sanchez, interview.

108. Bloom, interview; Matza, "Attacks"; Pascual Sanchez, interview; Carlos Rojas, interview by Domenic Vitiello, April 2, 2021.

109. Perez, interview, March 11, 2021; Perez, interview, March 18, 2021.

110. Perez, interview, March 11, 2021; Perez, interview, March 18, 2021.

111. Juntos, grant application to the Hilles Foundation, 2007; see also Juntos, grant application to the Fels Fund, 2010, in possession of the author; Juntos, grant application to the Hilles Foundation, 2010, in possession of the author; Steele, interview; Pascual Sanchez, interview.

112. Zac Steele, email to the author, November 1, 2020.

113. Steele, interview.

114. Juntos, grant application to the Fels Fund; Juntos, grant application to the Hilles Foundation, 2010; Steele, interview; Pascual Sanchez, interview.

115. Juntos, grant application to Bread and Roses Community Fund, 2010, in possession of the author.

116. Steele, interview; Nik Theodore and Nina Martin, "Migrant Civil Society: New Voices in the Struggle over Community Development," *Journal of Urban Affairs* 29, no. 3 (August 2007): 269-287; Garcia Hernandez, interview, May 3, 2013.

117. Ricardo Diaz Soto, correspondence with Domenic Vitiello, March 9, 2021; Carlos Pascual Sanchez, interview by Domenic Vitiello, March 14, 2021.

118. Diaz Soto, correspondence; Romero and Tlacopilco, interview.

119. Diaz Soto, correspondence; Romero and Tlacopilco, interview.

120. Pascual Sanchez, interview by Muñoz and Menon; Diaz Soto, correspondence.

121. Peter Pedemonti, interview by Domenic Vitiello, July 9, 2021.

122. Juntos, grant application to the Hilles Foundation, 2010; Pascual Sanchez, interview by Muñoz and Menon; Peter Pedemonti, interview by Daniel Schwartz, November 19, 2009; Jen Rock, interview by Daniel Schwartz, October 13, 2009; Alia Burton, notes from NSM meeting, October 16, 2008.

123. Zac Steele, interview by Daniel Schwartz, December 11, 2009.

124. Juntos, grant application to the Hilles Foundation, 2010; Pascual Sanchez, interview by Muñoz and Menon; Pedemonti, interview, July 9, 2021.

125. Peter Pedemonti, interview by Domenic Vitiello, March 29, 2017.

126. Tuzos Philadelphia, accessed June 30, 2020, https://www.tuzos-philadelphia.com/about-us.html.

127. Carlos Pascual Sanchez, interview by Domenic Vitiello, February 13, 2019; Iris Leon, "International Soccer 7," term paper for Urban Studies 670, May 9, 2010, in possession of the author; Fan Hong and J. A. Mangan, eds. *Soccer, Women, Sexual Liberation: Kicking Off a New Era* (Portland, OR: Frank Cass, 2004).

128. Leon, "International Soccer 7."

129. María Vazquez Castillo, "Of Anti-Immigrant, Sanctuary, and Repentance Cities," Progressive Planning, no. 178 (Winter 2009); Gerardo Sandoval, "Transforming Transit-Oriented Development Projects via Immigrant-Led Revitalization: The MacArthur Park Case," in *Immigration and Metropolitan Revitalization in the United States*, ed. Domenic Vitiello and Thomas J. Sugrue, 111–130 (Philadelphia: University of Pennsylvania Press, 2017).

130. Leon, "International Soccer 7."

131. Already by 2007 13 percent of over 5,000 babies at the hospital were born to mothers in the country illegally, the cost of which put significant strains on this and other medical providers. Stacey Burling, "Difficult Delivery for the Undocumented: Illegal Immigrants' Pregnancy Care Is Straining Local Hospitals," *Philadelphia Inquirer*, July 8, 2007.

132. Romero and Tlacopilco, interview; Alyssa Biederman, "'Para ser una promotora, tienes que venir de la comunidad, ese es el verdadero poder del modelo,'" *Generocity*, June 23, 2020, https://generocity.org/philly/2020/06/23/para-ser-una-promotora-tienes-que-venir-de-la-comunidad-ese-es-el-verdadero-poder-del-modelo/.

133. Pascual Sanchez, interview by Muñoz and Menon; Pascual Sanchez, interview by Domenic Vitiello; Alexandra Wolkoff, interview by Yary Muñoz and Natasha Menon, April 27, 2018; Jennifer Atlas, "Healthcare Access for Mexican Immigrants in South Philadelphia," in *Global Philadelphia: Immigrant Communities Old and New*, ed. Ayumi Takenaka and Mary Johnson Osirim, 178–195 (Philadelphia: Temple University Press, 2010).

134. Pascual Sanchez, interview by Muñoz and Menon; Wolkoff, interview.

135. Biederman, "'Para ser una promotora.'"

136. Ana Gamboa, "A Decade of 'Carnavalero' Pride on Display in South Philly," *Al Dia News*, April 25, 2016, https://aldianews.com/articles/local/philadelphia/decade-carnavalero-pride-display-south-philly/43125; Emma Restrepo and Jane Von Bergen, "Philly's Carnaval de Puebla Is Going Virtual. David Piña Wants You to See the Joy," *WHYY*, April 24, 2021, https://whyy.org/articles/phillys-carnaval-de-puebla-is-going-virtual-david-pina-wants-you-to-see-the-joy/; Ramirez and Osorio, interview.

137. Jaime Ventura, correspondence with Domenic Vitiello, January 13, 2021.

138. Pascual Sanchez, interview by Muñoz and Menon; Pascual Sanchez, interview by Vitiello; Fleisher Art Memorial, "Dia de los Muertos," accessed January 14, 2021, https://fleisher.community/programs/dia-de-los-muertos/.

139. Diaz Soto, correspondence.

140. Ramirez and Osorio, interview; Edwin Lopez Moya, "Edgar Ramirez: The Voice of Philatinos Radio in South Philly," *Al Dia News*, April 20, 2018, https://aldianews.com/articles/leaders/edgar-ramirez-voice-philatinos-radio-south-philly/52394; Emma Jacobs, "From a South Philly Basement, Mexican Immigrants Broadcast Globally Online," *WHYY NewsWorks*, May 23, 2014, http://www.newsworks.org/index.php/local/homepage-feature/68129-from-south-philly-basement-mexican-immigrants-broadcast-globally-online.

141. Bon Appetit, "An Undocumented Mexican Chef Runs One of the Country's Best New Restaurants," *Bon Appetit*, August 24, 2016, https://www.bonappetit.com /story/south-philly-barbacoa-cristina-martinez; Julia Kramer, "Best New Restaurants: South Philly Barbacoa," *Bon Appetit*, August 16, 2016, https://www.bonappetit .com/story/south-philly-barbacoa-philadelphia.

142. Carmen Guerrero, interview by Domenic Vitiello, October 8, 2020.

143. Craig LaBan, "A Collaboration for 'Radical' Change," *Philadelphia Inquirer*, November 12, 2020, https://www.inquirer.com/food/inq/dining-guide-cristina -martinez-ben-miller-peoples-kitchen-philadelphia-20201112.html.

144. Klein, "Alma del Mar."

145. Pascual Sanchez, interview Muñoz and Menon.

146. Ramirez and Osorio, interview.

147. Bethany Welch, interview by Mengyuan Bai, July 8, 2016; Bethany Welch and Maria Paula Ghiso, "Aquinas Center: Designing a Space of Radical Hospitality," in Gerald Campano, Maria Paula Ghiso, and Bethany Welch, *Partnering with Immigrant Communities: Action through Literacy* (New York: Teachers College Press, 2016), 27–38.

148. Oscar Gamble, "Norristown Latino Community Responds to President Obama's Immigration Initiative," *Times Herald* (Norristown, PA), November 21, 2014, https://www.timesherald.com/news/norristown-latino-community-responds-to -president-obama-s-immigration-initiative/article_21f2a5a2-9c13-524c-99c5 -ed21712771c6.html; Guerrero, interview. October 8, 2020.

149. Centro de Cultura, Arte, Trabajo y Educación translates as "Center for Culture, Art, Work and Education."

150. Holly Link, correspondence with Domenic Vitiello, February 19, 2021; CCATE, accessed November 12, 2020, https://www.ccate.org/.

151. White, interview; Ludy Soderman, interview by Domenic Vitiello, March 5, 2021; Partners for Families, "Montgomery County Latino Collaborative Hosted by Partners for Families," October 23, 2009, http://partnersforfamilies.blogspot.com /2009/10/montgomery-county-latino-collaborative.html.

152. Guerrero, interview, October 8, 2020.

153. Nelly Jiménez-Arévalo, interview by Domenic Vitiello, March 10, 2021.

154. Jiménez-Arévalo, interview.

155. In Spanish, CATA stood for El Comite de Apoyo a Los Trabajadores Agricolas.

156. Guerrero, interview, January 31, 2020; Guerrero, correspondence; see also Vourvoulias, "Carmen Guerrero."

157. Guerrero, correspondence.

158. Guerrero, interview, December 18, 2019; Guerrero, interview, January 31, 2020; Vourvoulias, "Carmen Guerrero."

159. Guerrero, correspondence.

160. Guerrero, interview, December 18, 2019; Vourvoulias, "Carmen Guerrero."

161. Guerrero, interview, December 18, 2019; Vourvoulias, "Carmen Guerrero."

162. Guerrero, interview, December 18, 2019; Vourvoulias, "Carmen Guerrero."

163. Guerrero, interview, November 8, 2019; Guerrero, interview, January 31, 2020; New Sanctuary Movement of Philadelphia (NSM), "Carmen Guerrero: Tireless Immigration Activist and Iron Warrior," June 1, 2018, https://www.sanctuaryphiladelphia .org/carmen-guerrero-tireless-immigration-activist-and-iron-warrior/.

164. Guerrero, interview, November 8, 2019; Guerrero, interview, January 31, 2020; NSM, "Carmen Guerrero"; Guerrero, correspondence; Vourvoulias, "Carmen Guerrero."

165. Guerrero, interview, November 8, 2019; Guerrero, interview, January 31, 2020.

166. Guerrero, interview, November 8, 2019; Guerrero, interview, January 31, 2020.

167. Sandoval-Strausz, *Barrio America*; Manuel Orozco and Rebecca Rouse, "Migrant Hometown Associations and Opportunities for Development," Migration Policy Institute, 2007; Marisol Raquel Gutierrez, "The Power of Transnational Organizing: Indigenous Migrant Politics in Oaxacalifornia," NACLA, 2010; Xochitl Bada, *Mexican Hometown Associations in Chicagoacan: From Local to Transnational Civic Engagement* (New Brunswick, NJ: Rutgers University Press, 2014).

168. Ramirez and Osorio, interview; see also Bloom, interview.

169. Sarah Lopez, *The Remittance Landscape: Spaces of Migration in Rural Mexico and Urban USA* (Chicago: University of Chicago Press, 2015).

170. Sandoval-Strausz, *Barrio America*; Lopez, *Remittance Landscape*.

171. Pascual Sanchez, interview by Muñoz and Menon.

172. Bloom, interview; Maximino Sandoval, interview by Domenic Vitiello, June 9, 2021.

173. Juntos, grant application to the Hilles Foundation, 2007.

174. Bloom, interview; Steele, interview by Juliana Pineda; Juntos, grant application to the Hilles Foundation, 2007; Juntos, grant application to the Hilles Foundation, 2010.

175. Jaime Ventura, interview by Domenic Vitiello, June 18, 2007; Jaime Ventura, interview by Domenic Vitiello, June 20, 2007; Bloom, interview; Sandoval, interview, June 9, 2021; Julie Shaw, "Exploring the Link from Philly to One Mexican Town," *Philadelphia Daily News*, June 1, 2012, https://www.inquirer.com/philly/hp/news_update/20120601_Exploring_the_link_from_Philly_to_1_Mexican_town.html.

176. Jaime Ventura, "Maize: A Brief History and a Look into the Future," January 2008, in possession of the author; see also Ventura, interview, June 18, 2007; Ventura, interview, June 20, 2007).

177. Bloom, interview; Ventura, interview, June 18, 2007; Ventura, interview, June 20, 2007; Ventura, interview, February 26, 2019; Juntos, grant application to the Hilles Foundation, 2007; Juntos, grant application to the Hilles Foundation, 2010.

178. Bloom, interview; Ventura, interview, June 18, 2007; Ventura, interview, June 20, 2007; Ventura, interview, February 26, 2019; Juntos, grant application to the Hilles Foundation, 2007; Juntos, grant application to the Hilles Foundation, 2010; Valeria Galetto, "Building Transnational Bridges: Remittances, Diaspora and Opportunities in Mexico," *Hispanics in Philanthropy*, 2011, https://hiponline.org/wp-content/uploads/2011/06/Building_Transnational_Bridges_2012_english-1.pdf; Pascual Sanchez, interview by Muñoz and Menon.

179. Ramirez and Osorio, interview.

180. Sandoval, interview; Craig LaBan, "Blue Corn: From a Mexican Family, 'A Fine Blend of Style and Authentic Substance,'" *Philadelphia Inquirer*, October 1, 2016, https://www.inquirer.com/philly/columnists/craig_laban/20161002_LaBan_review_Blue_Corn_Mexican_South_Philadelphia.html.

181. Domenic Vitiello and Rachel Van Tosh, "Liberian Reconstruction, Transnational Development, and Pan-African Community Revitalization," in *Immigration and Metropolitan Revitalization in the United States*, ed. Domenic Vitiello and Thomas J. Sug-

rue, 154–170 (Philadelphia: University of Pennsylvania Press, 2017); Mireille Fanon-Mendes France, "Mobilizing the Diaspora," interview, *Africities*, 2018, https://www.africities.org/news/mme-mireille-fanon-mendes-france-on-mobilizing-the-diaspora/.

182. Ventura, interview, February 26, 2019; Slow Food Foundation for Biodiversity, "Blue Cornmeal" (n.d.), accessed July 8, 2020, https://www.fondazioneslowfood.com/en/ark-of-taste-slow-food/blue-cornmeal/; Azure, "Original Mexican Superfuel," accessed July 8, 2020, https://www.azurefoods.uk; Juntos, grant application to the Hilles Foundation, 2010.

183. Ventura, interview, February 26, 2019; Janeth Gonzalez, "San Mateo Ozolco, del Sueño Americano a la Esperanza Azul," *La Campiña*, August 14, 2017, http://www.lacampinadepuebla.mx/index.php/agricultura/item/852-san-mateo-ozolco-del-sueno-americano-a-la-esperanza-azul; Claudia Rosas Sandoval, "Al Rescate del Maiz Azul," *Imagen Agropecuaria*, January 25, 2013, https://imagenagropecuaria.com/2013/al-rescate-del-maiz-azul/.

184. Jaime Ventura, presentation to City Planning 628, University of Pennsylvania, February 23, 2021.

185. Ventura, interview, February 26, 2019.

186. Vourvoulias, "Carmen Guerrero"; John Washington, "4 Years after the Forced Disappearance of 43 Students, a Father Is Still Looking," *Nation*, November 12, 2018, https://www.thenation.com/article/archive/ayotzinapa-mexico-students-disappearance/.

187. Guerrero, interview, January 31, 2020; Guerrero, correspondence.

188. Guerrero, interview, November 8, 2019; Guerrero, interview, January 31, 2020.

189. Abigail Hauslohner, "The Trump Administration's Immigration Jails Are Packed, But Deportations Are Lower Than in Obama Era," *Washington Post*, November 17, 2019, https://www.washingtonpost.com/immigration/the-trump-administrations-immigration-jails-are-packed-but-deportations-are-lower-than-in-obama-era/2019/11/17/27ad0e44-f057-11e9-89eb-ec56cd414732_story.html; John Gramlich, "How Border Apprehensions, ICE Arrests and Deportations Have Changed under Trump," Pew Research Center, March 2, 2020, https://www.pewresearch.org/fact-tank/2020/03/02/how-border-apprehensions-ice-arrests-and-deportations-have-changed-under-trump/; Zachary Wolf, "Yes, Obama Deported More People Than Trump But Context Is Everything," *CNN Politics*, July 13, 2019, https://www.cnn.com/2019/07/13/politics/obama-trump-deportations-illegal-immigration/index.html.

190. Suzanne Gamboa, "Donald Trump Announces Presidential Bid by Trashing Mexico, Mexicans," *NBC News*, June 16, 2015, https://www.nbcnews.com/news/latino/donald-trump-announces-presidential-bid-trashing-mexico-mexicans-n376521.

191. Robert J. Sampson, "Immigration and the New Social Transformation of the American City," in *Immigration and Metropolitan Revitalization in the United States*, ed. Domenic Vitiello and Thomas J. Sugrue, 11–24 (Philadelphia: University of Pennsylvania Press, 2017).

192. Tamara Keith, "Fact Check: Mexico Isn't Paying for the Border Wall, Military Unlikely to Build It," *NPR*, December 20, 2018, https://www.npr.org/2018/12/20/678557749/fact-check-border-wall-funding.

193. Michael Matza, "Fearing Raid on Immigrants, Organizers Cancel Cinco de Mayo Festival," *Philadelphia Inquirer*, March 20, 2017, https://www.inquirer.com/philly/news/Fearing-an-ICE-raid-organizers-cancel-a-Cinco-de-Mayo-celebration-.html.

194. Passel and Cohn, "Mexicans Decline"; Carlos Echeverria-Estrada and Jeanne Batalova, "Chinese Immigrants in the United States," *Migration Information Source* (Migration Policy Institute), January 15, 2020, https://www.migrationpolicy.org/article/chinese-immigrants-united-states.

195. Pascual Sanchez, interview by Muñoz and Menon.

196. Bloom, interview.

197. Benitez, "Philadelphia as a Re-Emerging Immigrant Gateway."

198. Ramirez and Osorio, interview; Dylan Purcell and Erin Arvedlund, "A Novel Year for the Mummers Parade," *Philadelphia Inquirer*, January 1, 2016, https://www.inquirer.com/philly/news/20160102_A_novel_year_for_the_Mummers_Parade.html.

199. Jeff Gammage, "Ten Years Later, Geno's 'Speak English' Sign Taken Down," *Philadelphia Inquirer*, October 13, 2016, https://www.inquirer.com/philly/news/20161014_Ten_years_later__Geno_s__Please_Speak_English__sign_taken_down.html.

200. Jacob Adelman, Kristen Graham, and David Maialetti, "'My Eyes Feel at Peace Now': Frank Rizzo Mural Is Erased, as Calls for Racial Justice Bring Change to Philly's Italian Market," *Philadelphia Inquirer*, June 7, 2020, https://www.inquirer.com/news/philadelphia/frank-rizzo-mural-philadelphia-italian-market-removed-george-floyd-20200607.html.

201. Chris Palmer, "Krasner Will Seek to Prevent Deportation of Immigrants Accused of Nonviolent Crimes," *Philadelphia Inquirer*, January 25, 2018, https://www.inquirer.com/philly/news/crime/philly-da-larry-krasner-caleb-arnold-prevent-deportation-immigrants-nonviolent-crimes-20180125.html?mobi=true.

202. Associated Press, "Judge Sides with Philadelphia in Sanctuary City Fight," *PBS News Hour*, June 6, 2018, https://www.pbs.org/newshour/nation/judge-sides-with-philadelphia-in-sanctuary-city-fight; Laura Benshoff, "Philly Pilots Program to Pay for Some Detained Immigrants' Legal Defense," *WHYY*, July 16, 2019, https://whyy.org/articles/philly-pilots-program-to-pay-for-some-detained-immigrants-legal-defense/; City of Philadelphia, "PHL City ID Cards Now Available to the Public." April 4, 2019, https://www.phila.gov/2019-04-04-phl-city-id-cards-now-available-to-the-public/.

203. Amy Chin-Arroyo and Solena Laigle, "Interlocking Systems: How Pennsylvania Counties and Local Police Are Assisting ICE to Deport Immigrants," (Temple University School of Law—Sheller Center for Social Justice and Juntos, 2019), in possession of the author.

204. Schwartz, "Recruiting for Sanctuary"; Jeff Gammage, "New Sanctuary Movement Has Been on a Dead Run since Trump's Election," *Philadelphia Inquirer*, December 14, 2017, https://www.inquirer.com/philly/news/new-sanctuary-movement-immigration-ice-trump-deportation-20171214.html.

205. Elie Wiesel, quoted in Marie Friedmann Marquardt, Susanna Snyder, and Manuel Vasquez, "Challenging Laws: Faith-Based Engagement with Unauthorized Immigration," in *Constructing Immigrant "Illegality": Critiques, Experiences, and Responses*, ed. Cecila Menjivar and Daniel Kanstroom, 272–297 (quote on p. 277) (New York: Cambridge University Press, 2014).

206. NSM, "Immigrants in Solidarity for #BlackLivesMatter," June 2, 2020, listserv email in possession of the author.

207. Ana Gamboa, "A New Life Opportunity for Angela Navarro," *Al Dia News*, January 19, 2015, https://aldianews.com/articles/local/philadelphia/new-life-opportunity-angela-navarro/37365.

208. Aline Barros, "More Undocumented People Find Sanctuary in US Churches," *Voice of America*, April 19, 2018, https://www.voanews.com/usa/more-undocumented-people-find-sanctuary-us-churches.

209. Laura Benshoff, "Two More Families Choose Sanctuary in a Philly Church over Separation, Deportation," *WHYY*, September 5, 2018, https://whyy.org/segments/two-more-families-choose-sanctuary-in-a-philly-church-over-separation-deportation/; NSM, "Sanctuary: Mobilizing Faith through Community Organizing" (n.d.), accessed July 10, 2020, https://www.sanctuaryphiladelphia.org.

210. NSM, "Sanctuary: Mobilizing Faith through Community Organizing"; NSM, "Action Alert: URGENT—3 Ways to Stop Anti-Sanctuary Bill in PA" (October 19, 2016); NSM, "Action Alert: Defend Philly as a Sanctuary City" (February 3, 2017), listserv email in possession of the author.

211. NSM, "Sanctuary"; NSM, "Share Your Check: Immigrant COVID Relief Fund," January 18, 2021, https://sanctuaryphiladelphia.ourpowerbase.net/civicrm/pcp/info.

212. Jeff Gammage, "Protesters Demand Devereux Agency Halt Its Plans for Migrant Children's Shelter in Philly Suburb," *Philadelphia Inquirer*, October 17, 2019, https://www.inquirer.com/news/migrant-children-immigration-trump-devereux-vision-quest-20191017.html; Jeff Gammage, "Court Rules for VisionQuest in Zoning Battle over Proposed Site to House Migrant Children in Philadelphia," *Philadelphia Inquirer*, November 1, 2019), https://www.inquirer.com/news/visionquest-shelter-unaccompanied-minors-immigration-bethany-devereux-20191101.html.

213. Juntos, "Why Philly Is NOT a Sanctuary City," January 13, 2017, listserv email in possession of the author.

214. City of Philadelphia, "Action Guide: Immigration Policies," January 8, 2018, https://www.phila.gov/2018-01-08-immigration-policies/; Julia Terruso, "Kenney: Philadelphia Stays a 'Sanctuary City' Despite Trump," *Philadelphia Inquirer*, November 10, 2016, https://www.inquirer.com/philly/news/politics/20161111_Kenney_Philadelphia_stays_a_sanctuary_city__despite_Trump.html.

215. David Gambacorta and Kavitha Surana, "No Sanctuary: Even in Philadelphia, One of the Most Determined Sanctuary Cities, Refuge Is Elusive," *ProPublica*, October 18, 2018, https://www.propublica.org/article/even-in-philadelphia-one-of-the-most-determined-sanctuary-cities-refuge-is-elusive.

216. Maddie Hanna, "Concern Rises Following ICE Arrest of Mother After She Dropped Off Child at South Philly School," *Philadelphia Inquirer*, February 18, 2020, https://fusion.inquirer.com/news/undocumented-immigrant-ice-arrest-school-philadelphia-kirkbride-elementary-20200218.html; Juntos, "Philadelphia Deserves Sanctuary Schools," February 11, 2021, https://www.vamosjuntos.org/ice-u.

217. Daniel Denvir, "The False Promise of Sanctuary Cities: For Many Undocumented Immigrants, the Protections Offered by Left-Leaning Cities Mean Nothing at All," *Slate*, February 17, 2017, https://slate.com/news-and-politics/2017/02/the-false-promise-of-sanctuary-cities.amp.

218. Emily Scott, *For All Who Hunger: Searching for Communion in a Shattered World* (New York: Random House, 2020).

219. Juntos, "Displacement in South Philadelphia," October 2, 2015, listserv email in possession of the author; Juntos, "Help Juntos Stay in the Community," July 14, 2017, listserv email in possession of the author.

220. NSM, "ACTION ALERT: Prayer Vigils this Friday, Aug 25," August 22, 2017, listserv email in possession of the author.

221. NSM, "ACTION ALERT: Call City Council to Support Emergency Housing Protection Package," Philadelphia, May 28, 2020.

222. The quote comes from FUMCOG's pastor in 2018, but it was often repeated by other members of NSM. "A New Sanctuary in Germantown," St. Vincent De Paul Church newsletter October 21, 2018, https://saint-vincent-church.org/wp-content/uploads/2018/10/st.-vincent-bulletin-102118-final-22-pgs.pdf.

223. NSM, "Statement on Sanctuary," 2017, https://www.sanctuaryphiladelphia.org/who-we-are-new-sanctuary/2017-statement-sanctuary/.

224. Rev. Dr. Renee McKenzie, sermon reprinted in "Carmela Libre: Grant Asylum to Mother & Children in Sanctuary at Church of the Advocate," December 13, 2017, https://www.sanctuaryphiladelphia.org/carmela-children-enter-sanctuary/.

225. NSM, "Carmen Guerrero."

## Conclusion

1. Mathew Frye Jacobson, *Barbarian Virtues: The United States Encounters Foreign Peoples at Home and Abroad, 1876–1917* (New York: Hill and Wang, 2000).

2. Thea Renda Abu El-Haj, *Unsettled Belonging: Educating Palestinian American Youth after 9/11* (Chicago: University of Chicago Press, 2015).

3. Scholars have explored and debated similar questions, for example, Alejandro Portes and Min Zhou, "The New Second Generation: Segmented Assimilation and Its Variants," *Annals of the American Academy of Political and Social Science* 530, no. 1 (1993):74–96.

4. Domenic Vitiello, "The Politics of Place in Immigrant and Receiving Communities," in *What's New about the "New" Immigration to the United States?* ed. Marilyn Halter, Marilynn Johnson, Katheryn Veins, and Conrad Wright, 83–110 (New York: Palgrave, 2014).

5. Judith Bernstein-Baker, presentation at University of Pennsylvania Urban Studies Public Conversation on Immigration to Philadelphia, January 24, 2006.

6. Thoai Nguyen, presentation to Refugee Inauguration Celebration, Nationalities Service Center, January 21, 2021.

7. The idea of global neighbors has been taken up particularly in certain faith communities; see, for example, Douglas Hicks and Mark Valeri, eds., *Global Neighbors: Christian Faith and Moral Obligation in Today's Economy* (Grand Rapids, MI: Eerdmans, 2008).

8. Ann Deslandes, "Sanctuary Cities Are as Old as the Bible," *JStor Daily*, March 22, 2017, https://daily.jstor.org/sanctuary-cities-as-old-as-bible/.

9. Chicago Religious Task Force on Central America and Tucson Ecumenical Council Central America Task Force, "Sanctuary," 37. This environmental vision of sanctuary is echoed in Frederick Steiner, "Expand Sanctuary Concept from Cities to Suburbs," Opinion section of *Philadelphia Inquirer*, December 18, 2016, downloaded from *ProQuest Historical Newspapers*, https://about.proquest.com/en/products-services/pq-hist-news/.

# INDEX

CPSIA information can be obtained
at www.ICGtesting.com
Printed in the USA
LVHW031213160822
726083LV00003B/171

9 781501 764806